2014 | THE LITTLE DATA BOOK ON INFORMATION AND COMMUNICATION TECHNOLOGY

THE WORLD BANK

International
Telecommunication
Union

ISBN (paper): 978-1-4648-0177-8
ISBN (electronic): 978-1-4648-0178-5
DOI: 10.1596/978-1-4648-0177-8

Design by Communications Development Incorporated, Washington, D.C.

Contents

Acknowledgments

The Little Data Book on Information and Communication Technology 2014 is a joint publication between the World Bank and the International Telecommunication Union (ITU).

For the World Bank team, the work was the result of close collaboration between the staff of the Development Data Group of the Development Economics Vice Presidency and the Transport, Water, and Information Communication Technologies Sector Unit of the World Bank. The Development Data Group team included Azita Amjadi, Federico Escaler, Buyant Erdene Khaltarkhuu, Leila Rafei, Jomo Tariku, and William Prince. The Information and Communication Technologies team included Tim Kelly and Kaoru Kimura. The work was carried out under the management of Haishan Fu and Jose Luis Irigoyen. Nora Ridolfi, Paola Scalabrin, and Janice Tuten from World Bank's Publishing and Knowledge Division oversaw publication and dissemination of the book.

The ITU contribution was provided by the ICT Data and Statistics Division of the Telecommunication Development Bureau. The team included Susan Teltscher (Head of Division), Vanessa Gray, Esperanza Magpantay, and Ivan Vallejo. Regulatory data were provided by the Regulatory and Market Environment Division of the Telecommunication Development Bureau. The team included Makhtar Fall (Head of Division), Nancy Sundberg, and Youlia Lozanova.

The World Bank and ITU acknowledge the data provided by other sources: IMF, Netcraft, OECD, UNCTAD, UNDESA/UNPAN, UNESCO, UNPD, and UNSD.

Preface

Since the late 1990s access to information and communication technologies (ICTs) has seen tremendous growth—driven primarily by the wireless technologies and liberalization of telecommunications markets. Mobile communications have evolved from simple voice and text services to diversified innovative applications and mobile broadband Internet. By the end of 2013, there were an estimated 6.8 billion mobile-cellular subscriptions globally. The number of individuals using the Internet has risen constantly and reached an estimated 2.7 billion while the number of fixed (wired)- broadband subscriptions reached almost 700 million at the end of 2013.

The impacts of ICTs cross all sectors. Research has shown that investment in information and communication technologies is associated with such economic benefits as higher productivity, lower costs, new economic opportunities, job creation, innovation, and increased trade. ICTs also help provide better services in health and education, and strengthen social cohesion.

The Little Data Book on Information and Communication Technology 2014 illustrates the progress of this revolution for 214 economies around the world. It provides comparable statistics on the sector for 2005 and 2012 across a range of indicators, enabling readers to readily compare economies.

This book includes indicators covering the economic and social context, the structure of the information and communication technology sector, sector efficiency and capacity, and sector performance related to access, usage, quality, affordability, trade, and applications. The glossary contains definitions of the terms used in the tables.

For more information and other World Bank data publications, visit our data Web site at data.worldbank.org or the Web site of the Information and Communication Technologies Department at www.worldbank.org/ict.

For more statistics on information and communication technology infrastructure, access and usage, as well as analytical reports such as the annual *Measuring the Information Society* report, visit ITU's Web site at www.itu.int/en/ITU-D/Statistics/Pages/default.aspx and the ITU ICT Eye at www.itu.int/icteye.

Data notes

The data in this book are for 2005 and 2012 or the most recent year unless otherwise noted in the table or the glossary.

- Growth rates are proportional changes from the previous year unless otherwise noted.

- Regional aggregates include data for low- and middle-income economies only.

- Figures in italics indicate data for years or periods other than those specified.

Symbols used:

..   indicates that data are not available or that aggregates cannot be calculated because of missing data.

0 or 0.0   indicates zero or small enough that the number would round to zero at the displayed number of decimal places.

$ indicates current U.S. dollars.

Lettered notes on some country tables can be found in the notes on page 232.

Data are shown for economies with populations greater than 30,000 or for smaller economies if they are members of the World Bank or the ITU. The term *country* (used interchangeably with *economy*) does not imply political independence or official recognition by the World Bank or the ITU but refers to any economy for which the authorities report separate social or economic statistics.

Aggregates for groups of economies are based on the World Bank's regional and income classifications. Because of missing data, aggregates should be treated as approximations of unknown totals or average values. The aggregation method for each indicator is noted in the glossary. Sums (s) are simple totals of available data. Weighted averages (w) are calculated using the value of the denominator or, in some cases, another indicator as the weight. Median (m) calculations are based on available data and exclude economies with populations below 1 million. For more information about aggregation methods visit datahelpdesk.worldbank.org.

The cutoff date for data is March 1, 2014.

Regional tables

The country composition of regions is based on the World Bank's analytical regions and may differ from common geographic usage. These regions include low- and middle-income economies only.

East Asia and Pacific

American Samoa, Cambodia, China, Fiji, Indonesia, Kiribati, Democratic People's Republic of Korea, Lao People's Democratic Republic, Malaysia, Marshall Islands, Federated States of Micronesia, Mongolia, Myanmar, Palau, Papua New Guinea, the Philippines, Samoa, Solomon Islands, Thailand, Timor-Leste, Tonga, Tuvalu, Vanuatu, Vietnam

Europe and Central Asia

Albania, Armenia, Azerbaijan, Belarus, Bosnia and Herzegovina, Bulgaria, Georgia, Hungary, Kazakhstan, Kosovo, Kyrgyz Republic, Former Yugoslav Republic of Macedonia, Moldova, Montenegro, Romania, Serbia, Tajikistan, Turkey, Turkmenistan, Ukraine, Uzbekistan

Latin America and the Caribbean

Argentina, Belize, Bolivia, Brazil, Colombia, Costa Rica, Cuba, Dominica, Dominican Republic, Ecuador, El Salvador, Grenada, Guatemala, Guyana, Haiti, Honduras, Jamaica, Mexico, Nicaragua, Panama, Paraguay, Peru, St. Lucia, St. Vincent and the Grenadines, Suriname, República Bolivariana de Venezuela

Middle East and North Africa

Algeria, Djibouti, Arab Republic of Egypt, Islamic Republic of Iran, Iraq, Jordan, Lebanon, Libya, Morocco, Syrian Arab Republic, Tunisia, West Bank and Gaza, Republic of Yemen

South Asia

Afghanistan, Bangladesh, Bhutan, India, Maldives, Nepal, Pakistan, Sri Lanka

Sub-Saharan Africa

Angola, Benin, Botswana, Burkina Faso, Burundi, Cabo Verde, Cameroon, Central African Republic, Chad, Comoros, Democratic Republic of Congo, Republic of Congo, Côte d'Ivoire, Eritrea, Ethiopia, Gabon, The Gambia, Ghana, Guinea, Guinea-Bissau, Kenya, Lesotho, Liberia, Madagascar, Malawi, Mali, Mauritania, Mauritius, Mozambique, Namibia, Niger, Nigeria, Rwanda, São Tomé and Príncipe, Senegal, Seychelles, Sierra Leone, Somalia, South Africa, South Sudan, Sudan, Swaziland, Tanzania, Togo, Uganda, Zambia, Zimbabwe

World

	2005	2012
Economic and social context		
Population (millions)	6,491	7,044
Urban population (% of total)	49	53
GNI per capita, *World Bank Atlas* method ($)	7,208	10,181
GDP growth, 2000–05 and 2005–12 (avg. annual %)	2.9	2.1
Adult literacy rate (% ages 15 and older)	82	84
Gross primary, secondary, tertiary school enrollment (%)	67	71
Sector structure		
Separate telecommunications/ICT regulator		
Status of main fixed-line telephone operator		
Level of competition (competition, partial comp., monopoly)		
International gateway(s)		
Mobile telephone service		
Internet service		
Foreign ownership (not allowed, restricted, allowed)		
Reg. treatment of VoIP (banned, closed, no framework, allowed)		
Sector efficiency and capacity		
Telecommunications revenue (% of GDP)	3.0	2.6
Telecommunications investment (% of revenue)	17.9	17.7
Sector performance		
Access		
Fixed-telephone subscriptions (per 100 people)	19.4	16.7
Mobile-cellular telephone subscriptions (per 100 people)	33.9	89.3
Fixed (wired)-broadband subscriptions (per 100 people)	3.4	9.2
Households with a computer (%)	27.6	40.3
Households with Internet access at home (%)	18.9	37.4
Usage		
Int'l. voice traffic, total (minutes/subscription/month)	..	7.1
Domestic mobile traffic (minutes/subscription/month)	..	..
Individuals using the Internet (%)	15.8	35.5
Quality		
Population covered by a mobile-cellular network (%)	67	93
Fixed (wired)-broadband subscriptions (% of total Internet)	49.7	93.3
International Internet bandwidth (bit/s per Internet user)	4,848	41,190
Affordability		
Fixed-telephone sub-basket ($ a month)	..	10.4
Mobile-cellular sub-basket ($ a month)	..	14.6
Fixed-broadband sub-basket ($ a month)	..	23.2
Trade		
ICT goods exports (% of total goods exports)	13.6	10.4
ICT goods imports (% of total goods imports)	13.8	11.2
ICT service exports (% of total service exports)	28.6	31.7
Applications		
Online service index (0–1, 1=highest presence)	0.45	0.41
Secure Internet servers (per million people)	64.9	160.4

East Asia & Pacific

	2005	2012
Economic and social context		
Population (millions)	1,893	1,992
Urban population (% of total)	42	50
GNI per capita, *World Bank Atlas* method ($)	1,614	4,884
GDP growth, 2000–05 and 2005–12 (avg. annual %)	8.4	9.1
Adult literacy rate (% ages 15 and older)	*91*	*94*
Gross primary, secondary, tertiary school enrollment (%)	67	71
Sector structure		
Separate telecommunications/ICT regulator		
Status of main fixed-line telephone operator		
Level of competition (competition, partial comp., monopoly)		
International gateway(s)		
Mobile telephone service		
Internet service		
Foreign ownership (not allowed, restricted, allowed)		
Reg. treatment of VoIP (banned, closed, no framework, allowed)		
Sector efficiency and capacity		
Telecommunications revenue (% of GDP)	3.2	2.2
Telecommunications investment (% of revenue)	*23.5*	*20.0*
Sector performance		
Access		
Fixed-telephone subscriptions (per 100 people)	20.9	17.0
Mobile-cellular telephone subscriptions (per 100 people)	28.1	88.9
Fixed (wired)-broadband subscriptions (per 100 people)	2.0	9.7
Households with a computer (%)	20.4	34.9
Households with Internet access at home (%)	9.0	30.9
Usage		
Int'l. voice traffic, total (minutes/subscription/month)	*1.3*	0.5
Domestic mobile traffic (minutes/subscription/month)	132	386
Individuals using the Internet (%)	8.3	36.2
Quality		
Population covered by a mobile-cellular network (%)	*93*	*99*
Fixed (wired)-broadband subscriptions (% of total Internet)	45.9	96.8
International Internet bandwidth (bit/s per Internet user)	975	5,993
Affordability		
Fixed-telephone sub-basket ($ a month)	..	5.2
Mobile-cellular sub-basket ($ a month)	..	7.7
Fixed-broadband sub-basket ($ a month)	..	22.5
Trade		
ICT goods exports (% of total goods exports)	29.6	24.3
ICT goods imports (% of total goods imports)	24.4	18.3
ICT service exports (% of total service exports)	24.1	32.9
Applications		
Online service index (0–1, 1=highest presence)	0.29	0.22
Secure Internet servers (per million people)	0.8	5.6

Europe & Central Asia

	2005	2012
Economic and social context		
Population (millions)	260	271
Urban population (% of total)	58	60
GNI per capita, *World Bank Atlas* method ($)	3,491	6,664
GDP growth, 2000–05 and 2005–12 (avg. annual %)	5.8	3.1
Adult literacy rate (% ages 15 and older)	97	98
Gross primary, secondary, tertiary school enrollment (%)	77	80
Sector structure		
Separate telecommunications/ICT regulator		
Status of main fixed-line telephone operator		
Level of competition (competition, partial comp., monopoly)		
International gateway(s)		
Mobile telephone service		
Internet service		
Foreign ownership (not allowed, restricted, allowed)		
Reg. treatment of VoIP (banned, closed, no framework, allowed)		
Sector efficiency and capacity		
Telecommunications revenue (% of GDP)	3.5	2.4
Telecommunications investment (% of revenue)	23.0	19.6
Sector performance		
Access		
Fixed-telephone subscriptions (per 100 people)	22.1	21.4
Mobile-cellular telephone subscriptions (per 100 people)	49.6	108.5
Fixed (wired)-broadband subscriptions (per 100 people)	1.2	10.1
Households with a computer (%)	14.7	44.8
Households with Internet access at home (%)	6.8	41.4
Usage		
Int'l. voice traffic, total (minutes/subscription/month)	..	..
Domestic mobile traffic (minutes/subscription/month)	..	95
Individuals using the Internet (%)	12.0	43.3
Quality		
Population covered by a mobile-cellular network (%)	92	99
Fixed (wired)-broadband subscriptions (% of total Internet)	30.7	92.2
International Internet bandwidth (bit/s per Internet user)	2,797	42,572
Affordability		
Fixed-telephone sub-basket ($ a month)	..	3.7
Mobile-cellular sub-basket ($ a month)	..	12.5
Fixed-broadband sub-basket ($ a month)	..	12.1
Trade		
ICT goods exports (% of total goods exports)	7.6	5.3
ICT goods imports (% of total goods imports)	8.0	6.7
ICT service exports (% of total service exports)	10.5	16.6
Applications		
Online service index (0–1, 1=highest presence)	0.46	0.46
Secure Internet servers (per million people)	7.8	42.0

Latin America & Caribbean

	2005	2012
Economic and social context		
Population (millions)	536	581
Urban population (% of total)	77	79
GNI per capita, *World Bank Atlas* method ($)	4,368	9,070
GDP growth, 2000–05 and 2005–12 (avg. annual %)	2.5	3.6
Adult literacy rate (% ages 15 and older)	90	91
Gross primary, secondary, tertiary school enrollment (%)	81	83
Sector structure		
Separate telecommunications/ICT regulator		
Status of main fixed-line telephone operator		
Level of competition (competition, partial comp., monopoly)		
International gateway(s)		
Mobile telephone service		
Internet service		
Foreign ownership (not allowed, restricted, allowed)		
Reg. treatment of VoIP (banned, closed, no framework, allowed)		
Sector efficiency and capacity		
Telecommunications revenue (% of GDP)	3.3	3.0
Telecommunications investment (% of revenue)	20.3	16.2
Sector performance		
Access		
Fixed-telephone subscriptions (per 100 people)	17.3	17.8
Mobile-cellular telephone subscriptions (per 100 people)	42.1	108.1
Fixed (wired)-broadband subscriptions (per 100 people)	1.4	8.0
Households with a computer (%)	16.8	38.7
Households with Internet access at home (%)	9.4	33.1
Usage		
Int'l. voice traffic, total (minutes/subscription/month)	..	..
Domestic mobile traffic (minutes/subscription/month)	43	93
Individuals using the Internet (%)	16.0	42.7
Quality		
Population covered by a mobile-cellular network (%)	89	99
Fixed (wired)-broadband subscriptions (% of total Internet)	53.8	89.3
International Internet bandwidth (bit/s per Internet user)	1,156	28,238
Affordability		
Fixed-telephone sub-basket ($ a month)	..	7.9
Mobile-cellular sub-basket ($ a month)	..	14.9
Fixed-broadband sub-basket ($ a month)	..	20.4
Trade		
ICT goods exports (% of total goods exports)	8.5	8.4
ICT goods imports (% of total goods imports)	13.7	12.6
ICT service exports (% of total service exports)	..	..
Applications		
Online service index (0–1, 1=highest presence)	0.47	0.43
Secure Internet servers (per million people)	9.8	36.4

Middle East & North Africa

	2005	2012
Economic and social context		
Population (millions)	301	340
Urban population (% of total)	58	60
GNI per capita, *World Bank Atlas* method ($)	1,996	*3,450*
GDP growth, 2000–05 and 2005–12 (avg. annual %)	4.5	4.2
Adult literacy rate (% ages 15 and older)	*68*	*77*
Gross primary, secondary, tertiary school enrollment (%)	68	*72*
Sector structure		
Separate telecommunications/ICT regulator		
Status of main fixed-line telephone operator		
Level of competition (competition, partial comp., monopoly)		
International gateway(s)		
Mobile telephone service		
Internet service		
Foreign ownership (not allowed, restricted, allowed)		
Reg. treatment of VoIP (banned, closed, no framework, allowed)		
Sector efficiency and capacity		
Telecommunications revenue (% of GDP)	3.2	*2.7*
Telecommunications investment (% of revenue)	21.7	*15.6*
Sector performance		
Access		
Fixed-telephone subscriptions (per 100 people)	14.4	16.1
Mobile-cellular telephone subscriptions (per 100 people)	22.4	95.1
Fixed (wired)-broadband subscriptions (per 100 people)	*0.4*	2.9
Households with a computer (%)	15.4	34.7
Households with Internet access at home (%)	8.9	27.9
Usage		
Int'l. voice traffic, total (minutes/subscription/month)	8.5	*6.1*
Domestic mobile traffic (minutes/subscription/month)	..	..
Individuals using the Internet (%)	8.5	30.7
Quality		
Population covered by a mobile-cellular network (%)	79	97
Fixed (wired)-broadband subscriptions (% of total Internet)	..	53.8
International Internet bandwidth (bit/s per Internet user)	645	7,114
Affordability		
Fixed-telephone sub-basket ($ a month)	..	4.5
Mobile-cellular sub-basket ($ a month)	..	10.9
Fixed-broadband sub-basket ($ a month)	..	14.4
Trade		
ICT goods exports (% of total goods exports)	0.7	*0.8*
ICT goods imports (% of total goods imports)	5.2	*4.1*
ICT service exports (% of total service exports)	..	..
Applications		
Online service index (0–1, 1=highest presence)	0.35	0.34
Secure Internet servers (per million people)	0.6	3.5

	2005	2012
Economic and social context		
Population (millions)	1,499	1,649
Urban population (% of total)	29	31
GNI per capita, *World Bank Atlas* method ($)	700	1,437
GDP growth, 2000–05 and 2005–12 (avg. annual %)	6.3	7.1
Adult literacy rate (% ages 15 and older)	*58*	*62*
Gross primary, secondary, tertiary school enrollment (%)	56	62
Sector structure		
Separate telecommunications/ICT regulator		
Status of main fixed-line telephone operator		
Level of competition (competition, partial comp., monopoly)		
International gateway(s)		
Mobile telephone service		
Internet service		
Foreign ownership (not allowed, restricted, allowed)		
Reg. treatment of VoIP (banned, closed, no framework, allowed)		
Sector efficiency and capacity		
Telecommunications revenue (% of GDP)	2.4	*2.3*
Telecommunications investment (% of revenue)	37.8	*36.3*
Sector performance		
Access		
Fixed-telephone subscriptions (per 100 people)	4.0	2.6
Mobile-cellular telephone subscriptions (per 100 people)	7.8	68.9
Fixed (wired)-broadband subscriptions (per 100 people)	0.1	1.1
Households with a computer (%)	2.0	10.3
Households with Internet access at home (%)	1.4	8.6
Usage		
Int'l. voice traffic, total (minutes/subscription/month)	*5.3*	*6.0*
Domestic mobile traffic (minutes/subscription/month)	..	..
Individuals using the Internet (%)	2.5	11.6
Quality		
Population covered by a mobile-cellular network (%)	37	*85*
Fixed (wired)-broadband subscriptions (% of total Internet)	14.9	56.9
International Internet bandwidth (bit/s per Internet user)	560	5,284
Affordability		
Fixed-telephone sub-basket ($ a month)	..	3.0
Mobile-cellular sub-basket ($ a month)	..	3.5
Fixed-broadband sub-basket ($ a month)	..	7.0
Trade		
ICT goods exports (% of total goods exports)	1.0	1.7
ICT goods imports (% of total goods imports)	7.6	5.0
ICT service exports (% of total service exports)	61.6	62.0
Applications		
Online service index (0–1, 1=highest presence)	0.31	0.36
Secure Internet servers (per million people)	0.5	3.3

Sub-Saharan Africa

	2005	2012
Economic and social context		
Population (millions)	757	911
Urban population (% of total)	34	37
GNI per capita, *World Bank Atlas* method ($)	763	1,350
GDP growth, 2000–05 and 2005–12 (avg. annual %)	4.6	4.7
Adult literacy rate (% ages 15 and older)	57	60
Gross primary, secondary, tertiary school enrollment (%)	52	58
Sector structure		
Separate telecommunications/ICT regulator		
Status of main fixed-line telephone operator		
Level of competition (competition, partial comp., monopoly)		
International gateway(s)		
Mobile telephone service		
Internet service		
Foreign ownership (not allowed, restricted, allowed)		
Reg. treatment of VoIP (banned, closed, no framework, allowed)		
Sector efficiency and capacity		
Telecommunications revenue (% of GDP)	4.7	3.8
Telecommunications investment (% of revenue)	..	23.8
Sector performance		
Access		
Fixed-telephone subscriptions (per 100 people)	1.5	1.2
Mobile-cellular telephone subscriptions (per 100 people)	12.0	59.3
Fixed (wired)-broadband subscriptions (per 100 people)	0.0	0.2
Households with a computer (%)	3.6	8.1
Households with Internet access at home (%)	1.1	8.0
Usage		
Int'l. voice traffic, total (minutes/subscription/month)	..	5.1
Domestic mobile traffic (minutes/subscription/month)	..	302
Individuals using the Internet (%)	2.1	14.8
Quality		
Population covered by a mobile-cellular network (%)	51	84
Fixed (wired)-broadband subscriptions (% of total Internet)	..	39.8
International Internet bandwidth (bit/s per Internet user)	232	6,430
Affordability		
Fixed-telephone sub-basket ($ a month)	..	10.5
Mobile-cellular sub-basket ($ a month)	..	14.6
Fixed-broadband sub-basket ($ a month)	..	46.6
Trade		
ICT goods exports (% of total goods exports)	0.6	0.5
ICT goods imports (% of total goods imports)	7.6	5.8
ICT service exports (% of total service exports)	12.5	14.4
Applications		
Online service index (0–1, 1=highest presence)	0.25	0.27
Secure Internet servers (per million people)	2.1	6.8

Income group tables

For operational and analytical purposes the World Bank's main criterion for classifying economies is gross national income (GNI) per capita. Every economy in *The Little Data Book on Information and Communication Technology* is classified as low income, middle income, or high income. Low- and middle-income economies are sometimes referred to as developing economies. The use of the term is convenient; it is not intended to imply that all economies in the group are experiencing similar development or that other economies have reached a preferred or final stage of development. Classification by income does not necessarily reflect development status. Note: Classifications are fixed during the World Bank's fiscal year (ending on June 30), thus countries remain in the categories in which they are classified irrespective of any revisions to their per capita income data.

Low-income economies are those with a GNI per capita of $1,035 or less in 2012.

Middle-income economies are those with a GNI per capita of more than $1,035 but less than $12,616. Lower-middle-income and upper-middle income economies are separated at a GNI per capita of $4,085.

High-income economies are those with a GNI per capita of $12,616 or more.

Euro area includes the member states of the Economic and Monetary Union of the European Union that have adopted the euro as their currency: Austria, Belgium, Cyprus, Estonia, Finland, France, Germany, Greece, Ireland, Italy, Latvia, Luxembourg, Malta, the Netherlands, Portugal, Slovak Republic, Slovenia, and Spain.

Low income

	2005	2012
Economic and social context		
Population (millions)	727	846
Urban population (% of total)	26	28
GNI per capita, *World Bank Atlas* method ($)	330	590
GDP growth, 2000–05 and 2005–12 (avg. annual %)	4.8	5.9
Adult literacy rate (% ages 15 and older)	57	61
Gross primary, secondary, tertiary school enrollment (%)	51	60
Sector structure		
Separate telecommunications/ICT regulator		
Status of main fixed-line telephone operator		
Level of competition (competition, partial comp., monopoly)		
International gateway(s)		
Mobile telephone service		
Internet service		
Foreign ownership (not allowed, restricted, allowed)		
Reg. treatment of VoIP (banned, closed, no framework, allowed)		
Sector efficiency and capacity		
Telecommunications revenue (% of GDP)	2.5	5.0
Telecommunications investment (% of revenue)	..	..
Sector performance		
Access		
Fixed-telephone subscriptions (per 100 people)	0.9	1.0
Mobile-cellular telephone subscriptions (per 100 people)	4.6	47.2
Fixed (wired)-broadband subscriptions (per 100 people)	0.0	0.2
Households with a computer (%)	1.0	4.2
Households with Internet access at home (%)	0.3	3.4
Usage		
Int'l. voice traffic, total (minutes/subscription/month)	..	..
Domestic mobile traffic (minutes/subscription/month)	..	70
Individuals using the Internet (%)	0.9	6.2
Quality		
Population covered by a mobile-cellular network (%)	51	..
Fixed (wired)-broadband subscriptions (% of total Internet)	4.5	30.9
International Internet bandwidth (bit/s per Internet user)	208	9,141
Affordability		
Fixed-telephone sub-basket ($ a month)	..	8.9
Mobile-cellular sub-basket ($ a month)	..	11.9
Fixed-broadband sub-basket ($ a month)	..	46.9
Trade		
ICT goods exports (% of total goods exports)	0.2	..
ICT goods imports (% of total goods imports)	4.8	..
ICT service exports (% of total service exports)	..	..
Applications		
Online service index (0–1, 1=highest presence)	0.22	0.20
Secure Internet servers (per million people)	0.1	1.1

Middle income

	2005	2012
Economic and social context		
Population (millions)	4,518	4,898
Urban population (% of total)	45	50
GNI per capita, *World Bank Atlas* method ($)	1,835	4,370
GDP growth, 2000–05 and 2005–12 (avg. annual %)	5.5	6.1
Adult literacy rate (% ages 15 and older)	*80*	*83*
Gross primary, secondary, tertiary school enrollment (%)	65	69
Sector structure		
Separate telecommunications/ICT regulator		
Status of main fixed-line telephone operator		
Level of competition (competition, partial comp., monopoly)		
International gateway(s)		
Mobile telephone service		
Internet service		
Foreign ownership (not allowed, restricted, allowed)		
Reg. treatment of VoIP (banned, closed, no framework, allowed)		
Sector efficiency and capacity		
Telecommunications revenue (% of GDP)	3.3	2.5
Telecommunications investment (% of revenue)	22.1	*20.0*
Sector performance		
Access		
Fixed-telephone subscriptions (per 100 people)	14.3	12.3
Mobile-cellular telephone subscriptions (per 100 people)	24.9	87.7
Fixed (wired)-broadband subscriptions (per 100 people)	1.2	6.0
Households with a computer (%)	14.9	29.3
Households with Internet access at home (%)	7.1	25.7
Usage		
Int'l. voice traffic, total (minutes/subscription/month)	*3.9*	*4.0*
Domestic mobile traffic (minutes/subscription/month)	..	..
Individuals using the Internet (%)	7.7	29.9
Quality		
Population covered by a mobile-cellular network (%)	*86*	*92*
Fixed (wired)-broadband subscriptions (% of total Internet)	42.2	91.8
International Internet bandwidth (bit/s per Internet user)	1,084	12,511
Affordability		
Fixed-telephone sub-basket ($ a month)	..	6.9
Mobile-cellular sub-basket ($ a month)	..	13.1
Fixed-broadband sub-basket ($ a month)	..	18.3
Trade		
ICT goods exports (% of total goods exports)	17.9	15.2
ICT goods imports (% of total goods imports)	16.5	13.1
ICT service exports (% of total service exports)	26.0	35.2
Applications		
Online service index (0–1, 1=highest presence)	0.42	0.37
Secure Internet servers (per million people)	2.4	11.3

Lower middle income

	2005	2012
Economic and social context		
Population (millions)	2,253	2,507
Urban population (% of total)	36	39
GNI per capita, *World Bank Atlas* method ($)	876	1,893
GDP growth, 2000–05 and 2005–12 (avg. annual %)	5.7	6.0
Adult literacy rate (% ages 15 and older)	68	71
Gross primary, secondary, tertiary school enrollment (%)	60	64
Sector structure		
Separate telecommunications/ICT regulator		
Status of main fixed-line telephone operator		
Level of competition (competition, partial comp., monopoly)		
International gateway(s)		
Mobile telephone service		
Internet service		
Foreign ownership (not allowed, restricted, allowed)		
Reg. treatment of VoIP (banned, closed, no framework, allowed)		
Sector efficiency and capacity		
Telecommunications revenue (% of GDP)	3.1	2.5
Telecommunications investment (% of revenue)	23.6	20.5
Sector performance		
Access		
Fixed-telephone subscriptions (per 100 people)	5.2	5.4
Mobile-cellular telephone subscriptions (per 100 people)	13.7	83.1
Fixed (wired)-broadband subscriptions (per 100 people)	0.1	1.4
Households with a computer (%)	3.5	15.0
Households with Internet access at home (%)	2.4	12.4
Usage		
Int'l. voice traffic, total (minutes/subscription/month)	6.9	6.5
Domestic mobile traffic (minutes/subscription/month)	..	..
Individuals using the Internet (%)	4.0	18.7
Quality		
Population covered by a mobile-cellular network (%)	50	86
Fixed (wired)-broadband subscriptions (% of total Internet)	10.7	58.2
International Internet bandwidth (bit/s per Internet user)	514	8,076
Affordability		
Fixed-telephone sub-basket ($ a month)	..	4.9
Mobile-cellular sub-basket ($ a month)	..	10.5
Fixed-broadband sub-basket ($ a month)	..	20.6
Trade		
ICT goods exports (% of total goods exports)	7.4	4.6
ICT goods imports (% of total goods imports)	9.7	7.2
ICT service exports (% of total service exports)	36.8	47.1
Applications		
Online service index (0–1, 1=highest presence)	0.35	0.32
Secure Internet servers (per million people)	0.7	4.4

Upper middle income

	2005	2012
Economic and social context		
Population (millions)	2,265	2,391
Urban population (% of total)	54	61
GNI per capita, *World Bank Atlas* method ($)	2,788	6,969
GDP growth, 2000–05 and 2005–12 (avg. annual %)	5.4	6.2
Adult literacy rate (% ages 15 and older)	91	94
Gross primary, secondary, tertiary school enrollment (%)	72	76
Sector structure		
Separate telecommunications/ICT regulator		
Status of main fixed-line telephone operator		
Level of competition (competition, partial comp., monopoly)		
International gateway(s)		
Mobile telephone service		
Internet service		
Foreign ownership (not allowed, restricted, allowed)		
Reg. treatment of VoIP (banned, closed, no framework, allowed)		
Sector efficiency and capacity		
Telecommunications revenue (% of GDP)	3.3	2.5
Telecommunications investment (% of revenue)	20.5	18.2
Sector performance		
Access		
Fixed-telephone subscriptions (per 100 people)	23.0	19.4
Mobile-cellular telephone subscriptions (per 100 people)	36.1	92.4
Fixed (wired)-broadband subscriptions (per 100 people)	2.3	10.8
Households with a computer (%)	22.0	40.6
Households with Internet access at home (%)	10.2	36.3
Usage		
Int'l. voice traffic, total (minutes/subscription/month)	2.6	1.3
Domestic mobile traffic (minutes/subscription/month)	98	284
Individuals using the Internet (%)	11.3	41.6
Quality		
Population covered by a mobile-cellular network (%)	94	99
Fixed (wired)-broadband subscriptions (% of total Internet)	49.7	95.5
International Internet bandwidth (bit/s per Internet user)	1,283	14,580
Affordability		
Fixed-telephone sub-basket ($ a month)	..	9.4
Mobile-cellular sub-basket ($ a month)	..	14.9
Fixed-broadband sub-basket ($ a month)	..	17.8
Trade		
ICT goods exports (% of total goods exports)	20.0	17.6
ICT goods imports (% of total goods imports)	18.5	14.7
ICT service exports (% of total service exports)	20.8	29.1
Applications		
Online service index (0–1, 1=highest presence)	0.47	0.42
Secure Internet servers (per million people)	4.1	18.5

Low and middle income

	2005	2012
Economic and social context		
Population (millions)	5,245	5,744
Urban population (% of total)	42	46
GNI per capita, *World Bank Atlas* method ($)	1,626	3,815
GDP growth, 2000–05 and 2005–12 (avg. annual %)	5.5	6.1
Adult literacy rate (% ages 15 and older)	78	80
Gross primary, secondary, tertiary school enrollment (%)	63	67
Sector structure		
Separate telecommunications/ICT regulator		
Status of main fixed-line telephone operator		
Level of competition (competition, partial comp., monopoly)		
International gateway(s)		
Mobile telephone service		
Internet service		
Foreign ownership (not allowed, restricted, allowed)		
Reg. treatment of VoIP (banned, closed, no framework, allowed)		
Sector efficiency and capacity		
Telecommunications revenue (% of GDP)	3.3	2.5
Telecommunications investment (% of revenue)	25.8	21.3
Sector performance		
Access		
Fixed-telephone subscriptions (per 100 people)	12.5	10.6
Mobile-cellular telephone subscriptions (per 100 people)	22.2	81.7
Fixed (wired)-broadband subscriptions (per 100 people)	1.0	5.3
Households with a computer (%)	13.7	26.4
Households with Internet access at home (%)	6.4	23.2
Usage		
Int'l. voice traffic, total (minutes/subscription/month)	..	4.3
Domestic mobile traffic (minutes/subscription/month)	..	..
Individuals using the Internet (%)	6.8	26.5
Quality		
Population covered by a mobile-cellular network (%)	84	91
Fixed (wired)-broadband subscriptions (% of total Internet)	42.0	91.1
International Internet bandwidth (bit/s per Internet user)	1,070	12,402
Affordability		
Fixed-telephone sub-basket ($ a month)	..	7.2
Mobile-cellular sub-basket ($ a month)	..	12.6
Fixed-broadband sub-basket ($ a month)	..	20.6
Trade		
ICT goods exports (% of total goods exports)	17.6	15.1
ICT goods imports (% of total goods imports)	16.3	12.9
ICT service exports (% of total service exports)	25.8	34.9
Applications		
Online service index (0–1, 1=highest presence)	0.35	0.33
Secure Internet servers (per million people)	2.2	9.8

High income

	2005	2012
Economic and social context		
Population (millions)	1,246	1,300
Urban population (% of total)	78	80
GNI per capita, *World Bank Atlas* method ($)	30,693	38,412
GDP growth, 2000–05 and 2005–12 (avg. annual %)	2.3	1.0
Adult literacy rate (% ages 15 and older)	..	..
Gross primary, secondary, tertiary school enrollment (%)	90	93
Sector structure		
Separate telecommunications/ICT regulator		
Status of main fixed-line telephone operator		
Level of competition (competition, partial comp., monopoly)		
International gateway(s)		
Mobile telephone service		
Internet service		
Foreign ownership (not allowed, restricted, allowed)		
Reg. treatment of VoIP (banned, closed, no framework, allowed)		
Sector efficiency and capacity		
Telecommunications revenue (% of GDP)	3.0	2.7
Telecommunications investment (% of revenue)	14.4	17.6
Sector performance		
Access		
Fixed-telephone subscriptions (per 100 people)	48.1	43.6
Mobile-cellular telephone subscriptions (per 100 people)	83.4	122.9
Fixed (wired)-broadband subscriptions (per 100 people)	13.5	26.2
Households with a computer (%)	60.1	77.7
Households with Internet access at home (%)	49.5	75.5
Usage		
Int'l. voice traffic, total (minutes/subscription/month)	..	..
Domestic mobile traffic (minutes/subscription/month)	..	114
Individuals using the Internet (%)	53.8	75.4
Quality		
Population covered by a mobile-cellular network (%)	98	100
Fixed (wired)-broadband subscriptions (% of total Internet)	37.9	95.9
International Internet bandwidth (bit/s per Internet user)	7,041	85,990
Affordability		
Fixed-telephone sub-basket ($ a month)	..	25.2
Mobile-cellular sub-basket ($ a month)	..	20.6
Fixed-broadband sub-basket ($ a month)	..	29.2
Trade		
ICT goods exports (% of total goods exports)	12.3	8.9
ICT goods imports (% of total goods imports)	13.1	10.8
ICT service exports (% of total service exports)	29.3	30.8
Applications		
Online service index (0–1, 1=highest presence)	0.66	0.67
Secure Internet servers (per million people)	313.4	827.6

Euro area

	2005	2012
Economic and social context		
Population (millions)	327	333
Urban population (% of total)	74	76
GNI per capita, *World Bank Atlas* method ($)	31,548	38,030
GDP growth, 2000–05 and 2005–12 (avg. annual %)	1.5	0.4
Adult literacy rate (% ages 15 and older)	..	99
Gross primary, secondary, tertiary school enrollment (%)	92	94
Sector structure		
Separate telecommunications/ICT regulator		
Status of main fixed-line telephone operator		
Level of competition (competition, partial comp., monopoly)		
International gateway(s)		
Mobile telephone service		
Internet service		
Foreign ownership (not allowed, restricted, allowed)		
Reg. treatment of VoIP (banned, closed, no framework, allowed)		
Sector efficiency and capacity		
Telecommunications revenue (% of GDP)	2.8	1.9
Telecommunications investment (% of revenue)	12.1	16.5
Sector performance		
Access		
Fixed-telephone subscriptions (per 100 people)	51.5	48.4
Mobile-cellular telephone subscriptions (per 100 people)	97.5	120.3
Fixed (wired)-broadband subscriptions (per 100 people)	13.2	29.7
Households with a computer (%)	58.2	79.2
Households with Internet access at home (%)	46.4	76.5
Usage		
Int'l. voice traffic, total (minutes/subscription/month)	..	..
Domestic mobile traffic (minutes/subscription/month)	84	117
Individuals using the Internet (%)	51.4	75.9
Quality		
Population covered by a mobile-cellular network (%)	99	99
Fixed (wired)-broadband subscriptions (% of total Internet)	58.6	97.6
International Internet bandwidth (bit/s per Internet user)	9,606	100,322
Affordability		
Fixed-telephone sub-basket ($ a month)	..	27.8
Mobile-cellular sub-basket ($ a month)	..	25.2
Fixed-broadband sub-basket ($ a month)	..	31.3
Trade		
ICT goods exports (% of total goods exports)	8.2	4.8
ICT goods imports (% of total goods imports)	10.1	6.9
ICT service exports (% of total service exports)	30.0	35.8
Applications		
Online service index (0–1, 1=highest presence)	0.70	0.66
Secure Internet servers (per million people)	144.1	662.3

Country tables

Cabo Verde

Cabo Verde is the new name for the country previously listed as Cape Verde.

China

Data for China do not include data for Hong Kong SAR, China; Macao SAR, China; or Taiwan, China.

Cyprus

GNI and GDP data and data calculated using GNI and GDP refer to the area controlled by the government of the Republic of Cyprus.

Georgia

GNI, GDP, and population data and data calculated using GNI, GDP, and population exclude Abkhazia and South Ossetia.

Kosovo, Montenegro, and Serbia

Montenegro declared independence from Serbia and Montenegro on June 3, 2006. Where available, data for each country are shown separately. However, some indicators for Serbia prior to 2006 include data for Montenegro. Moreover, data for most indicators for Serbia from 1999 onward exclude data for Kosovo, which in 1999 became a territory under international administration pursuant to UN Security Council Resolution 1244 (1999). Kosovo became a member of the World Bank on June 29, 2009, and its data are shown where available.

Moldova

GNI, GDP, and population data and data calculated using GNI, GDP, and population exclude Transnistria.

Morocco

GNI and GDP data and data calculated using GNI and GDP include Former Spanish Sahara.

South Sudan and Sudan

South Sudan declared its independence on July 9, 2011. Data are shown separately for South Sudan where available. However, data reported for Sudan include South Sudan unless otherwise noted.

Tanzania

GNI and GDP data and data calculated using GNI and GDP refer to mainland Tanzania only.

For more information, see *World Development Indicators 2014* or data.worldbank.org.

Afghanistan

South Asia			**Low income**

	Country data		Low-income group 2012
	2005	2012	2012
Economic and social context			
Population (millions)	25	30	846
Urban population (% of total)	22	24	28
GNI per capita, *World Bank Atlas* method ($)	250	680	590
GDP growth, 2000–05 and 2005–12 (avg. annual %)	6.2	10.5	5.9
Adult literacy rate (% ages 15 and older)	..	..	61
Gross primary, secondary, tertiary school enrollment (%)	53	62	60
Sector structure			
Separate telecommunications/ICT regulator	Yes	Yes	
Status of main fixed-line telephone operator	Public	Public	
Level of competition (competition, partial comp., monopoly)			
International gateway(s)	P	P	
Mobile telephone service	P	P	
Internet service	P	P	
Foreign ownership (not allowed, restricted, allowed)	A	A	
Reg. treatment of VoIP (banned, closed, no framework, allowed)	..	C	
Sector efficiency and capacity			
Telecommunications revenue (% of GDP)	6.0	..	5.0
Telecommunications investment (% of revenue)	37.8	..	..
Sector performance			
Access			
Fixed-telephone subscriptions (per 100 people)	0.2	0.0	1.0
Mobile-cellular telephone subscriptions (per 100 people)	4.8	60.4	47.2
Fixed (wired)-broadband subscriptions (per 100 people)	0.0	0.0	0.2
Households with a computer (%)	0.8	2.3[a]	4.2
Households with Internet access at home (%)	0.8	1.9[a]	3.4
Usage			
Int'l. voice traffic, total (minutes/subscription/month)	..	..	..
Domestic mobile traffic (minutes/subscription/month)	28.8	..	70.1
Individuals using the Internet (%)	1.2	5.5[a]	6.2
Quality			
Population covered by a mobile-cellular network (%)	72	85	..
Fixed (wired)-broadband subscriptions (% of total Internet)	18.3	50.0	30.9
International Internet bandwidth (bit/s per Internet user)	13	1,229	9,141
Affordability			
Fixed-telephone sub-basket ($ a month)	..	1.9	8.9
Mobile-cellular sub-basket ($ a month)	..	9.7	11.9
Fixed-broadband sub-basket ($ a month)	..	53.5	46.9
Trade			
ICT goods exports (% of total goods exports)	..	..	..
ICT goods imports (% of total goods imports)	..	0.2	..
ICT service exports (% of total service exports)	..	51.6	..
Applications			
Online service index (0–1, 1=highest presence)	0.20	0.24	0.20
Secure Internet servers (per million people)	0.0	1.0	1.1

Albania

Upper middle income

	Country data		Upper middle-income group
	2005	2012	2012
Economic and social context			
Population (millions)	3	3	2,391
Urban population (% of total)	47	54	61
GNI per capita, *World Bank Atlas* method ($)	2,540	4,030	6,969
GDP growth, 2000–05 and 2005–12 (avg. annual %)	5.3	4.4	6.2
Adult literacy rate (% ages 15 and older)	99	97	94
Gross primary, secondary, tertiary school enrollment (%)	66	..	76
Sector structure			
Separate telecommunications/ICT regulator	Yes	Yes	
Status of main fixed-line telephone operator	Public	Mixed	
Level of competition (competition, partial comp., monopoly)			
International gateway(s)	P	P	
Mobile telephone service	P	P	
Internet service	C	C	
Foreign ownership (not allowed, restricted, allowed)	R	R	
Reg. treatment of VoIP (banned, closed, no framework, allowed)	No	A	
Sector efficiency and capacity			
Telecommunications revenue (% of GDP)	6.1	4.3	2.5
Telecommunications investment (% of revenue)	11.2	28.4	18.2
Sector performance			
Access			
Fixed-telephone subscriptions (per 100 people)	8.7	9.9	19.4
Mobile-cellular telephone subscriptions (per 100 people)	47.9	110.7	92.4
Fixed (wired)-broadband subscriptions (per 100 people)	0.0	5.1	10.8
Households with a computer (%)	7.0	20.0[a]	40.6
Households with Internet access at home (%)	5.0	20.5[a]	36.3
Usage			
Int'l. voice traffic, total (minutes/subscription/month)	41.0	21.1	1.3
Domestic mobile traffic (minutes/subscription/month)	21.5	..	284.4
Individuals using the Internet (%)	6.0	54.7[a]	41.6
Quality			
Population covered by a mobile-cellular network (%)	91	99	99
Fixed (wired)-broadband subscriptions (% of total Internet)	25.0	91.8	95.5
International Internet bandwidth (bit/s per Internet user)	62	17,358	14,580
Affordability			
Fixed-telephone sub-basket ($ a month)	..	7.5	9.4
Mobile-cellular sub-basket ($ a month)	..	25.9	14.9
Fixed-broadband sub-basket ($ a month)	..	11.9	17.8
Trade			
ICT goods exports (% of total goods exports)	0.6	0.4	17.6
ICT goods imports (% of total goods imports)	3.8	3.0	14.7
ICT service exports (% of total service exports)	10.3	10.9	29.1
Applications			
Online service index (0–1, 1=highest presence)	0.47	0.42	0.42
Secure Internet servers (per million people)	0.3	16.1	18.5

Algeria

Middle East & North Africa			Upper middle income

	Country data		Upper middle-income group
	2005	**2012**	**2012**
Economic and social context			
Population (millions)	34	38	2,391
Urban population (% of total)	67	74	61
GNI per capita, *World Bank Atlas* method ($)	2,660	5,020	6,969
GDP growth, 2000–05 and 2005–12 (avg. annual %)	5.6	2.6	6.2
Adult literacy rate (% ages 15 and older)	73	..	94
Gross primary, secondary, tertiary school enrollment (%)	69	79	76
Sector structure			
Separate telecommunications/ICT regulator	Yes	Yes	
Status of main fixed-line telephone operator	Public	Public	
Level of competition (competition, partial comp., monopoly)			
International gateway(s)	P	P	
Mobile telephone service	P	P	
Internet service	C	C	
Foreign ownership (not allowed, restricted, allowed)	..	..	
Reg. treatment of VoIP (banned, closed, no framework, allowed)	A	A	
Sector efficiency and capacity			
Telecommunications revenue (% of GDP)	3.7	2.9	2.5
Telecommunications investment (% of revenue)	36.0	..	18.2
Sector performance			
Access			
Fixed-telephone subscriptions (per 100 people)	7.6	8.3	19.4
Mobile-cellular telephone subscriptions (per 100 people)	40.2	97.9	92.4
Fixed (wired)-broadband subscriptions (per 100 people)	0.4	2.9	10.8
Households with a computer (%)	7.1	24.2[a]	40.6
Households with Internet access at home (%)	1.2	19.4[a]	36.3
Usage			
Int'l. voice traffic, total (minutes/subscription/month)	8.1	6.8	1.3
Domestic mobile traffic (minutes/subscription/month)	12.4	191.1	284.4
Individuals using the Internet (%)	5.8	15.2[a]	41.6
Quality			
Population covered by a mobile-cellular network (%)	42	..	99
Fixed (wired)-broadband subscriptions (% of total Internet)	71.1	..	95.5
International Internet bandwidth (bit/s per Internet user)	79	7,679	14,580
Affordability			
Fixed-telephone sub-basket ($ a month)	..	6.4	9.4
Mobile-cellular sub-basket ($ a month)	..	14.1	14.9
Fixed-broadband sub-basket ($ a month)	..	14.1	17.8
Trade			
ICT goods exports (% of total goods exports)	0.0	0.0	17.6
ICT goods imports (% of total goods imports)	7.9	4.0	14.7
ICT service exports (% of total service exports)	29.2	59.4	29.1
Applications			
Online service index (0–1, 1=highest presence)	0.35	0.25	0.42
Secure Internet servers (per million people)	0.1	1.5	18.5

American Samoa

Upper middle income

	Country data		Upper middle-income group
	2005	2012	2012
Economic and social context			
Population (millions)	0.06	0.06	2,391
Urban population (% of total)	91	93	61
GNI per capita, *World Bank Atlas* method ($)	..	..	6,969
GDP growth, 2000–05 and 2005–12 (avg. annual %)	..	..	6.2
Adult literacy rate (% ages 15 and older)	..	..	94
Gross primary, secondary, tertiary school enrollment (%)	..	..	76
Sector structure			
Separate telecommunications/ICT regulator	..	..	
Status of main fixed-line telephone operator	..	..	
Level of competition (competition, partial comp., monopoly)			
International gateway(s)	..	..	
Mobile telephone service	..	..	
Internet service	..	..	
Foreign ownership (not allowed, restricted, allowed)	..	..	
Reg. treatment of VoIP (banned, closed, no framework, allowed)	..	..	
Sector efficiency and capacity			
Telecommunications revenue (% of GDP)	..	..	2.5
Telecommunications investment (% of revenue)	..	..	18.2
Sector performance			
Access			
Fixed-telephone subscriptions (per 100 people)	17.6	18.1	19.4
Mobile-cellular telephone subscriptions (per 100 people)	3.8	..	92.4
Fixed (wired)-broadband subscriptions (per 100 people)	..	..	10.8
Households with a computer (%)	..	..	40.6
Households with Internet access at home (%)	..	..	36.3
Usage			
Int'l. voice traffic, total (minutes/subscription/month)	..	..	1.3
Domestic mobile traffic (minutes/subscription/month)	..	..	284.4
Individuals using the Internet (%)	..	..	41.6
Quality			
Population covered by a mobile-cellular network (%)	..	..	99
Fixed (wired)-broadband subscriptions (% of total Internet)	..	..	95.5
International Internet bandwidth (bit/s per Internet user)	..	..	14,580
Affordability			
Fixed-telephone sub-basket ($ a month)	..	..	9.4
Mobile-cellular sub-basket ($ a month)	..	..	14.9
Fixed-broadband sub-basket ($ a month)	..	..	17.8
Trade			
ICT goods exports (% of total goods exports)	..	..	17.6
ICT goods imports (% of total goods imports)	..	..	14.7
ICT service exports (% of total service exports)	..	..	29.1
Applications			
Online service index (0–1, 1=highest presence)	..	..	0.42
Secure Internet servers (per million people)	69.1	36.4	18.5

Andorra

High income

	Country data		High-income group
	2005	2012	2012
Economic and social context			
Population (millions)	0.08	0.08	1,300
Urban population (% of total)	90	87	80
GNI per capita, *World Bank Atlas* method ($)	31,310	43,110	38,412
GDP growth, 2000–05 and 2005–12 (avg. annual %)	7.1	..	1.0
Adult literacy rate (% ages 15 and older)	..	..	..
Gross primary, secondary, tertiary school enrollment (%)	..	..	93
Sector structure			
Separate telecommunications/ICT regulator	No	No	
Status of main fixed-line telephone operator	Public	Public	
Level of competition (competition, partial comp., monopoly)			
International gateway(s)	..	M	
Mobile telephone service	M	M	
Internet service	..	M	
Foreign ownership (not allowed, restricted, allowed)	No	A	
Reg. treatment of VoIP (banned, closed, no framework, allowed)	..	..	
Sector efficiency and capacity			
Telecommunications revenue (% of GDP)	3.9	3.6	2.7
Telecommunications investment (% of revenue)	..	..	17.6
Sector performance			
Access			
Fixed-telephone subscriptions (per 100 people)	43.6	48.9	43.6
Mobile-cellular telephone subscriptions (per 100 people)	79.5	81.5	122.9
Fixed (wired)-broadband subscriptions (per 100 people)	12.7	34.3	26.2
Households with a computer (%)	..	..	77.7
Households with Internet access at home (%)	..	..	75.5
Usage			
Int'l. voice traffic, total (minutes/subscription/month)	112.6	80.2	..
Domestic mobile traffic (minutes/subscription/month)	65.4	53.6	113.6
Individuals using the Internet (%)	37.6	86.4[a]	75.4
Quality			
Population covered by a mobile-cellular network (%)	91	99	100
Fixed (wired)-broadband subscriptions (% of total Internet)	60.7	99.4	95.9
International Internet bandwidth (bit/s per Internet user)	13,750	38,388	85,990
Affordability			
Fixed-telephone sub-basket ($ a month)	..	..	25.2
Mobile-cellular sub-basket ($ a month)	..	..	20.6
Fixed-broadband sub-basket ($ a month)	..	..	29.2
Trade			
ICT goods exports (% of total goods exports)	18.8	..	8.9
ICT goods imports (% of total goods imports)	14.0	..	10.8
ICT service exports (% of total service exports)	..	..	30.8
Applications			
Online service index (0–1, 1=highest presence)	0.52	0.31	0.67
Secure Internet servers (per million people)	418.6	645.6	827.6

Angola

Sub-Saharan Africa		**Upper middle income**	

	Country data		Upper middle-income group
	2005	2012	2012
Economic and social context			
Population (millions)	17	21	2,391
Urban population (% of total)	54	60	61
GNI per capita, *World Bank Atlas* method ($)	1,270	4,580	6,969
GDP growth, 2000–05 and 2005–12 (avg. annual %)	10.1	9.4	6.2
Adult literacy rate (% ages 15 and older)	67	70	94
Gross primary, secondary, tertiary school enrollment (%)	..	73	76
Sector structure			
Separate telecommunications/ICT regulator	Yes	Yes	
Status of main fixed-line telephone operator	Public	Public	
Level of competition (competition, partial comp., monopoly)			
International gateway(s)	C	M	
Mobile telephone service	P	C	
Internet service	C	C	
Foreign ownership (not allowed, restricted, allowed)	R	R	
Reg. treatment of VoIP (banned, closed, no framework, allowed)	No	C	
Sector efficiency and capacity			
Telecommunications revenue (% of GDP)	2.2	..	2.5
Telecommunications investment (% of revenue)	25.3	..	18.2
Sector performance			
Access			
Fixed-telephone subscriptions (per 100 people)	0.6	1.5	19.4
Mobile-cellular telephone subscriptions (per 100 people)	9.7	47.1	92.4
Fixed (wired)-broadband subscriptions (per 100 people)	0.0	0.2	10.8
Households with a computer (%)	4.0	8.5[a]	40.6
Households with Internet access at home (%)	1.4[a]	7.2[a]	36.3
Usage			
Int'l. voice traffic, total (minutes/subscription/month)	..	..	1.3
Domestic mobile traffic (minutes/subscription/month)	..	..	284.4
Individuals using the Internet (%)	1.1	16.9[a]	41.6
Quality			
Population covered by a mobile-cellular network (%)	40	..	99
Fixed (wired)-broadband subscriptions (% of total Internet)	0.0	6.3	95.5
International Internet bandwidth (bit/s per Internet user)	359	567	14,580
Affordability			
Fixed-telephone sub-basket ($ a month)	..	16.9	9.4
Mobile-cellular sub-basket ($ a month)	..	20.0	14.9
Fixed-broadband sub-basket ($ a month)	..	53.2	17.8
Trade			
ICT goods exports (% of total goods exports)	..	..	17.6
ICT goods imports (% of total goods imports)	..	..	14.7
ICT service exports (% of total service exports)	9.3	4.5	29.1
Applications			
Online service index (0–1, 1=highest presence)	0.33	0.33	0.42
Secure Internet servers (per million people)	0.3	3.9	18.5

Antigua and Barbuda

High income

	Country data		High-income group
	2005	2012	2012
Economic and social context			
Population (millions)	0.08	0.09	1,300
Urban population (% of total)	31	30	80
GNI per capita, *World Bank Atlas* method ($)	12,000	12,480	38,412
GDP growth, 2000–05 and 2005–12 (avg. annual %)	3.9	-1.7	1.0
Adult literacy rate (% ages 15 and older)	99	99	..
Gross primary, secondary, tertiary school enrollment (%)	..	82	93
Sector structure			
Separate telecommunications/ICT regulator	No	No	
Status of main fixed-line telephone operator	Public	Public	
Level of competition (competition, partial comp., monopoly)			
International gateway(s)	M	P	
Mobile telephone service	C	P	
Internet service	C	P	
Foreign ownership (not allowed, restricted, allowed)	A	A	
Reg. treatment of VoIP (banned, closed, no framework, allowed)	B	A	
Sector efficiency and capacity			
Telecommunications revenue (% of GDP)	..	..	2.7
Telecommunications investment (% of revenue)	..	..	17.6
Sector performance			
Access			
Fixed-telephone subscriptions (per 100 people)	44.2	37.2	43.6
Mobile-cellular telephone subscriptions (per 100 people)	104.2	143.0	122.9
Fixed (wired)-broadband subscriptions (per 100 people)	1.0[a]	4.6	26.2
Households with a computer (%)	..	56.1[a]	77.7
Households with Internet access at home (%)	..	48.2[a]	75.5
Usage			
Int'l. voice traffic, total (minutes/subscription/month)	..	19.0	..
Domestic mobile traffic (minutes/subscription/month)	..	138.9	113.6
Individuals using the Internet (%)	27.0[a]	59.0[a]	75.4
Quality			
Population covered by a mobile-cellular network (%)	100	100	100
Fixed (wired)-broadband subscriptions (% of total Internet)	8.8	91.6	95.9
International Internet bandwidth (bit/s per Internet user)	24,896	97,620	85,990
Affordability			
Fixed-telephone sub-basket ($ a month)	..	12.8	25.2
Mobile-cellular sub-basket ($ a month)	..	25.3	20.6
Fixed-broadband sub-basket ($ a month)	..	54.9	29.2
Trade			
ICT goods exports (% of total goods exports)	4.6	11.6	8.9
ICT goods imports (% of total goods imports)	3.9	5.5	10.8
ICT service exports (% of total service exports)	9.6	6.5	30.8
Applications			
Online service index (0–1, 1=highest presence)	0.45	0.31	0.67
Secure Internet servers (per million people)	859.9	688.9	827.6

Argentina

	Country data		Upper middle-income group
	2005	2012	2012
Economic and social context			
Population (millions)	39	41	2,391
Urban population (% of total)	91	93	61
GNI per capita, *World Bank Atlas* method ($)	4,480	..	6,969
GDP growth, 2000–05 and 2005–12 (avg. annual %)	2.2	6.3	6.2
Adult literacy rate (% ages 15 and older)	97	98	94
Gross primary, secondary, tertiary school enrollment (%)	89	97	76
Sector structure			
Separate telecommunications/ICT regulator	Yes	Yes	
Status of main fixed-line telephone operator	Private	Private	
Level of competition (competition, partial comp., monopoly)			
International gateway(s)	..	..	
Mobile telephone service	C	C	
Internet service	C	C	
Foreign ownership (not allowed, restricted, allowed)	A	R	
Reg. treatment of VoIP (banned, closed, no framework, allowed)	A	A	
Sector efficiency and capacity			
Telecommunications revenue (% of GDP)	3.1	2.9	2.5
Telecommunications investment (% of revenue)	..	15.3	18.2
Sector performance			
Access			
Fixed-telephone subscriptions (per 100 people)	24.4	23.5	19.4
Mobile-cellular telephone subscriptions (per 100 people)	57.3	151.9	92.4
Fixed (wired)-broadband subscriptions (per 100 people)	2.4	10.9	10.8
Households with a computer (%)	32.0	56.0[a]	40.6
Households with Internet access at home (%)	13.3[a]	47.5[a]	36.3
Usage			
Int'l. voice traffic, total (minutes/subscription/month)	..	..	1.3
Domestic mobile traffic (minutes/subscription/month)	..	19.6	284.4
Individuals using the Internet (%)	17.7	55.8[a]	41.6
Quality			
Population covered by a mobile-cellular network (%)	94	..	99
Fixed (wired)-broadband subscriptions (% of total Internet)	38.3	92.2	95.5
International Internet bandwidth (bit/s per Internet user)	1,788	21,983	14,580
Affordability			
Fixed-telephone sub-basket ($ a month)	..	4.5	9.4
Mobile-cellular sub-basket ($ a month)	..	39.4	14.9
Fixed-broadband sub-basket ($ a month)	..	24.3	17.8
Trade			
ICT goods exports (% of total goods exports)	0.2	0.1	17.6
ICT goods imports (% of total goods imports)	11.6	8.3	14.7
ICT service exports (% of total service exports)	31.1	46.0	29.1
Applications			
Online service index (0–1, 1=highest presence)	0.58	0.53	0.42
Secure Internet servers (per million people)	10.8	42.9	18.5

Armenia

Lower middle income

	Country data		Lower middle-income group
	2005	2012	2012
Economic and social context			
Population (millions)	3	3	2,507
Urban population (% of total)	64	64	39
GNI per capita, *World Bank Atlas* method ($)	1,500	3,720	1,893
GDP growth, 2000–05 and 2005–12 (avg. annual %)	12.3	2.8	6.0
Adult literacy rate (% ages 15 and older)	99	100	71
Gross primary, secondary, tertiary school enrollment (%)	73	78	64
Sector structure			
Separate telecommunications/ICT regulator	No	Yes	
Status of main fixed-line telephone operator	Mixed	Mixed	
Level of competition (competition, partial comp., monopoly)			
International gateway(s)	..	..	
Mobile telephone service	P	P	
Internet service	C	C	
Foreign ownership (not allowed, restricted, allowed)	A	A	
Reg. treatment of VoIP (banned, closed, no framework, allowed)	C	A	
Sector efficiency and capacity			
Telecommunications revenue (% of GDP)	3.0	4.2	2.5
Telecommunications investment (% of revenue)	23.6	19.7	20.5
Sector performance			
Access			
Fixed-telephone subscriptions (per 100 people)	19.7	19.7	5.4
Mobile-cellular telephone subscriptions (per 100 people)	10.5	111.9	83.1
Fixed (wired)-broadband subscriptions (per 100 people)	0.1	6.7	1.4
Households with a computer (%)	5.5[a]	34.0[a]	15.0
Households with Internet access at home (%)	2.9[a]	25.4[a]	12.4
Usage			
Int'l. voice traffic, total (minutes/subscription/month)	..	20.5	6.5
Domestic mobile traffic (minutes/subscription/month)	58.0	171.7	..
Individuals using the Internet (%)	5.3	39.2[a]	18.7
Quality			
Population covered by a mobile-cellular network (%)	85	100	86
Fixed (wired)-broadband subscriptions (% of total Internet)	1.1	95.5	58.2
International Internet bandwidth (bit/s per Internet user)	459	40,373	8,076
Affordability			
Fixed-telephone sub-basket ($ a month)	..	3.0	4.9
Mobile-cellular sub-basket ($ a month)	..	8.8	10.5
Fixed-broadband sub-basket ($ a month)	..	12.1	20.6
Trade			
ICT goods exports (% of total goods exports)	0.3	1.3	4.6
ICT goods imports (% of total goods imports)	3.6	3.7	7.2
ICT service exports (% of total service exports)	14.3	13.5	47.1
Applications			
Online service index (0–1, 1=highest presence)	0.42	0.33	0.32
Secure Internet servers (per million people)	1.3	40.3	4.4

Aruba

	Country data		High-income group
	2005	2012	2012
Economic and social context			
Population (millions)	0.10	0.10	1,300
Urban population (% of total)	47	47	80
GNI per capita, World Bank Atlas method ($)	..	..	38,412
GDP growth, 2000–05 and 2005–12 (avg. annual %)	2.0	-3.9	1.0
Adult literacy rate (% ages 15 and older)	97	97	..
Gross primary, secondary, tertiary school enrollment (%)	84	84	93
Sector structure			
Separate telecommunications/ICT regulator	..	..	
Status of main fixed-line telephone operator	..	..	
Level of competition (competition, partial comp., monopoly)			
International gateway(s)	..	..	
Mobile telephone service	..	..	
Internet service	..	..	
Foreign ownership (not allowed, restricted, allowed)	..	..	
Reg. treatment of VoIP (banned, closed, no framework, allowed)	..	..	
Sector efficiency and capacity			
Telecommunications revenue (% of GDP)	53.0	5.6	2.7
Telecommunications investment (% of revenue)	1.2	15.8	17.6
Sector performance			
Access			
Fixed-telephone subscriptions (per 100 people)	38.2	35.2[a]	43.6
Mobile-cellular telephone subscriptions (per 100 people)	103.4	131.9[a]	122.9
Fixed (wired)-broadband subscriptions (per 100 people)	12.3	18.9	26.2
Households with a computer (%)	45.0	73.1[a]	77.7
Households with Internet access at home (%)	36.7	69.6[a]	75.5
Usage			
Int'l. voice traffic, total (minutes/subscription/month)	..	..	..
Domestic mobile traffic (minutes/subscription/month)	..	..	113.6
Individuals using the Internet (%)	25.4[a]	74.0[a]	75.4
Quality			
Population covered by a mobile-cellular network (%)	90	99	100
Fixed (wired)-broadband subscriptions (% of total Internet)	100.0	100.0	95.9
International Internet bandwidth (bit/s per Internet user)	7,084	67,578	85,990
Affordability			
Fixed-telephone sub-basket ($ a month)	..	..	25.2
Mobile-cellular sub-basket ($ a month)	..	..	20.6
Fixed-broadband sub-basket ($ a month)	..	..	29.2
Trade			
ICT goods exports (% of total goods exports)	..	0.7	8.9
ICT goods imports (% of total goods imports)	..	4.4	10.8
ICT service exports (% of total service exports)	10.2	13.9	30.8
Applications			
Online service index (0–1, 1=highest presence)	..	..	0.67
Secure Internet servers (per million people)	289.9	281.6	827.6

Australia

	Country data		High-income group
	2005	2012	2012
Economic and social context			
Population (millions)	20	23	1,300
Urban population (% of total)	88	89	80
GNI per capita, *World Bank Atlas* method ($)	30,280	59,260	38,412
GDP growth, 2000–05 and 2005–12 (avg. annual %)	3.4	2.8	1.0
Adult literacy rate (% ages 15 and older)	..	..	..
Gross primary, secondary, tertiary school enrollment (%)	112	112	93
Sector structure			
Separate telecommunications/ICT regulator	Yes	Yes	
Status of main fixed-line telephone operator	Mixed	Mixed	
Level of competition (competition, partial comp., monopoly)			
International gateway(s)	C	C	
Mobile telephone service	C	C	
Internet service	C	C	
Foreign ownership (not allowed, restricted, allowed)	A	A	
Reg. treatment of VoIP (banned, closed, no framework, allowed)	A	A	
Sector efficiency and capacity			
Telecommunications revenue (% of GDP)	3.8	2.9	2.7
Telecommunications investment (% of revenue)	16.7	20.5	17.6
Sector performance			
Access			
Fixed-telephone subscriptions (per 100 people)	49.3	45.4	43.6
Mobile-cellular telephone subscriptions (per 100 people)	89.8	105.6	122.9
Fixed (wired)-broadband subscriptions (per 100 people)	9.8	24.3	26.2
Households with a computer (%)	67.0	85.2[a]	77.7
Households with Internet access at home (%)	56.0	81.4[a]	75.5
Usage			
Int'l. voice traffic, total (minutes/subscription/month)	..	..	..
Domestic mobile traffic (minutes/subscription/month)	..	..	113.6
Individuals using the Internet (%)	63.0	82.3[a]	75.4
Quality			
Population covered by a mobile-cellular network (%)	98	99	100
Fixed (wired)-broadband subscriptions (% of total Internet)	33.7	92.9	95.9
International Internet bandwidth (bit/s per Internet user)	7,794	69,066	85,990
Affordability			
Fixed-telephone sub-basket ($ a month)	..	33.0	25.2
Mobile-cellular sub-basket ($ a month)	..	20.3	20.6
Fixed-broadband sub-basket ($ a month)	..	61.9	29.2
Trade			
ICT goods exports (% of total goods exports)	1.7	0.9	8.9
ICT goods imports (% of total goods imports)	11.8	8.9	10.8
ICT service exports (% of total service exports)	16.0	18.6	30.8
Applications			
Online service index (0–1, 1=highest presence)	0.81	0.86	0.67
Secure Internet servers (per million people)	498.1	1,265.3	827.6

Austria

	Country data		High-income group
	2005	2012	2012
Economic and social context			
Population (millions)	8	8	1,300
Urban population (% of total)	67	68	80
GNI per capita, World Bank Atlas method ($)	37,210	47,850	38,412
GDP growth, 2000–05 and 2005–12 (avg. annual %)	1.7	1.1	1.0
Adult literacy rate (% ages 15 and older)	..	..	..
Gross primary, secondary, tertiary school enrollment (%)	88	94	93
Sector structure			
Separate telecommunications/ICT regulator	Yes	Yes	
Status of main fixed-line telephone operator	Mixed	Mixed	
Level of competition (competition, partial comp., monopoly)			
International gateway(s)	C	C	
Mobile telephone service	C	C	
Internet service	C	C	
Foreign ownership (not allowed, restricted, allowed)	A	A	
Reg. treatment of VoIP (banned, closed, no framework, allowed)	A	A	
Sector efficiency and capacity			
Telecommunications revenue (% of GDP)	2.4	1.4	2.7
Telecommunications investment (% of revenue)	12.7	12.5	17.6
Sector performance			
Access			
Fixed-telephone subscriptions (per 100 people)	45.4	39.7	43.6
Mobile-cellular telephone subscriptions (per 100 people)	105.2	160.5	122.9
Fixed (wired)-broadband subscriptions (per 100 people)	14.2	25.0	26.2
Households with a computer (%)	63.1	81.0	77.7
Households with Internet access at home (%)	46.7	79.0	75.5
Usage			
Int'l. voice traffic, total (minutes/subscription/month)	16.1	..	..
Domestic mobile traffic (minutes/subscription/month)	107.5	140.0	113.6
Individuals using the Internet (%)	58.0	81.0	75.4
Quality			
Population covered by a mobile-cellular network (%)	99	99	100
Fixed (wired)-broadband subscriptions (% of total Internet)	66.3	85.4	95.9
International Internet bandwidth (bit/s per Internet user)	11,430	108,084	85,990
Affordability			
Fixed-telephone sub-basket ($ a month)	..	27.8	25.2
Mobile-cellular sub-basket ($ a month)	..	14.7	20.6
Fixed-broadband sub-basket ($ a month)	..	41.6	29.2
Trade			
ICT goods exports (% of total goods exports)	5.5	3.9	8.9
ICT goods imports (% of total goods imports)	7.7	5.1	10.8
ICT service exports (% of total service exports)	24.8	30.7	30.8
Applications			
Online service index (0–1, 1=highest presence)	0.74	0.75	0.67
Secure Internet servers (per million people)	231.7	1,079.2	827.6

Azerbaijan

Europe & Central Asia			Upper middle income

	Country data		Upper middle-income group
	2005	2012	2012

Economic and social context

Population (millions)	8	9	2,391
Urban population (% of total)	52	54	61
GNI per capita, *World Bank Atlas* method ($)	1,270	6,220	6,969
GDP growth, 2000–05 and 2005–12 (avg. annual %)	12.7	10.8	6.2
Adult literacy rate (% ages 15 and older)	100	100	94
Gross primary, secondary, tertiary school enrollment (%)	72	71	76

Sector structure

Separate telecommunications/ICT regulator	No	No	
Status of main fixed-line telephone operator	Public	Public	
Level of competition (competition, partial comp., monopoly)			
International gateway(s)	M	M	
Mobile telephone service	P	P	
Internet service	C	C	
Foreign ownership (not allowed, restricted, allowed)	R	R	
Reg. treatment of VoIP (banned, closed, no framework, allowed)	No	A	

Sector efficiency and capacity

Telecommunications revenue (% of GDP)	3.6	2.5	2.5
Telecommunications investment (% of revenue)	6.8	24.7	18.2

Sector performance
Access

Fixed-telephone subscriptions (per 100 people)	12.8	18.5	19.4
Mobile-cellular telephone subscriptions (per 100 people)	26.2	108.8	92.4
Fixed (wired)-broadband subscriptions (per 100 people)	0.0	14.1	10.8
Households with a computer (%)	7.3	45.0[a]	40.6
Households with Internet access at home (%)	6.3	46.8[a]	36.3

Usage

Int'l. voice traffic, total (minutes/subscription/month)	7.6	6.4	1.3
Domestic mobile traffic (minutes/subscription/month)	3.1	179.7	284.4
Individuals using the Internet (%)	8.0	54.2[a]	41.6

Quality

Population covered by a mobile-cellular network (%)	99	100	99
Fixed (wired)-broadband subscriptions (% of total Internet)	3.0	77.3	95.5
International Internet bandwidth (bit/s per Internet user)	436	40,591	14,580

Affordability

Fixed-telephone sub-basket ($ a month)	..	2.5	9.4
Mobile-cellular sub-basket ($ a month)	..	10.4	14.9
Fixed-broadband sub-basket ($ a month)	..	12.7	17.8

Trade

ICT goods exports (% of total goods exports)	0.0	0.0	17.6
ICT goods imports (% of total goods imports)	4.6	3.3	14.7
ICT service exports (% of total service exports)	38.8	15.0	29.1

Applications

Online service index (0–1, 1=highest presence)	0.46	0.37	0.42
Secure Internet servers (per million people)	0.5	8.6	18.5

Bahamas, The

	Country data		High-income group
	2005	2012	2012
Economic and social context			
Population (millions)	0.33	0.37	1,300
Urban population (% of total)	83	84	80
GNI per capita, *World Bank Atlas* method ($)	23,680	20,600	38,412
GDP growth, 2000–05 and 2005–12 (avg. annual %)	1.3	-0.3	1.0
Adult literacy rate (% ages 15 and older)	..	..	..
Gross primary, secondary, tertiary school enrollment (%)	..	..	93
Sector structure			
Separate telecommunications/ICT regulator	Yes	Yes	
Status of main fixed-line telephone operator	Public	Mixed	
Level of competition (competition, partial comp., monopoly)			
International gateway(s)	M	C	
Mobile telephone service	M	M	
Internet service	C	C	
Foreign ownership (not allowed, restricted, allowed)	A	A	
Reg. treatment of VoIP (banned, closed, no framework, allowed)	C	A	
Sector efficiency and capacity			
Telecommunications revenue (% of GDP)	..	..	2.7
Telecommunications investment (% of revenue)	..	..	17.6
Sector performance			
Access			
Fixed-telephone subscriptions (per 100 people)	40.4	36.3	43.6
Mobile-cellular telephone subscriptions (per 100 people)	69.2	80.7[a]	122.9
Fixed (wired)-broadband subscriptions (per 100 people)	4.1	4.2[a]	26.2
Households with a computer (%)	..	..	77.7
Households with Internet access at home (%)	..	..	75.5
Usage			
Int'l. voice traffic, total (minutes/subscription/month)	..	..	..
Domestic mobile traffic (minutes/subscription/month)	..	..	113.6
Individuals using the Internet (%)	25.0[a]	71.7[a]	75.4
Quality			
Population covered by a mobile-cellular network (%)	95	*100*	100
Fixed (wired)-broadband subscriptions (% of total Internet)	49.2	100.0	95.9
International Internet bandwidth (bit/s per Internet user)	1,094	3,747	85,990
Affordability			
Fixed-telephone sub-basket ($ a month)	..	16.3	25.2
Mobile-cellular sub-basket ($ a month)	..	17.5	20.6
Fixed-broadband sub-basket ($ a month)	..	30.0	29.2
Trade			
ICT goods exports (% of total goods exports)	0.3	0.2	8.9
ICT goods imports (% of total goods imports)	3.2	3.9	10.8
ICT service exports (% of total service exports)	..	..	30.8
Applications			
Online service index (0–1, 1=highest presence)	0.49	0.47	0.67
Secure Internet servers (per million people)	148.9	267.9	827.6

Bahrain

High income

	Country data		High-income group
	2005	2012	2012
Economic and social context			
Population (millions)	0.88	1	1,300
Urban population (% of total)	88	89	80
GNI per capita, World Bank Atlas method ($)	16,730	19,560	38,412
GDP growth, 2000–05 and 2005–12 (avg. annual %)	6.1	4.8	1.0
Adult literacy rate (% ages 15 and older)	87	95	..
Gross primary, secondary, tertiary school enrollment (%)	..	..	93
Sector structure			
Separate telecommunications/ICT regulator	Yes	Yes	
Status of main fixed-line telephone operator	Mixed	Mixed	
Level of competition (competition, partial comp., monopoly)			
International gateway(s)	C	C	
Mobile telephone service	P	P	
Internet service	C	C	
Foreign ownership (not allowed, restricted, allowed)	A	A	
Reg. treatment of VoIP (banned, closed, no framework, allowed)	C	A	
Sector efficiency and capacity			
Telecommunications revenue (% of GDP)	3.9	3.6	2.7
Telecommunications investment (% of revenue)	14.9	13.0	17.6
Sector performance			
Access			
Fixed-telephone subscriptions (per 100 people)	22.0	22.7	43.6
Mobile-cellular telephone subscriptions (per 100 people)	87.2	161.2	122.9
Fixed (wired)-broadband subscriptions (per 100 people)	2.4	13.2	26.2
Households with a computer (%)	44.0	92.7	77.7
Households with Internet access at home (%)	32.0	79.0	75.5
Usage			
Int'l. voice traffic, total (minutes/subscription/month)	..	100.6	..
Domestic mobile traffic (minutes/subscription/month)	117.3	227.6	113.6
Individuals using the Internet (%)	21.3	88.0	75.4
Quality			
Population covered by a mobile-cellular network (%)	100	100	100
Fixed (wired)-broadband subscriptions (% of total Internet)	42.6	100.0	95.9
International Internet bandwidth (bit/s per Internet user)	2,183	18,108	85,990
Affordability			
Fixed-telephone sub-basket ($ a month)	..	4.8	25.2
Mobile-cellular sub-basket ($ a month)	..	15.0	20.6
Fixed-broadband sub-basket ($ a month)	..	26.6	29.2
Trade			
ICT goods exports (% of total goods exports)	0.1	0.6	8.9
ICT goods imports (% of total goods imports)	2.1	3.3	10.8
ICT service exports (% of total service exports)	25.1	22.8	30.8
Applications			
Online service index (0–1, 1=highest presence)	0.57	0.86	0.67
Secure Internet servers (per million people)	39.8	141.9	827.6

Bangladesh

Low income

	Country data		Low-income group
	2005	2012	2012
Economic and social context			
Population (millions)	143	155	846
Urban population (% of total)	26	29	28
GNI per capita, *World Bank Atlas* method ($)	470	840	590
GDP growth, 2000–05 and 2005–12 (avg. annual %)	5.4	6.2	5.9
Adult literacy rate (% ages 15 and older)	47	58	61
Gross primary, secondary, tertiary school enrollment (%)	51	59	60
Sector structure			
Separate telecommunications/ICT regulator	Yes	Yes	
Status of main fixed-line telephone operator	Public	Public	
Level of competition (competition, partial comp., monopoly)			
International gateway(s)	M	P	
Mobile telephone service	C	C	
Internet service	C	C	
Foreign ownership (not allowed, restricted, allowed)	A	A	
Reg. treatment of VoIP (banned, closed, no framework, allowed)	B	A	
Sector efficiency and capacity			
Telecommunications revenue (% of GDP)	*1.5*	7.5	*5.0*
Telecommunications investment (% of revenue)	..	8.8	..
Sector performance			
Access			
Fixed-telephone subscriptions (per 100 people)	0.7	0.6	1.0
Mobile-cellular telephone subscriptions (per 100 people)	6.3	62.8	47.2
Fixed (wired)-broadband subscriptions (per 100 people)	0.0	0.4	0.2
Households with a computer (%)	1.4	4.8[a]	4.2
Households with Internet access at home (%)	0.2	3.2[a]	3.4
Usage			
Int'l. voice traffic, total (minutes/subscription/month)	..	21.3	..
Domestic mobile traffic (minutes/subscription/month)	..	96.2	70.1
Individuals using the Internet (%)	0.2[a]	6.3[a]	6.2
Quality			
Population covered by a mobile-cellular network (%)	80	99	..
Fixed (wired)-broadband subscriptions (% of total Internet)	0.0	25.8	*30.9*
International Internet bandwidth (bit/s per Internet user)	173	3,032	9,141
Affordability			
Fixed-telephone sub-basket ($ a month)	..	2.6	8.9
Mobile-cellular sub-basket ($ a month)	..	1.6	11.9
Fixed-broadband sub-basket ($ a month)	..	4.7	46.9
Trade			
ICT goods exports (% of total goods exports)	0.1	..	..
ICT goods imports (% of total goods imports)	6.2	..	..
ICT service exports (% of total service exports)	18.2	26.7	..
Applications			
Online service index (0–1, 1=highest presence)	0.29	0.44	0.20
Secure Internet servers (per million people)	0.0	0.8	1.1

Barbados

	Country data		High-income group 2012
	2005	2012	2012
Economic and social context			
Population (millions)	0.27	0.28	1,300
Urban population (% of total)	41	45	80
GNI per capita, *World Bank Atlas* method ($)	13,640	15,080	38,412
GDP growth, 2000–05 and 2005–12 (avg. annual %)	1.2	0.1	1.0
Adult literacy rate (% ages 15 and older)	..	..	..
Gross primary, secondary, tertiary school enrollment (%)	94	96	93
Sector structure			
Separate telecommunications/ICT regulator	Yes	Yes	
Status of main fixed-line telephone operator	Mixed	Mixed	
Level of competition (competition, partial comp., monopoly)			
International gateway(s)	P	..	
Mobile telephone service	C	P	
Internet service	C	..	
Foreign ownership (not allowed, restricted, allowed)	A	R	
Reg. treatment of VoIP (banned, closed, no framework, allowed)	No	A	
Sector efficiency and capacity			
Telecommunications revenue (% of GDP)	4.6	..	2.7
Telecommunications investment (% of revenue)	14.0	..	17.6
Sector performance			
Access			
Fixed-telephone subscriptions (per 100 people)	49.3	50.8	43.6
Mobile-cellular telephone subscriptions (per 100 people)	75.4	122.5[a]	122.9
Fixed (wired)-broadband subscriptions (per 100 people)	11.7	23.1[a]	26.2
Households with a computer (%)	42.6[a]	69.2[a]	77.7
Households with Internet access at home (%)	37.2[a]	62.9[a]	75.5
Usage			
Int'l. voice traffic, total (minutes/subscription/month)	..	..	..
Domestic mobile traffic (minutes/subscription/month)	..	..	113.6
Individuals using the Internet (%)	52.5[a]	73.3[a]	75.4
Quality			
Population covered by a mobile-cellular network (%)	100	99	100
Fixed (wired)-broadband subscriptions (% of total Internet)	71.2	94.0	95.9
International Internet bandwidth (bit/s per Internet user)	3,481	67,410	85,990
Affordability			
Fixed-telephone sub-basket ($ a month)	..	22.0	25.2
Mobile-cellular sub-basket ($ a month)	..	24.6	20.6
Fixed-broadband sub-basket ($ a month)	..	45.2	29.2
Trade			
ICT goods exports (% of total goods exports)	4.9	0.8	8.9
ICT goods imports (% of total goods imports)	7.8	4.4	10.8
ICT service exports (% of total service exports)	15.3	25.9	30.8
Applications			
Online service index (0–1, 1=highest presence)	0.57	0.37	0.67
Secure Internet servers (per million people)	204.7	340.4	827.6

Belarus

	Country data		Upper middle-income group
	2005	2012	2012
Economic and social context			
Population (millions)	10	9	2,391
Urban population (% of total)	72	75	61
GNI per capita, World Bank Atlas method ($)	2,810	6,530	6,969
GDP growth, 2000–05 and 2005–12 (avg. annual %)	7.6	6.1	6.2
Adult literacy rate (% ages 15 and older)	..	100	94
Gross primary, secondary, tertiary school enrollment (%)	..	100	76
Sector structure			
Separate telecommunications/ICT regulator	No	No	
Status of main fixed-line telephone operator	Public	Public	
Level of competition (competition, partial comp., monopoly)			
International gateway(s)	M	M	
Mobile telephone service	P	C	
Internet service	C	C	
Foreign ownership (not allowed, restricted, allowed)	R	R	
Reg. treatment of VoIP (banned, closed, no framework, allowed)	B	C	
Sector efficiency and capacity			
Telecommunications revenue (% of GDP)	1.3	1.7	2.5
Telecommunications investment (% of revenue)	41.3	26.8	18.2
Sector performance			
Access			
Fixed-telephone subscriptions (per 100 people)	34.0	46.9	19.4
Mobile-cellular telephone subscriptions (per 100 people)	42.4	113.5	92.4
Fixed (wired)-broadband subscriptions (per 100 people)	0.0	26.9	10.8
Households with a computer (%)	9.6	51.7	40.6
Households with Internet access at home (%)	7.0	48.3	36.3
Usage			
Int'l. voice traffic, total (minutes/subscription/month)	6.6	5.6	1.3
Domestic mobile traffic (minutes/subscription/month)	116.2	202.6	284.4
Individuals using the Internet (%)	19.7	46.9	41.6
Quality			
Population covered by a mobile-cellular network (%)	90	100	99
Fixed (wired)-broadband subscriptions (% of total Internet)	4.2	96.1	95.5
International Internet bandwidth (bit/s per Internet user)	1,356	79,337	14,580
Affordability			
Fixed-telephone sub-basket ($ a month)	..	1.4	9.4
Mobile-cellular sub-basket ($ a month)	..	8.4	14.9
Fixed-broadband sub-basket ($ a month)	..	11.9	17.8
Trade			
ICT goods exports (% of total goods exports)	1.0	0.6	17.6
ICT goods imports (% of total goods imports)	2.4	2.4	14.7
ICT service exports (% of total service exports)	15.0	18.0	29.1
Applications			
Online service index (0–1, 1=highest presence)	0.52	0.41	0.42
Secure Internet servers (per million people)	0.5	26.4	18.5

Belgium

	Country data		High-income group
	2005	2012	2012
Economic and social context			
Population (millions)	10	11	1,300
Urban population (% of total)	97	98	80
GNI per capita, *World Bank Atlas* method ($)	36,610	44,720	38,412
GDP growth, 2000–05 and 2005–12 (avg. annual %)	1.6	0.9	1.0
Adult literacy rate (% ages 15 and older)	..	..	..
Gross primary, secondary, tertiary school enrollment (%)	93	95	93
Sector structure			
Separate telecommunications/ICT regulator	Yes	Yes	
Status of main fixed-line telephone operator	Mixed	Mixed	
Level of competition (competition, partial comp., monopoly)			
International gateway(s)	..	C	
Mobile telephone service	P	C	
Internet service	C	C	
Foreign ownership (not allowed, restricted, allowed)	A	A	
Reg. treatment of VoIP (banned, closed, no framework, allowed)	A	A	
Sector efficiency and capacity			
Telecommunications revenue (% of GDP)	3.0	1.6	2.7
Telecommunications investment (% of revenue)	11.6	20.4	17.6
Sector performance			
Access			
Fixed-telephone subscriptions (per 100 people)	45.6	41.9	43.6
Mobile-cellular telephone subscriptions (per 100 people)	91.4	111.3	122.9
Fixed (wired)-broadband subscriptions (per 100 people)	19.1	33.3	26.2
Households with a computer (%)	57.0	80.0	77.7
Households with Internet access at home (%)	50.2	78.0	75.5
Usage			
Int'l. voice traffic, total (minutes/subscription/month)	..	..	..
Domestic mobile traffic (minutes/subscription/month)	70.2	92.5	113.6
Individuals using the Internet (%)	55.8[a]	82.0	75.4
Quality			
Population covered by a mobile-cellular network (%)	99	100	100
Fixed (wired)-broadband subscriptions (% of total Internet)	88.1	99.7	95.9
International Internet bandwidth (bit/s per Internet user)	20,038	180,389	85,990
Affordability			
Fixed-telephone sub-basket ($ a month)	..	36.1	25.2
Mobile-cellular sub-basket ($ a month)	..	39.7	20.6
Fixed-broadband sub-basket ($ a month)	..	34.7	29.2
Trade			
ICT goods exports (% of total goods exports)	3.9	2.1	8.9
ICT goods imports (% of total goods imports)	4.6	3.1	10.8
ICT service exports (% of total service exports)	34.5	43.1	30.8
Applications			
Online service index (0–1, 1=highest presence)	0.68	0.65	0.67
Secure Internet servers (per million people)	117.9	749.3	827.6

Belize

Latin America & Caribbean			Upper middle income

	Country data		Upper middle-income group
	2005	2012	2012
Economic and social context			
Population (millions)	0.27	0.32	2,391
Urban population (% of total)	46	45	61
GNI per capita, World Bank Atlas method ($)	4,770	4,490	6,969
GDP growth, 2000–05 and 2005–12 (avg. annual %)	5.7	2.8	6.2
Adult literacy rate (% ages 15 and older)	..	..	94
Gross primary, secondary, tertiary school enrollment (%)	79	82	76
Sector structure			
Separate telecommunications/ICT regulator	Yes	Yes	
Status of main fixed-line telephone operator	Mixed	Mixed	
Level of competition (competition, partial comp., monopoly)			
International gateway(s)	..	C	
Mobile telephone service	M	C	
Internet service	M	C	
Foreign ownership (not allowed, restricted, allowed)	R	R	
Reg. treatment of VoIP (banned, closed, no framework, allowed)	No	C	
Sector efficiency and capacity			
Telecommunications revenue (% of GDP)	5.7	4.8	2.5
Telecommunications investment (% of revenue)	23.8	19.4	18.2
Sector performance			
Access			
Fixed-telephone subscriptions (per 100 people)	12.4	7.8	19.4
Mobile-cellular telephone subscriptions (per 100 people)	35.3	53.2	92.4
Fixed (wired)-broadband subscriptions (per 100 people)	1.8	3.1	10.8
Households with a computer (%)	..	..	40.6
Households with Internet access at home (%)	..	..	36.3
Usage			
Int'l. voice traffic, total (minutes/subscription/month)	..	34.3	1.3
Domestic mobile traffic (minutes/subscription/month)	15.3	..	284.4
Individuals using the Internet (%)	9.2	25.0[a]	41.6
Quality			
Population covered by a mobile-cellular network (%)	..	..	99
Fixed (wired)-broadband subscriptions (% of total Internet)	73.5	71.7	95.5
International Internet bandwidth (bit/s per Internet user)	5,390	34,562	14,580
Affordability			
Fixed-telephone sub-basket ($ a month)	..	19.2	9.4
Mobile-cellular sub-basket ($ a month)	..	31.3	14.9
Fixed-broadband sub-basket ($ a month)	..	50.0	17.8
Trade			
ICT goods exports (% of total goods exports)	0.0	0.5	17.6
ICT goods imports (% of total goods imports)	5.9	3.6	14.7
ICT service exports (% of total service exports)	12.3	11.0	29.1
Applications			
Online service index (0–1, 1=highest presence)	0.41	0.40	0.42
Secure Internet servers (per million people)	275.8	177.7	18.5

Benin

	Country data		Low-income group
	2005	2012	2012
Economic and social context			
Population (millions)	8	10	846
Urban population (% of total)	41	46	28
GNI per capita, *World Bank Atlas* method ($)	530	750	590
GDP growth, 2000–05 and 2005–12 (avg. annual %)	4.0	3.8	5.9
Adult literacy rate (% ages 15 and older)	29	..	61
Gross primary, secondary, tertiary school enrollment (%)	54	68	60
Sector structure			
Separate telecommunications/ICT regulator	Yes	Yes	
Status of main fixed-line telephone operator	Public	Public	
Level of competition (competition, partial comp., monopoly)			
International gateway(s)	..	P	
Mobile telephone service	C	C	
Internet service	..	P	
Foreign ownership (not allowed, restricted, allowed)	..	A	
Reg. treatment of VoIP (banned, closed, no framework, allowed)	No	B	
Sector efficiency and capacity			
Telecommunications revenue (% of GDP)	1.4	6.3	5.0
Telecommunications investment (% of revenue)	35.0	32.2	..
Sector performance			
Access			
Fixed-telephone subscriptions (per 100 people)	0.9	1.6	1.0
Mobile-cellular telephone subscriptions (per 100 people)	7.3	83.7	47.2
Fixed (wired)-broadband subscriptions (per 100 people)	0.0	0.1	0.2
Households with a computer (%)	1.6[a]	4.2[a]	4.2
Households with Internet access at home (%)	0.0[a]	2.4[a]	3.4
Usage			
Int'l. voice traffic, total (minutes/subscription/month)	..	6.4	..
Domestic mobile traffic (minutes/subscription/month)	..	30.9	70.1
Individuals using the Internet (%)	1.3	3.8[a]	6.2
Quality			
Population covered by a mobile-cellular network (%)	43	99	..
Fixed (wired)-broadband subscriptions (% of total Internet)	2.9	11.9	30.9
International Internet bandwidth (bit/s per Internet user)	452	3,249	9,141
Affordability			
Fixed-telephone sub-basket ($ a month)	..	13.4	8.9
Mobile-cellular sub-basket ($ a month)	..	14.4	11.9
Fixed-broadband sub-basket ($ a month)	..	53.0	46.9
Trade			
ICT goods exports (% of total goods exports)	0.0	0.0	..
ICT goods imports (% of total goods imports)	2.9	1.3	..
ICT service exports (% of total service exports)	20.1	21.1	..
Applications			
Online service index (0–1, 1=highest presence)	0.19	0.20	0.20
Secure Internet servers (per million people)	0.1	1.1	1.1

Bermuda

	Country data		High-income group
	2005	2012	2012
Economic and social context			
Population (millions)	0.06	0.06	1,300
Urban population (% of total)	100	100	80
GNI per capita, *World Bank Atlas* method ($)	117,640	104,590	38,412
GDP growth, 2000–05 and 2005–12 (avg. annual %)	2.3	-1.2	1.0
Adult literacy rate (% ages 15 and older)	..	..	..
Gross primary, secondary, tertiary school enrollment (%)	71	68	93
Sector structure			
Separate telecommunications/ICT regulator	..	..	
Status of main fixed-line telephone operator	..	..	
Level of competition (competition, partial comp., monopoly)			
International gateway(s)	..	..	
Mobile telephone service	..	..	
Internet service	..	..	
Foreign ownership (not allowed, restricted, allowed)	..	..	
Reg. treatment of VoIP (banned, closed, no framework, allowed)	..	..	
Sector efficiency and capacity			
Telecommunications revenue (% of GDP)	3.9	..	2.7
Telecommunications investment (% of revenue)	11.3	..	17.6
Sector performance			
Access			
Fixed-telephone subscriptions (per 100 people)	81.8	105.8	43.6
Mobile-cellular telephone subscriptions (per 100 people)	82.2	139.5	122.9
Fixed (wired)-broadband subscriptions (per 100 people)	28.8	61.7	26.2
Households with a computer (%)	67.9	97.2[a]	77.7
Households with Internet access at home (%)	62.8[a]	95.0[a]	75.5
Usage			
Int'l. voice traffic, total (minutes/subscription/month)	..	..	..
Domestic mobile traffic (minutes/subscription/month)	194.8	..	113.6
Individuals using the Internet (%)	65.4	91.3[a]	75.4
Quality			
Population covered by a mobile-cellular network (%)	98	..	100
Fixed (wired)-broadband subscriptions (% of total Internet)	59.8	..	95.9
International Internet bandwidth (bit/s per Internet user)	10,554	..	85,990
Affordability			
Fixed-telephone sub-basket ($ a month)	..	..	25.2
Mobile-cellular sub-basket ($ a month)	..	..	20.6
Fixed-broadband sub-basket ($ a month)	..	..	29.2
Trade			
ICT goods exports (% of total goods exports)	..	6.6	8.9
ICT goods imports (% of total goods imports)	..	3.6	10.8
ICT service exports (% of total service exports)	37.2	40.4	30.8
Applications			
Online service index (0–1, 1=highest presence)	..	..	0.67
Secure Internet servers (per million people)	1,699.0	5,015.0	827.6

Bhutan

	Country data		Lower middle-income group
	2005	2012	2012
Economic and social context			
Population (millions)	0.65	0.74	2,507
Urban population (% of total)	31	36	39
GNI per capita, *World Bank Atlas* method ($)	1,230	2,420	1,893
GDP growth, 2000–05 and 2005–12 (avg. annual %)	7.9	9.3	6.0
Adult literacy rate (% ages 15 and older)	53	..	71
Gross primary, secondary, tertiary school enrollment (%)	54	69	64
Sector structure			
Separate telecommunications/ICT regulator	Yes	Yes	
Status of main fixed-line telephone operator	Public	Public	
Level of competition (competition, partial comp., monopoly)			
International gateway(s)	M	C	
Mobile telephone service	M	C	
Internet service	P	C	
Foreign ownership (not allowed, restricted, allowed)	R	R	
Reg. treatment of VoIP (banned, closed, no framework, allowed)	B	A	
Sector efficiency and capacity			
Telecommunications revenue (% of GDP)	2.0	2.8	2.5
Telecommunications investment (% of revenue)	*81.1*	35.1	20.5
Sector performance			
Access			
Fixed-telephone subscriptions (per 100 people)	5.1	3.6	5.4
Mobile-cellular telephone subscriptions (per 100 people)	5.5	75.6	83.1
Fixed (wired)-broadband subscriptions (per 100 people)	0.0	2.3	1.4
Households with a computer (%)	2.6	16.4	15.0
Households with Internet access at home (%)	1.2	11.6	12.4
Usage			
Int'l. voice traffic, total (minutes/subscription/month)	..	21.3	6.5
Domestic mobile traffic (minutes/subscription/month)	*56.1*	44.6	..
Individuals using the Internet (%)	3.8	25.4[a]	18.7
Quality			
Population covered by a mobile-cellular network (%)	5	100	86
Fixed (wired)-broadband subscriptions (% of total Internet)	0.0	98.1	58.2
International Internet bandwidth (bit/s per Internet user)	240	3,286	8,076
Affordability			
Fixed-telephone sub-basket ($ a month)	..	1.7	4.9
Mobile-cellular sub-basket ($ a month)	..	3.5	10.5
Fixed-broadband sub-basket ($ a month)	..	10.7	20.6
Trade			
ICT goods exports (% of total goods exports)	0.9	15.9	4.6
ICT goods imports (% of total goods imports)	5.3	2.4	7.2
ICT service exports (% of total service exports)	5.8	3.9	47.1
Applications			
Online service index (0–1, 1=highest presence)	0.31	0.35	0.32
Secure Internet servers (per million people)	..	9.3	4.4

Bolivia

Latin America & Caribbean　　　　　　　　　**Lower middle income**

	Country data		Lower middle-income group
	2005	2012	2012
Economic and social context			
Population (millions)	9	10	2,507
Urban population (% of total)	64	67	39
GNI per capita, *World Bank Atlas* method ($)	1,000	2,220	1,893
GDP growth, 2000–05 and 2005–12 (avg. annual %)	3.1	4.7	6.0
Adult literacy rate (% ages 15 and older)	91	91	71
Gross primary, secondary, tertiary school enrollment (%)	79	..	64
Sector structure			
Separate telecommunications/ICT regulator	Yes	Yes	
Status of main fixed-line telephone operator	Private	Public	
Level of competition (competition, partial comp., monopoly)			
International gateway(s)	..	..	
Mobile telephone service	C	C	
Internet service	C	C	
Foreign ownership (not allowed, restricted, allowed)	R	No	
Reg. treatment of VoIP (banned, closed, no framework, allowed)	B	A	
Sector efficiency and capacity			
Telecommunications revenue (% of GDP)	5.6	4.8	2.5
Telecommunications investment (% of revenue)	3.8	21.1	20.5
Sector performance			
Access			
Fixed-telephone subscriptions (per 100 people)	6.9	8.4	5.4
Mobile-cellular telephone subscriptions (per 100 people)	25.9	90.4	83.1
Fixed (wired)-broadband subscriptions (per 100 people)	0.1	1.1	1.4
Households with a computer (%)	12.1	25.9[a]	15.0
Households with Internet access at home (%)	3.5	10.0[a]	12.4
Usage			
Int'l. voice traffic, total (minutes/subscription/month)	..	5.8	6.5
Domestic mobile traffic (minutes/subscription/month)	20.8	33.4	..
Individuals using the Internet (%)	5.2	34.2[a]	18.7
Quality			
Population covered by a mobile-cellular network (%)	46	95	86
Fixed (wired)-broadband subscriptions (% of total Internet)	18.1	81.1	58.2
International Internet bandwidth (bit/s per Internet user)	814	5,176	8,076
Affordability			
Fixed-telephone sub-basket ($ a month)	..	24.0	4.9
Mobile-cellular sub-basket ($ a month)	..	11.8	10.5
Fixed-broadband sub-basket ($ a month)	..	24.5	20.6
Trade			
ICT goods exports (% of total goods exports)	0.0	0.0	4.6
ICT goods imports (% of total goods imports)	3.9	3.2	7.2
ICT service exports (% of total service exports)	6.6	11.8	47.1
Applications			
Online service index (0–1, 1=highest presence)	0.49	0.41	0.32
Secure Internet servers (per million people)	2.4	8.9	4.4

Bosnia and Herzegovina

Europe & Central Asia			Upper middle income

	Country data		Upper middle-income group
	2005	2012	2012
Economic and social context			
Population (millions)	4	4	2,391
Urban population (% of total)	45	49	61
GNI per capita, World Bank Atlas method ($)	2,940	4,750	6,969
GDP growth, 2000-05 and 2005-12 (avg. annual %)	5.0	2.1	6.2
Adult literacy rate (% ages 15 and older)	97	98	94
Gross primary, secondary, tertiary school enrollment (%)	..	..	76
Sector structure			
Separate telecommunications/ICT regulator	Yes	Yes	
Status of main fixed-line telephone operator	Public	Mixed	
Level of competition (competition, partial comp., monopoly)			
International gateway(s)	..	..	
Mobile telephone service	P	P	
Internet service	C	C	
Foreign ownership (not allowed, restricted, allowed)	A	A	
Reg. treatment of VoIP (banned, closed, no framework, allowed)	B	A	
Sector efficiency and capacity			
Telecommunications revenue (% of GDP)	6.1	4.7	2.5
Telecommunications investment (% of revenue)	36.5	22.7	18.2
Sector performance			
Access			
Fixed-telephone subscriptions (per 100 people)	25.0	23.1	19.4
Mobile-cellular telephone subscriptions (per 100 people)	41.1	87.6	92.4
Fixed (wired)-broadband subscriptions (per 100 people)	0.4	10.6	10.8
Households with a computer (%)	20.0	39.8[a]	40.6
Households with Internet access at home (%)	6.2[a]	39.7[a]	36.3
Usage			
Int'l. voice traffic, total (minutes/subscription/month)	..	20.4	1.3
Domestic mobile traffic (minutes/subscription/month)	36.3	59.2	284.4
Individuals using the Internet (%)	21.3	65.4[a]	41.6
Quality			
Population covered by a mobile-cellular network (%)	97	100	99
Fixed (wired)-broadband subscriptions (% of total Internet)	7.6	83.3	95.5
International Internet bandwidth (bit/s per Internet user)	187	23,945	14,580
Affordability			
Fixed-telephone sub-basket ($ a month)	..	10.4	9.4
Mobile-cellular sub-basket ($ a month)	..	15.4	14.9
Fixed-broadband sub-basket ($ a month)	..	8.3	17.8
Trade			
ICT goods exports (% of total goods exports)	0.3	0.2	17.6
ICT goods imports (% of total goods imports)	4.2	2.7	14.7
ICT service exports (% of total service exports)	18.1	5.5	29.1
Applications			
Online service index (0-1, 1=highest presence)	0.45	0.37	0.42
Secure Internet servers (per million people)	3.4	24.0	18.5

Botswana

	Country data		Upper middle-income group
Sub-Saharan Africa			**Upper middle income**
	2005	2012	2012
Economic and social context			
Population (millions)	2	2	2,391
Urban population (% of total)	57	62	61
GNI per capita, *World Bank Atlas* method ($)	4,730	7,650	6,969
GDP growth, 2000–05 and 2005–12 (avg. annual %)	3.9	3.7	6.2
Adult literacy rate (% ages 15 and older)	81	85	94
Gross primary, secondary, tertiary school enrollment (%)	71	..	76
Sector structure			
Separate telecommunications/ICT regulator	Yes	Yes	
Status of main fixed-line telephone operator	Public	Public	
Level of competition (competition, partial comp., monopoly)			
International gateway(s)	M	P	
Mobile telephone service	C	P	
Internet service	C	C	
Foreign ownership (not allowed, restricted, allowed)	A	A	
Reg. treatment of VoIP (banned, closed, no framework, allowed)	B	A	
Sector efficiency and capacity			
Telecommunications revenue (% of GDP)	3.2	4.2	2.5
Telecommunications investment (% of revenue)	48.9	14.4	18.2
Sector performance			
Access			
Fixed-telephone subscriptions (per 100 people)	7.3	8.0	19.4
Mobile-cellular telephone subscriptions (per 100 people)	30.1	153.8	92.4
Fixed (wired)-broadband subscriptions (per 100 people)	0.1	0.9	10.8
Households with a computer (%)	6.5[a]	12.3[a]	40.6
Households with Internet access at home (%)	0.1[a]	9.1[a]	36.3
Usage			
Int'l. voice traffic, total (minutes/subscription/month)	..	..	1.3
Domestic mobile traffic (minutes/subscription/month)	45.5	56.4	284.4
Individuals using the Internet (%)	3.3[a]	11.5[a]	41.6
Quality			
Population covered by a mobile-cellular network (%)	99	96	99
Fixed (wired)-broadband subscriptions (% of total Internet)	..	100.0	95.5
International Internet bandwidth (bit/s per Internet user)	490	6,509	14,580
Affordability			
Fixed-telephone sub-basket ($ a month)	..	17.9	9.4
Mobile-cellular sub-basket ($ a month)	..	13.0	14.9
Fixed-broadband sub-basket ($ a month)	..	57.3	17.8
Trade			
ICT goods exports (% of total goods exports)	0.2	0.2	17.6
ICT goods imports (% of total goods imports)	4.7	2.4	14.7
ICT service exports (% of total service exports)	12.8	40.9	29.1
Applications			
Online service index (0–1, 1=highest presence)	0.36	0.36	0.42
Secure Internet servers (per million people)	1.6	10.4	18.5

Brazil

Upper middle income

	Country data		Upper middle-income group
	2005	2012	2012
Economic and social context			
Population (millions)	186	199	2,391
Urban population (% of total)	83	85	61
GNI per capita, World Bank Atlas method ($)	3,960	11,630	6,969
GDP growth, 2000–05 and 2005–12 (avg. annual %)	2.8	3.8	6.2
Adult literacy rate (% ages 15 and older)	90	90	94
Gross primary, secondary, tertiary school enrollment (%)	..	..	76
Sector structure			
Separate telecommunications/ICT regulator	Yes	Yes	
Status of main fixed-line telephone operator	Private	Private	
Level of competition (competition, partial comp., monopoly)			
International gateway(s)	..	C	
Mobile telephone service	C	C	
Internet service	C	C	
Foreign ownership (not allowed, restricted, allowed)	A	A	
Reg. treatment of VoIP (banned, closed, no framework, allowed)	A	A	
Sector efficiency and capacity			
Telecommunications revenue (% of GDP)	4.1	2.9	2.5
Telecommunications investment (% of revenue)	17.4	13.1	18.2
Sector performance			
Access			
Fixed-telephone subscriptions (per 100 people)	21.4	22.3	19.4
Mobile-cellular telephone subscriptions (per 100 people)	46.3	125.0	92.4
Fixed (wired)-broadband subscriptions (per 100 people)	1.7	9.2	10.8
Households with a computer (%)	18.5	49.9[a]	40.6
Households with Internet access at home (%)	13.6	45.4[a]	36.3
Usage			
Int'l. voice traffic, total (minutes/subscription/month)	..	0.2	1.3
Domestic mobile traffic (minutes/subscription/month)	30.9	56.9	284.4
Individuals using the Internet (%)	21.0	49.8[a]	41.6
Quality			
Population covered by a mobile-cellular network (%)	88	100	99
Fixed (wired)-broadband subscriptions (% of total Internet)	74.1	81.4	95.5
International Internet bandwidth (bit/s per Internet user)	716	44,837	14,580
Affordability			
Fixed-telephone sub-basket ($ a month)	..	29.8	9.4
Mobile-cellular sub-basket ($ a month)	..	60.2	14.9
Fixed-broadband sub-basket ($ a month)	..	17.8	17.8
Trade			
ICT goods exports (% of total goods exports)	3.1	0.5	17.6
ICT goods imports (% of total goods imports)	12.1	8.8	14.7
ICT service exports (% of total service exports)	43.0	55.7	29.1
Applications			
Online service index (0–1, 1=highest presence)	0.57	0.67	0.42
Secure Internet servers (per million people)	14.2	57.4	18.5

Brunei Darussalam

High income

	Country data		High-income group
	2005	2012	2012
Economic and social context			
Population (millions)	0.37	0.41	1,300
Urban population (% of total)	74	76	80
GNI per capita, *World Bank Atlas* method ($)	22,920	31,590	38,412
GDP growth, 2000–05 and 2005–12 (avg. annual %)	2.2	0.6	1.0
Adult literacy rate (% ages 15 and older)	93	95	..
Gross primary, secondary, tertiary school enrollment (%)	81	81	93
Sector structure			
Separate telecommunications/ICT regulator	Yes	Yes	
Status of main fixed-line telephone operator	Public	Public	
Level of competition (competition, partial comp., monopoly)			
International gateway(s)	P	P	
Mobile telephone service	M	M	
Internet service	P	P	
Foreign ownership (not allowed, restricted, allowed)	R	R	
Reg. treatment of VoIP (banned, closed, no framework, allowed)	A	A	
Sector efficiency and capacity			
Telecommunications revenue (% of GDP)	..	..	2.7
Telecommunications investment (% of revenue)	..	..	17.6
Sector performance			
Access			
Fixed-telephone subscriptions (per 100 people)	22.8	17.2	43.6
Mobile-cellular telephone subscriptions (per 100 people)	63.3	113.9	122.9
Fixed (wired)-broadband subscriptions (per 100 people)	2.2	4.8	26.2
Households with a computer (%)	55.0	86.9[a]	77.7
Households with Internet access at home (%)	50.0	72.4[a]	75.5
Usage			
Int'l. voice traffic, total (minutes/subscription/month)	..	..	..
Domestic mobile traffic (minutes/subscription/month)	..	..	113.6
Individuals using the Internet (%)	36.5	60.3[a]	75.4
Quality			
Population covered by a mobile-cellular network (%)	..	..	100
Fixed (wired)-broadband subscriptions (% of total Internet)	45.2	84.5	95.9
International Internet bandwidth (bit/s per Internet user)	4,138	39,925	85,990
Affordability			
Fixed-telephone sub-basket ($ a month)	..	12.5	25.2
Mobile-cellular sub-basket ($ a month)	..	20.8	20.6
Fixed-broadband sub-basket ($ a month)	..	51.7	29.2
Trade			
ICT goods exports (% of total goods exports)	0.1	0.3	8.9
ICT goods imports (% of total goods imports)	6.1	4.1	10.8
ICT service exports (% of total service exports)	17.0	21.4	30.8
Applications			
Online service index (0–1, 1=highest presence)	0.47	0.59	0.67
Secure Internet servers (per million people)	13.6	117.2	827.6

Bulgaria

Europe & Central Asia   **Upper middle income**

	Country data		Upper middle-income group
	2005	2012	2012
Economic and social context			
Population (millions)	8	7	2,391
Urban population (% of total)	70	74	61
GNI per capita, *World Bank Atlas* method ($)	3,640	6,840	6,969
GDP growth, 2000–05 and 2005–12 (avg. annual %)	5.5	1.8	6.2
Adult literacy rate (% ages 15 and older)	98	98	94
Gross primary, secondary, tertiary school enrollment (%)	77	82	76
Sector structure			
Separate telecommunications/ICT regulator	Yes	Yes	
Status of main fixed-line telephone operator	Mixed	Mixed	
Level of competition (competition, partial comp., monopoly)			
International gateway(s)	..	P	
Mobile telephone service	P	P	
Internet service	C	C	
Foreign ownership (not allowed, restricted, allowed)	A	A	
Reg. treatment of VoIP (banned, closed, no framework, allowed)	No	A	
Sector efficiency and capacity			
Telecommunications revenue (% of GDP)	6.0	3.0	2.5
Telecommunications investment (% of revenue)	34.5	23.9	18.2
Sector performance			
Access			
Fixed-telephone subscriptions (per 100 people)	32.4	29.3	19.4
Mobile-cellular telephone subscriptions (per 100 people)	81.3	148.1	92.4
Fixed (wired)-broadband subscriptions (per 100 people)	2.2	17.9	10.8
Households with a computer (%)	17.9[a]	52.0	40.6
Households with Internet access at home (%)	13.3[a]	51.0	36.3
Usage			
Int'l. voice traffic, total (minutes/subscription/month)	5.9	6.8	1.3
Domestic mobile traffic (minutes/subscription/month)	37.8	122.8	284.4
Individuals using the Internet (%)	20.0	55.1	41.6
Quality			
Population covered by a mobile-cellular network (%)	100	100	99
Fixed (wired)-broadband subscriptions (% of total Internet)	80.0	100.0	95.5
International Internet bandwidth (bit/s per Internet user)	888	85,424	14,580
Affordability			
Fixed-telephone sub-basket ($ a month)	..	11.9	9.4
Mobile-cellular sub-basket ($ a month)	..	34.8	14.9
Fixed-broadband sub-basket ($ a month)	..	10.5	17.8
Trade			
ICT goods exports (% of total goods exports)	1.5	2.0	17.6
ICT goods imports (% of total goods imports)	5.5	6.2	14.7
ICT service exports (% of total service exports)	12.5	22.8	29.1
Applications			
Online service index (0–1, 1=highest presence)	0.57	0.49	0.42
Secure Internet servers (per million people)	8.7	146.8	18.5

Burkina Faso

Sub-Saharan Africa   **Low income**

	Country data		Low-income group
	2005	2012	2012
Economic and social context			
Population (millions)	13	16	846
Urban population (% of total)	22	27	28
GNI per capita, World Bank Atlas method ($)	410	670	590
GDP growth, 2000–05 and 2005–12 (avg. annual %)	6.4	5.5	5.9
Adult literacy rate (% ages 15 and older)	24	..	61
Gross primary, secondary, tertiary school enrollment (%)	29	45	60
Sector structure			
Separate telecommunications/ICT regulator	Yes	Yes	
Status of main fixed-line telephone operator	Public	Mixed	
Level of competition (competition, partial comp., monopoly)			
International gateway(s)	M	C	
Mobile telephone service	C	C	
Internet service	C	C	
Foreign ownership (not allowed, restricted, allowed)	R	R	
Reg. treatment of VoIP (banned, closed, no framework, allowed)	B	C	
Sector efficiency and capacity			
Telecommunications revenue (% of GDP)	3.5	..	5.0
Telecommunications investment (% of revenue)	55.8	..	..
Sector performance			
Access			
Fixed-telephone subscriptions (per 100 people)	0.7	0.9	1.0
Mobile-cellular telephone subscriptions (per 100 people)	4.7	60.6	47.2
Fixed (wired)-broadband subscriptions (per 100 people)	0.0	0.1	0.2
Households with a computer (%)	1.4	3.4a	4.2
Households with Internet access at home (%)	0.0a	2.8a	3.4
Usage			
Int'l. voice traffic, total (minutes/subscription/month)	..	..	..
Domestic mobile traffic (minutes/subscription/month)	27.7	30.2	70.1
Individuals using the Internet (%)	0.5	3.7a	6.2
Quality			
Population covered by a mobile-cellular network (%)	26	..	..
Fixed (wired)-broadband subscriptions (% of total Internet)	4.6	47.7	30.9
International Internet bandwidth (bit/s per Internet user)	1,142	1,812	9,141
Affordability			
Fixed-telephone sub-basket ($ a month)	..	14.8	8.9
Mobile-cellular sub-basket ($ a month)	..	12.2	11.9
Fixed-broadband sub-basket ($ a month)	..	46.6	46.9
Trade			
ICT goods exports (% of total goods exports)	0.2	0.0	..
ICT goods imports (% of total goods imports)	4.5	3.2	..
ICT service exports (% of total service exports)	8.9	21.1	..
Applications			
Online service index (0–1, 1=highest presence)	0.15	0.29	0.20
Secure Internet servers (per million people)	0.1	0.8	1.1

Burundi

	Country data 2005	Country data 2012	Low-income group 2012
Economic and social context			
Population (millions)	8	10	846
Urban population (% of total)	9	11	28
GNI per capita, *World Bank Atlas* method ($)	130	240	590
GDP growth, 2000–05 and 2005–12 (avg. annual %)	2.2	4.3	5.9
Adult literacy rate (% ages 15 and older)	59	87	61
Gross primary, secondary, tertiary school enrollment (%)	36	59	60
Sector structure			
Separate telecommunications/ICT regulator	Yes	Yes	
Status of main fixed-line telephone operator	Public	Public	
Level of competition (competition, partial comp., monopoly)			
International gateway(s)	..	C	
Mobile telephone service	C	C	
Internet service	C	C	
Foreign ownership (not allowed, restricted, allowed)	A	A	
Reg. treatment of VoIP (banned, closed, no framework, allowed)	B	B	
Sector efficiency and capacity			
Telecommunications revenue (% of GDP)	..	2.3	5.0
Telecommunications investment (% of revenue)	..	..	..
Sector performance			
Access			
Fixed-telephone subscriptions (per 100 people)	0.4[a]	0.2	1.0
Mobile-cellular telephone subscriptions (per 100 people)	2.0	22.8	47.2
Fixed (wired)-broadband subscriptions (per 100 people)	0.0	0.0	0.2
Households with a computer (%)	..	0.1[a]	4.2
Households with Internet access at home (%)	..	0.1[a]	3.4
Usage			
Int'l. voice traffic, total (minutes/subscription/month)	..	..	..
Domestic mobile traffic (minutes/subscription/month)	..	35.1	70.1
Individuals using the Internet (%)	0.5	1.2[a]	6.2
Quality			
Population covered by a mobile-cellular network (%)	82	83	..
Fixed (wired)-broadband subscriptions (% of total Internet)	0.0	0.6	30.9
International Internet bandwidth (bit/s per Internet user)	95	3,462	9,141
Affordability			
Fixed-telephone sub-basket ($ a month)	..	..	8.9
Mobile-cellular sub-basket ($ a month)	..	..	11.9
Fixed-broadband sub-basket ($ a month)	..	..	46.9
Trade			
ICT goods exports (% of total goods exports)	0.1	0.2	..
ICT goods imports (% of total goods imports)	5.6	1.9	..
ICT service exports (% of total service exports)	..	6.6	..
Applications			
Online service index (0–1, 1=highest presence)	0.18	0.15	0.20
Secure Internet servers (per million people)	0.1	0.3	1.1

Cabo Verde

Lower middle income

	Country data		Lower middle-income group
	2005	2012	2012
Economic and social context			
Population (millions)	0.48	0.49	2,507
Urban population (% of total)	58	63	39
GNI per capita, *World Bank Atlas* method ($)	2,330	3,830	1,893
GDP growth, 2000–05 and 2005–12 (avg. annual %)	5.9	5.9	6.0
Adult literacy rate (% ages 15 and older)	*80*	*85*	*71*
Gross primary, secondary, tertiary school enrollment (%)	71	77	64
Sector structure			
Separate telecommunications/ICT regulator	Yes	Yes	
Status of main fixed-line telephone operator	Mixed	Mixed	
Level of competition (competition, partial comp., monopoly)			
International gateway(s)	M	C	
Mobile telephone service	C	C	
Internet service	C	C	
Foreign ownership (not allowed, restricted, allowed)	R	A	
Reg. treatment of VoIP (banned, closed, no framework, allowed)	B	A	
Sector efficiency and capacity			
Telecommunications revenue (% of GDP)	6.7	7.9	2.5
Telecommunications investment (% of revenue)	*19.1*	*23.9*	*20.5*
Sector performance			
Access			
Fixed-telephone subscriptions (per 100 people)	15.0	14.2	5.4
Mobile-cellular telephone subscriptions (per 100 people)	17.1	86.0	83.1
Fixed (wired)-broadband subscriptions (per 100 people)	0.2	4.0	1.4
Households with a computer (%)	6.7[a]	26.5[a]	15.0
Households with Internet access at home (%)	1.4[a]	13.7[a]	12.4
Usage			
Int'l. voice traffic, total (minutes/subscription/month)	*33.8*	*22.6*	*6.5*
Domestic mobile traffic (minutes/subscription/month)	46.6	72.1	..
Individuals using the Internet (%)	6.1	34.7[a]	18.7
Quality			
Population covered by a mobile-cellular network (%)	85	96	*86*
Fixed (wired)-broadband subscriptions (% of total Internet)	14.4	100.0	*58.2*
International Internet bandwidth (bit/s per Internet user)	482	6,317	8,076
Affordability			
Fixed-telephone sub-basket ($ a month)	..	10.8	4.9
Mobile-cellular sub-basket ($ a month)	..	32.9	10.5
Fixed-broadband sub-basket ($ a month)	..	33.3	20.6
Trade			
ICT goods exports (% of total goods exports)	0.5	..	4.6
ICT goods imports (% of total goods imports)	3.9	3.7	7.2
ICT service exports (% of total service exports)	7.8	4.6	47.1
Applications			
Online service index (0–1, 1=highest presence)	0.42	0.44	0.32
Secure Internet servers (per million people)	*2.1*	*26.1*	*4.4*

Cambodia

Low income

	Country data 2005	Country data 2012	Low-income group 2012
Economic and social context			
Population (millions)	13	15	846
Urban population (% of total)	19	20	28
GNI per capita, *World Bank Atlas* method ($)	460	880	590
GDP growth, 2000–05 and 2005–12 (avg. annual %)	9.1	6.2	5.9
Adult literacy rate (% ages 15 and older)	74	74	61
Gross primary, secondary, tertiary school enrollment (%)	62	64	60
Sector structure			
Separate telecommunications/ICT regulator	No	Yes	
Status of main fixed-line telephone operator	Public	Public	
Level of competition (competition, partial comp., monopoly)			
International gateway(s)	..	C	
Mobile telephone service	P	C	
Internet service	P	C	
Foreign ownership (not allowed, restricted, allowed)	R	A	
Reg. treatment of VoIP (banned, closed, no framework, allowed)	B	A	
Sector efficiency and capacity			
Telecommunications revenue (% of GDP)	0.4	5.5	5.0
Telecommunications investment (% of revenue)	..	69.8	..
Sector performance			
Access			
Fixed-telephone subscriptions (per 100 people)	0.2	3.9	1.0
Mobile-cellular telephone subscriptions (per 100 people)	8.0	128.5	47.2
Fixed (wired)-broadband subscriptions (per 100 people)	0.0	0.2	0.2
Households with a computer (%)	1.8a	5.4a	4.2
Households with Internet access at home (%)	..	3.9a	3.4
Usage			
Int'l. voice traffic, total (minutes/subscription/month)	..	..	..
Domestic mobile traffic (minutes/subscription/month)	11.1	..	70.1
Individuals using the Internet (%)	0.3	4.9a	6.2
Quality			
Population covered by a mobile-cellular network (%)	75	99	..
Fixed (wired)-broadband subscriptions (% of total Internet)	11.7	46.8	30.9
International Internet bandwidth (bit/s per Internet user)	425	13,619	9,141
Affordability			
Fixed-telephone sub-basket ($ a month)	..	3.8	8.9
Mobile-cellular sub-basket ($ a month)	..	7.5	11.9
Fixed-broadband sub-basket ($ a month)	..	23.5	46.9
Trade			
ICT goods exports (% of total goods exports)	0.0	0.2	..
ICT goods imports (% of total goods imports)	2.3	1.7	..
ICT service exports (% of total service exports)	6.5	8.4	..
Applications			
Online service index (0–1, 1=highest presence)	0.30	0.19	0.20
Secure Internet servers (per million people)	0.1	2.0	1.1

Cameroon

	Country data		Lower middle-income group
	2005	2012	2012
Economic and social context			
Population (millions)	18	22	2,507
Urban population (% of total)	49	53	39
GNI per capita, *World Bank Atlas* method ($)	900	1,170	1,893
GDP growth, 2000–05 and 2005–12 (avg. annual %)	3.8	3.2	6.0
Adult literacy rate (% ages 15 and older)	*71*	*71*	*71*
Gross primary, secondary, tertiary school enrollment (%)	*51*	*62*	*64*
Sector structure			
Separate telecommunications/ICT regulator	Yes	Yes	
Status of main fixed-line telephone operator	Public	Public	
Level of competition (competition, partial comp., monopoly)			
International gateway(s)	..	..	
Mobile telephone service	C	C	
Internet service	C	C	
Foreign ownership (not allowed, restricted, allowed)	A	A	
Reg. treatment of VoIP (banned, closed, no framework, allowed)	B	B	
Sector efficiency and capacity			
Telecommunications revenue (% of GDP)	3.1	*3.5*	*2.5*
Telecommunications investment (% of revenue)	28.3	*24.2*	*20.5*
Sector performance			
Access			
Fixed-telephone subscriptions (per 100 people)	0.6	3.4	5.4
Mobile-cellular telephone subscriptions (per 100 people)	12.4	60.4	83.1
Fixed (wired)-broadband subscriptions (per 100 people)	0.0	0.6	1.4
Households with a computer (%)	3.0	8.3[a]	15.0
Households with Internet access at home (%)	1.1[a]	3.5[a]	12.4
Usage			
Int'l. voice traffic, total (minutes/subscription/month)	..	4.4	6.5
Domestic mobile traffic (minutes/subscription/month)	1.6	9.3	..
Individuals using the Internet (%)	1.4	5.7[a]	18.7
Quality			
Population covered by a mobile-cellular network (%)	54	..	86
Fixed (wired)-broadband subscriptions (% of total Internet)	1.3	..	58.2
International Internet bandwidth (bit/s per Internet user)	609	260	8,076
Affordability			
Fixed-telephone sub-basket ($ a month)	..	*17.9*	4.9
Mobile-cellular sub-basket ($ a month)	..	*18.8*	10.5
Fixed-broadband sub-basket ($ a month)	..	*58.1*	20.6
Trade			
ICT goods exports (% of total goods exports)	0.0	0.0	4.6
ICT goods imports (% of total goods imports)	3.3	2.7	7.2
ICT service exports (% of total service exports)	19.1	29.7	47.1
Applications			
Online service index (0–1, 1=highest presence)	0.27	0.30	0.32
Secure Internet servers (per million people)	0.1	1.5	4.4

Canada

High income

	Country data		High-income group
	2005	2012	2012
Economic and social context			
Population (millions)	32	35	1,300
Urban population (% of total)	80	81	80
GNI per capita, *World Bank Atlas* method ($)	33,110	51,570	38,412
GDP growth, 2000–05 and 2005–12 (avg. annual %)	2.5	1.2	1.0
Adult literacy rate (% ages 15 and older)	..	..	..
Gross primary, secondary, tertiary school enrollment (%)	..	..	93
Sector structure			
Separate telecommunications/ICT regulator	Yes	Yes	
Status of main fixed-line telephone operator	Public	Private	
Level of competition (competition, partial comp., monopoly)			
International gateway(s)	C	C	
Mobile telephone service	C	C	
Internet service	C	C	
Foreign ownership (not allowed, restricted, allowed)	R	R	
Reg. treatment of VoIP (banned, closed, no framework, allowed)	A	A	
Sector efficiency and capacity			
Telecommunications revenue (% of GDP)	2.5	2.5	2.7
Telecommunications investment (% of revenue)	16.2	21.9	17.6
Sector performance			
Access			
Fixed-telephone subscriptions (per 100 people)	56.3	50.7	43.6
Mobile-cellular telephone subscriptions (per 100 people)	52.8	80.1	122.9
Fixed (wired)-broadband subscriptions (per 100 people)	21.7	32.5	26.2
Households with a computer (%)	72.0	86.6[a]	77.7
Households with Internet access at home (%)	64.3	83.0[a]	75.5
Usage			
Int'l. voice traffic, total (minutes/subscription/month)	..	..	..
Domestic mobile traffic (minutes/subscription/month)	..	357.1	*113.6*
Individuals using the Internet (%)	71.7	86.8[a]	75.4
Quality			
Population covered by a mobile-cellular network (%)	97	99	100
Fixed (wired)-broadband subscriptions (% of total Internet)	78.9	97.9	*95.9*
International Internet bandwidth (bit/s per Internet user)	9,411	100,505	85,990
Affordability			
Fixed-telephone sub-basket ($ a month)	..	29.3	25.2
Mobile-cellular sub-basket ($ a month)	..	40.8	20.6
Fixed-broadband sub-basket ($ a month)	..	40.4	29.2
Trade			
ICT goods exports (% of total goods exports)	3.9	2.3	8.9
ICT goods imports (% of total goods imports)	9.1	7.3	10.8
ICT service exports (% of total service exports)	39.3	41.2	30.8
Applications			
Online service index (0–1, 1=highest presence)	0.82	0.89	0.67
Secure Internet servers (per million people)	569.1	1,040.6	827.6

Cayman Islands

High income

	Country data		High-income group
	2005	2012	2012
Economic and social context			
Population (millions)	0.05	0.06	1,300
Urban population (% of total)	100	100	80
GNI per capita, *World Bank Atlas* method ($)	..	..	38,412
GDP growth, 2000–05 and 2005–12 (avg. annual %)	..	..	1.0
Adult literacy rate (% ages 15 and older)	99	..	..
Gross primary, secondary, tertiary school enrollment (%)	..	..	93
Sector structure			
Separate telecommunications/ICT regulator	..	..	
Status of main fixed-line telephone operator	..	..	
Level of competition (competition, partial comp., monopoly)			
International gateway(s)	..	..	
Mobile telephone service	..	..	
Internet service	..	..	
Foreign ownership (not allowed, restricted, allowed)	..	..	
Reg. treatment of VoIP (banned, closed, no framework, allowed)	No	*No*	
Sector efficiency and capacity			
Telecommunications revenue (% of GDP)	..	..	2.7
Telecommunications investment (% of revenue)	..	..	17.6
Sector performance			
Access			
Fixed-telephone subscriptions (per 100 people)	78.2[a]	65.0	43.6
Mobile-cellular telephone subscriptions (per 100 people)	166.5	171.7	122.9
Fixed (wired)-broadband subscriptions (per 100 people)	..	33.6	26.2
Households with a computer (%)	54.8	74.5[a]	77.7
Households with Internet access at home (%)	50.7[a]	66.0[a]	75.5
Usage			
Int'l. voice traffic, total (minutes/subscription/month)	..	..	..
Domestic mobile traffic (minutes/subscription/month)	..	..	113.6
Individuals using the Internet (%)	38.0	74.1[a]	75.4
Quality			
Population covered by a mobile-cellular network (%)	100	100	100
Fixed (wired)-broadband subscriptions (% of total Internet)	..	..	95.9
International Internet bandwidth (bit/s per Internet user)	..	..	85,990
Affordability			
Fixed-telephone sub-basket ($ a month)	..	..	25.2
Mobile-cellular sub-basket ($ a month)	..	..	20.6
Fixed-broadband sub-basket ($ a month)	..	..	29.2
Trade			
ICT goods exports (% of total goods exports)	..	..	8.9
ICT goods imports (% of total goods imports)	..	..	10.8
ICT service exports (% of total service exports)	..	..	30.8
Applications			
Online service index (0–1, 1=highest presence)	..	..	0.67
Secure Internet servers (per million people)	843.2	2,103.4	827.6

Central African Republic

	Country data		Low-income group
	2005	2012	2012
Economic and social context			
Population (millions)	4	5	846
Urban population (% of total)	38	39	28
GNI per capita, World Bank Atlas method ($)	340	510	590
GDP growth, 2000–05 and 2005–12 (avg. annual %)	1.5	6.7	5.9
Adult literacy rate (% ages 15 and older)	51	57	61
Gross primary, secondary, tertiary school enrollment (%)	..	43	60
Sector structure			
Separate telecommunications/ICT regulator	Yes	Yes	
Status of main fixed-line telephone operator	Mixed	Mixed	
Level of competition (competition, partial comp., monopoly)			
International gateway(s)	..	C	
Mobile telephone service	C	C	
Internet service	C	C	
Foreign ownership (not allowed, restricted, allowed)	..	A	
Reg. treatment of VoIP (banned, closed, no framework, allowed)	..	C	
Sector efficiency and capacity			
Telecommunications revenue (% of GDP)	1.1	2.2	5.0
Telecommunications investment (% of revenue)	..	56.3	..
Sector performance			
Access			
Fixed-telephone subscriptions (per 100 people)	0.3	0.0	1.0
Mobile-cellular telephone subscriptions (per 100 people)	2.5	25.3	47.2
Fixed (wired)-broadband subscriptions (per 100 people)	0.0	0.0	0.2
Households with a computer (%)	..	2.9[a]	4.2
Households with Internet access at home (%)	..	2.4[a]	3.4
Usage			
Int'l. voice traffic, total (minutes/subscription/month)	..	5.2	..
Domestic mobile traffic (minutes/subscription/month)	..	29.8	70.1
Individuals using the Internet (%)	0.3[a]	3.0[a]	6.2
Quality			
Population covered by a mobile-cellular network (%)	19	63	
Fixed (wired)-broadband subscriptions (% of total Internet)	0.0	0.0	30.9
International Internet bandwidth (bit/s per Internet user)	145	162	9,141
Affordability			
Fixed-telephone sub-basket ($ a month)	..	10.1	8.9
Mobile-cellular sub-basket ($ a month)	..	12.9	11.9
Fixed-broadband sub-basket ($ a month)	..	1,329.5	46.9
Trade			
ICT goods exports (% of total goods exports)	0.0	0.2	..
ICT goods imports (% of total goods imports)	2.4	5.9	..
ICT service exports (% of total service exports)	..	..	..
Applications			
Online service index (0–1, 1=highest presence)	0.14	0.00	0.20
Secure Internet servers (per million people)	0.2	0.2	1.1

Chad

                  Low income

	Country data		Low-income group
	2005	**2012**	**2012**
Economic and social context			
Population (millions)	10	12	846
Urban population (% of total)	22	22	28
GNI per capita, *World Bank Atlas* method ($)	360	770	590
GDP growth, 2000–05 and 2005–12 (avg. annual %)	17.2	4.9	5.9
Adult literacy rate (% ages 15 and older)	28	35	61
Gross primary, secondary, tertiary school enrollment (%)	36	47	60
Sector structure			
Separate telecommunications/ICT regulator	Yes	Yes	
Status of main fixed-line telephone operator	Public	Public	
Level of competition (competition, partial comp., monopoly)			
International gateway(s)	..	..	
Mobile telephone service	C	..	
Internet service	C	C	
Foreign ownership (not allowed, restricted, allowed)	A	A	
Reg. treatment of VoIP (banned, closed, no framework, allowed)	B	B	
Sector efficiency and capacity			
Telecommunications revenue (% of GDP)	..	2.1	5.0
Telecommunications investment (% of revenue)	..	..	..
Sector performance			
Access			
Fixed-telephone subscriptions (per 100 people)	0.1	0.2	1.0
Mobile-cellular telephone subscriptions (per 100 people)	2.1	35.4	47.2
Fixed (wired)-broadband subscriptions (per 100 people)	0.0	0.2	0.2
Households with a computer (%)	..	2.5[a]	4.2
Households with Internet access at home (%)	..	2.3[a]	3.4
Usage			
Int'l. voice traffic, total (minutes/subscription/month)	..	3.4	..
Domestic mobile traffic (minutes/subscription/month)	..	..	70.1
Individuals using the Internet (%)	0.4	2.1[a]	6.2
Quality			
Population covered by a mobile-cellular network (%)	24	36	..
Fixed (wired)-broadband subscriptions (% of total Internet)	0.0	100.0	30.9
International Internet bandwidth (bit/s per Internet user)	88	490	9,141
Affordability			
Fixed-telephone sub-basket ($ a month)	..	16.7	8.9
Mobile-cellular sub-basket ($ a month)	..	15.4	11.9
Fixed-broadband sub-basket ($ a month)	..	11.8	46.9
Trade			
ICT goods exports (% of total goods exports)	..	..	..
ICT goods imports (% of total goods imports)	..	..	..
ICT service exports (% of total service exports)	..	..	..
Applications			
Online service index (0–1, 1=highest presence)	0.10	0.10	0.20
Secure Internet servers (per million people)	..	..	1.1

Channel Islands

	Country data		High-income group
	2005	2012	2012
Economic and social context			
Population (millions)	0.15	0.16	1,300
Urban population (% of total)	31	31	80
GNI per capita, World Bank Atlas method ($)	55,320	..	38,412
GDP growth, 2000–05 and 2005–12 (avg. annual %)	-1.2	..	1.0
Adult literacy rate (% ages 15 and older)	..	..	..
Gross primary, secondary, tertiary school enrollment (%)	..	..	93
Sector structure			
Separate telecommunications/ICT regulator	..	..	
Status of main fixed-line telephone operator	..	..	
Level of competition (competition, partial comp., monopoly)			
International gateway(s)	..	..	
Mobile telephone service	..	..	
Internet service	..	..	
Foreign ownership (not allowed, restricted, allowed)	..	..	
Reg. treatment of VoIP (banned, closed, no framework, allowed)	..	..	
Sector efficiency and capacity			
Telecommunications revenue (% of GDP)	..	..	2.7
Telecommunications investment (% of revenue)	..	..	17.6
Sector performance			
Access			
Fixed-telephone subscriptions (per 100 people)	..	..	43.6
Mobile-cellular telephone subscriptions (per 100 people)	..	..	122.9
Fixed (wired)-broadband subscriptions (per 100 people)	..	..	26.2
Households with a computer (%)	..	..	77.7
Households with Internet access at home (%)	..	..	75.5
Usage			
Int'l. voice traffic, total (minutes/subscription/month)	..	..	..
Domestic mobile traffic (minutes/subscription/month)	..	..	113.6
Individuals using the Internet (%)	..	..	75.4
Quality			
Population covered by a mobile-cellular network (%)	..	..	100
Fixed (wired)-broadband subscriptions (% of total Internet)	..	..	95.9
International Internet bandwidth (bit/s per Internet user)	..	..	85,990
Affordability			
Fixed-telephone sub-basket ($ a month)	..	..	25.2
Mobile-cellular sub-basket ($ a month)	..	..	20.6
Fixed-broadband sub-basket ($ a month)	..	..	29.2
Trade			
ICT goods exports (% of total goods exports)	..	..	8.9
ICT goods imports (% of total goods imports)	..	..	10.8
ICT service exports (% of total service exports)	..	..	30.8
Applications			
Online service index (0–1, 1=highest presence)	..	..	0.67
Secure Internet servers (per million people)	..	..	827.6

Chile

	Country data		High-income group
	2005	2012	2012
Economic and social context			
Population (millions)	16	17	1,300
Urban population (% of total)	88	89	80
GNI per capita, *World Bank Atlas* method ($)	6,250	14,310	38,412
GDP growth, 2000–05 and 2005–12 (avg. annual %)	4.2	3.8	1.0
Adult literacy rate (% ages 15 and older)	96	99	..
Gross primary, secondary, tertiary school enrollment (%)	83	88	93
Sector structure			
Separate telecommunications/ICT regulator	Yes	Yes	
Status of main fixed-line telephone operator	Private	Private	
Level of competition (competition, partial comp., monopoly)			
International gateway(s)	C	C	
Mobile telephone service	C	C	
Internet service	C	C	
Foreign ownership (not allowed, restricted, allowed)	A	A	
Reg. treatment of VoIP (banned, closed, no framework, allowed)	No	A	
Sector efficiency and capacity			
Telecommunications revenue (% of GDP)	..	..	2.7
Telecommunications investment (% of revenue)	..	..	17.6
Sector performance			
Access			
Fixed-telephone subscriptions (per 100 people)	21.0	18.8	43.6
Mobile-cellular telephone subscriptions (per 100 people)	64.7	138.2	122.9
Fixed (wired)-broadband subscriptions (per 100 people)	4.3	12.4	26.2
Households with a computer (%)	30.1[a]	53.7[a]	77.7
Households with Internet access at home (%)	16.7[a]	45.3[a]	75.5
Usage			
Int'l. voice traffic, total (minutes/subscription/month)	3.7	1.9	..
Domestic mobile traffic (minutes/subscription/month)	55.9	91.5	113.6
Individuals using the Internet (%)	31.2[a]	61.4[a]	75.4
Quality			
Population covered by a mobile-cellular network (%)	100	100	100
Fixed (wired)-broadband subscriptions (% of total Internet)	78.2	98.9	95.9
International Internet bandwidth (bit/s per Internet user)	2,494	40,460	85,990
Affordability			
Fixed-telephone sub-basket ($ a month)	..	35.1	25.2
Mobile-cellular sub-basket ($ a month)	..	22.8	20.6
Fixed-broadband sub-basket ($ a month)	..	25.8	29.2
Trade			
ICT goods exports (% of total goods exports)	0.5	0.3	8.9
ICT goods imports (% of total goods imports)	8.2	7.3	10.8
ICT service exports (% of total service exports)	18.4	21.1	30.8
Applications			
Online service index (0–1, 1=highest presence)	0.58	0.75	0.67
Secure Internet servers (per million people)	21.0	93.6	827.6

China

East Asia & Pacific			**Upper middle income**

	Country data		Upper middle-income group
	2005	**2012**	**2012**
Economic and social context			
Population (millions)	1,304	1,351	2,391
Urban population (% of total)	43	52	61
GNI per capita, *World Bank Atlas* method ($)	1,740	5,720	6,969
GDP growth, 2000–05 and 2005–12 (avg. annual %)	9.8	10.4	6.2
Adult literacy rate (% ages 15 and older)	91	95	94
Gross primary, secondary, tertiary school enrollment (%)	64	74	76
Sector structure			
Separate telecommunications/ICT regulator	No	No	
Status of main fixed-line telephone operator	Mixed	Mixed	
Level of competition (competition, partial comp., monopoly)			
International gateway(s)	..	P	
Mobile telephone service	P	..	
Internet service	C	..	
Foreign ownership (not allowed, restricted, allowed)	R	R	
Reg. treatment of VoIP (banned, closed, no framework, allowed)	B	C	
Sector efficiency and capacity			
Telecommunications revenue (% of GDP)	3.2	2.1	2.5
Telecommunications investment (% of revenue)	35.9	33.6	18.2
Sector performance			
Access			
Fixed-telephone subscriptions (per 100 people)	26.6	20.2	19.4
Mobile-cellular telephone subscriptions (per 100 people)	29.8	80.8	92.4
Fixed (wired)-broadband subscriptions (per 100 people)	2.8	12.7	10.8
Households with a computer (%)	25.0	40.9a	40.6
Households with Internet access at home (%)	11.0	37.4a	36.3
Usage			
Int'l. voice traffic, total (minutes/subscription/month)	1.3	0.4	1.3
Domestic mobile traffic (minutes/subscription/month)	132.5	415.4	284.4
Individuals using the Internet (%)	8.5	42.3a	41.6
Quality			
Population covered by a mobile-cellular network (%)	97	99	99
Fixed (wired)-broadband subscriptions (% of total Internet)	51.2	96.8	95.5
International Internet bandwidth (bit/s per Internet user)	1,211	3,261	14,580
Affordability			
Fixed-telephone sub-basket ($ a month)	..	4.9	9.4
Mobile-cellular sub-basket ($ a month)	..	2.3	14.9
Fixed-broadband sub-basket ($ a month)	..	23.2	17.8
Trade			
ICT goods exports (% of total goods exports)	30.7	27.1	17.6
ICT goods imports (% of total goods imports)	25.3	19.6	14.7
ICT service exports (% of total service exports)	24.9	34.9	29.1
Applications			
Online service index (0–1, 1=highest presence)	0.50	0.53	0.42
Secure Internet servers (per million people)	0.3	3.9	18.5

Colombia

	Country data		Upper middle-income group
Latin America & Caribbean			**Upper middle income**
	2005	2012	2012
Economic and social context			
Population (millions)	43	48	2,391
Urban population (% of total)	74	76	61
GNI per capita, *World Bank Atlas* method ($)	2,930	7,020	6,969
GDP growth, 2000–05 and 2005–12 (avg. annual %)	3.7	4.5	6.2
Adult literacy rate (% ages 15 and older)	93	94	94
Gross primary, secondary, tertiary school enrollment (%)	79	82	76
Sector structure			
Separate telecommunications/ICT regulator	Yes	Yes	
Status of main fixed-line telephone operator	Public	Mixed	
Level of competition (competition, partial comp., monopoly)			
International gateway(s)	..	C	
Mobile telephone service	P	C	
Internet service	C	C	
Foreign ownership (not allowed, restricted, allowed)	R	A	
Reg. treatment of VoIP (banned, closed, no framework, allowed)	No	A	
Sector efficiency and capacity			
Telecommunications revenue (% of GDP)	4.3	5.4	2.5
Telecommunications investment (% of revenue)	..	17.8	18.2
Sector performance			
Access			
Fixed-telephone subscriptions (per 100 people)	17.8	13.0	19.4
Mobile-cellular telephone subscriptions (per 100 people)	50.6	102.9	92.4
Fixed (wired)-broadband subscriptions (per 100 people)	0.7	8.2	10.8
Households with a computer (%)	14.6	38.4	40.6
Households with Internet access at home (%)	6.2	32.1	36.3
Usage			
Int'l. voice traffic, total (minutes/subscription/month)	..	5.7	1.3
Domestic mobile traffic (minutes/subscription/month)	48.4	353.4	284.4
Individuals using the Internet (%)	11.0	49.0	41.6
Quality			
Population covered by a mobile-cellular network (%)	82	100	99
Fixed (wired)-broadband subscriptions (% of total Internet)	46.3	99.9	95.5
International Internet bandwidth (bit/s per Internet user)	4,686	20,370	14,580
Affordability			
Fixed-telephone sub-basket ($ a month)	..	10.0	9.4
Mobile-cellular sub-basket ($ a month)	..	22.7	14.9
Fixed-broadband sub-basket ($ a month)	..	18.7	17.8
Trade			
ICT goods exports (% of total goods exports)	0.2	0.1	17.6
ICT goods imports (% of total goods imports)	13.0	9.0	14.7
ICT service exports (% of total service exports)	14.6	18.6	29.1
Applications			
Online service index (0–1, 1=highest presence)	0.53	0.84	0.42
Secure Internet servers (per million people)	4.4	33.5	18.5

Comoros

	Country data		Low-income group
	2005	2012	2012
Economic and social context			
Population (millions)	0.60	0.72	846
Urban population (% of total)	28	28	28
GNI per capita, *World Bank Atlas* method ($)	650	840	590
GDP growth, 2000–05 and 2005–12 (avg. annual %)	2.6	1.6	5.9
Adult literacy rate (% ages 15 and older)	68	76	61
Gross primary, secondary, tertiary school enrollment (%)	64	78	60
Sector structure			
Separate telecommunications/ICT regulator	No	Yes	
Status of main fixed-line telephone operator	Public	Public	
Level of competition (competition, partial comp., monopoly)			
International gateway(s)	..	M	
Mobile telephone service	..	M	
Internet service	M	M	
Foreign ownership (not allowed, restricted, allowed)	No	A	
Reg. treatment of VoIP (banned, closed, no framework, allowed)	B	C	
Sector efficiency and capacity			
Telecommunications revenue (% of GDP)	4.0	5.5	5.0
Telecommunications investment (% of revenue)	25.6	13.8	..
Sector performance			
Access			
Fixed-telephone subscriptions (per 100 people)	2.8	3.3[a]	1.0
Mobile-cellular telephone subscriptions (per 100 people)	2.6	39.5	47.2
Fixed (wired)-broadband subscriptions (per 100 people)	0.0	0.2	0.2
Households with a computer (%)	3.0	6.4[a]	4.2
Households with Internet access at home (%)	0.8[a]	3.4[a]	3.4
Usage			
Int'l. voice traffic, total (minutes/subscription/month)	..	..	..
Domestic mobile traffic (minutes/subscription/month)	..	49.4	70.1
Individuals using the Internet (%)	2.0[a]	6.0[a]	6.2
Quality			
Population covered by a mobile-cellular network (%)	40	..	..
Fixed (wired)-broadband subscriptions (% of total Internet)	0.3	60.6	30.9
International Internet bandwidth (bit/s per Internet user)	166	7,231	9,141
Affordability			
Fixed-telephone sub-basket ($ a month)	..	10.0	8.9
Mobile-cellular sub-basket ($ a month)	..	13.5	11.9
Fixed-broadband sub-basket ($ a month)	..	80.2	46.9
Trade			
ICT goods exports (% of total goods exports)	0.0	0.9	..
ICT goods imports (% of total goods imports)	2.7	7.0	..
ICT service exports (% of total service exports)	..	..	..
Applications			
Online service index (0–1, 1=highest presence)	0.19	0.08	0.20
Secure Internet servers (per million people)	5.0	1.4	1.1

Congo, Dem. Rep.

Sub-Saharan Africa   **Low income**

	Country data		Low-income group
	2005	2012	2012
Economic and social context			
Population (millions)	54	66	846
Urban population (% of total)	31	35	28
GNI per capita, *World Bank Atlas* method ($)	130	230	590
GDP growth, 2000–05 and 2005–12 (avg. annual %)	4.6	5.8	5.9
Adult literacy rate (% ages 15 and older)	61	..	61
Gross primary, secondary, tertiary school enrollment (%)	53	63	60
Sector structure			
Separate telecommunications/ICT regulator	Yes	Yes	
Status of main fixed-line telephone operator	Public	Public	
Level of competition (competition, partial comp., monopoly)			
International gateway(s)	..	C	
Mobile telephone service	C	C	
Internet service	C	C	
Foreign ownership (not allowed, restricted, allowed)	No	R	
Reg. treatment of VoIP (banned, closed, no framework, allowed)	B	A	
Sector efficiency and capacity			
Telecommunications revenue (% of GDP)	5.5	5.8	5.0
Telecommunications investment (% of revenue)	89.2	49.4	..
Sector performance			
Access			
Fixed-telephone subscriptions (per 100 people)	0.0	0.1	1.0
Mobile-cellular telephone subscriptions (per 100 people)	5.1	30.6	47.2
Fixed (wired)-broadband subscriptions (per 100 people)	0.0	0.0	0.2
Households with a computer (%)	0.2[a]	1.3[a]	4.2
Households with Internet access at home (%)	0.2[a]	1.3[a]	3.4
Usage			
Int'l. voice traffic, total (minutes/subscription/month)	9.5	3.0	..
Domestic mobile traffic (minutes/subscription/month)	51.2	35.6	70.1
Individuals using the Internet (%)	0.2[a]	1.7[a]	6.2
Quality			
Population covered by a mobile-cellular network (%)	50	50	..
Fixed (wired)-broadband subscriptions (% of total Internet)	6.3	..	30.9
International Internet bandwidth (bit/s per Internet user)	39	725	9,141
Affordability			
Fixed-telephone sub-basket ($ a month)	..	9.9	8.9
Mobile-cellular sub-basket ($ a month)	..	11.9	11.9
Fixed-broadband sub-basket ($ a month)	..	400.2	46.9
Trade			
ICT goods exports (% of total goods exports)	..	..	..
ICT goods imports (% of total goods imports)	..	..	..
ICT service exports (% of total service exports)	..	..	..
Applications			
Online service index (0–1, 1=highest presence)	0.22	0.18	0.20
Secure Internet servers (per million people)	0.1	0.3	1.1

Congo, Rep.

Sub-Saharan Africa			Lower middle income

	Country data		Lower middle-income group
	2005	2012	2012
Economic and social context			
Population (millions)	4	4	2,507
Urban population (% of total)	61	64	39
GNI per capita, *World Bank Atlas* method ($)	970	2,550	1,893
GDP growth, 2000–05 and 2005–12 (avg. annual %)	3.7	5.0	6.0
Adult literacy rate (% ages 15 and older)	..	..	71
Gross primary, secondary, tertiary school enrollment (%)	55	66	64
Sector structure			
Separate telecommunications/ICT regulator	No	Yes	
Status of main fixed-line telephone operator	Public	Public	
Level of competition (competition, partial comp., monopoly)			
International gateway(s)	..	C	
Mobile telephone service	C	C	
Internet service	..	C	
Foreign ownership (not allowed, restricted, allowed)	..	A	
Reg. treatment of VoIP (banned, closed, no framework, allowed)	B	C	
Sector efficiency and capacity			
Telecommunications revenue (% of GDP)	2.7	3.2	2.5
Telecommunications investment (% of revenue)	..	23.4	20.5
Sector performance			
Access			
Fixed-telephone subscriptions (per 100 people)	0.4	0.3	5.4
Mobile-cellular telephone subscriptions (per 100 people)	15.8	98.8	83.1
Fixed (wired)-broadband subscriptions (per 100 people)	0.0	0.0	1.4
Households with a computer (%)	1.4	4.3[a]	15.0
Households with Internet access at home (%)	0.1[a]	1.3[a]	12.4
Usage			
Int'l. voice traffic, total (minutes/subscription/month)	..	9.5	6.5
Domestic mobile traffic (minutes/subscription/month)	..	40.9	..
Individuals using the Internet (%)	1.5[a]	6.1[a]	18.7
Quality			
Population covered by a mobile-cellular network (%)	39	95	86
Fixed (wired)-broadband subscriptions (% of total Internet)	0.0	14.3	58.2
International Internet bandwidth (bit/s per Internet user)	19	204	8,076
Affordability			
Fixed-telephone sub-basket ($ a month)	..	..	4.9
Mobile-cellular sub-basket ($ a month)	..	..	10.5
Fixed-broadband sub-basket ($ a month)	..	..	20.6
Trade			
ICT goods exports (% of total goods exports)	0.0	0.0	4.6
ICT goods imports (% of total goods imports)	1.0	0.9	7.2
ICT service exports (% of total service exports)	..	..	47.1
Applications			
Online service index (0–1, 1=highest presence)	0.27	0.08	0.32
Secure Internet servers (per million people)	0.6	1.1	4.4

Costa Rica

	Country data		Upper middle-income group
	2005	2012	2012
Economic and social context			
Population (millions)	4	5	2,391
Urban population (% of total)	62	65	61
GNI per capita, *World Bank Atlas* method ($)	4,810	8,820	6,969
GDP growth, 2000–05 and 2005–12 (avg. annual %)	4.3	4.1	6.2
Adult literacy rate (% ages 15 and older)	95	96	94
Gross primary, secondary, tertiary school enrollment (%)	74	85	76
Sector structure			
Separate telecommunications/ICT regulator	Yes	Yes	
Status of main fixed-line telephone operator	Public	Public	
Level of competition (competition, partial comp., monopoly)			
International gateway(s)	..	C	
Mobile telephone service	M	C	
Internet service	M	C	
Foreign ownership (not allowed, restricted, allowed)	R	R	
Reg. treatment of VoIP (banned, closed, no framework, allowed)	B	A	
Sector efficiency and capacity			
Telecommunications revenue (% of GDP)	2.3	2.3	2.5
Telecommunications investment (% of revenue)	25.8	98.2	18.2
Sector performance			
Access			
Fixed-telephone subscriptions (per 100 people)	32.1	20.7	19.4
Mobile-cellular telephone subscriptions (per 100 people)	25.5	111.9	92.4
Fixed (wired)-broadband subscriptions (per 100 people)	1.0	9.3	10.8
Households with a computer (%)	27.0	49.0	40.6
Households with Internet access at home (%)	10.2	47.3	36.3
Usage			
Int'l. voice traffic, total (minutes/subscription/month)	19.2	13.0	1.3
Domestic mobile traffic (minutes/subscription/month)	152.2	120.0	284.4
Individuals using the Internet (%)	22.1	47.5	41.6
Quality			
Population covered by a mobile-cellular network (%)	86	70	99
Fixed (wired)-broadband subscriptions (% of total Internet)	60.6	100.0	95.5
International Internet bandwidth (bit/s per Internet user)	687	29,890	14,580
Affordability			
Fixed-telephone sub-basket ($ a month)	..	4.7	9.4
Mobile-cellular sub-basket ($ a month)	..	3.8	14.9
Fixed-broadband sub-basket ($ a month)	..	15.8	17.8
Trade			
ICT goods exports (% of total goods exports)	23.7	19.4	17.6
ICT goods imports (% of total goods imports)	23.7	18.3	14.7
ICT service exports (% of total service exports)	13.3	32.2	29.1
Applications			
Online service index (0–1, 1=highest presence)	0.51	0.50	0.42
Secure Internet servers (per million people)	61.8	79.0	18.5

Côte d'Ivoire

Sub-Saharan Africa			Lower middle income

	Country data		Lower middle-income group
	2005	2012	2012
Economic and social context			
Population (millions)	17	20	2,507
Urban population (% of total)	47	52	39
GNI per capita, *World Bank Atlas* method ($)	900	1,220	1,893
GDP growth, 2000–05 and 2005–12 (avg. annual %)	-0.2	1.9	6.0
Adult literacy rate (% ages 15 and older)	49	57	71
Gross primary, secondary, tertiary school enrollment (%)	..	..	64
Sector structure			
Separate telecommunications/ICT regulator	Yes	Yes	
Status of main fixed-line telephone operator	Mixed	Mixed	
Level of competition (competition, partial comp., monopoly)			
International gateway(s)	..	M	
Mobile telephone service	P	P	
Internet service	C	C	
Foreign ownership (not allowed, restricted, allowed)	A	A	
Reg. treatment of VoIP (banned, closed, no framework, allowed)	B	No	
Sector efficiency and capacity			
Telecommunications revenue (% of GDP)	5.0	7.0	2.5
Telecommunications investment (% of revenue)	29.1	15.4	20.5
Sector performance			
Access			
Fixed-telephone subscriptions (per 100 people)	1.5	1.4	5.4
Mobile-cellular telephone subscriptions (per 100 people)	13.5	91.2	83.1
Fixed (wired)-broadband subscriptions (per 100 people)	0.0	0.1	1.4
Households with a computer (%)	1.3	2.3[a]	15.0
Households with Internet access at home (%)	0.2[a]	1.3[a]	12.4
Usage			
Int'l. voice traffic, total (minutes/subscription/month)	..	5.9	6.5
Domestic mobile traffic (minutes/subscription/month)	106.4	66.5	..
Individuals using the Internet (%)	1.0	2.4[a]	18.7
Quality			
Population covered by a mobile-cellular network (%)	55	95	86
Fixed (wired)-broadband subscriptions (% of total Internet)	6.9	..	58.2
International Internet bandwidth (bit/s per Internet user)	307	16,950	8,076
Affordability			
Fixed-telephone sub-basket ($ a month)	..	20.7	4.9
Mobile-cellular sub-basket ($ a month)	..	20.1	10.5
Fixed-broadband sub-basket ($ a month)	..	42.4	20.6
Trade			
ICT goods exports (% of total goods exports)	0.6	0.1	4.6
ICT goods imports (% of total goods imports)	3.8	3.1	7.2
ICT service exports (% of total service exports)	33.7	28.5	47.1
Applications			
Online service index (0–1, 1=highest presence)	0.19	0.33	0.32
Secure Internet servers (per million people)	0.3	2.0	4.4

Croatia

High income

	Country data		High-income group 2012
	2005	2012	2012
Economic and social context			
Population (millions)	4	4	1,300
Urban population (% of total)	56	58	80
GNI per capita, World Bank Atlas method ($)	9,690	13,490	38,412
GDP growth, 2000–05 and 2005–12 (avg. annual %)	4.6	-0.4	1.0
Adult literacy rate (% ages 15 and older)	98	99	..
Gross primary, secondary, tertiary school enrollment (%)	79	85	93
Sector structure			
Separate telecommunications/ICT regulator	Yes	Yes	
Status of main fixed-line telephone operator	Mixed	Mixed	
Level of competition (competition, partial comp., monopoly)			
International gateway(s)	C	C	
Mobile telephone service	C	C	
Internet service	C	C	
Foreign ownership (not allowed, restricted, allowed)	A	A	
Reg. treatment of VoIP (banned, closed, no framework, allowed)	A	A	
Sector efficiency and capacity			
Telecommunications revenue (% of GDP)	4.9	3.6	2.7
Telecommunications investment (% of revenue)	14.5	18.3	17.6
Sector performance			
Access			
Fixed-telephone subscriptions (per 100 people)	42.9	37.9	43.6
Mobile-cellular telephone subscriptions (per 100 people)	83.2	115.4	122.9
Fixed (wired)-broadband subscriptions (per 100 people)	2.6	20.7	26.2
Households with a computer (%)	32.7	68.0	77.7
Households with Internet access at home (%)	25.0	66.0	75.5
Usage			
Int'l. voice traffic, total (minutes/subscription/month)	16.5	8.4	..
Domestic mobile traffic (minutes/subscription/month)	65.7	115.0	113.6
Individuals using the Internet (%)	33.1	63.0	75.4
Quality			
Population covered by a mobile-cellular network (%)	100	100	100
Fixed (wired)-broadband subscriptions (% of total Internet)	12.2	95.6	95.9
International Internet bandwidth (bit/s per Internet user)	3,280	28,743	85,990
Affordability			
Fixed-telephone sub-basket ($ a month)	..	15.3	25.2
Mobile-cellular sub-basket ($ a month)	..	17.6	20.6
Fixed-broadband sub-basket ($ a month)	..	19.0	29.2
Trade			
ICT goods exports (% of total goods exports)	2.6	1.9	8.9
ICT goods imports (% of total goods imports)	6.1	4.4	10.8
ICT service exports (% of total service exports)	12.5	14.5	30.8
Applications			
Online service index (0–1, 1=highest presence)	0.57	0.64	0.67
Secure Internet servers (per million people)	39.6	188.5	827.6

The Little Data Book on Information and Communication Technology 2014 **65**

Cuba

Latin America & Caribbean			Upper middle income

	Country data		Upper middle-income group
	2005	2012	2012
Economic and social context			
Population (millions)	11	11	2,391
Urban population (% of total)	76	75	61
GNI per capita, *World Bank Atlas* method ($)	3,950	5,890	6,969
GDP growth, 2000–05 and 2005–12 (avg. annual %)	4.6	4.4	6.2
Adult literacy rate (% ages 15 and older)	100	100	94
Gross primary, secondary, tertiary school enrollment (%)	86	85	76
Sector structure			
Separate telecommunications/ICT regulator	No	No	
Status of main fixed-line telephone operator	Private	Mixed	
Level of competition (competition, partial comp., monopoly)			
International gateway(s)	..	..	
Mobile telephone service	M	M	
Internet service	P	P	
Foreign ownership (not allowed, restricted, allowed)	R	R	
Reg. treatment of VoIP (banned, closed, no framework, allowed)	B	A	
Sector efficiency and capacity			
Telecommunications revenue (% of GDP)	2.9	..	2.5
Telecommunications investment (% of revenue)	7.5	..	18.2
Sector performance			
Access			
Fixed-telephone subscriptions (per 100 people)	7.6	10.8	19.4
Mobile-cellular telephone subscriptions (per 100 people)	1.2	14.9	92.4
Fixed (wired)-broadband subscriptions (per 100 people)	0.0	0.0	10.8
Households with a computer (%)	0.2[a]	4.6[a]	40.6
Households with Internet access at home (%)	0.0	3.8[a]	36.3
Usage			
Int'l. voice traffic, total (minutes/subscription/month)	26.5	11.9	1.3
Domestic mobile traffic (minutes/subscription/month)	53.0	36.6	284.4
Individuals using the Internet (%)	9.7	25.6[a]	41.6
Quality			
Population covered by a mobile-cellular network (%)	71	85	99
Fixed (wired)-broadband subscriptions (% of total Internet)	5.8	11.9	95.5
International Internet bandwidth (bit/s per Internet user)	95	158	14,580
Affordability			
Fixed-telephone sub-basket ($ a month)	..	0.3	9.4
Mobile-cellular sub-basket ($ a month)	..	26.5	14.9
Fixed-broadband sub-basket ($ a month)	..	1,760.4	17.8
Trade			
ICT goods exports (% of total goods exports)	0.9	..	17.6
ICT goods imports (% of total goods imports)	2.6	..	14.7
ICT service exports (% of total service exports)	..	..	29.1
Applications			
Online service index (0–1, 1=highest presence)	0.40	0.31	0.42
Secure Internet servers (per million people)	0.1	0.4	18.5

Curaçao

High income

	Country data		High-income group
	2005	2012	2012
Economic and social context			
Population (millions)	0.14	0.15	1,300
Urban population (% of total)	..	..	80
GNI per capita, *World Bank Atlas* method ($)	..	..	38,412
GDP growth, 2000–05 and 2005–12 (avg. annual %)	..	..	1.0
Adult literacy rate (% ages 15 and older)	..	..	..
Gross primary, secondary, tertiary school enrollment (%)	..	..	93
Sector structure			
Separate telecommunications/ICT regulator	..	..	
Status of main fixed-line telephone operator	..	..	
Level of competition (competition, partial comp., monopoly)			
International gateway(s)	..	..	
Mobile telephone service	..	..	
Internet service	..	..	
Foreign ownership (not allowed, restricted, allowed)	..	..	
Reg. treatment of VoIP (banned, closed, no framework, allowed)	..	..	
Sector efficiency and capacity			
Telecommunications revenue (% of GDP)	..	..	2.7
Telecommunications investment (% of revenue)	..	..	17.6
Sector performance			
Access			
Fixed-telephone subscriptions (per 100 people)	..	..	43.6
Mobile-cellular telephone subscriptions (per 100 people)	..	..	122.9
Fixed (wired)-broadband subscriptions (per 100 people)	..	..	26.2
Households with a computer (%)	..	..	77.7
Households with Internet access at home (%)	..	..	75.5
Usage			
Int'l. voice traffic, total (minutes/subscription/month)	..	..	..
Domestic mobile traffic (minutes/subscription/month)	..	..	*113.6*
Individuals using the Internet (%)	..	..	75.4
Quality			
Population covered by a mobile-cellular network (%)	..	..	100
Fixed (wired)-broadband subscriptions (% of total Internet)	..	..	*95.9*
International Internet bandwidth (bit/s per Internet user)	..	..	85,990
Affordability			
Fixed-telephone sub-basket ($ a month)	..	..	25.2
Mobile-cellular sub-basket ($ a month)	..	..	20.6
Fixed-broadband sub-basket ($ a month)	..	..	29.2
Trade			
ICT goods exports (% of total goods exports)	..	..	8.9
ICT goods imports (% of total goods imports)	..	..	10.8
ICT service exports (% of total service exports)	..	..	30.8
Applications			
Online service index (0–1, 1=highest presence)	..	..	0.67
Secure Internet servers (per million people)	..	187.5	827.6

Cyprus

	Country data		High-income group
	2005	2012	2012
Economic and social context			
Population (millions)	1	1	1,300
Urban population (% of total)	69	71	80
GNI per capita, *World Bank Atlas* method ($)	21,490	26,110	38,412
GDP growth, 2000–05 and 2005–12 (avg. annual %)	3.1	1.5	1.0
Adult literacy rate (% ages 15 and older)	97	99	..
Gross primary, secondary, tertiary school enrollment (%)	78	78	93
Sector structure			
Separate telecommunications/ICT regulator	Yes	Yes	
Status of main fixed-line telephone operator	Public	Public	
Level of competition (competition, partial comp., monopoly)			
International gateway(s)	..	C	
Mobile telephone service	P	P	
Internet service	C	C	
Foreign ownership (not allowed, restricted, allowed)	A	A	
Reg. treatment of VoIP (banned, closed, no framework, allowed)	No	A	
Sector efficiency and capacity			
Telecommunications revenue (% of GDP)	2.9	3.1	2.7
Telecommunications investment (% of revenue)	15.0	11.9	17.6
Sector performance			
Access			
Fixed-telephone subscriptions (per 100 people)	40.7	33.1	43.6
Mobile-cellular telephone subscriptions (per 100 people)	75.8	98.4	122.9
Fixed (wired)-broadband subscriptions (per 100 people)	3.1	19.2	26.2
Households with a computer (%)	46.0	70.0	77.7
Households with Internet access at home (%)	31.7	62.0	75.5
Usage			
Int'l. voice traffic, total (minutes/subscription/month)	57.5	40.2	..
Domestic mobile traffic (minutes/subscription/month)	174.0	228.7	113.6
Individuals using the Internet (%)	32.8	61.0	75.4
Quality			
Population covered by a mobile-cellular network (%)	100	100	100
Fixed (wired)-broadband subscriptions (% of total Internet)	35.0	96.5	95.9
International Internet bandwidth (bit/s per Internet user)	1,328	69,698	85,990
Affordability			
Fixed-telephone sub-basket ($ a month)	..	25.2	25.2
Mobile-cellular sub-basket ($ a month)	..	8.4	20.6
Fixed-broadband sub-basket ($ a month)	..	21.9	29.2
Trade			
ICT goods exports (% of total goods exports)	25.0	3.5	8.9
ICT goods imports (% of total goods imports)	10.8	4.1	10.8
ICT service exports (% of total service exports)	21.1	25.1	30.8
Applications			
Online service index (0–1, 1=highest presence)	0.60	0.56	0.67
Secure Internet servers (per million people)	175.3	621.4	827.6

Czech Republic

High income

	Country data		High-income group
	2005	2012	2012
Economic and social context			
Population (millions)	10	11	1,300
Urban population (% of total)	74	73	80
GNI per capita, World Bank Atlas method ($)	11,920	18,130	38,412
GDP growth, 2000–05 and 2005–12 (avg. annual %)	3.9	1.6	1.0
Adult literacy rate (% ages 15 and older)	..	..	..
Gross primary, secondary, tertiary school enrollment (%)	83	88	93
Sector structure			
Separate telecommunications/ICT regulator	Yes	Yes	
Status of main fixed-line telephone operator	Private	Private	
Level of competition (competition, partial comp., monopoly)			
International gateway(s)	C	..	
Mobile telephone service	C	P	
Internet service	C	C	
Foreign ownership (not allowed, restricted, allowed)	A	R	
Reg. treatment of VoIP (banned, closed, no framework, allowed)	A	A	
Sector efficiency and capacity			
Telecommunications revenue (% of GDP)	3.8	1.9	2.7
Telecommunications investment (% of revenue)	11.7	20.8	17.6
Sector performance			
Access			
Fixed-telephone subscriptions (per 100 people)	31.4	19.9	43.6
Mobile-cellular telephone subscriptions (per 100 people)	115.1	126.8	122.9
Fixed (wired)-broadband subscriptions (per 100 people)	6.9	16.4	26.2
Households with a computer (%)	30.0	75.0[a]	77.7
Households with Internet access at home (%)	19.1	71.0	75.5
Usage			
Int'l. voice traffic, total (minutes/subscription/month)	7.4	9.7	..
Domestic mobile traffic (minutes/subscription/month)	50.3	97.8	113.6
Individuals using the Internet (%)	35.3	75.0	75.4
Quality			
Population covered by a mobile-cellular network (%)	100	100	100
Fixed (wired)-broadband subscriptions (% of total Internet)	30.1	100.0	95.9
International Internet bandwidth (bit/s per Internet user)	13,620	100,062	85,990
Affordability			
Fixed-telephone sub-basket ($ a month)	..	29.1	25.2
Mobile-cellular sub-basket ($ a month)	..	27.7	20.6
Fixed-broadband sub-basket ($ a month)	..	22.6	29.2
Trade			
ICT goods exports (% of total goods exports)	11.1	14.5	8.9
ICT goods imports (% of total goods imports)	11.2	14.7	10.8
ICT service exports (% of total service exports)	24.4	36.1	30.8
Applications			
Online service index (0–1, 1=highest presence)	0.67	0.54	0.67
Secure Internet servers (per million people)	41.6	559.3	827.6

Denmark

	Country data		High-income group
	2005	2012	2012
Economic and social context			
Population (millions)	5	6	1,300
Urban population (% of total)	86	87	80
GNI per capita, *World Bank Atlas* method ($)	48,590	59,870	38,412
GDP growth, 2000–05 and 2005–12 (avg. annual %)	1.2	-0.4	1.0
Adult literacy rate (% ages 15 and older)	..	..	..
Gross primary, secondary, tertiary school enrollment (%)	103	*100*	93
Sector structure			
Separate telecommunications/ICT regulator	Yes	Yes	
Status of main fixed-line telephone operator	Private	Private	
Level of competition (competition, partial comp., monopoly)			
International gateway(s)	C	C	
Mobile telephone service	P	P	
Internet service	C	C	
Foreign ownership (not allowed, restricted, allowed)	A	A	
Reg. treatment of VoIP (banned, closed, no framework, allowed)	A	A	
Sector efficiency and capacity			
Telecommunications revenue (% of GDP)	2.6	2.0	2.7
Telecommunications investment (% of revenue)	17.2	17.2	17.6
Sector performance			
Access			
Fixed-telephone subscriptions (per 100 people)	61.8	43.4	43.6
Mobile-cellular telephone subscriptions (per 100 people)	100.6	117.6	122.9
Fixed (wired)-broadband subscriptions (per 100 people)	24.8	38.8	26.2
Households with a computer (%)	84.0	92.2[a]	77.7
Households with Internet access at home (%)	74.9	92.0	75.5
Usage			
Int'l. voice traffic, total (minutes/subscription/month)	..	18.2	..
Domestic mobile traffic (minutes/subscription/month)	99.1	146.1	*113.6*
Individuals using the Internet (%)	82.7	93.0	75.4
Quality			
Population covered by a mobile-cellular network (%)	..	..	100
Fixed (wired)-broadband subscriptions (% of total Internet)	74.3	96.3	95.9
International Internet bandwidth (bit/s per Internet user)	42,041	174,801	85,990
Affordability			
Fixed-telephone sub-basket ($ a month)	..	30.5	25.2
Mobile-cellular sub-basket ($ a month)	..	10.3	20.6
Fixed-broadband sub-basket ($ a month)	..	46.4	29.2
Trade			
ICT goods exports (% of total goods exports)	7.1	3.5	8.9
ICT goods imports (% of total goods imports)	12.4	8.2	10.8
ICT service exports (% of total service exports)	..	..	30.8
Applications			
Online service index (0–1, 1=highest presence)	0.91	0.86	0.67
Secure Internet servers (per million people)	411.3	2,104.5	827.6

Djibouti

	Country data		Lower middle-income group
	2005	2012	2012
Economic and social context			
Population (millions)	0.78	0.86	2,507
Urban population (% of total)	77	77	39
GNI per capita, *World Bank Atlas* method ($)	1,030	..	1,893
GDP growth, 2000–05 and 2005–12 (avg. annual %)	3.0	..	6.0
Adult literacy rate (% ages 15 and older)	..	..	71
Gross primary, secondary, tertiary school enrollment (%)	25	37	64
Sector structure			
Separate telecommunications/ICT regulator	No	No	
Status of main fixed-line telephone operator	Public	Public	
Level of competition (competition, partial comp., monopoly)			
International gateway(s)	..	M	
Mobile telephone service	..	M	
Internet service	M	M	
Foreign ownership (not allowed, restricted, allowed)	No	No	
Reg. treatment of VoIP (banned, closed, no framework, allowed)	B	C	
Sector efficiency and capacity			
Telecommunications revenue (% of GDP)	4.8	..	2.5
Telecommunications investment (% of revenue)	25.6	14.3[a]	20.5
Sector performance			
Access			
Fixed-telephone subscriptions (per 100 people)	1.4	2.3	5.4
Mobile-cellular telephone subscriptions (per 100 people)	5.7	24.7	83.1
Fixed (wired)-broadband subscriptions (per 100 people)	0.0	1.7	1.4
Households with a computer (%)	6.8	15.5[a]	15.0
Households with Internet access at home (%)	0.6	5.1[a]	12.4
Usage			
Int'l. voice traffic, total (minutes/subscription/month)	..	124.9	6.5
Domestic mobile traffic (minutes/subscription/month)	50.2	32.0	..
Individuals using the Internet (%)	1.0	8.3[a]	18.7
Quality			
Population covered by a mobile-cellular network (%)	75	95	86
Fixed (wired)-broadband subscriptions (% of total Internet)	1.2	79.6	58.2
International Internet bandwidth (bit/s per Internet user)	6,076	11,960	8,076
Affordability			
Fixed-telephone sub-basket ($ a month)	..	6.9	4.9
Mobile-cellular sub-basket ($ a month)	..	13.2	10.5
Fixed-broadband sub-basket ($ a month)	..	31.6	20.6
Trade			
ICT goods exports (% of total goods exports)	..	0.1	4.6
ICT goods imports (% of total goods imports)	..	5.4	7.2
ICT service exports (% of total service exports)	5.1	..	47.1
Applications			
Online service index (0–1, 1=highest presence)	0.23	0.20	0.32
Secure Internet servers (per million people)	1.3	4.6	4.4

Dominica

Latin America & Caribbean			Upper middle income
	Country data		Upper middle-income group
	2005	2012	2012
Economic and social context			
Population (millions)	0.07	0.07	2,391
Urban population (% of total)	67	67	61
GNI per capita, *World Bank Atlas* method ($)	4,980	6,440	6,969
GDP growth, 2000–05 and 2005–12 (avg. annual %)	1.9	3.3	6.2
Adult literacy rate (% ages 15 and older)	..	..	94
Gross primary, secondary, tertiary school enrollment (%)	..	..	76
Sector structure			
Separate telecommunications/ICT regulator	Yes	Yes	
Status of main fixed-line telephone operator	Mixed	Private	
Level of competition (competition, partial comp., monopoly)			
International gateway(s)	..	C	
Mobile telephone service	M	C	
Internet service	..	C	
Foreign ownership (not allowed, restricted, allowed)	R	A	
Reg. treatment of VoIP (banned, closed, no framework, allowed)	No	A	
Sector efficiency and capacity			
Telecommunications revenue (% of GDP)	8.4	7.8	2.5
Telecommunications investment (% of revenue)	18.0	12.5	18.2
Sector performance			
Access			
Fixed-telephone subscriptions (per 100 people)	26.9	20.3	19.4
Mobile-cellular telephone subscriptions (per 100 people)	73.7	152.5	92.4
Fixed (wired)-broadband subscriptions (per 100 people)	4.8	11.9	10.8
Households with a computer (%)	..	..	40.6
Households with Internet access at home (%)	..	..	36.3
Usage			
Int'l. voice traffic, total (minutes/subscription/month)	41.2	14.6	1.3
Domestic mobile traffic (minutes/subscription/month)	38.4	112.1	284.4
Individuals using the Internet (%)	38.5[a]	55.2[a]	41.6
Quality			
Population covered by a mobile-cellular network (%)	..	90	99
Fixed (wired)-broadband subscriptions (% of total Internet)	54.0	97.2	95.5
International Internet bandwidth (bit/s per Internet user)	1,407	65,734	14,580
Affordability			
Fixed-telephone sub-basket ($ a month)	..	10.7	9.4
Mobile-cellular sub-basket ($ a month)	..	15.4	14.9
Fixed-broadband sub-basket ($ a month)	..	33.0	17.8
Trade			
ICT goods exports (% of total goods exports)	0.2	7.8	17.6
ICT goods imports (% of total goods imports)	8.3	4.3	14.7
ICT service exports (% of total service exports)	25.9	14.5	29.1
Applications			
Online service index (0–1, 1=highest presence)	0.37	0.29	0.42
Secure Internet servers (per million people)	113.4	430.6	18.5

Dominican Republic

Latin America & Caribbean			Upper middle income

	Country data		Upper middle-income group
	2005	2012	2012

Economic and social context
Population (millions)	9	10	2,391
Urban population (% of total)	66	70	61
GNI per capita, World Bank Atlas method ($)	2,880	5,470	6,969
GDP growth, 2000–05 and 2005–12 (avg. annual %)	3.1	6.0	6.2
Adult literacy rate (% ages 15 and older)	88	90	94
Gross primary, secondary, tertiary school enrollment (%)	..	..	76

Sector structure
Separate telecommunications/ICT regulator	Yes	Yes	
Status of main fixed-line telephone operator	Private	Private	
Level of competition (competition, partial comp., monopoly)			
International gateway(s)	C	C	
Mobile telephone service	C	C	
Internet service	C	C	
Foreign ownership (not allowed, restricted, allowed)	A	A	
Reg. treatment of VoIP (banned, closed, no framework, allowed)	No	A	

Sector efficiency and capacity
Telecommunications revenue (% of GDP)	0.4	3.3	2.5
Telecommunications investment (% of revenue)	192.0	16.1	18.2

Sector performance
Access
Fixed-telephone subscriptions (per 100 people)	9.6	10.4	19.4
Mobile-cellular telephone subscriptions (per 100 people)	38.8	86.9	92.4
Fixed (wired)-broadband subscriptions (per 100 people)	0.6	4.3	10.8
Households with a computer (%)	8.7	19.8[a]	40.6
Households with Internet access at home (%)	3.1	13.7[a]	36.3

Usage
Int'l. voice traffic, total (minutes/subscription/month)	..	12.8	1.3
Domestic mobile traffic (minutes/subscription/month)	..	26.1	284.4
Individuals using the Internet (%)	11.5	45.0[a]	41.6

Quality
Population covered by a mobile-cellular network (%)	..	95	99
Fixed (wired)-broadband subscriptions (% of total Internet)	45.1	90.4	95.5
International Internet bandwidth (bit/s per Internet user)	2,889	14,874	14,580

Affordability
Fixed-telephone sub-basket ($ a month)	..	16.6	9.4
Mobile-cellular sub-basket ($ a month)	..	14.9	14.9
Fixed-broadband sub-basket ($ a month)	..	23.3	17.8

Trade
ICT goods exports (% of total goods exports)	7.2	0.9	17.6
ICT goods imports (% of total goods imports)	4.2	3.2	14.7
ICT service exports (% of total service exports)	2.8	4.3	29.1

Applications
Online service index (0–1, 1=highest presence)	0.49	0.54	0.42
Secure Internet servers (per million people)	5.6	20.4	18.5

Ecuador

	Country data		Upper middle-income group
	2005	2012	2012
Economic and social context			
Population (millions)	14	15	2,391
Urban population (% of total)	64	68	61
GNI per capita, *World Bank Atlas* method ($)	2,890	5,170	6,969
GDP growth, 2000–05 and 2005–12 (avg. annual %)	4.8	4.0	6.2
Adult literacy rate (% ages 15 and older)	*84*	*92*	*94*
Gross primary, secondary, tertiary school enrollment (%)	..	..	76
Sector structure			
Separate telecommunications/ICT regulator	Yes	Yes	
Status of main fixed-line telephone operator	Public	Public	
Level of competition (competition, partial comp., monopoly)			
International gateway(s)	..	C	
Mobile telephone service	P	C	
Internet service	C	C	
Foreign ownership (not allowed, restricted, allowed)	A	A	
Reg. treatment of VoIP (banned, closed, no framework, allowed)	No	A	
Sector efficiency and capacity			
Telecommunications revenue (% of GDP)	3.4	*2.3*	2.5
Telecommunications investment (% of revenue)	..	*13.9*	18.2
Sector performance			
Access			
Fixed-telephone subscriptions (per 100 people)	12.2	14.9	19.4
Mobile-cellular telephone subscriptions (per 100 people)	45.3	106.2	92.4
Fixed (wired)-broadband subscriptions (per 100 people)	0.2	5.3	10.8
Households with a computer (%)	*17.9*	32.2	40.6
Households with Internet access at home (%)	2.5	22.5	36.3
Usage			
Int'l. voice traffic, total (minutes/subscription/month)	..	4.4	1.3
Domestic mobile traffic (minutes/subscription/month)	..	77.6	284.4
Individuals using the Internet (%)	6.0[a]	35.1	41.6
Quality			
Population covered by a mobile-cellular network (%)	80	96	99
Fixed (wired)-broadband subscriptions (% of total Internet)	19.5	94.2	95.5
International Internet bandwidth (bit/s per Internet user)	2,422	31,804	14,580
Affordability			
Fixed-telephone sub-basket ($ a month)	..	6.9	9.4
Mobile-cellular sub-basket ($ a month)	..	17.1	14.9
Fixed-broadband sub-basket ($ a month)	..	20.2	17.8
Trade			
ICT goods exports (% of total goods exports)	0.2	0.1	17.6
ICT goods imports (% of total goods imports)	11.1	6.4	14.7
ICT service exports (% of total service exports)	..	..	29.1
Applications			
Online service index (0–1, 1=highest presence)	0.48	0.46	0.42
Secure Internet servers (per million people)	3.9	24.5	18.5

Egypt, Arab Rep.

Middle East & North Africa   **Lower middle income**

	Country data		Lower middle-income group
	2005	2012	2012
Economic and social context			
Population (millions)	72	81	2,507
Urban population (% of total)	43	44	39
GNI per capita, World Bank Atlas method ($)	1,290	2,980	1,893
GDP growth, 2000–05 and 2005–12 (avg. annual %)	3.4	5.1	6.0
Adult literacy rate (% ages 15 and older)	71	74	71
Gross primary, secondary, tertiary school enrollment (%)	76	77	64
Sector structure			
Separate telecommunications/ICT regulator	Yes	Yes	
Status of main fixed-line telephone operator	Mixed	Mixed	
Level of competition (competition, partial comp., monopoly)			
International gateway(s)	M	P	
Mobile telephone service	P	C	
Internet service	C	C	
Foreign ownership (not allowed, restricted, allowed)	A	A	
Reg. treatment of VoIP (banned, closed, no framework, allowed)	No	A	
Sector efficiency and capacity			
Telecommunications revenue (% of GDP)	3.8	2.8	2.5
Telecommunications investment (% of revenue)	35.2	33.4	20.5
Sector performance			
Access			
Fixed-telephone subscriptions (per 100 people)	14.5	10.6	5.4
Mobile-cellular telephone subscriptions (per 100 people)	19.0	119.9	83.1
Fixed (wired)-broadband subscriptions (per 100 people)	0.2	2.8	1.4
Households with a computer (%)	..	37.9	15.0
Households with Internet access at home (%)	15.3	32.3	12.4
Usage			
Int'l. voice traffic, total (minutes/subscription/month)	7.6	5.5	6.5
Domestic mobile traffic (minutes/subscription/month)	36.0	119.6	..
Individuals using the Internet (%)	12.8	44.1	18.7
Quality			
Population covered by a mobile-cellular network (%)	92	100	86
Fixed (wired)-broadband subscriptions (% of total Internet)	5.5	93.8	58.2
International Internet bandwidth (bit/s per Internet user)	413	4,242	8,076
Affordability			
Fixed-telephone sub-basket ($ a month)	..	3.0	4.9
Mobile-cellular sub-basket ($ a month)	..	6.3	10.5
Fixed-broadband sub-basket ($ a month)	..	7.6	20.6
Trade			
ICT goods exports (% of total goods exports)	0.1	0.2	4.6
ICT goods imports (% of total goods imports)	4.4	3.4	7.2
ICT service exports (% of total service exports)	13.2	7.3	47.1
Applications			
Online service index (0–1, 1=highest presence)	0.48	0.60	0.32
Secure Internet servers (per million people)	0.5	3.5	4.4

El Salvador

Latin America & Caribbean			Lower middle income

	Country data		Lower middle-income group
	2005	2012	2012
Economic and social context			
Population (millions)	6	6	2,507
Urban population (% of total)	62	65	39
GNI per capita, *World Bank Atlas* method ($)	2,810	3,590	1,893
GDP growth, 2000–05 and 2005–12 (avg. annual %)	2.3	1.2	6.0
Adult literacy rate (% ages 15 and older)	84	84	71
Gross primary, secondary, tertiary school enrollment (%)	72	71	64
Sector structure			
Separate telecommunications/ICT regulator	Yes	Yes	
Status of main fixed-line telephone operator	Mixed	Mixed	
Level of competition (competition, partial comp., monopoly)			
International gateway(s)	..	C	
Mobile telephone service	C	C	
Internet service	C	C	
Foreign ownership (not allowed, restricted, allowed)	A	A	
Reg. treatment of VoIP (banned, closed, no framework, allowed)	No	A	
Sector efficiency and capacity			
Telecommunications revenue (% of GDP)	4.1	3.8	2.5
Telecommunications investment (% of revenue)	13.6	17.7	20.5
Sector performance			
Access			
Fixed-telephone subscriptions (per 100 people)	16.0	16.8	5.4
Mobile-cellular telephone subscriptions (per 100 people)	39.7	137.3	83.1
Fixed (wired)-broadband subscriptions (per 100 people)	0.7	3.8	1.4
Households with a computer (%)	7.4	15.3[a]	15.0
Households with Internet access at home (%)	2.1	15.0[a]	12.4
Usage			
Int'l. voice traffic, total (minutes/subscription/month)	..	27.5	6.5
Domestic mobile traffic (minutes/subscription/month)	33.2	86.9	..
Individuals using the Internet (%)	4.2[a]	25.5[a]	18.7
Quality			
Population covered by a mobile-cellular network (%)	95	..	86
Fixed (wired)-broadband subscriptions (% of total Internet)	33.2	99.3	58.2
International Internet bandwidth (bit/s per Internet user)	608	6,850	8,076
Affordability			
Fixed-telephone sub-basket ($ a month)	..	6.9	4.9
Mobile-cellular sub-basket ($ a month)	..	14.7	10.5
Fixed-broadband sub-basket ($ a month)	..	20.3	20.6
Trade			
ICT goods exports (% of total goods exports)	0.2	0.4	4.6
ICT goods imports (% of total goods imports)	3.6	5.0	7.2
ICT service exports (% of total service exports)	8.4	11.5	47.1
Applications			
Online service index (0–1, 1=highest presence)	0.50	0.67	0.32
Secure Internet servers (per million people)	6.1	18.8	4.4

Equatorial Guinea

High income

	Country data		High-income group
	2005	**2012**	**2012**
Economic and social context			
Population (millions)	0.60	0.74	1,300
Urban population (% of total)	39	40	80
GNI per capita, World Bank Atlas method ($)	5,250	13,560	38,412
GDP growth, 2000–05 and 2005–12 (avg. annual %)	26.0	3.1	1.0
Adult literacy rate (% ages 15 and older)	88	94	..
Gross primary, secondary, tertiary school enrollment (%)	..	..	93
Sector structure			
Separate telecommunications/ICT regulator	No	Yes	
Status of main fixed-line telephone operator	Mixed	Mixed	
Level of competition (competition, partial comp., monopoly)			
International gateway(s)	..	P	
Mobile telephone service	..	C	
Internet service	M	C	
Foreign ownership (not allowed, restricted, allowed)	No	R	
Reg. treatment of VoIP (banned, closed, no framework, allowed)	B	No	
Sector efficiency and capacity			
Telecommunications revenue (% of GDP)	..	..	2.7
Telecommunications investment (% of revenue)	..	..	17.6
Sector performance			
Access			
Fixed-telephone subscriptions (per 100 people)	1.7	2.0	43.6
Mobile-cellular telephone subscriptions (per 100 people)	16.1	68.1	122.9
Fixed (wired)-broadband subscriptions (per 100 people)	0.0	0.2	26.2
Households with a computer (%)	..	..	77.7
Households with Internet access at home (%)	..	..	75.5
Usage			
Int'l. voice traffic, total (minutes/subscription/month)	..	..	..
Domestic mobile traffic (minutes/subscription/month)	..	..	113.6
Individuals using the Internet (%)	1.1	13.9[a]	75.4
Quality			
Population covered by a mobile-cellular network (%)	..	..	100
Fixed (wired)-broadband subscriptions (% of total Internet)	15.0	..	95.9
International Internet bandwidth (bit/s per Internet user)	2,421	2,123	85,990
Affordability			
Fixed-telephone sub-basket ($ a month)	..	..	25.2
Mobile-cellular sub-basket ($ a month)	..	..	20.6
Fixed-broadband sub-basket ($ a month)	..	..	29.2
Trade			
ICT goods exports (% of total goods exports)	..	..	8.9
ICT goods imports (% of total goods imports)	..	..	10.8
ICT service exports (% of total service exports)	..	..	30.8
Applications			
Online service index (0–1, 1=highest presence)	0.29	0.10	0.67
Secure Internet servers (per million people)	..	1.3	827.6

Eritrea

	Country data		Low-income group
	2005	2012	2012
Economic and social context			
Population (millions)	5	6	846
Urban population (% of total)	19	22	28
GNI per capita, *World Bank Atlas* method ($)	230	450	590
GDP growth, 2000–05 and 2005–12 (avg. annual %)	1.9	1.2	5.9
Adult literacy rate (% ages 15 and older)	53	69	61
Gross primary, secondary, tertiary school enrollment (%)	30	25	60
Sector structure			
Separate telecommunications/ICT regulator	Yes	Yes	
Status of main fixed-line telephone operator	Public	Public	
Level of competition (competition, partial comp., monopoly)			
International gateway(s)	M	*M*	
Mobile telephone service	P	*P*	
Internet service	P	*P*	
Foreign ownership (not allowed, restricted, allowed)	..	..	
Reg. treatment of VoIP (banned, closed, no framework, allowed)	B	B	
Sector efficiency and capacity			
Telecommunications revenue (% of GDP)	3.1	*3.1*	5.0
Telecommunications investment (% of revenue)	57.6	*70.0*	..
Sector performance			
Access			
Fixed-telephone subscriptions (per 100 people)	0.8	1.0	1.0
Mobile-cellular telephone subscriptions (per 100 people)	0.8	5.0	47.2
Fixed (wired)-broadband subscriptions (per 100 people)	0.0	0.0	0.2
Households with a computer (%)	0.2	1.5[a]	4.2
Households with Internet access at home (%)	0.2[a]	1.1[a]	3.4
Usage			
Int'l. voice traffic, total (minutes/subscription/month)	..	76.5	..
Domestic mobile traffic (minutes/subscription/month)	*81.4*	88.7	70.1
Individuals using the Internet (%)	0.4[a]	0.8[a]	6.2
Quality			
Population covered by a mobile-cellular network (%)	2	85	..
Fixed (wired)-broadband subscriptions (% of total Internet)	0.0	13.0	*30.9*
International Internet bandwidth (bit/s per Internet user)	562	1,284	9,141
Affordability			
Fixed-telephone sub-basket ($ a month)	..	4.1	8.9
Mobile-cellular sub-basket ($ a month)	..	11.8	11.9
Fixed-broadband sub-basket ($ a month)	..	1,596.5	46.9
Trade			
ICT goods exports (% of total goods exports)	0.2	..	..
ICT goods imports (% of total goods imports)	3.0	..	..
ICT service exports (% of total service exports)	..	..	..
Applications			
Online service index (0–1, 1=highest presence)	0.20	0.21	0.20
Secure Internet servers (per million people)	..	..	1.1

Estonia

	Country data		High-income group
	2005	2012	2012
Economic and social context			
Population (millions)	1	1	1,300
Urban population (% of total)	69	70	80
GNI per capita, World Bank Atlas method ($)	9,690	16,270	38,412
GDP growth, 2000–05 and 2005–12 (avg. annual %)	7.1	0.3	1.0
Adult literacy rate (% ages 15 and older)	100	100	..
Gross primary, secondary, tertiary school enrollment (%)	95	96	93
Sector structure			
Separate telecommunications/ICT regulator	Yes	Yes	
Status of main fixed-line telephone operator	Mixed	Mixed	
Level of competition (competition, partial comp., monopoly)			
International gateway(s)	C	..	
Mobile telephone service	C	C	
Internet service	C	C	
Foreign ownership (not allowed, restricted, allowed)	A	A	
Reg. treatment of VoIP (banned, closed, no framework, allowed)	A	A	
Sector efficiency and capacity			
Telecommunications revenue (% of GDP)	5.5	2.6	2.7
Telecommunications investment (% of revenue)	8.2	26.0	17.6
Sector performance			
Access			
Fixed-telephone subscriptions (per 100 people)	33.4	34.7	43.6
Mobile-cellular telephone subscriptions (per 100 people)	109.1	160.4	122.9
Fixed (wired)-broadband subscriptions (per 100 people)	13.5	25.5	26.2
Households with a computer (%)	43.0	76.0	77.7
Households with Internet access at home (%)	38.7	75.0	75.5
Usage			
Int'l. voice traffic, total (minutes/subscription/month)	6.9	9.0	..
Domestic mobile traffic (minutes/subscription/month)	75.0	115.0	113.6
Individuals using the Internet (%)	61.5	79.0	75.4
Quality			
Population covered by a mobile-cellular network (%)	99	100	100
Fixed (wired)-broadband subscriptions (% of total Internet)	91.0	95.6	95.9
International Internet bandwidth (bit/s per Internet user)	5,895	26,478	85,990
Affordability			
Fixed-telephone sub-basket ($ a month)	..	12.8	25.2
Mobile-cellular sub-basket ($ a month)	..	24.6	20.6
Fixed-broadband sub-basket ($ a month)	..	22.2	29.2
Trade			
ICT goods exports (% of total goods exports)	17.0	10.9	8.9
ICT goods imports (% of total goods imports)	13.0	10.7	10.8
ICT service exports (% of total service exports)	17.2	26.2	30.8
Applications			
Online service index (0–1, 1=highest presence)	0.76	0.82	0.67
Secure Internet servers (per million people)	101.4	749.2	827.6

Ethiopia

Sub-Saharan Africa		**Low income**

	Country data		Low-income group 2012
	2005	2012	2012
Economic and social context			
Population (millions)	76	92	846
Urban population (% of total)	16	17	28
GNI per capita, *World Bank Atlas* method ($)	160	380	590
GDP growth, 2000–05 and 2005–12 (avg. annual %)	5.6	9.7	5.9
Adult literacy rate (% ages 15 and older)	30	..	61
Gross primary, secondary, tertiary school enrollment (%)	43	..	60
Sector structure			
Separate telecommunications/ICT regulator	Yes	No	
Status of main fixed-line telephone operator	Public	Public	
Level of competition (competition, partial comp., monopoly)			
International gateway(s)	M	M	
Mobile telephone service	M	M	
Internet service	M	M	
Foreign ownership (not allowed, restricted, allowed)	No	No	
Reg. treatment of VoIP (banned, closed, no framework, allowed)	B	B	
Sector efficiency and capacity			
Telecommunications revenue (% of GDP)	2.2	1.7	5.0
Telecommunications investment (% of revenue)	82.1	36.2	..
Sector performance			
Access			
Fixed-telephone subscriptions (per 100 people)	0.8	0.9	1.0
Mobile-cellular telephone subscriptions (per 100 people)	0.5	22.4	47.2
Fixed (wired)-broadband subscriptions (per 100 people)	0.0	0.0	0.2
Households with a computer (%)	0.2	2.1[a]	4.2
Households with Internet access at home (%)	0.0[a]	1.9[a]	3.4
Usage			
Int'l. voice traffic, total (minutes/subscription/month)	13.5	3.1	..
Domestic mobile traffic (minutes/subscription/month)	90.9	55.8	70.1
Individuals using the Internet (%)	0.2	1.5[a]	6.2
Quality			
Population covered by a mobile-cellular network (%)	10	73	..
Fixed (wired)-broadband subscriptions (% of total Internet)	0.3	3.2	30.9
International Internet bandwidth (bit/s per Internet user)	347	4,779	9,141
Affordability			
Fixed-telephone sub-basket ($ a month)	..	1.0	8.9
Mobile-cellular sub-basket ($ a month)	..	3.8	11.9
Fixed-broadband sub-basket ($ a month)	..	23.7	46.9
Trade			
ICT goods exports (% of total goods exports)	0.0	0.2	..
ICT goods imports (% of total goods imports)	7.0	3.5	..
ICT service exports (% of total service exports)	10.9	6.5	..
Applications			
Online service index (0–1, 1=highest presence)	0.19	0.47	0.20
Secure Internet servers (per million people)	0.0	0.2	1.1

Faeroe Islands

High income

	Country data		High-income group
	2005	2012	2012
Economic and social context			
Population (millions)	0.05	0.05	1,300
Urban population (% of total)	40	41	80
GNI per capita, *World Bank Atlas* method ($)	..	..	38,412
GDP growth, 2000–05 and 2005–12 (avg. annual %)	..	..	1.0
Adult literacy rate (% ages 15 and older)	..	..	..
Gross primary, secondary, tertiary school enrollment (%)	..	..	93
Sector structure			
Separate telecommunications/ICT regulator	..	..	
Status of main fixed-line telephone operator	..	..	
Level of competition (competition, partial comp., monopoly)			
International gateway(s)	..	..	
Mobile telephone service	..	..	
Internet service	..	..	
Foreign ownership (not allowed, restricted, allowed)	..	..	
Reg. treatment of VoIP (banned, closed, no framework, allowed)	..	..	
Sector efficiency and capacity			
Telecommunications revenue (% of GDP)	3.5	..	2.7
Telecommunications investment (% of revenue)	..	..	17.6
Sector performance			
Access			
Fixed-telephone subscriptions (per 100 people)	48.5	37.7	43.6
Mobile-cellular telephone subscriptions (per 100 people)	85.5	118.6	122.9
Fixed (wired)-broadband subscriptions (per 100 people)	11.9	33.0	26.2
Households with a computer (%)	..	..	77.7
Households with Internet access at home (%)	..	..	75.5
Usage			
Int'l. voice traffic, total (minutes/subscription/month)	..	..	..
Domestic mobile traffic (minutes/subscription/month)	73.1	122.4	113.6
Individuals using the Internet (%)	67.9[a]	85.3[a]	75.4
Quality			
Population covered by a mobile-cellular network (%)	100	100	100
Fixed (wired)-broadband subscriptions (% of total Internet)	49.2	100.0	95.9
International Internet bandwidth (bit/s per Internet user)	4,793	..	85,990
Affordability			
Fixed-telephone sub-basket ($ a month)	..	..	25.2
Mobile-cellular sub-basket ($ a month)	..	..	20.6
Fixed-broadband sub-basket ($ a month)	..	..	29.2
Trade			
ICT goods exports (% of total goods exports)	0.0	0.0	8.9
ICT goods imports (% of total goods imports)	4.3	4.3	10.8
ICT service exports (% of total service exports)	30.1	25.8	30.8
Applications			
Online service index (0–1, 1=highest presence)	..	..	0.67
Secure Internet servers (per million people)	61.5	1,632.7	827.6

Fiji

		Country data	Upper middle-income group
East Asia & Pacific			Upper middle income
	2005	**2012**	**2012**

Economic and social context
	2005	2012	2012
Population (millions)	0.82	0.87	2,391
Urban population (% of total)	50	53	61
GNI per capita, *World Bank Atlas* method ($)	3,590	4,110	6,969
GDP growth, 2000–05 and 2005–12 (avg. annual %)	2.6	0.4	6.2
Adult literacy rate (% ages 15 and older)	..	..	94
Gross primary, secondary, tertiary school enrollment (%)	78	88	76

Sector structure
	2005	2012	2012
Separate telecommunications/ICT regulator	No	Yes	
Status of main fixed-line telephone operator	Mixed	Mixed	
Level of competition (competition, partial comp., monopoly)			
International gateway(s)	..	C	
Mobile telephone service	M	C	
Internet service	..	C	
Foreign ownership (not allowed, restricted, allowed)	..	A	
Reg. treatment of VoIP (banned, closed, no framework, allowed)	B	A	

Sector efficiency and capacity
	2005	2012	2012
Telecommunications revenue (% of GDP)	4.7	..	2.5
Telecommunications investment (% of revenue)	20.2	..	18.2

Sector performance
Access
	2005	2012	2012
Fixed-telephone subscriptions (per 100 people)	13.7	10.1	19.4
Mobile-cellular telephone subscriptions (per 100 people)	24.9	98.2	92.4
Fixed (wired)-broadband subscriptions (per 100 people)	0.9	1.5	10.8
Households with a computer (%)	13.0	31.7[a]	40.6
Households with Internet access at home (%)	8.0	24.4[a]	36.3

Usage
	2005	2012	2012
Int'l. voice traffic, total (minutes/subscription/month)	..	..	1.3
Domestic mobile traffic (minutes/subscription/month)	..	..	284.4
Individuals using the Internet (%)	8.5	33.7[a]	41.6

Quality
	2005	2012	2012
Population covered by a mobile-cellular network (%)	60	..	99
Fixed (wired)-broadband subscriptions (% of total Internet)	52.6	59.6	95.5
International Internet bandwidth (bit/s per Internet user)	1,036	9,232	14,580

Affordability
	2005	2012	2012
Fixed-telephone sub-basket ($ a month)	..	6.9	9.4
Mobile-cellular sub-basket ($ a month)	..	21.1	14.9
Fixed-broadband sub-basket ($ a month)	..	19.5	17.8

Trade
	2005	2012	2012
ICT goods exports (% of total goods exports)	0.3	0.8	17.6
ICT goods imports (% of total goods imports)	4.7	4.2	14.7
ICT service exports (% of total service exports)	5.4	4.3	29.1

Applications
	2005	2012	2012
Online service index (0–1, 1=highest presence)	0.42	0.36	0.42
Secure Internet servers (per million people)	8.5	30.6	18.5

Finland

	Country data		High-income group
	2005	2012	2012
Economic and social context			
Population (millions)	5	5	1,300
Urban population (% of total)	83	84	80
GNI per capita, World Bank Atlas method ($)	38,550	46,490	38,412
GDP growth, 2000–05 and 2005–12 (avg. annual %)	2.6	0.4	1.0
Adult literacy rate (% ages 15 and older)	..	..	..
Gross primary, secondary, tertiary school enrollment (%)	101	101	93
Sector structure			
Separate telecommunications/ICT regulator	Yes	Yes	
Status of main fixed-line telephone operator	Mixed	Mixed	
Level of competition (competition, partial comp., monopoly)			
International gateway(s)	C	C	
Mobile telephone service	P	C	
Internet service	C	C	
Foreign ownership (not allowed, restricted, allowed)	A	A	
Reg. treatment of VoIP (banned, closed, no framework, allowed)	A	A	
Sector efficiency and capacity			
Telecommunications revenue (% of GDP)	2.7	2.0	2.7
Telecommunications investment (% of revenue)	9.8	15.0	17.6
Sector performance			
Access			
Fixed-telephone subscriptions (per 100 people)	40.4	16.4	43.6
Mobile-cellular telephone subscriptions (per 100 people)	100.5	172.3	122.9
Fixed (wired)-broadband subscriptions (per 100 people)	22.4	30.3	26.2
Households with a computer (%)	63.9	88.0	77.7
Households with Internet access at home (%)	54.1	87.0	75.5
Usage			
Int'l. voice traffic, total (minutes/subscription/month)	..	..	..
Domestic mobile traffic (minutes/subscription/month)	171.5	177.5	113.6
Individuals using the Internet (%)	74.5	91.0	75.4
Quality			
Population covered by a mobile-cellular network (%)	99	100	100
Fixed (wired)-broadband subscriptions (% of total Internet)	57.1	..	95.9
International Internet bandwidth (bit/s per Internet user)	5,788	159,294	85,990
Affordability			
Fixed-telephone sub-basket ($ a month)	..	31.4	25.2
Mobile-cellular sub-basket ($ a month)	..	13.8	20.6
Fixed-broadband sub-basket ($ a month)	..	37.4	29.2
Trade			
ICT goods exports (% of total goods exports)	20.3	4.0	8.9
ICT goods imports (% of total goods imports)	14.3	6.9	10.8
ICT service exports (% of total service exports)	32.3	45.7	30.8
Applications			
Online service index (0–1, 1=highest presence)	0.75	0.88	0.67
Secure Internet servers (per million people)	308.2	1,554.7	827.6

France

	Country data		High-income group
	2005	2012	2012
Economic and social context			
Population (millions)	63	66	1,300
Urban population (% of total)	82	86	80
GNI per capita, *World Bank Atlas* method ($)	34,850	41,750	38,412
GDP growth, 2000–05 and 2005–12 (avg. annual %)	1.5	0.5	1.0
Adult literacy rate (% ages 15 and older)	..	..	..
Gross primary, secondary, tertiary school enrollment (%)	93	94	93
Sector structure			
Separate telecommunications/ICT regulator	Yes	Yes	
Status of main fixed-line telephone operator	Mixed	Mixed	
Level of competition (competition, partial comp., monopoly)			
International gateway(s)	C	C	
Mobile telephone service	C	C	
Internet service	C	C	
Foreign ownership (not allowed, restricted, allowed)	A	R	
Reg. treatment of VoIP (banned, closed, no framework, allowed)	A	A	
Sector efficiency and capacity			
Telecommunications revenue (% of GDP)	2.4	2.1	2.7
Telecommunications investment (% of revenue)	15.6	17.6	17.6
Sector performance			
Access			
Fixed-telephone subscriptions (per 100 people)	54.9	61.5	43.6
Mobile-cellular telephone subscriptions (per 100 people)	78.3	97.4	122.9
Fixed (wired)-broadband subscriptions (per 100 people)	15.4	37.5	26.2
Households with a computer (%)	54.3[a]	81.0	77.7
Households with Internet access at home (%)	34.4	80.0	75.5
Usage			
Int'l. voice traffic, total (minutes/subscription/month)	13.6	19.5	..
Domestic mobile traffic (minutes/subscription/month)	138.0	160.4	113.6
Individuals using the Internet (%)	42.9	83.0	75.4
Quality			
Population covered by a mobile-cellular network (%)	99	99	100
Fixed (wired)-broadband subscriptions (% of total Internet)	71.7	99.1	95.9
International Internet bandwidth (bit/s per Internet user)	7,593	83,918	85,990
Affordability			
Fixed-telephone sub-basket ($ a month)	..	28.1	25.2
Mobile-cellular sub-basket ($ a month)	..	42.2	20.6
Fixed-broadband sub-basket ($ a month)	..	29.2	29.2
Trade			
ICT goods exports (% of total goods exports)	6.3	4.1	8.9
ICT goods imports (% of total goods imports)	8.5	6.2	10.8
ICT service exports (% of total service exports)	23.8	32.6	30.8
Applications			
Online service index (0–1, 1=highest presence)	0.80	0.88	0.67
Secure Internet servers (per million people)	76.1	487.0	827.6

French Polynesia

High income

	Country data		High-income group
	2005	2012	2012
Economic and social context			
Population (millions)	0.25	0.27	1,300
Urban population (% of total)	52	51	80
GNI per capita, *World Bank Atlas* method ($)	..	..	38,412
GDP growth, 2000–05 and 2005–12 (avg. annual %)	..	..	1.0
Adult literacy rate (% ages 15 and older)	..	..	..
Gross primary, secondary, tertiary school enrollment (%)	..	..	93
Sector structure			
Separate telecommunications/ICT regulator	..	..	
Status of main fixed-line telephone operator	..	..	
Level of competition (competition, partial comp., monopoly)			
International gateway(s)	..	..	
Mobile telephone service	..	..	
Internet service	..	..	
Foreign ownership (not allowed, restricted, allowed)	..	..	
Reg. treatment of VoIP (banned, closed, no framework, allowed)	..	..	
Sector efficiency and capacity			
Telecommunications revenue (% of GDP)	..	..	2.7
Telecommunications investment (% of revenue)	..	..	17.6
Sector performance			
Access			
Fixed-telephone subscriptions (per 100 people)	20.9	20.1	43.6
Mobile-cellular telephone subscriptions (per 100 people)	47.1	82.5	122.9
Fixed (wired)-broadband subscriptions (per 100 people)	4.3	14.7	26.2
Households with a computer (%)	45.0	..	77.7
Households with Internet access at home (%)	..	..	75.5
Usage			
Int'l. voice traffic, total (minutes/subscription/month)	9.1	9.4	..
Domestic mobile traffic (minutes/subscription/month)	116.7	103.8	113.6
Individuals using the Internet (%)	21.5	52.9[a]	75.4
Quality			
Population covered by a mobile-cellular network (%)	96	98	100
Fixed (wired)-broadband subscriptions (% of total Internet)	59.5	98.5	95.9
International Internet bandwidth (bit/s per Internet user)	1,639	13,814	85,990
Affordability			
Fixed-telephone sub-basket ($ a month)	..	..	25.2
Mobile-cellular sub-basket ($ a month)	..	..	20.6
Fixed-broadband sub-basket ($ a month)	..	..	29.2
Trade			
ICT goods exports (% of total goods exports)	0.2	0.4	8.9
ICT goods imports (% of total goods imports)	5.1	5.2	10.8
ICT service exports (% of total service exports)	13.5	9.7	30.8
Applications			
Online service index (0–1, 1=highest presence)	..	..	0.67
Secure Internet servers (per million people)	58.9	133.6	827.6

Gabon

	Country data		Upper middle-income group
	2005	2012	2012
Economic and social context			
Population (millions)	1	2	2,391
Urban population (% of total)	83	86	61
GNI per capita, *World Bank Atlas* method ($)	5,080	10,040	6,969
GDP growth, 2000–05 and 2005–12 (avg. annual %)	1.6	3.1	6.2
Adult literacy rate (% ages 15 and older)	84	89	94
Gross primary, secondary, tertiary school enrollment (%)	..	..	76
Sector structure			
Separate telecommunications/ICT regulator	Yes	Yes	
Status of main fixed-line telephone operator	Public	Mixed	
Level of competition (competition, partial comp., monopoly)			
International gateway(s)	..	C	
Mobile telephone service	C	C	
Internet service	C	C	
Foreign ownership (not allowed, restricted, allowed)	A	A	
Reg. treatment of VoIP (banned, closed, no framework, allowed)	B	C	
Sector efficiency and capacity			
Telecommunications revenue (% of GDP)	1.7	..	2.5
Telecommunications investment (% of revenue)	12.4	..	18.2
Sector performance			
Access			
Fixed-telephone subscriptions (per 100 people)	2.8	1.0	19.4
Mobile-cellular telephone subscriptions (per 100 people)	53.4	179.5[a]	92.4
Fixed (wired)-broadband subscriptions (per 100 people)	0.1	0.3[a]	10.8
Households with a computer (%)	3.0	10.1[a]	40.6
Households with Internet access at home (%)	2.0	7.9[a]	36.3
Usage			
Int'l. voice traffic, total (minutes/subscription/month)	..	1.6	1.3
Domestic mobile traffic (minutes/subscription/month)	..	..	284.4
Individuals using the Internet (%)	4.9	8.6[a]	41.6
Quality			
Population covered by a mobile-cellular network (%)	78	..	99
Fixed (wired)-broadband subscriptions (% of total Internet)	17.7	18.4	95.5
International Internet bandwidth (bit/s per Internet user)	2,963	5,509	14,580
Affordability			
Fixed-telephone sub-basket ($ a month)	..	52.9	9.4
Mobile-cellular sub-basket ($ a month)	..	23.3	14.9
Fixed-broadband sub-basket ($ a month)	..	31.8	17.8
Trade			
ICT goods exports (% of total goods exports)	0.0	0.0	17.6
ICT goods imports (% of total goods imports)	3.7	3.5	14.7
ICT service exports (% of total service exports)	37.7	..	29.1
Applications			
Online service index (0–1, 1=highest presence)	0.32	0.19	0.42
Secure Internet servers (per million people)	5.8	9.6	18.5

Gambia, The

	Country data		Low-income group
	2005	2012	2012
Economic and social context			
Population (millions)	1	2	846
Urban population (% of total)	53	58	28
GNI per capita, *World Bank Atlas* method ($)	410	510	590
GDP growth, 2000–05 and 2005–12 (avg. annual %)	3.2	3.8	5.9
Adult literacy rate (% ages 15 and older)	37	51	61
Gross primary, secondary, tertiary school enrollment (%)	..	58	60
Sector structure			
Separate telecommunications/ICT regulator	Yes	Yes	
Status of main fixed-line telephone operator	Public	Public	
Level of competition (competition, partial comp., monopoly)			
International gateway(s)	M	M	
Mobile telephone service	P	C	
Internet service	C	C	
Foreign ownership (not allowed, restricted, allowed)	A	A	
Reg. treatment of VoIP (banned, closed, no framework, allowed)	B	B	
Sector efficiency and capacity			
Telecommunications revenue (% of GDP)	..	..	5.0
Telecommunications investment (% of revenue)	..	..	..
Sector performance			
Access			
Fixed-telephone subscriptions (per 100 people)	3.1	3.6	1.0
Mobile-cellular telephone subscriptions (per 100 people)	17.2	85.2	47.2
Fixed (wired)-broadband subscriptions (per 100 people)	0.0	0.0	0.2
Households with a computer (%)	2.3	7.4[a]	4.2
Households with Internet access at home (%)	1.0[a]	6.7[a]	3.4
Usage			
Int'l. voice traffic, total (minutes/subscription/month)	..	..	..
Domestic mobile traffic (minutes/subscription/month)	14.7	..	70.1
Individuals using the Internet (%)	3.8[a]	12.4[a]	6.2
Quality			
Population covered by a mobile-cellular network (%)	70	..	..
Fixed (wired)-broadband subscriptions (% of total Internet)	7.6	..	30.9
International Internet bandwidth (bit/s per Internet user)	165	2,117	9,141
Affordability			
Fixed-telephone sub-basket ($ a month)	..	3.5	8.9
Mobile-cellular sub-basket ($ a month)	..	6.0	11.9
Fixed-broadband sub-basket ($ a month)	..	280.3	46.9
Trade			
ICT goods exports (% of total goods exports)	1.2	0.1	..
ICT goods imports (% of total goods imports)	5.0	1.9	..
ICT service exports (% of total service exports)	..	..	..
Applications			
Online service index (0–1, 1=highest presence)	0.23	0.32	0.20
Secure Internet servers (per million people)	1.3	4.3	1.1

Georgia

Lower middle income

	Country data		Lower middle-income group
	2005	2012	2012
Economic and social context			
Population (millions)	4	4	2,507
Urban population (% of total)	52	53	39
GNI per capita, *World Bank Atlas* method ($)	1,360	3,290	1,893
GDP growth, 2000–05 and 2005–12 (avg. annual %)	7.5	4.7	6.0
Adult literacy rate (% ages 15 and older)	100	100	71
Gross primary, secondary, tertiary school enrollment (%)	77	72	64
Sector structure			
Separate telecommunications/ICT regulator	Yes	Yes	
Status of main fixed-line telephone operator	Public	Mixed	
Level of competition (competition, partial comp., monopoly)			
International gateway(s)	..	C	
Mobile telephone service	C	C	
Internet service	C	C	
Foreign ownership (not allowed, restricted, allowed)	A	A	
Reg. treatment of VoIP (banned, closed, no framework, allowed)	A	No	
Sector efficiency and capacity			
Telecommunications revenue (% of GDP)	6.2	2.7	2.5
Telecommunications investment (% of revenue)	30.9	19.6	20.5
Sector performance			
Access			
Fixed-telephone subscriptions (per 100 people)	12.7	29.3	5.4
Mobile-cellular telephone subscriptions (per 100 people)	26.2	107.8	83.1
Fixed (wired)-broadband subscriptions (per 100 people)	0.1	8.7	1.4
Households with a computer (%)	1.8[a]	32.7	15.0
Households with Internet access at home (%)	1.0[a]	32.0	12.4
Usage			
Int'l. voice traffic, total (minutes/subscription/month)	..	6.1	6.5
Domestic mobile traffic (minutes/subscription/month)	..	116.5	..
Individuals using the Internet (%)	6.1[a]	45.5[a]	18.7
Quality			
Population covered by a mobile-cellular network (%)	95	99	86
Fixed (wired)-broadband subscriptions (% of total Internet)	1.3	100.0	58.2
International Internet bandwidth (bit/s per Internet user)	118	52,946	8,076
Affordability			
Fixed-telephone sub-basket ($ a month)	..	2.4	4.9
Mobile-cellular sub-basket ($ a month)	..	6.0	10.5
Fixed-broadband sub-basket ($ a month)	..	11.9	20.6
Trade			
ICT goods exports (% of total goods exports)	0.1	0.5	4.6
ICT goods imports (% of total goods imports)	4.4	4.9	7.2
ICT service exports (% of total service exports)	4.0	4.6	47.1
Applications			
Online service index (0–1, 1=highest presence)	0.46	0.60	0.32
Secure Internet servers (per million people)	4.6	29.3	4.4

Germany

	Country data		High-income group
	2005	2012	2012
Economic and social context			
Population (millions)	82	80	1,300
Urban population (% of total)	73	74	80
GNI per capita, World Bank Atlas method ($)	34,780	45,070	38,412
GDP growth, 2000–05 and 2005–12 (avg. annual %)	0.5	1.2	1.0
Adult literacy rate (% ages 15 and older)	..	..	..
Gross primary, secondary, tertiary school enrollment (%)	..	90	93
Sector structure			
Separate telecommunications/ICT regulator	Yes	Yes	
Status of main fixed-line telephone operator	Private	Mixed	
Level of competition (competition, partial comp., monopoly)			
International gateway(s)	C	C	
Mobile telephone service	C	C	
Internet service	C	C	
Foreign ownership (not allowed, restricted, allowed)	A	A	
Reg. treatment of VoIP (banned, closed, no framework, allowed)	A	A	
Sector efficiency and capacity			
Telecommunications revenue (% of GDP)	3.0	1.5	2.7
Telecommunications investment (% of revenue)	8.6	15.3	17.6
Sector performance			
Access			
Fixed-telephone subscriptions (per 100 people)	65.4	60.5	43.6
Mobile-cellular telephone subscriptions (per 100 people)	94.6	111.6	122.9
Fixed (wired)-broadband subscriptions (per 100 people)	12.9	33.7	26.2
Households with a computer (%)	70.0	87.0	77.7
Households with Internet access at home (%)	61.6	85.0	75.5
Usage			
Int'l. voice traffic, total (minutes/subscription/month)	..	..	..
Domestic mobile traffic (minutes/subscription/month)	43.0	99.1	113.6
Individuals using the Internet (%)	68.7	84.0	75.4
Quality			
Population covered by a mobile-cellular network (%)	99	99	100
Fixed (wired)-broadband subscriptions (% of total Internet)	53.9	..	95.9
International Internet bandwidth (bit/s per Internet user)	9,827	74,793	85,990
Affordability			
Fixed-telephone sub-basket ($ a month)	..	28.6	25.2
Mobile-cellular sub-basket ($ a month)	..	18.9	20.6
Fixed-broadband sub-basket ($ a month)	..	41.7	29.2
Trade			
ICT goods exports (% of total goods exports)	7.9	4.4	8.9
ICT goods imports (% of total goods imports)	11.5	7.6	10.8
ICT service exports (% of total service exports)	29.7	33.7	30.8
Applications			
Online service index (0–1, 1=highest presence)	0.71	0.75	0.67
Secure Internet servers (per million people)	274.2	1,060.5	827.6

Ghana

Sub-Saharan Africa			**Lower middle income**

	Country data		Lower middle-income group
	2005	**2012**	**2012**
Economic and social context			
Population (millions)	21	25	2,507
Urban population (% of total)	48	53	39
GNI per capita, *World Bank Atlas* method ($)	470	1,550	1,893
GDP growth, 2000–05 and 2005–12 (avg. annual %)	5.1	7.9	6.0
Adult literacy rate (% ages 15 and older)	58	71	71
Gross primary, secondary, tertiary school enrollment (%)	54	66	64
Sector structure			
Separate telecommunications/ICT regulator	Yes	Yes	
Status of main fixed-line telephone operator	Mixed	Mixed	
Level of competition (competition, partial comp., monopoly)			
International gateway(s)	..	C	
Mobile telephone service	P	C	
Internet service	C	C	
Foreign ownership (not allowed, restricted, allowed)	A	A	
Reg. treatment of VoIP (banned, closed, no framework, allowed)	C	C	
Sector efficiency and capacity			
Telecommunications revenue (% of GDP)	..	2.4	2.5
Telecommunications investment (% of revenue)	..	98.7	20.5
Sector performance			
Access			
Fixed-telephone subscriptions (per 100 people)	1.5	1.1	5.4
Mobile-cellular telephone subscriptions (per 100 people)	13.4	101.0	83.1
Fixed (wired)-broadband subscriptions (per 100 people)	0.0	0.3	1.4
Households with a computer (%)	2.0	13.8	15.0
Households with Internet access at home (%)	0.2[a]	11.0[a]	12.4
Usage			
Int'l. voice traffic, total (minutes/subscription/month)	14.6	6.5	6.5
Domestic mobile traffic (minutes/subscription/month)	..	67.5	..
Individuals using the Internet (%)	1.8	17.1[a]	18.7
Quality			
Population covered by a mobile-cellular network (%)	59	87	86
Fixed (wired)-broadband subscriptions (% of total Internet)	17.8	100.0	58.2
International Internet bandwidth (bit/s per Internet user)	429	230	8,076
Affordability			
Fixed-telephone sub-basket ($ a month)	..	5.2	4.9
Mobile-cellular sub-basket ($ a month)	..	6.6	10.5
Fixed-broadband sub-basket ($ a month)	..	43.0	20.6
Trade			
ICT goods exports (% of total goods exports)	0.0	0.1	4.6
ICT goods imports (% of total goods imports)	4.8	4.4	7.2
ICT service exports (% of total service exports)	..	..	47.1
Applications			
Online service index (0–1, 1=highest presence)	0.30	0.30	0.32
Secure Internet servers (per million people)	0.1	2.6	4.4

Greece

High income

	Country data		High-income group
	2005	2012	2012
Economic and social context			
Population (millions)	11	11	1,300
Urban population (% of total)	60	62	80
GNI per capita, *World Bank Atlas* method ($)	21,400	23,660	38,412
GDP growth, 2000–05 and 2005–12 (avg. annual %)	4.2	-2.2	1.0
Adult literacy rate (% ages 15 and older)	96	97	..
Gross primary, secondary, tertiary school enrollment (%)	100	..	93
Sector structure			
Separate telecommunications/ICT regulator	Yes	Yes	
Status of main fixed-line telephone operator	Mixed	Mixed	
Level of competition (competition, partial comp., monopoly)			
International gateway(s)	C	C	
Mobile telephone service	P	P	
Internet service	C	C	
Foreign ownership (not allowed, restricted, allowed)	A	A	
Reg. treatment of VoIP (banned, closed, no framework, allowed)	A	A	
Sector efficiency and capacity			
Telecommunications revenue (% of GDP)	4.0	3.1	2.7
Telecommunications investment (% of revenue)	9.4	12.2	17.6
Sector performance			
Access			
Fixed-telephone subscriptions (per 100 people)	57.2	49.1	43.6
Mobile-cellular telephone subscriptions (per 100 people)	92.9	120.0	122.9
Fixed (wired)-broadband subscriptions (per 100 people)	1.5	24.1	26.2
Households with a computer (%)	33.0	57.4	77.7
Households with Internet access at home (%)	21.7	54.0	75.5
Usage			
Int'l. voice traffic, total (minutes/subscription/month)	13.9	13.9	..
Domestic mobile traffic (minutes/subscription/month)	49.3	34.0	113.6
Individuals using the Internet (%)	24.0	56.0	75.4
Quality			
Population covered by a mobile-cellular network (%)	100[a]	100	100
Fixed (wired)-broadband subscriptions (% of total Internet)	18.1	98.7	95.9
International Internet bandwidth (bit/s per Internet user)	2,458	64,208	85,990
Affordability			
Fixed-telephone sub-basket ($ a month)	..	25.4	25.2
Mobile-cellular sub-basket ($ a month)	..	43.3	20.6
Fixed-broadband sub-basket ($ a month)	..	23.7	29.2
Trade			
ICT goods exports (% of total goods exports)	2.8	1.7	8.9
ICT goods imports (% of total goods imports)	5.7	5.1	10.8
ICT service exports (% of total service exports)	6.6	7.9	30.8
Applications			
Online service index (0–1, 1=highest presence)	0.57	0.58	0.67
Secure Internet servers (per million people)	31.4	133.1	827.6

Greenland

High income

	Country data		High-income group
	2005	2012	2012
Economic and social context			
Population (millions)	0.06	0.06	1,300
Urban population (% of total)	83	85	80
GNI per capita, *World Bank Atlas* method ($)	29,690	26,020	38,412
GDP growth, 2000–05 and 2005–12 (avg. annual %)	0.7	1.5	1.0
Adult literacy rate (% ages 15 and older)	..	..	..
Gross primary, secondary, tertiary school enrollment (%)	..	..	93
Sector structure			
Separate telecommunications/ICT regulator	..	..	
Status of main fixed-line telephone operator	..	..	
Level of competition (competition, partial comp., monopoly)			
International gateway(s)	..	..	
Mobile telephone service	..	..	
Internet service	..	..	
Foreign ownership (not allowed, restricted, allowed)	..	..	
Reg. treatment of VoIP (banned, closed, no framework, allowed)	..	..	
Sector efficiency and capacity			
Telecommunications revenue (% of GDP)	..	..	2.7
Telecommunications investment (% of revenue)	..	..	17.6
Sector performance			
Access			
Fixed-telephone subscriptions (per 100 people)	56.5	33.3	43.6
Mobile-cellular telephone subscriptions (per 100 people)	81.6	104.7	122.9
Fixed (wired)-broadband subscriptions (per 100 people)	12.5	19.9	26.2
Households with a computer (%)	..	..	77.7
Households with Internet access at home (%)	32.0	76.7[a]	75.5
Usage			
Int'l. voice traffic, total (minutes/subscription/month)	..	..	..
Domestic mobile traffic (minutes/subscription/month)	..	87.9	113.6
Individuals using the Internet (%)	57.7	64.9[a]	75.4
Quality			
Population covered by a mobile-cellular network (%)	90	100	100
Fixed (wired)-broadband subscriptions (% of total Internet)	100.0	100.0	95.9
International Internet bandwidth (bit/s per Internet user)	913	18,995	85,990
Affordability			
Fixed-telephone sub-basket ($ a month)	..	..	25.2
Mobile-cellular sub-basket ($ a month)	..	..	20.6
Fixed-broadband sub-basket ($ a month)	..	..	29.2
Trade			
ICT goods exports (% of total goods exports)	0.1	0.0	8.9
ICT goods imports (% of total goods imports)	5.6	3.9	10.8
ICT service exports (% of total service exports)	..	..	30.8
Applications			
Online service index (0–1, 1=highest presence)	..	..	0.67
Secure Internet servers (per million people)	212.2	1,478.6	827.6

Grenada

Latin America & Caribbean   **Upper middle income**

	Country data		Upper middle-income group
	2005	2012	2012
Economic and social context			
Population (millions)	0.10	0.11	2,391
Urban population (% of total)	37	39	61
GNI per capita, *World Bank Atlas* method ($)	6,800	7,220	6,969
GDP growth, 2000-05 and 2005-12 (avg. annual %)	4.6	-0.4	6.2
Adult literacy rate (% ages 15 and older)	..	..	94
Gross primary, secondary, tertiary school enrollment (%)	..	91	76
Sector structure			
Separate telecommunications/ICT regulator	Yes	Yes	
Status of main fixed-line telephone operator	Mixed	Mixed	
Level of competition (competition, partial comp., monopoly)			
International gateway(s)	..	..	
Mobile telephone service	M	C	
Internet service	..	C	
Foreign ownership (not allowed, restricted, allowed)	..	A	
Reg. treatment of VoIP (banned, closed, no framework, allowed)	No	No	
Sector efficiency and capacity			
Telecommunications revenue (% of GDP)	5.8	6.7	2.5
Telecommunications investment (% of revenue)	19.1	13.4	18.2
Sector performance			
Access			
Fixed-telephone subscriptions (per 100 people)	26.6	27.0[a]	19.4
Mobile-cellular telephone subscriptions (per 100 people)	45.5	121.3	92.4
Fixed (wired)-broadband subscriptions (per 100 people)	3.1	13.7[a]	10.8
Households with a computer (%)	..	..	40.6
Households with Internet access at home (%)	..	..	36.3
Usage			
Int'l. voice traffic, total (minutes/subscription/month)	100.5	46.6	1.3
Domestic mobile traffic (minutes/subscription/month)	133.5	200.9	284.4
Individuals using the Internet (%)	20.5[a]	42.1[a]	41.6
Quality			
Population covered by a mobile-cellular network (%)	..	..	99
Fixed (wired)-broadband subscriptions (% of total Internet)	57.3	100.0	95.5
International Internet bandwidth (bit/s per Internet user)	19,463	90,094	14,580
Affordability			
Fixed-telephone sub-basket ($ a month)	..	13.4	9.4
Mobile-cellular sub-basket ($ a month)	..	14.7	14.9
Fixed-broadband sub-basket ($ a month)	..	29.4	17.8
Trade			
ICT goods exports (% of total goods exports)	1.5	2.0	17.6
ICT goods imports (% of total goods imports)	4.8	4.4	14.7
ICT service exports (% of total service exports)	15.8	15.9	29.1
Applications			
Online service index (0-1, 1=highest presence)	0.45	0.35	0.42
Secure Internet servers (per million people)	29.1	28.3	18.5

Guam

	Country data		High-income group
	2005	2012	2012
Economic and social context			
Population (millions)	0.16	0.16	1,300
Urban population (% of total)	93	93	80
GNI per capita, World Bank Atlas method ($)	..	..	38,412
GDP growth, 2000–05 and 2005–12 (avg. annual %)	..	..	1.0
Adult literacy rate (% ages 15 and older)	..	..	..
Gross primary, secondary, tertiary school enrollment (%)	..	..	93
Sector structure			
Separate telecommunications/ICT regulator	..	..	
Status of main fixed-line telephone operator	..	..	
Level of competition (competition, partial comp., monopoly)			
International gateway(s)	..	..	
Mobile telephone service	..	..	
Internet service	..	..	
Foreign ownership (not allowed, restricted, allowed)	..	..	
Reg. treatment of VoIP (banned, closed, no framework, allowed)	..	..	
Sector efficiency and capacity			
Telecommunications revenue (% of GDP)	..	..	2.7
Telecommunications investment (% of revenue)	..	..	17.6
Sector performance			
Access			
Fixed-telephone subscriptions (per 100 people)	41.4	41.2	43.6
Mobile-cellular telephone subscriptions (per 100 people)	61.9	..	122.9
Fixed (wired)-broadband subscriptions (per 100 people)	1.7	1.9	26.2
Households with a computer (%)	..	..	77.7
Households with Internet access at home (%)	..	..	75.5
Usage			
Int'l. voice traffic, total (minutes/subscription/month)	..	..	..
Domestic mobile traffic (minutes/subscription/month)	..	..	113.6
Individuals using the Internet (%)	38.6	61.5[a]	75.4
Quality			
Population covered by a mobile-cellular network (%)	..	..	100
Fixed (wired)-broadband subscriptions (% of total Internet)	..	..	95.9
International Internet bandwidth (bit/s per Internet user)	..	..	85,990
Affordability			
Fixed-telephone sub-basket ($ a month)	..	..	25.2
Mobile-cellular sub-basket ($ a month)	..	..	20.6
Fixed-broadband sub-basket ($ a month)	..	..	29.2
Trade			
ICT goods exports (% of total goods exports)	..	..	8.9
ICT goods imports (% of total goods imports)	..	..	10.8
ICT service exports (% of total service exports)	..	..	30.8
Applications			
Online service index (0–1, 1=highest presence)	..	..	0.67
Secure Internet servers (per million people)	113.6	242.4	827.6

Guatemala

	Country data		Lower middle-income group
	2005	2012	2012
Economic and social context			
Population (millions)	13	15	2,507
Urban population (% of total)	47	50	39
GNI per capita, *World Bank Atlas* method ($)	2,070	3,120	1,893
GDP growth, 2000–05 and 2005–12 (avg. annual %)	3.1	3.4	6.0
Adult literacy rate (% ages 15 and older)	69	76	71
Gross primary, secondary, tertiary school enrollment (%)	71	..	64
Sector structure			
Separate telecommunications/ICT regulator	Yes	Yes	
Status of main fixed-line telephone operator	Private	Private	
Level of competition (competition, partial comp., monopoly)			
International gateway(s)	..	C	
Mobile telephone service	C	C	
Internet service	C	C	
Foreign ownership (not allowed, restricted, allowed)	A	A	
Reg. treatment of VoIP (banned, closed, no framework, allowed)	No	A	
Sector efficiency and capacity			
Telecommunications revenue (% of GDP)	..	..	2.5
Telecommunications investment (% of revenue)	..	..	20.5
Sector performance			
Access			
Fixed-telephone subscriptions (per 100 people)	9.8	11.6	5.4
Mobile-cellular telephone subscriptions (per 100 people)	35.6	137.8	83.1
Fixed (wired)-broadband subscriptions (per 100 people)	0.2	1.8	1.4
Households with a computer (%)	8.4	19.2a	15.0
Households with Internet access at home (%)	2.1	9.3a	12.4
Usage			
Int'l. voice traffic, total (minutes/subscription/month)	32.1	11.5	6.5
Domestic mobile traffic (minutes/subscription/month)	51.4	77.6	..
Individuals using the Internet (%)	5.7	16.0a	18.7
Quality			
Population covered by a mobile-cellular network (%)	76	100	86
Fixed (wired)-broadband subscriptions (% of total Internet)	..	..	58.2
International Internet bandwidth (bit/s per Internet user)	977	6,630	8,076
Affordability			
Fixed-telephone sub-basket ($ a month)	..	5.8	4.9
Mobile-cellular sub-basket ($ a month)	..	19.8	10.5
Fixed-broadband sub-basket ($ a month)	..	20.6	20.6
Trade			
ICT goods exports (% of total goods exports)	0.3	0.3	4.6
ICT goods imports (% of total goods imports)	6.0	5.7	7.2
ICT service exports (% of total service exports)	19.3	21.9	47.1
Applications			
Online service index (0–1, 1=highest presence)	0.43	0.46	0.32
Secure Internet servers (per million people)	5.5	13.3	4.4

Guinea

	Country data		Low-income group
	2005	2012	2012
Economic and social context			
Population (millions)	10	11	846
Urban population (% of total)	33	36	28
GNI per capita, *World Bank Atlas* method ($)	340	440	590
GDP growth, 2000–05 and 2005–12 (avg. annual %)	3.0	2.5	5.9
Adult literacy rate (% ages 15 and older)	30	25	61
Gross primary, secondary, tertiary school enrollment (%)	44	52	60
Sector structure			
Separate telecommunications/ICT regulator	No	Yes	
Status of main fixed-line telephone operator	Mixed	Mixed	
Level of competition (competition, partial comp., monopoly)			
International gateway(s)	..	C	
Mobile telephone service	P	C	
Internet service	C	C	
Foreign ownership (not allowed, restricted, allowed)	..	R	
Reg. treatment of VoIP (banned, closed, no framework, allowed)	No	A	
Sector efficiency and capacity			
Telecommunications revenue (% of GDP)	..	..	5.0
Telecommunications investment (% of revenue)	..	..	..
Sector performance			
Access			
Fixed-telephone subscriptions (per 100 people)	0.3	0.2	1.0
Mobile-cellular telephone subscriptions (per 100 people)	2.0	41.8	47.2
Fixed (wired)-broadband subscriptions (per 100 people)	0.0	0.0	0.2
Households with a computer (%)	..	2.1[a]	4.2
Households with Internet access at home (%)	0.0[a]	1.3[a]	3.4
Usage			
Int'l. voice traffic, total (minutes/subscription/month)	..	..	..
Domestic mobile traffic (minutes/subscription/month)	..	..	70.1
Individuals using the Internet (%)	0.5	1.5[a]	6.2
Quality			
Population covered by a mobile-cellular network (%)	80	80	..
Fixed (wired)-broadband subscriptions (% of total Internet)	0.0	..	30.9
International Internet bandwidth (bit/s per Internet user)	39	2,051	9,141
Affordability			
Fixed-telephone sub-basket ($ a month)	..	1.6	8.9
Mobile-cellular sub-basket ($ a month)	..	4.1	11.9
Fixed-broadband sub-basket ($ a month)	..	800.0	46.9
Trade			
ICT goods exports (% of total goods exports)	0.0	0.0	..
ICT goods imports (% of total goods imports)	0.7	5.2	..
ICT service exports (% of total service exports)	1.1	64.9	..
Applications			
Online service index (0–1, 1=highest presence)	0.14	0.00	0.20
Secure Internet servers (per million people)	..	0.1	1.1

Guinea-Bissau

	Country data		Low-income group
	2005	2012	2012
Economic and social context			
Population (millions)	1	2	846
Urban population (% of total)	40	45	28
GNI per capita, *World Bank Atlas* method ($)	390	510	590
GDP growth, 2000–05 and 2005–12 (avg. annual %)	0.7	3.1	5.9
Adult literacy rate (% ages 15 and older)	41	55	61
Gross primary, secondary, tertiary school enrollment (%)	59	..	60
Sector structure			
Separate telecommunications/ICT regulator	Yes	Yes	
Status of main fixed-line telephone operator	Mixed	Mixed	
Level of competition (competition, partial comp., monopoly)			
International gateway(s)	P	P	
Mobile telephone service	P	P	
Internet service	C	C	
Foreign ownership (not allowed, restricted, allowed)	A	A	
Reg. treatment of VoIP (banned, closed, no framework, allowed)	B	B	
Sector efficiency and capacity			
Telecommunications revenue (% of GDP)	..	..	5.0
Telecommunications investment (% of revenue)	..	..	..
Sector performance			
Access			
Fixed-telephone subscriptions (per 100 people)	0.7	0.3	1.0
Mobile-cellular telephone subscriptions (per 100 people)	7.0	63.1	47.2
Fixed (wired)-broadband subscriptions (per 100 people)	0.0	0.0	0.2
Households with a computer (%)	..	2.3a	4.2
Households with Internet access at home (%)	0.7	1.6a	3.4
Usage			
Int'l. voice traffic, total (minutes/subscription/month)	..	..	..
Domestic mobile traffic (minutes/subscription/month)	..	..	70.1
Individuals using the Internet (%)	1.9	2.9a	6.2
Quality			
Population covered by a mobile-cellular network (%)	65	65	..
Fixed (wired)-broadband subscriptions (% of total Internet)	..	0.0	30.9
International Internet bandwidth (bit/s per Internet user)	2	3,220	9,141
Affordability			
Fixed-telephone sub-basket ($ a month)	..	..	8.9
Mobile-cellular sub-basket ($ a month)	..	..	11.9
Fixed-broadband sub-basket ($ a month)	..	..	46.9
Trade			
ICT goods exports (% of total goods exports)	..	..	..
ICT goods imports (% of total goods imports)	1.8	..	..
ICT service exports (% of total service exports)	10.5	55.4	..
Applications			
Online service index (0–1, 1=highest presence)	0.15	0.10	0.20
Secure Internet servers (per million people)	..	1.2	1.1

Guyana

Latin America & Caribbean			Lower middle income

	Country data		Lower middle-income group
	2005	2012	2012
Economic and social context			
Population (millions)	0.76	0.80	2,507
Urban population (% of total)	28	28	39
GNI per capita, *World Bank Atlas* method ($)	1,070	3,410	1,893
GDP growth, 2000–05 and 2005–12 (avg. annual %)	0.8	2.8	6.0
Adult literacy rate (% ages 15 and older)	..	85	71
Gross primary, secondary, tertiary school enrollment (%)	77	68	64
Sector structure			
Separate telecommunications/ICT regulator	Yes	Yes	
Status of main fixed-line telephone operator	Mixed	Mixed	
Level of competition (competition, partial comp., monopoly)			
International gateway(s)	..	M	
Mobile telephone service	C	P	
Internet service	..	P	
Foreign ownership (not allowed, restricted, allowed)	..	..	
Reg. treatment of VoIP (banned, closed, no framework, allowed)	B	C	
Sector efficiency and capacity			
Telecommunications revenue (% of GDP)	6.3	5.2	2.5
Telecommunications investment (% of revenue)	50.0	19.2	20.5
Sector performance			
Access			
Fixed-telephone subscriptions (per 100 people)	14.5	19.4	5.4
Mobile-cellular telephone subscriptions (per 100 people)	37.0	68.8	83.1
Fixed (wired)-broadband subscriptions (per 100 people)	0.3	3.7	1.4
Households with a computer (%)	11.6[a]	22.9[a]	15.0
Households with Internet access at home (%)	10.4[a]	20.6[a]	12.4
Usage			
Int'l. voice traffic, total (minutes/subscription/month)	21.7	15.1	6.5
Domestic mobile traffic (minutes/subscription/month)	24.7	35.2	..
Individuals using the Internet (%)	13.8[a]	33.0[a]	18.7
Quality			
Population covered by a mobile-cellular network (%)	95	97	86
Fixed (wired)-broadband subscriptions (% of total Internet)	4.2	68.2	58.2
International Internet bandwidth (bit/s per Internet user)	339	8,382	8,076
Affordability			
Fixed-telephone sub-basket ($ a month)	..	3.1	4.9
Mobile-cellular sub-basket ($ a month)	..	9.0	10.5
Fixed-broadband sub-basket ($ a month)	..	24.5	20.6
Trade			
ICT goods exports (% of total goods exports)	0.0	0.1	4.6
ICT goods imports (% of total goods imports)	1.9	5.8	7.2
ICT service exports (% of total service exports)	42.4	41.4	47.1
Applications			
Online service index (0–1, 1=highest presence)	0.44	0.25	0.32
Secure Internet servers (per million people)	1.3	12.5	4.4

Haiti

	Country data		Low-income group
	2005	2012	2012
Economic and social context			
Population (millions)	9	10	846
Urban population (% of total)	44	55	28
GNI per capita, *World Bank Atlas* method ($)	410	760	590
GDP growth, 2000–05 and 2005–12 (avg. annual %)	-0.7	1.4	5.9
Adult literacy rate (% ages 15 and older)	49	..	61
Gross primary, secondary, tertiary school enrollment (%)	..	..	60
Sector structure			
Separate telecommunications/ICT regulator	Yes	Yes	
Status of main fixed-line telephone operator	Public	Mixed	
Level of competition (competition, partial comp., monopoly)			
International gateway(s)	..	C	
Mobile telephone service	P	C	
Internet service	C	C	
Foreign ownership (not allowed, restricted, allowed)	..	R	
Reg. treatment of VoIP (banned, closed, no framework, allowed)	No	A	
Sector efficiency and capacity			
Telecommunications revenue (% of GDP)	..	3.7	5.0
Telecommunications investment (% of revenue)	..	..	..
Sector performance			
Access			
Fixed-telephone subscriptions (per 100 people)	1.6	0.5	1.0
Mobile-cellular telephone subscriptions (per 100 people)	5.4	59.9	47.2
Fixed (wired)-broadband subscriptions (per 100 people)	0.0	0.0	0.2
Households with a computer (%)	2.0	7.3[a]	4.2
Households with Internet access at home (%)	1.0	3.4[a]	3.4
Usage			
Int'l. voice traffic, total (minutes/subscription/month)	..	..	..
Domestic mobile traffic (minutes/subscription/month)	..	..	70.1
Individuals using the Internet (%)	6.4[a]	9.8[a]	6.2
Quality			
Population covered by a mobile-cellular network (%)	..	..	..
Fixed (wired)-broadband subscriptions (% of total Internet)	0.0	..	30.9
International Internet bandwidth (bit/s per Internet user)	229	..	9,141
Affordability			
Fixed-telephone sub-basket ($ a month)	..	5.6	8.9
Mobile-cellular sub-basket ($ a month)	..	12.6	11.9
Fixed-broadband sub-basket ($ a month)	..	47.8	46.9
Trade			
ICT goods exports (% of total goods exports)	..	..	..
ICT goods imports (% of total goods imports)	..	..	..
ICT service exports (% of total service exports)	..	..	..
Applications			
Online service index (0–1, 1=highest presence)	0.21	0.09	0.20
Secure Internet servers (per million people)	0.6	1.1	1.1

Honduras

| Latin America & Caribbean | | | Lower middle income |

	Country data		Lower middle-income group
	2005	2012	2012
Economic and social context			
Population (millions)	7	8	2,507
Urban population (% of total)	49	53	39
GNI per capita, *World Bank Atlas* method ($)	1,380	2,120	1,893
GDP growth, 2000–05 and 2005–12 (avg. annual %)	4.7	3.2	6.0
Adult literacy rate (% ages 15 and older)	84	85	71
Gross primary, secondary, tertiary school enrollment (%)	..	71	64
Sector structure			
Separate telecommunications/ICT regulator	Yes	Yes	
Status of main fixed-line telephone operator	Public	Public	
Level of competition (competition, partial comp., monopoly)			
International gateway(s)	..	..	
Mobile telephone service	M	C	
Internet service	C	C	
Foreign ownership (not allowed, restricted, allowed)	A	R	
Reg. treatment of VoIP (banned, closed, no framework, allowed)	B	C	
Sector efficiency and capacity			
Telecommunications revenue (% of GDP)	5.1	5.4	2.5
Telecommunications investment (% of revenue)	23.5	9.1	20.5
Sector performance			
Access			
Fixed-telephone subscriptions (per 100 people)	7.2	7.7	5.4
Mobile-cellular telephone subscriptions (per 100 people)	18.6	92.9	83.1
Fixed (wired)-broadband subscriptions (per 100 people)	0.0	0.8	1.4
Households with a computer (%)	6.3	15.1[a]	15.0
Households with Internet access at home (%)	1.5	13.2[a]	12.4
Usage			
Int'l. voice traffic, total (minutes/subscription/month)	25.3	24.7	6.5
Domestic mobile traffic (minutes/subscription/month)	43.0	186.5	..
Individuals using the Internet (%)	6.5	18.1[a]	18.7
Quality			
Population covered by a mobile-cellular network (%)	90	..	86
Fixed (wired)-broadband subscriptions (% of total Internet)	0.0	81.1	58.2
International Internet bandwidth (bit/s per Internet user)	1,115	4,173	8,076
Affordability			
Fixed-telephone sub-basket ($ a month)	..	6.3	4.9
Mobile-cellular sub-basket ($ a month)	..	17.0	10.5
Fixed-broadband sub-basket ($ a month)	..	19.0	20.6
Trade			
ICT goods exports (% of total goods exports)	1.1	0.3	4.6
ICT goods imports (% of total goods imports)	5.6	5.0	7.2
ICT service exports (% of total service exports)	8.1	11.2	47.1
Applications			
Online service index (0–1, 1=highest presence)	0.40	0.38	0.32
Secure Internet servers (per million people)	4.3	9.1	4.4

Hong Kong SAR, China

High income

	Country data		High-income group
	2005	2012	2012
Economic and social context			
Population (millions)	7	7	1,300
Urban population (% of total)	100	100	80
GNI per capita, World Bank Atlas method ($)	28,890	36,560	38,412
GDP growth, 2000–05 and 2005–12 (avg. annual %)	4.2	3.4	1.0
Adult literacy rate (% ages 15 and older)	..	..	..
Gross primary, secondary, tertiary school enrollment (%)	72	90	93
Sector structure			
Separate telecommunications/ICT regulator	..	Yes	
Status of main fixed-line telephone operator	..	..	
Level of competition (competition, partial comp., monopoly)			
International gateway(s)	..	..	
Mobile telephone service	..	..	
Internet service	..	..	
Foreign ownership (not allowed, restricted, allowed)	..	..	
Reg. treatment of VoIP (banned, closed, no framework, allowed)	A	A	
Sector efficiency and capacity			
Telecommunications revenue (% of GDP)	3.6	3.6	2.7
Telecommunications investment (% of revenue)	18.3	12.9	17.6
Sector performance			
Access			
Fixed-telephone subscriptions (per 100 people)	55.0	61.3	43.6
Mobile-cellular telephone subscriptions (per 100 people)	123.9	229.2	122.9
Fixed (wired)-broadband subscriptions (per 100 people)	24.1	31.2	26.2
Households with a computer (%)	70.1	80.3	77.7
Households with Internet access at home (%)	64.6	78.6	75.5
Usage			
Int'l. voice traffic, total (minutes/subscription/month)	..	61.2	..
Domestic mobile traffic (minutes/subscription/month)	..	102.5	113.6
Individuals using the Internet (%)	56.9	72.8	75.4
Quality			
Population covered by a mobile-cellular network (%)	100	100	100
Fixed (wired)-broadband subscriptions (% of total Internet)	63.1	75.6	95.9
International Internet bandwidth (bit/s per Internet user)	16,723	1,426,554	85,990
Affordability			
Fixed-telephone sub-basket ($ a month)	..	14.1	25.2
Mobile-cellular sub-basket ($ a month)	..	1.8	20.6
Fixed-broadband sub-basket ($ a month)	..	21.6	29.2
Trade			
ICT goods exports (% of total goods exports)	38.3	42.2	8.9
ICT goods imports (% of total goods imports)	38.2	40.8	10.8
ICT service exports (% of total service exports)	18.4	15.3	30.8
Applications			
Online service index (0–1, 1=highest presence)	..	..	0.67
Secure Internet servers (per million people)	162.3	627.0	827.6

Hungary

<table>
<tr><td>**Europe & Central Asia**</td><td colspan="3">**Upper middle income**</td></tr>
</table>

	Country data		Upper middle-income group
	2005	2012	2012
Economic and social context			
Population (millions)	10	10	2,391
Urban population (% of total)	66	70	61
GNI per capita, *World Bank Atlas* method ($)	10,220	12,410	6,969
GDP growth, 2000–05 and 2005–12 (avg. annual %)	4.2	-0.5	6.2
Adult literacy rate (% ages 15 and older)	99	99	94
Gross primary, secondary, tertiary school enrollment (%)	89	90	76
Sector structure			
Separate telecommunications/ICT regulator	Yes	Yes	
Status of main fixed-line telephone operator	Private	Private	
Level of competition (competition, partial comp., monopoly)			
International gateway(s)	C	C	
Mobile telephone service	P	P	
Internet service	C	C	
Foreign ownership (not allowed, restricted, allowed)	A	A	
Reg. treatment of VoIP (banned, closed, no framework, allowed)	A	A	
Sector efficiency and capacity			
Telecommunications revenue (% of GDP)	4.6	3.4	2.5
Telecommunications investment (% of revenue)	9.1	15.8	18.2
Sector performance			
Access			
Fixed-telephone subscriptions (per 100 people)	33.8	29.7	19.4
Mobile-cellular telephone subscriptions (per 100 people)	92.3	116.1	92.4
Fixed (wired)-broadband subscriptions (per 100 people)	6.5	22.9	10.8
Households with a computer (%)	42.0	71.0	40.6
Households with Internet access at home (%)	22.1	69.0	36.3
Usage			
Int'l. voice traffic, total (minutes/subscription/month)	6.8	8.9	1.3
Domestic mobile traffic (minutes/subscription/month)	84.5	129.5	284.4
Individuals using the Internet (%)	39.0	72.0	41.6
Quality			
Population covered by a mobile-cellular network (%)	99	99	99
Fixed (wired)-broadband subscriptions (% of total Internet)	66.7	99.4	95.5
International Internet bandwidth (bit/s per Internet user)	8,896	15,314	14,580
Affordability			
Fixed-telephone sub-basket ($ a month)	..	25.3	9.4
Mobile-cellular sub-basket ($ a month)	..	25.1	14.9
Fixed-broadband sub-basket ($ a month)	..	31.0	17.8
Trade			
ICT goods exports (% of total goods exports)	25.6	17.4	17.6
ICT goods imports (% of total goods imports)	18.7	16.2	14.7
ICT service exports (% of total service exports)	20.3	27.7	29.1
Applications			
Online service index (0–1, 1=highest presence)	0.65	0.69	0.42
Secure Internet servers (per million people)	30.0	248.7	18.5

Iceland

High income

	Country data		High-income group
	2005	2012	2012
Economic and social context			
Population (millions)	0.30	0.32	1,300
Urban population (% of total)	93	94	80
GNI per capita, World Bank Atlas method ($)	49,620	38,270	38,412
GDP growth, 2000–05 and 2005–12 (avg. annual %)	4.0	-0.1	1.0
Adult literacy rate (% ages 15 and older)	..	..	..
Gross primary, secondary, tertiary school enrollment (%)	95	98	93
Sector structure			
Separate telecommunications/ICT regulator	Yes	Yes	
Status of main fixed-line telephone operator	Mixed	Private	
Level of competition (competition, partial comp., monopoly)			
International gateway(s)	..	C	
Mobile telephone service	C	C	
Internet service	C	C	
Foreign ownership (not allowed, restricted, allowed)	A	A	
Reg. treatment of VoIP (banned, closed, no framework, allowed)	C	A	
Sector efficiency and capacity			
Telecommunications revenue (% of GDP)	2.8	2.0	2.7
Telecommunications investment (% of revenue)	19.5	14.6	17.6
Sector performance			
Access			
Fixed-telephone subscriptions (per 100 people)	65.3	55.2	43.6
Mobile-cellular telephone subscriptions (per 100 people)	95.4	108.1	122.9
Fixed (wired)-broadband subscriptions (per 100 people)	26.3	34.3	26.2
Households with a computer (%)	89.0	96.0	77.7
Households with Internet access at home (%)	84.4	95.0	75.5
Usage			
Int'l. voice traffic, total (minutes/subscription/month)	18.7	13.9	..
Domestic mobile traffic (minutes/subscription/month)	125.4	178.7	113.6
Individuals using the Internet (%)	87.0	96.2	75.4
Quality			
Population covered by a mobile-cellular network (%)	99	99	100
Fixed (wired)-broadband subscriptions (% of total Internet)	89.6	95.9	95.9
International Internet bandwidth (bit/s per Internet user)	4,803	318,962	85,990
Affordability			
Fixed-telephone sub-basket ($ a month)	..	21.0	25.2
Mobile-cellular sub-basket ($ a month)	..	21.9	20.6
Fixed-broadband sub-basket ($ a month)	..	31.8	29.2
Trade			
ICT goods exports (% of total goods exports)	0.1	0.2	8.9
ICT goods imports (% of total goods imports)	6.4	4.1	10.8
ICT service exports (% of total service exports)	21.4	27.1	30.8
Applications			
Online service index (0–1, 1=highest presence)	0.72	0.54	0.67
Secure Internet servers (per million people)	1,004.3	2,869.3	827.6

India

South Asia			**Lower middle income**

	Country data		Lower middle-income group
	2005	**2012**	**2012**
Economic and social context			
Population (millions)	1,127	1,237	2,507
Urban population (% of total)	29	32	39
GNI per capita, *World Bank Atlas* method ($)	740	1,550	1,893
GDP growth, 2000–05 and 2005–12 (avg. annual %)	6.7	7.6	6.0
Adult literacy rate (% ages 15 and older)	63	..	71
Gross primary, secondary, tertiary school enrollment (%)	63	70	64
Sector structure			
Separate telecommunications/ICT regulator	Yes	Yes	
Status of main fixed-line telephone operator	Mixed	Mixed	
Level of competition (competition, partial comp., monopoly)			
International gateway(s)	C	C	
Mobile telephone service	C	C	
Internet service	C	C	
Foreign ownership (not allowed, restricted, allowed)	R	R	
Reg. treatment of VoIP (banned, closed, no framework, allowed)	A	A	
Sector efficiency and capacity			
Telecommunications revenue (% of GDP)	2.4	2.1	2.5
Telecommunications investment (% of revenue)	42.8	17.6	20.5
Sector performance			
Access			
Fixed-telephone subscriptions (per 100 people)	4.5	2.5	5.4
Mobile-cellular telephone subscriptions (per 100 people)	8.0	69.9	83.1
Fixed (wired)-broadband subscriptions (per 100 people)	0.1	1.2	1.4
Households with a computer (%)	2.0[a]	10.9[a]	15.0
Households with Internet access at home (%)	1.6[a]	9.5[a]	12.4
Usage			
Int'l. voice traffic, total (minutes/subscription/month)	5.6	4.9	6.5
Domestic mobile traffic (minutes/subscription/month)	..	..	..
Individuals using the Internet (%)	2.4[a]	12.6[a]	18.7
Quality			
Population covered by a mobile-cellular network (%)	31	83	86
Fixed (wired)-broadband subscriptions (% of total Internet)	19.4	59.1	58.2
International Internet bandwidth (bit/s per Internet user)	743	5,277	8,076
Affordability			
Fixed-telephone sub-basket ($ a month)	..	3.2	4.9
Mobile-cellular sub-basket ($ a month)	..	3.5	10.5
Fixed-broadband sub-basket ($ a month)	..	6.0	20.6
Trade			
ICT goods exports (% of total goods exports)	1.1	2.0	4.6
ICT goods imports (% of total goods imports)	7.6	5.3	7.2
ICT service exports (% of total service exports)	67.2	65.9	47.1
Applications			
Online service index (0–1, 1=highest presence)	0.38	0.54	0.32
Secure Internet servers (per million people)	0.6	3.9	4.4

Indonesia

Lower middle income

	Country data		Lower middle-income group
	2005	2012	2012
Economic and social context			
Population (millions)	224	247	2,507
Urban population (% of total)	46	51	39
GNI per capita, *World Bank Atlas* method ($)	1,230	3,420	1,893
GDP growth, 2000–05 and 2005–12 (avg. annual %)	4.7	5.9	6.0
Adult literacy rate (% ages 15 and older)	92	93	71
Gross primary, secondary, tertiary school enrollment (%)	67	77	64
Sector structure			
Separate telecommunications/ICT regulator	Yes	Yes	
Status of main fixed-line telephone operator	Mixed	Mixed	
Level of competition (competition, partial comp., monopoly)			
International gateway(s)	C	C	
Mobile telephone service	C	C	
Internet service	C	C	
Foreign ownership (not allowed, restricted, allowed)	..	..	
Reg. treatment of VoIP (banned, closed, no framework, allowed)	A	A	
Sector efficiency and capacity			
Telecommunications revenue (% of GDP)	2.2	1.9	2.5
Telecommunications investment (% of revenue)	28.3	18.6	20.5
Sector performance			
Access			
Fixed-telephone subscriptions (per 100 people)	6.0	15.4	5.4
Mobile-cellular telephone subscriptions (per 100 people)	20.9	114.2	83.1
Fixed (wired)-broadband subscriptions (per 100 people)	0.0	1.2	1.4
Households with a computer (%)	3.7	15.1	15.0
Households with Internet access at home (%)	1.0	6.5	12.4
Usage			
Int'l. voice traffic, total (minutes/subscription/month)	..	..	6.5
Domestic mobile traffic (minutes/subscription/month)	..	..	..
Individuals using the Internet (%)	3.6	15.4	18.7
Quality			
Population covered by a mobile-cellular network (%)	90	100	86
Fixed (wired)-broadband subscriptions (% of total Internet)	5.8	57.5	58.2
International Internet bandwidth (bit/s per Internet user)	186	17,063	8,076
Affordability			
Fixed-telephone sub-basket ($ a month)	..	4.8	4.9
Mobile-cellular sub-basket ($ a month)	..	7.9	10.5
Fixed-broadband sub-basket ($ a month)	..	22.2	20.6
Trade			
ICT goods exports (% of total goods exports)	8.1	4.1	4.6
ICT goods imports (% of total goods imports)	3.6	7.1	7.2
ICT service exports (% of total service exports)	29.7	38.2	47.1
Applications			
Online service index (0–1, 1=highest presence)	0.41	0.50	0.32
Secure Internet servers (per million people)	0.5	4.1	4.4

Iran, Islamic Rep.

Middle East & North Africa   **Upper middle income**

	Country data		Upper middle-income group
	2005	2012	2012
Economic and social context			
Population (millions)	70	76	2,391
Urban population (% of total)	68	69	61
GNI per capita, *World Bank Atlas* method ($)	2,530	*4,330*	6,969
GDP growth, 2000–05 and 2005–12 (avg. annual %)	5.9	3.7	6.2
Adult literacy rate (% ages 15 and older)	82	85	94
Gross primary, secondary, tertiary school enrollment (%)	64	87	76
Sector structure			
Separate telecommunications/ICT regulator	Yes	Yes	
Status of main fixed-line telephone operator	Public	Public	
Level of competition (competition, partial comp., monopoly)			
International gateway(s)	M	*M*	
Mobile telephone service	P	*C*	
Internet service	P	*C*	
Foreign ownership (not allowed, restricted, allowed)	R	R	
Reg. treatment of VoIP (banned, closed, no framework, allowed)	B	B	
Sector efficiency and capacity			
Telecommunications revenue (% of GDP)	1.4	*2.0*	2.5
Telecommunications investment (% of revenue)	74.5	*95.4*	18.2
Sector performance			
Access			
Fixed-telephone subscriptions (per 100 people)	29.0	37.6	19.4
Mobile-cellular telephone subscriptions (per 100 people)	12.1	76.1	92.4
Fixed (wired)-broadband subscriptions (per 100 people)	*0.1*	4.0	10.8
Households with a computer (%)	19.0[a]	37.0[a]	40.6
Households with Internet access at home (%)	6.6[a]	26.5[a]	36.3
Usage			
Int'l. voice traffic, total (minutes/subscription/month)	2.9	2.6	1.3
Domestic mobile traffic (minutes/subscription/month)	..	109.4	284.4
Individuals using the Internet (%)	8.1[a]	26.0[a]	41.6
Quality			
Population covered by a mobile-cellular network (%)	75	96	99
Fixed (wired)-broadband subscriptions (% of total Internet)	..	*33.8*	95.5
International Internet bandwidth (bit/s per Internet user)	600	3,731	14,580
Affordability			
Fixed-telephone sub-basket ($ a month)	..	0.2	9.4
Mobile-cellular sub-basket ($ a month)	..	5.0	14.9
Fixed-broadband sub-basket ($ a month)	..	17.8	17.8
Trade			
ICT goods exports (% of total goods exports)	0.0	*0.0*	17.6
ICT goods imports (% of total goods imports)	4.6	*4.6*	14.7
ICT service exports (% of total service exports)	..	..	29.1
Applications			
Online service index (0–1, 1=highest presence)	0.41	0.49	0.42
Secure Internet servers (per million people)	0.3	1.3	18.5

Iraq

	Country data		Upper middle-income group
	2005	2012	2012
Economic and social context			
Population (millions)	27	33	2,391
Urban population (% of total)	67	66	61
GNI per capita, *World Bank Atlas* method ($)	1,990	6,130	6,969
GDP growth, 2000–05 and 2005–12 (avg. annual %)	-1.1	6.7	6.2
Adult literacy rate (% ages 15 and older)	74	78	94
Gross primary, secondary, tertiary school enrollment (%)	63	..	76
Sector structure			
Separate telecommunications/ICT regulator	Yes	Yes	
Status of main fixed-line telephone operator	Public	Public	
Level of competition (competition, partial comp., monopoly)			
International gateway(s)	..	M	
Mobile telephone service	..	P	
Internet service	..	P	
Foreign ownership (not allowed, restricted, allowed)	..	R	
Reg. treatment of VoIP (banned, closed, no framework, allowed)	B	B	
Sector efficiency and capacity			
Telecommunications revenue (% of GDP)	..	..	2.5
Telecommunications investment (% of revenue)	..	..	18.2
Sector performance			
Access			
Fixed-telephone subscriptions (per 100 people)	4.1	5.7[a]	19.4
Mobile-cellular telephone subscriptions (per 100 people)	5.6	81.6[a]	92.4
Fixed (wired)-broadband subscriptions (per 100 people)	0.0	0.0	10.8
Households with a computer (%)	5.0	23.3[a]	40.6
Households with Internet access at home (%)	..	15.6[a]	36.3
Usage			
Int'l. voice traffic, total (minutes/subscription/month)	..	..	1.3
Domestic mobile traffic (minutes/subscription/month)	..	..	284.4
Individuals using the Internet (%)	0.9[a]	7.1[a]	41.6
Quality			
Population covered by a mobile-cellular network (%)	68	..	99
Fixed (wired)-broadband subscriptions (% of total Internet)	72.1	28.5	95.5
International Internet bandwidth (bit/s per Internet user)	130	43	14,580
Affordability			
Fixed-telephone sub-basket ($ a month)	..	0.4	9.4
Mobile-cellular sub-basket ($ a month)	..	12.5	14.9
Fixed-broadband sub-basket ($ a month)	..	211.3	17.8
Trade			
ICT goods exports (% of total goods exports)	..	..	17.6
ICT goods imports (% of total goods imports)	..	..	14.7
ICT service exports (% of total service exports)	5.0	12.0	29.1
Applications			
Online service index (0–1, 1=highest presence)	0.27	0.29	0.42
Secure Internet servers (per million people)	0.0	0.3	18.5

Ireland

	Country data		High-income group
	2005	2012	2012
Economic and social context			
Population (millions)	4	5	1,300
Urban population (% of total)	60	63	80
GNI per capita, World Bank Atlas method ($)	42,380	39,020	38,412
GDP growth, 2000–05 and 2005–12 (avg. annual %)	4.7	-0.4	1.0
Adult literacy rate (% ages 15 and older)	..	..	..
Gross primary, secondary, tertiary school enrollment (%)	96	106	93
Sector structure			
Separate telecommunications/ICT regulator	Yes	Yes	
Status of main fixed-line telephone operator	Private	Private	
Level of competition (competition, partial comp., monopoly)			
International gateway(s)	C	C	
Mobile telephone service	C	C	
Internet service	C	C	
Foreign ownership (not allowed, restricted, allowed)	A	R	
Reg. treatment of VoIP (banned, closed, no framework, allowed)	A	A	
Sector efficiency and capacity			
Telecommunications revenue (% of GDP)	2.4	1.6	2.7
Telecommunications investment (% of revenue)	10.1	23.9	17.6
Sector performance			
Access			
Fixed-telephone subscriptions (per 100 people)	49.4	43.9	43.6
Mobile-cellular telephone subscriptions (per 100 people)	102.7	107.2	122.9
Fixed (wired)-broadband subscriptions (per 100 people)	7.8	22.7	26.2
Households with a computer (%)	55.0	83.0	77.7
Households with Internet access at home (%)	47.2	81.0	75.5
Usage			
Int'l. voice traffic, total (minutes/subscription/month)	..	..	..
Domestic mobile traffic (minutes/subscription/month)	115.4	167.1	113.6
Individuals using the Internet (%)	41.6	79.0	75.4
Quality			
Population covered by a mobile-cellular network (%)	99	99	100
Fixed (wired)-broadband subscriptions (% of total Internet)	34.8	93.1	95.9
International Internet bandwidth (bit/s per Internet user)	14,211	97,097	85,990
Affordability			
Fixed-telephone sub-basket ($ a month)	..	27.8	25.2
Mobile-cellular sub-basket ($ a month)	..	46.0	20.6
Fixed-broadband sub-basket ($ a month)	..	34.8	29.2
Trade			
ICT goods exports (% of total goods exports)	22.4	5.8	8.9
ICT goods imports (% of total goods imports)	23.8	9.0	10.8
ICT service exports (% of total service exports)	57.1	66.3	30.8
Applications			
Online service index (0–1, 1=highest presence)	0.73	0.54	0.67
Secure Internet servers (per million people)	353.9	700.5	827.6

Isle of Man

	Country data		High-income group
	2005	2012	2012
Economic and social context			
Population (millions)	0.08	0.09	1,300
Urban population (% of total)	51	51	80
GNI per capita, World Bank Atlas method ($)	38,440	..	38,412
GDP growth, 2000–05 and 2005–12 (avg. annual %)	5.8	..	1.0
Adult literacy rate (% ages 15 and older)	..	..	..
Gross primary, secondary, tertiary school enrollment (%)	..	..	93
Sector structure			
Separate telecommunications/ICT regulator	..	..	
Status of main fixed-line telephone operator	..	..	
Level of competition (competition, partial comp., monopoly)			
International gateway(s)	..	..	
Mobile telephone service	..	..	
Internet service	..	..	
Foreign ownership (not allowed, restricted, allowed)	..	..	
Reg. treatment of VoIP (banned, closed, no framework, allowed)	..	..	
Sector efficiency and capacity			
Telecommunications revenue (% of GDP)	..	..	2.7
Telecommunications investment (% of revenue)	..	..	17.6
Sector performance			
Access			
Fixed-telephone subscriptions (per 100 people)	..	..	43.6
Mobile-cellular telephone subscriptions (per 100 people)	..	..	122.9
Fixed (wired)-broadband subscriptions (per 100 people)	..	..	26.2
Households with a computer (%)	..	..	77.7
Households with Internet access at home (%)	..	..	75.5
Usage			
Int'l. voice traffic, total (minutes/subscription/month)	..	..	..
Domestic mobile traffic (minutes/subscription/month)	..	..	*113.6*
Individuals using the Internet (%)	..	..	75.4
Quality			
Population covered by a mobile-cellular network (%)	..	..	100
Fixed (wired)-broadband subscriptions (% of total Internet)	..	..	95.9
International Internet bandwidth (bit/s per Internet user)	..	..	85,990
Affordability			
Fixed-telephone sub-basket ($ a month)	..	..	25.2
Mobile-cellular sub-basket ($ a month)	..	..	20.6
Fixed-broadband sub-basket ($ a month)	..	..	29.2
Trade			
ICT goods exports (% of total goods exports)	..	..	8.9
ICT goods imports (% of total goods imports)	..	..	10.8
ICT service exports (% of total service exports)	..	..	30.8
Applications			
Online service index (0–1, 1=highest presence)	..	..	0.67
Secure Internet servers (per million people)	24.9	2,220.9	827.6

Israel

	Country data		High-income group
	2005	2012	2012
Economic and social context			
Population (millions)	7	8	1,300
Urban population (% of total)	92	92	80
GNI per capita, *World Bank Atlas* method ($)	20,140	32,030	38,412
GDP growth, 2000–05 and 2005–12 (avg. annual %)	2.0	4.4	1.0
Adult literacy rate (% ages 15 and older)	..	..	..
Gross primary, secondary, tertiary school enrollment (%)	92	92	93
Sector structure			
Separate telecommunications/ICT regulator	No	No	
Status of main fixed-line telephone operator	Mixed	Mixed	
Level of competition (competition, partial comp., monopoly)			
International gateway(s)	..	C	
Mobile telephone service	C	C	
Internet service	C	C	
Foreign ownership (not allowed, restricted, allowed)	R	R	
Reg. treatment of VoIP (banned, closed, no framework, allowed)	A	A	
Sector efficiency and capacity			
Telecommunications revenue (% of GDP)	4.1	2.6	2.7
Telecommunications investment (% of revenue)	..	12.0	17.6
Sector performance			
Access			
Fixed-telephone subscriptions (per 100 people)	44.5	47.0	43.6
Mobile-cellular telephone subscriptions (per 100 people)	117.5	120.7	122.9
Fixed (wired)-broadband subscriptions (per 100 people)	18.6	25.3	26.2
Households with a computer (%)	60.0	82.1[a]	77.7
Households with Internet access at home (%)	42.0	73.4[a]	75.5
Usage			
Int'l. voice traffic, total (minutes/subscription/month)	..	..	..
Domestic mobile traffic (minutes/subscription/month)	..	..	113.6
Individuals using the Internet (%)	25.2	73.4[a]	75.4
Quality			
Population covered by a mobile-cellular network (%)	99	99	100
Fixed (wired)-broadband subscriptions (% of total Internet)	73.3	100.0	95.9
International Internet bandwidth (bit/s per Internet user)	10,218	56,170	85,990
Affordability			
Fixed-telephone sub-basket ($ a month)	..	18.2	25.2
Mobile-cellular sub-basket ($ a month)	..	36.2	20.6
Fixed-broadband sub-basket ($ a month)	..	38.3	29.2
Trade			
ICT goods exports (% of total goods exports)	7.5	11.7	8.9
ICT goods imports (% of total goods imports)	9.7	8.9	10.8
ICT service exports (% of total service exports)	55.4	59.3	30.8
Applications			
Online service index (0–1, 1=highest presence)	0.74	0.85	0.67
Secure Internet servers (per million people)	162.8	275.4	827.6

Italy

	Country data		High-income group
	2005	2012	2012
Economic and social context			
Population (millions)	59	60	1,300
Urban population (% of total)	68	69	80
GNI per capita, World Bank Atlas method ($)	30,880	34,640	38,412
GDP growth, 2000–05 and 2005–12 (avg. annual %)	0.9	-0.7	1.0
Adult literacy rate (% ages 15 and older)	98	99	..
Gross primary, secondary, tertiary school enrollment (%)	90	90	93
Sector structure			
Separate telecommunications/ICT regulator	Yes	Yes	
Status of main fixed-line telephone operator	Mixed	Mixed	
Level of competition (competition, partial comp., monopoly)			
International gateway(s)	..	..	
Mobile telephone service	C	P	
Internet service	C	C	
Foreign ownership (not allowed, restricted, allowed)	A	A	
Reg. treatment of VoIP (banned, closed, no framework, allowed)	A	A	
Sector efficiency and capacity			
Telecommunications revenue (% of GDP)	2.4	1.8	2.7
Telecommunications investment (% of revenue)	23.2	21.3	17.6
Sector performance			
Access			
Fixed-telephone subscriptions (per 100 people)	42.7	35.4	43.6
Mobile-cellular telephone subscriptions (per 100 people)	121.9	159.8	122.9
Fixed (wired)-broadband subscriptions (per 100 people)	11.6	22.1	26.2
Households with a computer (%)	46.0	67.0	77.7
Households with Internet access at home (%)	38.6	63.0	75.5
Usage			
Int'l. voice traffic, total (minutes/subscription/month)	..	..	..
Domestic mobile traffic (minutes/subscription/month)	87.7	108.8	113.6
Individuals using the Internet (%)	35.0	58.0	75.4
Quality			
Population covered by a mobile-cellular network (%)	100	99	100
Fixed (wired)-broadband subscriptions (% of total Internet)	38.5	97.5	95.9
International Internet bandwidth (bit/s per Internet user)	5,834	76,346	85,990
Affordability			
Fixed-telephone sub-basket ($ a month)	..	28.8	25.2
Mobile-cellular sub-basket ($ a month)	..	31.9	20.6
Fixed-broadband sub-basket ($ a month)	..	28.0	29.2
Trade			
ICT goods exports (% of total goods exports)	3.1	2.1	8.9
ICT goods imports (% of total goods imports)	7.1	6.2	10.8
ICT service exports (% of total service exports)	34.2	34.9	30.8
Applications			
Online service index (0–1, 1=highest presence)	0.67	0.58	0.67
Secure Internet servers (per million people)	44.2	200.3	827.6

Jamaica

Latin America & Caribbean			Upper middle income

	Country data		Upper middle-income group
	2005	2012	2012
Economic and social context			
Population (millions)	3	3	2,391
Urban population (% of total)	52	52	61
GNI per capita, *World Bank Atlas* method ($)	..	5,130	6,969
GDP growth, 2000–05 and 2005–12 (avg. annual %)	..	-1.0	6.2
Adult literacy rate (% ages 15 and older)	..	87	94
Gross primary, secondary, tertiary school enrollment (%)	80	..	76
Sector structure			
Separate telecommunications/ICT regulator	Yes	Yes	
Status of main fixed-line telephone operator	Mixed	Mixed	
Level of competition (competition, partial comp., monopoly)			
International gateway(s)	C	C	
Mobile telephone service	C	C	
Internet service	C	C	
Foreign ownership (not allowed, restricted, allowed)	A	A	
Reg. treatment of VoIP (banned, closed, no framework, allowed)	No	A	
Sector efficiency and capacity			
Telecommunications revenue (% of GDP)	6.6	4.2	2.5
Telecommunications investment (% of revenue)	19.0	23.2	18.2
Sector performance			
Access			
Fixed-telephone subscriptions (per 100 people)	11.9	9.6	19.4
Mobile-cellular telephone subscriptions (per 100 people)	73.9	96.3	92.4
Fixed (wired)-broadband subscriptions (per 100 people)	1.7	4.3	10.8
Households with a computer (%)	12.7[a]	32.6[a]	40.6
Households with Internet access at home (%)	5.1[a]	23.0[a]	36.3
Usage			
Int'l. voice traffic, total (minutes/subscription/month)	41.3	80.8	1.3
Domestic mobile traffic (minutes/subscription/month)	33.5	194.7	284.4
Individuals using the Internet (%)	12.8[a]	46.5[a]	41.6
Quality			
Population covered by a mobile-cellular network (%)	95	..	99
Fixed (wired)-broadband subscriptions (% of total Internet)	96.4	97.9	95.5
International Internet bandwidth (bit/s per Internet user)	5,826	20,193	14,580
Affordability			
Fixed-telephone sub-basket ($ a month)	..	15.0	9.4
Mobile-cellular sub-basket ($ a month)	..	10.5	14.9
Fixed-broadband sub-basket ($ a month)	..	29.2	17.8
Trade			
ICT goods exports (% of total goods exports)	0.3	0.4	17.6
ICT goods imports (% of total goods imports)	5.0	2.5	14.7
ICT service exports (% of total service exports)	8.3	9.4	29.1
Applications			
Online service index (0–1, 1=highest presence)	0.47	0.31	0.42
Secure Internet servers (per million people)	14.4	44.3	18.5

Japan

High income

	Country data		High-income group
	2005	2012	2012
Economic and social context			
Population (millions)	128	128	1,300
Urban population (% of total)	86	92	80
GNI per capita, *World Bank Atlas* method ($)	39,140	47,870	38,412
GDP growth, 2000–05 and 2005–12 (avg. annual %)	1.3	0.1	1.0
Adult literacy rate (% ages 15 and older)	..	..	..
Gross primary, secondary, tertiary school enrollment (%)	86	89	93
Sector structure			
Separate telecommunications/ICT regulator	No	No	
Status of main fixed-line telephone operator	Private	Private	
Level of competition (competition, partial comp., monopoly)			
International gateway(s)	C	C	
Mobile telephone service	C	C	
Internet service	C	C	
Foreign ownership (not allowed, restricted, allowed)	A	A	
Reg. treatment of VoIP (banned, closed, no framework, allowed)	A	A	
Sector efficiency and capacity			
Telecommunications revenue (% of GDP)	2.9	2.8	2.7
Telecommunications investment (% of revenue)	14.3	10.8	17.6
Sector performance			
Access			
Fixed-telephone subscriptions (per 100 people)	45.7	50.5	43.6
Mobile-cellular telephone subscriptions (per 100 people)	76.0	110.9	122.9
Fixed (wired)-broadband subscriptions (per 100 people)	18.4	27.7	26.2
Households with a computer (%)	80.5	80.0	77.7
Households with Internet access at home (%)	57.0	86.0	75.5
Usage			
Int'l. voice traffic, total (minutes/subscription/month)	23.6	1.9	..
Domestic mobile traffic (minutes/subscription/month)	97.6	90.4	113.6
Individuals using the Internet (%)	66.9	79.1	75.4
Quality			
Population covered by a mobile-cellular network (%)	99	100	100
Fixed (wired)-broadband subscriptions (% of total Internet)	44.0	89.9	95.9
International Internet bandwidth (bit/s per Internet user)	2,589	32,827	85,990
Affordability			
Fixed-telephone sub-basket ($ a month)	..	29.0	25.2
Mobile-cellular sub-basket ($ a month)	..	30.7	20.6
Fixed-broadband sub-basket ($ a month)	..	26.6	29.2
Trade			
ICT goods exports (% of total goods exports)	16.9	9.1	8.9
ICT goods imports (% of total goods imports)	13.5	10.2	10.8
ICT service exports (% of total service exports)	19.8	20.7	30.8
Applications			
Online service index (0–1, 1=highest presence)	0.77	0.86	0.67
Secure Internet servers (per million people)	257.7	741.6	827.6

Jordan

Middle East & North Africa   **Upper middle income**

	Country data		Upper middle-income group
	2005	2012	2012
Economic and social context			
Population (millions)	5	6	2,391
Urban population (% of total)	81	83	61
GNI per capita, World Bank Atlas method ($)	2,490	4,670	6,969
GDP growth, 2000–05 and 2005–12 (avg. annual %)	6.3	5.2	6.2
Adult literacy rate (% ages 15 and older)	91	96	94
Gross primary, secondary, tertiary school enrollment (%)	83	79	76
Sector structure			
Separate telecommunications/ICT regulator	Yes	Yes	
Status of main fixed-line telephone operator	Mixed	Mixed	
Level of competition (competition, partial comp., monopoly)			
International gateway(s)	C	C	
Mobile telephone service	P	P	
Internet service	C	C	
Foreign ownership (not allowed, restricted, allowed)	A	A	
Reg. treatment of VoIP (banned, closed, no framework, allowed)	A	A	
Sector efficiency and capacity			
Telecommunications revenue (% of GDP)	8.5	5.4	2.5
Telecommunications investment (% of revenue)	20.5	12.0	18.2
Sector performance			
Access			
Fixed-telephone subscriptions (per 100 people)	12.0	6.2	19.4
Mobile-cellular telephone subscriptions (per 100 people)	59.9	128.2	92.4
Fixed (wired)-broadband subscriptions (per 100 people)	0.4	2.8	10.8
Households with a computer (%)	23.0	54.6ª	40.6
Households with Internet access at home (%)	8.0	43.6ª	36.3
Usage			
Int'l. voice traffic, total (minutes/subscription/month)	15.4	16.0	1.3
Domestic mobile traffic (minutes/subscription/month)	111.8	297.2	284.4
Individuals using the Internet (%)	12.9	41.0ª	41.6
Quality			
Population covered by a mobile-cellular network (%)	99	99	99
Fixed (wired)-broadband subscriptions (% of total Internet)	12.0	99.6	95.5
International Internet bandwidth (bit/s per Internet user)	457	5,219	14,580
Affordability			
Fixed-telephone sub-basket ($ a month)	..	9.4	9.4
Mobile-cellular sub-basket ($ a month)	..	7.8	14.9
Fixed-broadband sub-basket ($ a month)	..	18.7	17.8
Trade			
ICT goods exports (% of total goods exports)	3.2	1.5	17.6
ICT goods imports (% of total goods imports)	6.9	4.1	14.7
ICT service exports (% of total service exports)	..	..	29.1
Applications			
Online service index (0–1, 1=highest presence)	0.55	0.39	0.42
Secure Internet servers (per million people)	3.7	25.8	18.5

Kazakhstan

Europe & Central Asia   **Upper middle income**

	Country data 2005	Country data 2012	Upper middle-income group 2012
Economic and social context			
Population (millions)	15	17	2,391
Urban population (% of total)	55	54	61
GNI per capita, *World Bank Atlas* method ($)	2,930	9,780	6,969
GDP growth, 2000–05 and 2005–12 (avg. annual %)	10.1	5.7	6.2
Adult literacy rate (% ages 15 and older)	..	100	94
Gross primary, secondary, tertiary school enrollment (%)	92	92	76
Sector structure			
Separate telecommunications/ICT regulator	Yes	No	
Status of main fixed-line telephone operator	Mixed	Mixed	
Level of competition (competition, partial comp., monopoly)			
International gateway(s)	..	C	
Mobile telephone service	C	P	
Internet service	..	C	
Foreign ownership (not allowed, restricted, allowed)	..	R	
Reg. treatment of VoIP (banned, closed, no framework, allowed)	No	A	
Sector efficiency and capacity			
Telecommunications revenue (% of GDP)	2.8	2.0	2.5
Telecommunications investment (% of revenue)	5.3	18.0	18.2
Sector performance			
Access			
Fixed-telephone subscriptions (per 100 people)	18.0	26.8	19.4
Mobile-cellular telephone subscriptions (per 100 people)	35.8	185.8	92.4
Fixed (wired)-broadband subscriptions (per 100 people)	0.0	9.8	10.8
Households with a computer (%)	15.6[a]	63.0[a]	40.6
Households with Internet access at home (%)	5.0	52.6[a]	36.3
Usage			
Int'l. voice traffic, total (minutes/subscription/month)	7.2	..	1.3
Domestic mobile traffic (minutes/subscription/month)	41.1	97.0	284.4
Individuals using the Internet (%)	3.0	53.3[a]	41.6
Quality			
Population covered by a mobile-cellular network (%)	81	95	99
Fixed (wired)-broadband subscriptions (% of total Internet)	1.0	96.5	95.5
International Internet bandwidth (bit/s per Internet user)	108	32,028	14,580
Affordability			
Fixed-telephone sub-basket ($ a month)	..	3.2	9.4
Mobile-cellular sub-basket ($ a month)	..	11.3	14.9
Fixed-broadband sub-basket ($ a month)	..	13.2	17.8
Trade			
ICT goods exports (% of total goods exports)	0.1	0.4	17.6
ICT goods imports (% of total goods imports)	4.0	5.8	14.7
ICT service exports (% of total service exports)	11.2	10.6	29.1
Applications			
Online service index (0–1, 1=highest presence)	0.47	0.78	0.42
Secure Internet servers (per million people)	0.9	9.5	18.5

Kenya

	Country data		Low-income group
	2005	2012	2012
Economic and social context			
Population (millions)	36	43	846
Urban population (% of total)	22	24	28
GNI per capita, *World Bank Atlas* method ($)	520	860	590
GDP growth, 2000–05 and 2005–12 (avg. annual %)	3.4	4.3	5.9
Adult literacy rate (% ages 15 and older)	72	..	61
Gross primary, secondary, tertiary school enrollment (%)	59	67	60
Sector structure			
Separate telecommunications/ICT regulator	Yes	Yes	
Status of main fixed-line telephone operator	Public	Mixed	
Level of competition (competition, partial comp., monopoly)			
International gateway(s)	P	C	
Mobile telephone service	P	C	
Internet service	C	C	
Foreign ownership (not allowed, restricted, allowed)	R	R	
Reg. treatment of VoIP (banned, closed, no framework, allowed)	A	A	
Sector efficiency and capacity			
Telecommunications revenue (% of GDP)	4.7	4.1	5.0
Telecommunications investment (% of revenue)	76.3	48.0	..
Sector performance			
Access			
Fixed-telephone subscriptions (per 100 people)	0.8	0.6	1.0
Mobile-cellular telephone subscriptions (per 100 people)	12.9	71.2	47.2
Fixed (wired)-broadband subscriptions (per 100 people)	0.0	0.1	0.2
Households with a computer (%)	2.6	10.8a	4.2
Households with Internet access at home (%)	1.2	11.5a	3.4
Usage			
Int'l. voice traffic, total (minutes/subscription/month)	3.8	3.8	..
Domestic mobile traffic (minutes/subscription/month)	12.7	78.1	70.1
Individuals using the Internet (%)	3.1	32.1a	6.2
Quality			
Population covered by a mobile-cellular network (%)	62	89	..
Fixed (wired)-broadband subscriptions (% of total Internet)	6.7	61.6	30.9
International Internet bandwidth (bit/s per Internet user)	102	23,715	9,141
Affordability			
Fixed-telephone sub-basket ($ a month)	..	12.6	8.9
Mobile-cellular sub-basket ($ a month)	..	3.7	11.9
Fixed-broadband sub-basket ($ a month)	..	33.7	46.9
Trade			
ICT goods exports (% of total goods exports)	0.2	1.4	..
ICT goods imports (% of total goods imports)	4.1	7.2	..
ICT service exports (% of total service exports)	..	..	..
Applications			
Online service index (0–1, 1=highest presence)	0.35	0.43	0.20
Secure Internet servers (per million people)	0.3	4.8	1.1

Kiribati

Lower middle income

	Country data		Lower middle-income group
	2005	2012	2012
Economic and social context			
Population (millions)	0.09	0.10	2,507
Urban population (% of total)	44	44	39
GNI per capita, World Bank Atlas method ($)	1,800	2,520	1,893
GDP growth, 2000–05 and 2005–12 (avg. annual %)	2.0	1.5	6.0
Adult literacy rate (% ages 15 and older)	..	..	71
Gross primary, secondary, tertiary school enrollment (%)	77	75	64
Sector structure			
Separate telecommunications/ICT regulator	No	Yes	
Status of main fixed-line telephone operator	Public	Public	
Level of competition (competition, partial comp., monopoly)			
International gateway(s)	..	..	
Mobile telephone service	..	P	
Internet service	..	C	
Foreign ownership (not allowed, restricted, allowed)	..	..	
Reg. treatment of VoIP (banned, closed, no framework, allowed)	No	No	
Sector efficiency and capacity			
Telecommunications revenue (% of GDP)	..	..	2.5
Telecommunications investment (% of revenue)	..	..	20.5
Sector performance			
Access			
Fixed-telephone subscriptions (per 100 people)	4.6	8.9	5.4
Mobile-cellular telephone subscriptions (per 100 people)	0.7	15.9	83.1
Fixed (wired)-broadband subscriptions (per 100 people)	0.4	1.0	1.4
Households with a computer (%)	6.0	..	15.0
Households with Internet access at home (%)	2.5	..	12.4
Usage			
Int'l. voice traffic, total (minutes/subscription/month)	..	..	6.5
Domestic mobile traffic (minutes/subscription/month)	..	..	..
Individuals using the Internet (%)	4.0[a]	10.7[a]	18.7
Quality			
Population covered by a mobile-cellular network (%)	..	..	86
Fixed (wired)-broadband subscriptions (% of total Internet)	..	..	58.2
International Internet bandwidth (bit/s per Internet user)	..	4,155	8,076
Affordability			
Fixed-telephone sub-basket ($ a month)	..	12.9	4.9
Mobile-cellular sub-basket ($ a month)	..	18.1	10.5
Fixed-broadband sub-basket ($ a month)	..	428.3	20.6
Trade			
ICT goods exports (% of total goods exports)	0.9	1.9	4.6
ICT goods imports (% of total goods imports)	1.3	1.5	7.2
ICT service exports (% of total service exports)	..	..	47.1
Applications			
Online service index (0–1, 1=highest presence)	0.00	0.07	0.32
Secure Internet servers (per million people)	..	9.8	4.4

Korea, Dem. People's Rep.

East Asia & Pacific   **Low income**

	Country data		Low-income group
	2005	2012	2012
Economic and social context			
Population (millions)	24	25	846
Urban population (% of total)	60	60	28
GNI per capita, *World Bank Atlas* method ($)	..	..	590
GDP growth, 2000–05 and 2005–12 (avg. annual %)	..	..	5.9
Adult literacy rate (% ages 15 and older)	..	*100*	61
Gross primary, secondary, tertiary school enrollment (%)	..	..	60
Sector structure			
Separate telecommunications/ICT regulator	No	No	
Status of main fixed-line telephone operator	Public	Public	
Level of competition (competition, partial comp., monopoly)			
International gateway(s)	..	..	
Mobile telephone service	..	..	
Internet service	..	..	
Foreign ownership (not allowed, restricted, allowed)	..	No	
Reg. treatment of VoIP (banned, closed, no framework, allowed)	B	B	
Sector efficiency and capacity			
Telecommunications revenue (% of GDP)	..	..	5.0
Telecommunications investment (% of revenue)	..	..	..
Sector performance			
Access			
Fixed-telephone subscriptions (per 100 people)	4.2	4.8	1.0
Mobile-cellular telephone subscriptions (per 100 people)	0.0	6.9	47.2
Fixed (wired)-broadband subscriptions (per 100 people)	0.0	0.0	0.2
Households with a computer (%)	..	..	4.2
Households with Internet access at home (%)	..	..	3.4
Usage			
Int'l. voice traffic, total (minutes/subscription/month)	..	..	..
Domestic mobile traffic (minutes/subscription/month)	..	..	70.1
Individuals using the Internet (%)	0.0	0.0[a]	6.2
Quality			
Population covered by a mobile-cellular network (%)	0	..	..
Fixed (wired)-broadband subscriptions (% of total Internet)	..	..	30.9
International Internet bandwidth (bit/s per Internet user)	..	..	9,141
Affordability			
Fixed-telephone sub-basket ($ a month)	..	..	8.9
Mobile-cellular sub-basket ($ a month)	..	..	11.9
Fixed-broadband sub-basket ($ a month)	..	..	46.9
Trade			
ICT goods exports (% of total goods exports)	..	..	..
ICT goods imports (% of total goods imports)	..	..	..
ICT service exports (% of total service exports)	..	..	..
Applications			
Online service index (0–1, 1=highest presence)	0.00	0.12	0.20*
Secure Internet servers (per million people)	..	0.0	1.1

Korea, Rep.

High income

	Country data		High-income group
	2005	2012	2012
Economic and social context			
Population (millions)	48	50	1,300
Urban population (% of total)	81	83	80
GNI per capita, *World Bank Atlas* method ($)	16,900	22,670	38,412
GDP growth, 2000–05 and 2005–12 (avg. annual %)	4.5	3.4	1.0
Adult literacy rate (% ages 15 and older)	..	..	..
Gross primary, secondary, tertiary school enrollment (%)	98	*100*	93
Sector structure			
Separate telecommunications/ICT regulator	Yes	Yes	
Status of main fixed-line telephone operator	Private	Private	
Level of competition (competition, partial comp., monopoly)			
International gateway(s)	..	C	
Mobile telephone service	C	P	
Internet service	C	C	
Foreign ownership (not allowed, restricted, allowed)	R	R	
Reg. treatment of VoIP (banned, closed, no framework, allowed)	A	A	
Sector efficiency and capacity			
Telecommunications revenue (% of GDP)	4.7	4.3	2.7
Telecommunications investment (% of revenue)	14.4	15.7	17.6
Sector performance			
Access			
Fixed-telephone subscriptions (per 100 people)	50.8	61.4	43.6
Mobile-cellular telephone subscriptions (per 100 people)	81.5	109.4	122.9
Fixed (wired)-broadband subscriptions (per 100 people)	25.9	37.2	26.2
Households with a computer (%)	79.7[a]	82.3	77.7
Households with Internet access at home (%)	92.7	97.4	75.5
Usage			
Int'l. voice traffic, total (minutes/subscription/month)	*3.2*	3.2	..
Domestic mobile traffic (minutes/subscription/month)	175.8	163.0	*113.6*
Individuals using the Internet (%)	73.5	84.1	75.4
Quality			
Population covered by a mobile-cellular network (%)	80	100	100
Fixed (wired)-broadband subscriptions (% of total Internet)	100.0	100.0	*95.9*
International Internet bandwidth (bit/s per Internet user)	1,440	25,815	85,990
Affordability			
Fixed-telephone sub-basket ($ a month)	..	6.1	25.2
Mobile-cellular sub-basket ($ a month)	..	7.4	20.6
Fixed-broadband sub-basket ($ a month)	..	27.1	29.2
Trade			
ICT goods exports (% of total goods exports)	30.0	17.2	8.9
ICT goods imports (% of total goods imports)	15.2	9.8	10.8
ICT service exports (% of total service exports)	19.9	21.6	30.8
Applications			
Online service index (0–1, 1=highest presence)	0.83	1.00	0.67
Secure Internet servers (per million people)	20.0	1,999.1	827.6

Kosovo

	Country data		Lower middle-income group
	2005	**2012**	**2012**

| **Europe & Central Asia** | | **Lower middle income** | |

	2005	**2012**	**2012**
Economic and social context			
Population (millions)	2	2	2,507
Urban population (% of total)	..	..	39
GNI per capita, *World Bank Atlas* method ($)	2,520	3,600	1,893
GDP growth, 2000–05 and 2005–12 (avg. annual %)	6.4	4.7	6.0
Adult literacy rate (% ages 15 and older)	..	..	71
Gross primary, secondary, tertiary school enrollment (%)	..	..	64
Sector structure			
Separate telecommunications/ICT regulator	..	..	
Status of main fixed-line telephone operator	..	..	
Level of competition (competition, partial comp., monopoly)			
International gateway(s)	..	..	
Mobile telephone service	..	..	
Internet service	..	..	
Foreign ownership (not allowed, restricted, allowed)	..	..	
Reg. treatment of VoIP (banned, closed, no framework, allowed)	..	..	
Sector efficiency and capacity			
Telecommunications revenue (% of GDP)	..	..	2.5
Telecommunications investment (% of revenue)	..	..	20.5
Sector performance			
Access			
Fixed-telephone subscriptions (per 100 people)	..	..	5.4
Mobile-cellular telephone subscriptions (per 100 people)	..	..	83.1
Fixed (wired)-broadband subscriptions (per 100 people)	..	..	1.4
Households with a computer (%)	..	..	15.0
Households with Internet access at home (%)	..	..	12.4
Usage			
Int'l. voice traffic, total (minutes/subscription/month)	..	..	6.5
Domestic mobile traffic (minutes/subscription/month)	..	..	..
Individuals using the Internet (%)	..	..	18.7
Quality			
Population covered by a mobile-cellular network (%)	..	..	86
Fixed (wired)-broadband subscriptions (% of total Internet)	..	..	58.2
International Internet bandwidth (bit/s per Internet user)	..	..	8,076
Affordability			
Fixed-telephone sub-basket ($ a month)	..	..	4.9
Mobile-cellular sub-basket ($ a month)	..	..	10.5
Fixed-broadband sub-basket ($ a month)	..	..	20.6
Trade			
ICT goods exports (% of total goods exports)	..	..	4.6
ICT goods imports (% of total goods imports)	..	..	7.2
ICT service exports (% of total service exports)	4.7	20.7	47.1
Applications			
Online service index (0–1, 1=highest presence)	..	..	0.32
Secure Internet servers (per million people)	..	..	4.4

Kuwait

	Country data		High-income group
	2005	2012	2012
Economic and social context			
Population (millions)	2	3	1,300
Urban population (% of total)	98	98	80
GNI per capita, World Bank Atlas method ($)	34,160	44,880	38,412
GDP growth, 2000–05 and 2005–12 (avg. annual %)	9.0	1.4	1.0
Adult literacy rate (% ages 15 and older)	93	94	..
Gross primary, secondary, tertiary school enrollment (%)	86	..	93
Sector structure			
Separate telecommunications/ICT regulator	No	No	
Status of main fixed-line telephone operator	Public	Public	
Level of competition (competition, partial comp., monopoly)			
International gateway(s)	M	M	
Mobile telephone service	P	M	
Internet service	P	P	
Foreign ownership (not allowed, restricted, allowed)	R	R	
Reg. treatment of VoIP (banned, closed, no framework, allowed)	B	B	
Sector efficiency and capacity			
Telecommunications revenue (% of GDP)	3.5	..	2.7
Telecommunications investment (% of revenue)	27.0	..	17.6
Sector performance			
Access			
Fixed-telephone subscriptions (per 100 people)	22.0	15.7	43.6
Mobile-cellular telephone subscriptions (per 100 people)	60.2	156.9	122.9
Fixed (wired)-broadband subscriptions (per 100 people)	1.1	1.4	26.2
Households with a computer (%)	32.0	75.0[a]	77.7
Households with Internet access at home (%)	27.0	65.2[a]	75.5
Usage			
Int'l. voice traffic, total (minutes/subscription/month)	..	..	..
Domestic mobile traffic (minutes/subscription/month)	..	..	113.6
Individuals using the Internet (%)	25.9	79.2[a]	75.4
Quality			
Population covered by a mobile-cellular network (%)	100	100[a]	100
Fixed (wired)-broadband subscriptions (% of total Internet)	8.8	..	95.9
International Internet bandwidth (bit/s per Internet user)	1,481	5,444	85,990
Affordability			
Fixed-telephone sub-basket ($ a month)	..	8.6	25.2
Mobile-cellular sub-basket ($ a month)	..	7.8	20.6
Fixed-broadband sub-basket ($ a month)	..	19.2	29.2
Trade			
ICT goods exports (% of total goods exports)	0.2	0.3	8.9
ICT goods imports (% of total goods imports)	5.0	6.4	10.8
ICT service exports (% of total service exports)	52.2	34.5	30.8
Applications			
Online service index (0–1, 1=highest presence)	0.52	0.58	0.67
Secure Internet servers (per million people)	34.8	184.9	827.6

Kyrgyz Republic

Europe & Central Asia			Low income

	Country data		Low-income group
	2005	2012	2012
Economic and social context			
Population (millions)	5	6	846
Urban population (% of total)	35	35	28
GNI per capita, *World Bank Atlas* method ($)	450	990	590
GDP growth, 2000–05 and 2005–12 (avg. annual %)	4.1	4.2	5.9
Adult literacy rate (% ages 15 and older)	..	99	61
Gross primary, secondary, tertiary school enrollment (%)	79	75	60
Sector structure			
Separate telecommunications/ICT regulator	Yes	Yes	
Status of main fixed-line telephone operator	Mixed	Mixed	
Level of competition (competition, partial comp., monopoly)			
International gateway(s)	C	C	
Mobile telephone service	C	C	
Internet service	C	C	
Foreign ownership (not allowed, restricted, allowed)	R	A	
Reg. treatment of VoIP (banned, closed, no framework, allowed)	No	No	
Sector efficiency and capacity			
Telecommunications revenue (% of GDP)	4.5	6.7	5.0
Telecommunications investment (% of revenue)	3.2	18.6	..
Sector performance			
Access			
Fixed-telephone subscriptions (per 100 people)	8.7	8.9	1.0
Mobile-cellular telephone subscriptions (per 100 people)	10.7	124.2	47.2
Fixed (wired)-broadband subscriptions (per 100 people)	0.0	0.9	0.2
Households with a computer (%)	1.0[a]	6.9[a]	4.2
Households with Internet access at home (%)	0.8[a]	6.3[a]	3.4
Usage			
Int'l. voice traffic, total (minutes/subscription/month)	..	14.8	..
Domestic mobile traffic (minutes/subscription/month)	..	394.7	70.1
Individuals using the Internet (%)	10.5	21.7[a]	6.2
Quality			
Population covered by a mobile-cellular network (%)	42	98	..
Fixed (wired)-broadband subscriptions (% of total Internet)	16.2	33.6	30.9
International Internet bandwidth (bit/s per Internet user)	516	3,875	9,141
Affordability			
Fixed-telephone sub-basket ($ a month)	..	1.4	8.9
Mobile-cellular sub-basket ($ a month)	..	5.7	11.9
Fixed-broadband sub-basket ($ a month)	..	12.5	46.9
Trade			
ICT goods exports (% of total goods exports)	0.1	0.1	..
ICT goods imports (% of total goods imports)	3.3	2.3	..
ICT service exports (% of total service exports)	26.4	15.9	..
Applications			
Online service index (0–1, 1=highest presence)	0.42	0.42	0.20
Secure Internet servers (per million people)	0.6	5.5	1.1

Lao PDR

	Country data		Lower middle-income group
	2005	2012	2012
Economic and social context			
Population (millions)	6	7	2,507
Urban population (% of total)	27	35	39
GNI per capita, *World Bank Atlas* method ($)	450	1,270	1,893
GDP growth, 2000–05 and 2005–12 (avg. annual %)	6.2	8.0	6.0
Adult literacy rate (% ages 15 and older)	73	..	71
Gross primary, secondary, tertiary school enrollment (%)	58	60	64
Sector structure			
Separate telecommunications/ICT regulator	No	Yes	
Status of main fixed-line telephone operator	Public	Mixed	
Level of competition (competition, partial comp., monopoly)			
International gateway(s)	M	*M*	
Mobile telephone service	P	*P*	
Internet service	P	*P*	
Foreign ownership (not allowed, restricted, allowed)	R	R	
Reg. treatment of VoIP (banned, closed, no framework, allowed)	B	No	
Sector efficiency and capacity			
Telecommunications revenue (% of GDP)	1.7	*1.7*	2.5
Telecommunications investment (% of revenue)	63.0	*8.9*	20.5
Sector performance			
Access			
Fixed-telephone subscriptions (per 100 people)	1.6	1.8	5.4
Mobile-cellular telephone subscriptions (per 100 people)	11.4	64.7	83.1
Fixed (wired)-broadband subscriptions (per 100 people)	0.0	0.1	1.4
Households with a computer (%)	2.0	8.7[a]	15.0
Households with Internet access at home (%)	1.0	5.1[a]	12.4
Usage			
Int'l. voice traffic, total (minutes/subscription/month)	..	5.9	6.5
Domestic mobile traffic (minutes/subscription/month)	59.6	11.2	..
Individuals using the Internet (%)	0.9	10.7[a]	18.7
Quality			
Population covered by a mobile-cellular network (%)	55	72	86
Fixed (wired)-broadband subscriptions (% of total Internet)	5.0	27.6	58.2
International Internet bandwidth (bit/s per Internet user)	406	9,397	8,076
Affordability			
Fixed-telephone sub-basket ($ a month)	..	4.6	4.9
Mobile-cellular sub-basket ($ a month)	..	6.2	10.5
Fixed-broadband sub-basket ($ a month)	..	97.2	20.6
Trade			
ICT goods exports (% of total goods exports)	..	..	4.6
ICT goods imports (% of total goods imports)	..	..	7.2
ICT service exports (% of total service exports)	..	..	47.1
Applications			
Online service index (0–1, 1=highest presence)	0.24	0.22	0.32
Secure Internet servers (per million people)	0.3	1.0	4.4

Latvia

	Country data		High-income group
	2005	2012	2012
Economic and social context			
Population (millions)	2	2	1,300
Urban population (% of total)	68	68	80
GNI per capita, *World Bank Atlas* method ($)	7,000	14,060	38,412
GDP growth, 2000–05 and 2005–12 (avg. annual %)	8.0	-1.1	1.0
Adult literacy rate (% ages 15 and older)	*100*	*100*	..
Gross primary, secondary, tertiary school enrollment (%)	95	89	93
Sector structure			
Separate telecommunications/ICT regulator	Yes	Yes	
Status of main fixed-line telephone operator	Mixed	Mixed	
Level of competition (competition, partial comp., monopoly)			
International gateway(s)	..	..	
Mobile telephone service	C	P	
Internet service	C	C	
Foreign ownership (not allowed, restricted, allowed)	A	A	
Reg. treatment of VoIP (banned, closed, no framework, allowed)	A	A	
Sector efficiency and capacity			
Telecommunications revenue (% of GDP)	*4.0*	3.6	2.7
Telecommunications investment (% of revenue)	..	25.9	17.6
Sector performance			
Access			
Fixed-telephone subscriptions (per 100 people)	32.8	24.3[a]	43.6
Mobile-cellular telephone subscriptions (per 100 people)	84.0	112.1[a]	122.9
Fixed (wired)-broadband subscriptions (per 100 people)	2.7	23.3[a]	26.2
Households with a computer (%)	32.0	70.0	77.7
Households with Internet access at home (%)	30.5	69.0	75.5
Usage			
Int'l. voice traffic, total (minutes/subscription/month)	3.7	..	..
Domestic mobile traffic (minutes/subscription/month)	72.2	..	113.6
Individuals using the Internet (%)	46.0	74.0	75.4
Quality			
Population covered by a mobile-cellular network (%)	98	..	100
Fixed (wired)-broadband subscriptions (% of total Internet)	83.2	..	95.9
International Internet bandwidth (bit/s per Internet user)	2,713	59,027	85,990
Affordability			
Fixed-telephone sub-basket ($ a month)	..	10.9	25.2
Mobile-cellular sub-basket ($ a month)	..	13.3	20.6
Fixed-broadband sub-basket ($ a month)	..	13.8	29.2
Trade			
ICT goods exports (% of total goods exports)	2.0	6.1	8.9
ICT goods imports (% of total goods imports)	5.8	6.0	10.8
ICT service exports (% of total service exports)	15.9	20.5	30.8
Applications			
Online service index (0–1, 1=highest presence)	0.59	0.59	0.67
Secure Internet servers (per million people)	38.9	266.1	827.6

Lebanon

Upper middle income

	Country data		Upper middle-income group
	2005	2012	2012
Economic and social context			
Population (millions)	4	4	2,391
Urban population (% of total)	87	87	61
GNI per capita, *World Bank Atlas* method ($)	5,800	9,190	6,969
GDP growth, 2000–05 and 2005–12 (avg. annual %)	4.0	6.1	6.2
Adult literacy rate (% ages 15 and older)	90	..	94
Gross primary, secondary, tertiary school enrollment (%)	78	75	76
Sector structure			
Separate telecommunications/ICT regulator	No	Yes	
Status of main fixed-line telephone operator	Public	Public	
Level of competition (competition, partial comp., monopoly)			
International gateway(s)	..	M	
Mobile telephone service	C	M	
Internet service	C	C	
Foreign ownership (not allowed, restricted, allowed)	..	R	
Reg. treatment of VoIP (banned, closed, no framework, allowed)	B	B	
Sector efficiency and capacity			
Telecommunications revenue (% of GDP)	7.9	..	2.5
Telecommunications investment (% of revenue)	..	..	18.2
Sector performance			
Access			
Fixed-telephone subscriptions (per 100 people)	15.9	18.7	19.4
Mobile-cellular telephone subscriptions (per 100 people)	24.9	80.8	92.4
Fixed (wired)-broadband subscriptions (per 100 people)	3.3	9.7	10.8
Households with a computer (%)	24.0	79.7[a]	40.6
Households with Internet access at home (%)	4.4	64.0[a]	36.3
Usage			
Int'l. voice traffic, total (minutes/subscription/month)	88.5	44.4	1.3
Domestic mobile traffic (minutes/subscription/month)	190.6	189.4	284.4
Individuals using the Internet (%)	10.1	61.2[a]	41.6
Quality			
Population covered by a mobile-cellular network (%)	100	99	99
Fixed (wired)-broadband subscriptions (% of total Internet)	56.5	61.9	95.5
International Internet bandwidth (bit/s per Internet user)	717	18,445	14,580
Affordability			
Fixed-telephone sub-basket ($ a month)	..	10.3	9.4
Mobile-cellular sub-basket ($ a month)	..	20.9	14.9
Fixed-broadband sub-basket ($ a month)	..	17.6	17.8
Trade			
ICT goods exports (% of total goods exports)	1.8	0.6	17.6
ICT goods imports (% of total goods imports)	3.3	2.2	14.7
ICT service exports (% of total service exports)	42.4	56.8	29.1
Applications			
Online service index (0–1, 1=highest presence)	0.48	0.48	0.42
Secure Internet servers (per million people)	8.5	39.8	18.5

Lesotho

Sub-Saharan Africa   **Lower middle income**

	Country data		Lower middle-income group
	2005	2012	2012
Economic and social context			
Population (millions)	2	2	2,507
Urban population (% of total)	23	28	39
GNI per capita, *World Bank Atlas* method ($)	910	1,380	1,893
GDP growth, 2000–05 and 2005–12 (avg. annual %)	2.8	5.0	6.0
Adult literacy rate (% ages 15 and older)	86	76	71
Gross primary, secondary, tertiary school enrollment (%)	64	65	64
Sector structure			
Separate telecommunications/ICT regulator	Yes	Yes	
Status of main fixed-line telephone operator	Mixed	Mixed	
Level of competition (competition, partial comp., monopoly)			
International gateway(s)	M	C	
Mobile telephone service	C	C	
Internet service	C	C	
Foreign ownership (not allowed, restricted, allowed)	A	A	
Reg. treatment of VoIP (banned, closed, no framework, allowed)	B	No	
Sector efficiency and capacity			
Telecommunications revenue (% of GDP)	0.6	4.5	2.5
Telecommunications investment (% of revenue)	20.9	12.2	20.5
Sector performance			
Access			
Fixed-telephone subscriptions (per 100 people)	2.5	2.5	5.4
Mobile-cellular telephone subscriptions (per 100 people)	13.0	75.3	83.1
Fixed (wired)-broadband subscriptions (per 100 people)	0.0	0.1	1.4
Households with a computer (%)	3.0	5.9a	15.0
Households with Internet access at home (%)	0.6	3.7a	12.4
Usage			
Int'l. voice traffic, total (minutes/subscription/month)	..	31.1	6.5
Domestic mobile traffic (minutes/subscription/month)	26.2	21.4	..
Individuals using the Internet (%)	2.6a	4.6a	18.7
Quality			
Population covered by a mobile-cellular network (%)	29	81	86
Fixed (wired)-broadband subscriptions (% of total Internet)	1.8	4.1	58.2
International Internet bandwidth (bit/s per Internet user)	86	6,330	8,076
Affordability			
Fixed-telephone sub-basket ($ a month)	..	13.8	4.9
Mobile-cellular sub-basket ($ a month)	..	19.8	10.5
Fixed-broadband sub-basket ($ a month)	..	85.4	20.6
Trade			
ICT goods exports (% of total goods exports)	3.3	5.8	4.6
ICT goods imports (% of total goods imports)	1.1	2.7	7.2
ICT service exports (% of total service exports)	11.9	18.0	47.1
Applications			
Online service index (0–1, 1=highest presence)	0.38	0.30	0.32
Secure Internet servers (per million people)	0.5	0.5	4.4

Liberia

	Country data		Low-income group
	2005	2012	2012
Economic and social context			
Population (millions)	3	4	846
Urban population (% of total)	46	49	28
GNI per capita, *World Bank Atlas* method ($)	120	370	590
GDP growth, 2000–05 and 2005–12 (avg. annual %)	-1.0	11.6	5.9
Adult literacy rate (% ages 15 and older)	55	..	61
Gross primary, secondary, tertiary school enrollment (%)	..	..	60
Sector structure			
Separate telecommunications/ICT regulator	Yes	Yes	
Status of main fixed-line telephone operator	Public	Public	
Level of competition (competition, partial comp., monopoly)			
International gateway(s)	..	C	
Mobile telephone service	C	P	
Internet service	..	C	
Foreign ownership (not allowed, restricted, allowed)	A	No	
Reg. treatment of VoIP (banned, closed, no framework, allowed)	B	C	
Sector efficiency and capacity			
Telecommunications revenue (% of GDP)	8.1	..	5.0
Telecommunications investment (% of revenue)	..	..	..
Sector performance			
Access			
Fixed-telephone subscriptions (per 100 people)	0.1	0.0	1.0
Mobile-cellular telephone subscriptions (per 100 people)	4.9	57.1	47.2
Fixed (wired)-broadband subscriptions (per 100 people)	0.0	0.0	0.2
Households with a computer (%)	0.8	2.0[a]	4.2
Households with Internet access at home (%)	..	1.5[a]	3.4
Usage			
Int'l. voice traffic, total (minutes/subscription/month)	..	11.1	..
Domestic mobile traffic (minutes/subscription/month)	0.0	52.0	70.1
Individuals using the Internet (%)	0.6[a]	3.8[a]	6.2
Quality			
Population covered by a mobile-cellular network (%)	16	..	..
Fixed (wired)-broadband subscriptions (% of total Internet)	..	..	30.9
International Internet bandwidth (bit/s per Internet user)	..	2,006	9,141
Affordability			
Fixed-telephone sub-basket ($ a month)	..	..	8.9
Mobile-cellular sub-basket ($ a month)	..	..	11.9
Fixed-broadband sub-basket ($ a month)	..	..	46.9
Trade			
ICT goods exports (% of total goods exports)	..	..	..
ICT goods imports (% of total goods imports)	..	..	..
ICT service exports (% of total service exports)	..	..	..
Applications			
Online service index (0–1, 1=highest presence)	0.22	0.19	0.20
Secure Internet servers (per million people)	..	0.9	1.1

Libya

	Country data		Upper middle-income group
	2005	2012	2012
Economic and social context			
Population (millions)	6	6	2,391
Urban population (% of total)	77	78	61
GNI per capita, *World Bank Atlas* method ($)	6,660	*12,930*	6,969
GDP growth, 2000–05 and 2005–12 (avg. annual %)	4.7	4.5	6.2
Adult literacy rate (% ages 15 and older)	*86*	*90*	94
Gross primary, secondary, tertiary school enrollment (%)	*94*	..	76
Sector structure			
Separate telecommunications/ICT regulator	No	Yes	
Status of main fixed-line telephone operator	Public	Public	
Level of competition (competition, partial comp., monopoly)			
International gateway(s)	..	..	
Mobile telephone service	*M*	*M*	
Internet service	..	..	
Foreign ownership (not allowed, restricted, allowed)	..	..	
Reg. treatment of VoIP (banned, closed, no framework, allowed)	B	B	
Sector efficiency and capacity			
Telecommunications revenue (% of GDP)	..	..	2.5
Telecommunications investment (% of revenue)	..	..	18.2
Sector performance			
Access			
Fixed-telephone subscriptions (per 100 people)	15.2[a]	13.2[a]	19.4
Mobile-cellular telephone subscriptions (per 100 people)	35.7	155.8[a]	92.4
Fixed (wired)-broadband subscriptions (per 100 people)	0.0	1.1[a]	10.8
Households with a computer (%)	5.0	17.6[a]	40.6
Households with Internet access at home (%)	3.0	13.7[a]	36.3
Usage			
Int'l. voice traffic, total (minutes/subscription/month)	13.4	..	1.3
Domestic mobile traffic (minutes/subscription/month)	84.0	..	284.4
Individuals using the Internet (%)	3.9[a]	14.0[a]	41.6
Quality			
Population covered by a mobile-cellular network (%)	71	98	99
Fixed (wired)-broadband subscriptions (% of total Internet)	..	8.2	95.5
International Internet bandwidth (bit/s per Internet user)	456	14,044	14,580
Affordability			
Fixed-telephone sub-basket ($ a month)	..	..	9.4
Mobile-cellular sub-basket ($ a month)	..	..	14.9
Fixed-broadband sub-basket ($ a month)	..	..	17.8
Trade			
ICT goods exports (% of total goods exports)	..	..	17.6
ICT goods imports (% of total goods imports)	4.8	3.6	14.7
ICT service exports (% of total service exports)	..	..	29.1
Applications			
Online service index (0–1, 1=highest presence)	0.35	0.00	0.42
Secure Internet servers (per million people)	0.2	3.4	18.5

Liechtenstein

	Country data		High-income group
	2005	2012	2012
Economic and social context			
Population (millions)	0.03	0.04	1,300
Urban population (% of total)	15	14	80
GNI per capita, *World Bank Atlas* method ($)	92,660	136,770	38,412
GDP growth, 2000–05 and 2005–12 (avg. annual %)	0.5	3.0	1.0
Adult literacy rate (% ages 15 and older)	..	..	..
Gross primary, secondary, tertiary school enrollment (%)	86	88	93
Sector structure			
Separate telecommunications/ICT regulator	Yes	Yes	
Status of main fixed-line telephone operator	Public	Public	
Level of competition (competition, partial comp., monopoly)			
International gateway(s)	..	C	
Mobile telephone service	P	C	
Internet service	C	C	
Foreign ownership (not allowed, restricted, allowed)	..	A	
Reg. treatment of VoIP (banned, closed, no framework, allowed)	..	..	
Sector efficiency and capacity			
Telecommunications revenue (% of GDP)	0.8	..	2.7
Telecommunications investment (% of revenue)	..	..	17.6
Sector performance			
Access			
Fixed-telephone subscriptions (per 100 people)	57.6	50.4	43.6
Mobile-cellular telephone subscriptions (per 100 people)	79.2	97.4	122.9
Fixed (wired)-broadband subscriptions (per 100 people)	24.8	30.5	26.2
Households with a computer (%)	..	..	77.7
Households with Internet access at home (%)	..	..	75.5
Usage			
Int'l. voice traffic, total (minutes/subscription/month)	..	..	..
Domestic mobile traffic (minutes/subscription/month)	..	11.7	113.6
Individuals using the Internet (%)	63.4	89.4[a]	75.4
Quality			
Population covered by a mobile-cellular network (%)	94	100	100
Fixed (wired)-broadband subscriptions (% of total Internet)	54.9	92.7	95.9
International Internet bandwidth (bit/s per Internet user)	6,813	6,022	85,990
Affordability			
Fixed-telephone sub-basket ($ a month)	..	29.0	25.2
Mobile-cellular sub-basket ($ a month)	..	23.4	20.6
Fixed-broadband sub-basket ($ a month)	..	47.1	29.2
Trade			
ICT goods exports (% of total goods exports)	..	..	8.9
ICT goods imports (% of total goods imports)	..	..	10.8
ICT service exports (% of total service exports)	..	..	30.8
Applications			
Online service index (0–1, 1=highest presence)	0.55	0.59	0.67
Secure Internet servers (per million people)	1,410.5	8,216.2	827.6

Lithuania

	Country data		High-income group
	2005	2012	2012
Economic and social context			
Population (millions)	3	3	1,300
Urban population (% of total)	67	67	80
GNI per capita, *World Bank Atlas* method ($)	7,590	13,820	38,412
GDP growth, 2000–05 and 2005–12 (avg. annual %)	8.0	0.8	1.0
Adult literacy rate (% ages 15 and older)	*100*	*100*	*..*
Gross primary, secondary, tertiary school enrollment (%)	96	97	93
Sector structure			
Separate telecommunications/ICT regulator	Yes	Yes	
Status of main fixed-line telephone operator	Mixed	Mixed	
Level of competition (competition, partial comp., monopoly)			
International gateway(s)	C	..	
Mobile telephone service	C	C	
Internet service	C	C	
Foreign ownership (not allowed, restricted, allowed)	A	A	
Reg. treatment of VoIP (banned, closed, no framework, allowed)	A	A	
Sector efficiency and capacity			
Telecommunications revenue (% of GDP)	3.5	1.7	2.7
Telecommunications investment (% of revenue)	15.6	138.3	17.6
Sector performance			
Access			
Fixed-telephone subscriptions (per 100 people)	24.4	22.3	43.6
Mobile-cellular telephone subscriptions (per 100 people)	132.5	165.1	122.9
Fixed (wired)-broadband subscriptions (per 100 people)	7.1	21.1	26.2
Households with a computer (%)	32.0	64.0	77.7
Households with Internet access at home (%)	15.8	62.0	75.5
Usage			
Int'l. voice traffic, total (minutes/subscription/month)	6.0	6.1	..
Domestic mobile traffic (minutes/subscription/month)	55.7	124.5	*113.6*
Individuals using the Internet (%)	36.2	68.0	75.4
Quality			
Population covered by a mobile-cellular network (%)	100	98	100
Fixed (wired)-broadband subscriptions (% of total Internet)	90.9	99.4	*95.9*
International Internet bandwidth (bit/s per Internet user)	4,188	76,193	85,990
Affordability			
Fixed-telephone sub-basket ($ a month)	..	13.9	25.2
Mobile-cellular sub-basket ($ a month)	..	10.8	20.6
Fixed-broadband sub-basket ($ a month)	..	12.1	29.2
Trade			
ICT goods exports (% of total goods exports)	5.3	2.3	8.9
ICT goods imports (% of total goods imports)	6.4	3.6	10.8
ICT service exports (% of total service exports)	8.2	9.0	30.8
Applications			
Online service index (0–1, 1=highest presence)	0.66	0.70	0.67
Secure Internet servers (per million people)	22.3	248.6	827.6

Luxembourg

	Country data		High-income group
	2005	2012	2012
Economic and social context			
Population (millions)	0.47	0.53	1,300
Urban population (% of total)	84	86	80
GNI per capita, World Bank Atlas method ($)	69,180	71,640	38,412
GDP growth, 2000–05 and 2005–12 (avg. annual %)	3.5	0.9	1.0
Adult literacy rate (% ages 15 and older)	..	..	..
Gross primary, secondary, tertiary school enrollment (%)	76	78	93
Sector structure			
Separate telecommunications/ICT regulator	Yes	Yes	
Status of main fixed-line telephone operator	Public	Public	
Level of competition (competition, partial comp., monopoly)			
International gateway(s)	C	C	
Mobile telephone service	C	C	
Internet service	C	C	
Foreign ownership (not allowed, restricted, allowed)	A	A	
Reg. treatment of VoIP (banned, closed, no framework, allowed)	A	A	
Sector efficiency and capacity			
Telecommunications revenue (% of GDP)	1.5	1.2	2.7
Telecommunications investment (% of revenue)	18.3	25.9	17.6
Sector performance			
Access			
Fixed-telephone subscriptions (per 100 people)	53.4	50.9	43.6
Mobile-cellular telephone subscriptions (per 100 people)	111.4	145.4	122.9
Fixed (wired)-broadband subscriptions (per 100 people)	15.3	32.4	26.2
Households with a computer (%)	75.0	92.0	77.7
Households with Internet access at home (%)	64.6	93.0	75.5
Usage			
Int'l. voice traffic, total (minutes/subscription/month)	74.2	69.1	..
Domestic mobile traffic (minutes/subscription/month)	79.7	84.4	113.6
Individuals using the Internet (%)	70.0	92.0	75.4
Quality			
Population covered by a mobile-cellular network (%)	99	100	100
Fixed (wired)-broadband subscriptions (% of total Internet)	58.9	100.0	95.9
International Internet bandwidth (bit/s per Internet user)	29,486	4,088,456	85,990
Affordability			
Fixed-telephone sub-basket ($ a month)	..	28.5	25.2
Mobile-cellular sub-basket ($ a month)	..	27.7	20.6
Fixed-broadband sub-basket ($ a month)	..	40.3	29.2
Trade			
ICT goods exports (% of total goods exports)	7.9	2.7	8.9
ICT goods imports (% of total goods imports)	8.4	4.1	10.8
ICT service exports (% of total service exports)	16.4	21.7	30.8
Applications			
Online service index (0–1, 1=highest presence)	0.75	0.70	0.67
Secure Internet servers (per million people)	473.0	2,258.1	827.6

Macao SAR, China

High income

	Country data		High-income group
	2005	2012	2012
Economic and social context			
Population (millions)	0.47	0.56	1,300
Urban population (% of total)	100	100	80
GNI per capita, *World Bank Atlas* method ($)	24,080	55,720	38,412
GDP growth, 2000–05 and 2005–12 (avg. annual %)	12.8	12.6	1.0
Adult literacy rate (% ages 15 and older)	93	96	..
Gross primary, secondary, tertiary school enrollment (%)	92	82	93
Sector structure			
Separate telecommunications/ICT regulator	..	..	
Status of main fixed-line telephone operator	..	..	
Level of competition (competition, partial comp., monopoly)			
International gateway(s)	..	..	
Mobile telephone service	..	..	
Internet service	..	..	
Foreign ownership (not allowed, restricted, allowed)	..	..	
Reg. treatment of VoIP (banned, closed, no framework, allowed)	No	No	
Sector efficiency and capacity			
Telecommunications revenue (% of GDP)	2.5	1.7	2.7
Telecommunications investment (% of revenue)	16.8	11.2	17.6
Sector performance			
Access			
Fixed-telephone subscriptions (per 100 people)	37.3	29.2	43.6
Mobile-cellular telephone subscriptions (per 100 people)	113.8	289.8	122.9
Fixed (wired)-broadband subscriptions (per 100 people)	14.5	26.0	26.2
Households with a computer (%)	68.1	85.8[a]	77.7
Households with Internet access at home (%)	56.9[a]	81.0[a]	75.5
Usage			
Int'l. voice traffic, total (minutes/subscription/month)	37.5	30.1	..
Domestic mobile traffic (minutes/subscription/month)	123.1	..	113.6
Individuals using the Internet (%)	34.9	64.3[a]	75.4
Quality			
Population covered by a mobile-cellular network (%)	100	100	100
Fixed (wired)-broadband subscriptions (% of total Internet)	76.8	99.6	95.9
International Internet bandwidth (bit/s per Internet user)	9,803	59,233	85,990
Affordability			
Fixed-telephone sub-basket ($ a month)	..	8.4	25.2
Mobile-cellular sub-basket ($ a month)	..	5.7	20.6
Fixed-broadband sub-basket ($ a month)	..	7.9	29.2
Trade			
ICT goods exports (% of total goods exports)	2.8	14.9	8.9
ICT goods imports (% of total goods imports)	9.7	14.5	10.8
ICT service exports (% of total service exports)	0.9	1.3	30.8
Applications			
Online service index (0–1, 1=highest presence)	..	..	0.67
Secure Internet servers (per million people)	55.5	311.0	827.6

Macedonia, FYR

Europe & Central Asia			Upper middle income

	Country data		Upper middle-income group
	2005	2012	2012
Economic and social context			
Population (millions)	2	2	2,391
Urban population (% of total)	59	59	61
GNI per capita, World Bank Atlas method ($)	2,830	4,620	6,969
GDP growth, 2000–05 and 2005–12 (avg. annual %)	1.9	2.9	6.2
Adult literacy rate (% ages 15 and older)	96	97	94
Gross primary, secondary, tertiary school enrollment (%)	68	70	76
Sector structure			
Separate telecommunications/ICT regulator	Yes	Yes	
Status of main fixed-line telephone operator	Mixed	Mixed	
Level of competition (competition, partial comp., monopoly)			
International gateway(s)	M	..	
Mobile telephone service	C	C	
Internet service	C	C	
Foreign ownership (not allowed, restricted, allowed)	A	..	
Reg. treatment of VoIP (banned, closed, no framework, allowed)	No	A	
Sector efficiency and capacity			
Telecommunications revenue (% of GDP)	5.5	4.9	2.5
Telecommunications investment (% of revenue)	9.8	14.0	18.2
Sector performance			
Access			
Fixed-telephone subscriptions (per 100 people)	25.5	19.4	19.4
Mobile-cellular telephone subscriptions (per 100 people)	54.1	106.2	92.4
Fixed (wired)-broadband subscriptions (per 100 people)	0.6	13.7	10.8
Households with a computer (%)	24.9	58.4a	40.6
Households with Internet access at home (%)	12.5	56.8a	36.3
Usage			
Int'l. voice traffic, total (minutes/subscription/month)	..	9.0	1.3
Domestic mobile traffic (minutes/subscription/month)	28.7	149.3	284.4
Individuals using the Internet (%)	26.5a	63.1a	41.6
Quality			
Population covered by a mobile-cellular network (%)	99	100	99
Fixed (wired)-broadband subscriptions (% of total Internet)	11.5	92.2	95.5
International Internet bandwidth (bit/s per Internet user)	62	30,836	14,580
Affordability			
Fixed-telephone sub-basket ($ a month)	..	9.1	9.4
Mobile-cellular sub-basket ($ a month)	..	13.3	14.9
Fixed-broadband sub-basket ($ a month)	..	13.5	17.8
Trade			
ICT goods exports (% of total goods exports)	0.4	0.3	17.6
ICT goods imports (% of total goods imports)	4.3	4.0	14.7
ICT service exports (% of total service exports)	20.7	24.0	29.1
Applications			
Online service index (0–1, 1=highest presence)	0.49	0.45	0.42
Secure Internet servers (per million people)	0.5	51.7	18.5

Madagascar

	Country data		Low-income group
	2005	2012	2012
Economic and social context			
Population (millions)	18	22	846
Urban population (% of total)	29	33	28
GNI per capita, *World Bank Atlas* method ($)	290	430	590
GDP growth, 2000–05 and 2005–12 (avg. annual %)	2.0	2.3	5.9
Adult literacy rate (% ages 15 and older)	*71*	*64*	*61*
Gross primary, secondary, tertiary school enrollment (%)	60	66	60
Sector structure			
Separate telecommunications/ICT regulator	Yes	Yes	
Status of main fixed-line telephone operator	Mixed	Mixed	
Level of competition (competition, partial comp., monopoly)			
International gateway(s)	C	..	
Mobile telephone service	C	*C*	
Internet service	C	*C*	
Foreign ownership (not allowed, restricted, allowed)	R	R	
Reg. treatment of VoIP (banned, closed, no framework, allowed)	B	C	
Sector efficiency and capacity			
Telecommunications revenue (% of GDP)	2.6	3.2	*5.0*
Telecommunications investment (% of revenue)	*32.8*	31.3	..
Sector performance			
Access			
Fixed-telephone subscriptions (per 100 people)	0.5	1.1	1.0
Mobile-cellular telephone subscriptions (per 100 people)	2.8	39.4	47.2
Fixed (wired)-broadband subscriptions (per 100 people)	0.0	0.0	0.2
Households with a computer (%)	0.5	2.9[a]	4.2
Households with Internet access at home (%)	0.4[a]	2.7[a]	3.4
Usage			
Int'l. voice traffic, total (minutes/subscription/month)	14.7	0.9	..
Domestic mobile traffic (minutes/subscription/month)	7.7	2.4	70.1
Individuals using the Internet (%)	0.6[a]	2.1[a]	6.2
Quality			
Population covered by a mobile-cellular network (%)	23	..	..
Fixed (wired)-broadband subscriptions (% of total Internet)	0.0	65.0	*30.9*
International Internet bandwidth (bit/s per Internet user)	327	493	9,141
Affordability			
Fixed-telephone sub-basket ($ a month)	..	8.8	8.9
Mobile-cellular sub-basket ($ a month)	..	17.7	11.9
Fixed-broadband sub-basket ($ a month)	..	63.7	46.9
Trade			
ICT goods exports (% of total goods exports)	0.3	0.1	..
ICT goods imports (% of total goods imports)	4.6	2.4	..
ICT service exports (% of total service exports)	19.6	..	..
Applications			
Online service index (0–1, 1=highest presence)	0.31	0.32	0.20
Secure Internet servers (per million people)	0.2	0.7	1.1

Malawi

Low income

	Country data		Low-income group
	2005	2012	2012
Economic and social context			
Population (millions)	13	16	846
Urban population (% of total)	15	16	28
GNI per capita, *World Bank Atlas* method ($)	220	320	590
GDP growth, 2000–05 and 2005–12 (avg. annual %)	2.5	3.6	5.9
Adult literacy rate (% ages 15 and older)	..	61	61
Gross primary, secondary, tertiary school enrollment (%)	64	69	60
Sector structure			
Separate telecommunications/ICT regulator	Yes	Yes	
Status of main fixed-line telephone operator	Public	Mixed	
Level of competition (competition, partial comp., monopoly)			
International gateway(s)	..	C	
Mobile telephone service	P	P	
Internet service	P	P	
Foreign ownership (not allowed, restricted, allowed)	R	R	
Reg. treatment of VoIP (banned, closed, no framework, allowed)	B	C	
Sector efficiency and capacity			
Telecommunications revenue (% of GDP)	3.4	3.4	5.0
Telecommunications investment (% of revenue)	..	..	..
Sector performance			
Access			
Fixed-telephone subscriptions (per 100 people)	0.8	1.4	1.0
Mobile-cellular telephone subscriptions (per 100 people)	3.3	29.2	47.2
Fixed (wired)-broadband subscriptions (per 100 people)	0.0	0.0	0.2
Households with a computer (%)	..	4.0	4.2
Households with Internet access at home (%)	..	5.5	3.4
Usage			
Int'l. voice traffic, total (minutes/subscription/month)	..	..	..
Domestic mobile traffic (minutes/subscription/month)	..	5.2	70.1
Individuals using the Internet (%)	0.4	4.4[a]	6.2
Quality			
Population covered by a mobile-cellular network (%)	70	85	..
Fixed (wired)-broadband subscriptions (% of total Internet)	2.7	0.3	30.9
International Internet bandwidth (bit/s per Internet user)	392	2,803	9,141
Affordability			
Fixed-telephone sub-basket ($ a month)	..	21.5	8.9
Mobile-cellular sub-basket ($ a month)	..	21.0	11.9
Fixed-broadband sub-basket ($ a month)	..	48.1	46.9
Trade			
ICT goods exports (% of total goods exports)	0.2	0.2	..
ICT goods imports (% of total goods imports)	3.5	3.5	..
ICT service exports (% of total service exports)	6.7	27.1	..
Applications			
Online service index (0–1, 1=highest presence)	0.29	0.22	0.20
Secure Internet servers (per million people)	0.2	0.9	1.1

Malaysia

East Asia & Pacific			Upper middle income

	Country data		Upper middle-income group
	2005	2012	2012
Economic and social context			
Population (millions)	26	29	2,391
Urban population (% of total)	68	73	61
GNI per capita, *World Bank Atlas* method ($)	5,240	9,820	6,969
GDP growth, 2000–05 and 2005–12 (avg. annual %)	5.1	4.4	6.2
Adult literacy rate (% ages 15 and older)	89	93	94
Gross primary, secondary, tertiary school enrollment (%)	71	..	76
Sector structure			
Separate telecommunications/ICT regulator	Yes	Yes	
Status of main fixed-line telephone operator	Mixed	Private	
Level of competition (competition, partial comp., monopoly)			
International gateway(s)	C	C	
Mobile telephone service	C	C	
Internet service	C	C	
Foreign ownership (not allowed, restricted, allowed)	R	R	
Reg. treatment of VoIP (banned, closed, no framework, allowed)	A	A	
Sector efficiency and capacity			
Telecommunications revenue (% of GDP)	4.6	4.6	2.5
Telecommunications investment (% of revenue)	22.5	14.4	18.2
Sector performance			
Access			
Fixed-telephone subscriptions (per 100 people)	16.9	15.7	19.4
Mobile-cellular telephone subscriptions (per 100 people)	75.6	141.3	92.4
Fixed (wired)-broadband subscriptions (per 100 people)	1.9	8.4	10.8
Households with a computer (%)	28.2	66.9	40.6
Households with Internet access at home (%)	15.0[a]	64.7	36.3
Usage			
Int'l. voice traffic, total (minutes/subscription/month)	..	..	1.3
Domestic mobile traffic (minutes/subscription/month)	..	..	284.4
Individuals using the Internet (%)	48.6	65.8	41.6
Quality			
Population covered by a mobile-cellular network (%)	93	97	99
Fixed (wired)-broadband subscriptions (% of total Internet)	11.6	27.6	95.5
International Internet bandwidth (bit/s per Internet user)	254	16,424	14,580
Affordability			
Fixed-telephone sub-basket ($ a month)	..	5.4	9.4
Mobile-cellular sub-basket ($ a month)	..	7.4	14.9
Fixed-broadband sub-basket ($ a month)	..	21.6	17.8
Trade			
ICT goods exports (% of total goods exports)	43.4	27.9	17.6
ICT goods imports (% of total goods imports)	38.0	23.1	14.7
ICT service exports (% of total service exports)	19.4	27.9	29.1
Applications			
Online service index (0–1, 1=highest presence)	0.61	0.79	0.42
Secure Internet servers (per million people)	14.6	66.8	18.5

Maldives

	Country data		Upper middle-income group
	2005	2012	2012
Economic and social context			
Population (millions)	0.30	0.34	2,391
Urban population (% of total)	34	42	61
GNI per capita, *World Bank Atlas* method ($)	3,420	5,750	6,969
GDP growth, 2000–05 and 2005–12 (avg. annual %)	7.1	7.0	6.2
Adult literacy rate (% ages 15 and older)	98	..	94
Gross primary, secondary, tertiary school enrollment (%)	77	..	76
Sector structure			
Separate telecommunications/ICT regulator	Yes	Yes	
Status of main fixed-line telephone operator	Mixed	Mixed	
Level of competition (competition, partial comp., monopoly)			
International gateway(s)	..	..	
Mobile telephone service	M	P	
Internet service	M	..	
Foreign ownership (not allowed, restricted, allowed)	..	A	
Reg. treatment of VoIP (banned, closed, no framework, allowed)	B	C	
Sector efficiency and capacity			
Telecommunications revenue (% of GDP)	9.6	..	2.5
Telecommunications investment (% of revenue)	15.2	..	18.2
Sector performance			
Access			
Fixed-telephone subscriptions (per 100 people)	10.9	6.8	19.4
Mobile-cellular telephone subscriptions (per 100 people)	68.4	165.6	92.4
Fixed (wired)-broadband subscriptions (per 100 people)	1.1	5.3	10.8
Households with a computer (%)	26.1[a]	67.2[a]	40.6
Households with Internet access at home (%)	7.0[a]	34.3[a]	36.3
Usage			
Int'l. voice traffic, total (minutes/subscription/month)	..	32.7	1.3
Domestic mobile traffic (minutes/subscription/month)	55.8	218.4	284.4
Individuals using the Internet (%)	6.9	38.9[a]	41.6
Quality			
Population covered by a mobile-cellular network (%)	91	100	99
Fixed (wired)-broadband subscriptions (% of total Internet)	71.7	100.0	95.5
International Internet bandwidth (bit/s per Internet user)	2,593	25,479	14,580
Affordability			
Fixed-telephone sub-basket ($ a month)	..	3.6	9.4
Mobile-cellular sub-basket ($ a month)	..	6.0	14.9
Fixed-broadband sub-basket ($ a month)	..	8.2	17.8
Trade			
ICT goods exports (% of total goods exports)	0.2	..	17.6
ICT goods imports (% of total goods imports)	11.2	4.3	14.7
ICT service exports (% of total service exports)	..	..	29.1
Applications			
Online service index (0–1, 1=highest presence)	0.45	0.33	0.42
Secure Internet servers (per million people)	6.7	87.0	18.5

Mali

	Country data 2005	Country data 2012	Low-income group 2012
Economic and social context			
Population (millions)	12	15	846
Urban population (% of total)	31	36	28
GNI per capita, *World Bank Atlas* method ($)	440	660	590
GDP growth, 2000–05 and 2005–12 (avg. annual %)	5.9	4.4	5.9
Adult literacy rate (% ages 15 and older)	26	33	61
Gross primary, secondary, tertiary school enrollment (%)	48	57	60
Sector structure			
Separate telecommunications/ICT regulator	Yes	Yes	
Status of main fixed-line telephone operator	Public	Mixed	
Level of competition (competition, partial comp., monopoly)			
International gateway(s)	..	P	
Mobile telephone service	P	P	
Internet service	C	C	
Foreign ownership (not allowed, restricted, allowed)	..	A	
Reg. treatment of VoIP (banned, closed, no framework, allowed)	B	B	
Sector efficiency and capacity			
Telecommunications revenue (% of GDP)	4.7	6.3	5.0
Telecommunications investment (% of revenue)	25.8	24.2	..
Sector performance			
Access			
Fixed-telephone subscriptions (per 100 people)	0.6	0.8	1.0
Mobile-cellular telephone subscriptions (per 100 people)	6.4	98.4	47.2
Fixed (wired)-broadband subscriptions (per 100 people)	0.0	0.0	0.2
Households with a computer (%)	1.0[a]	7.7[a]	4.2
Households with Internet access at home (%)	0.7[a]	2.5[a]	3.4
Usage			
Int'l. voice traffic, total (minutes/subscription/month)	5.0	5.2	..
Domestic mobile traffic (minutes/subscription/month)	9.9	19.3	70.1
Individuals using the Internet (%)	0.5	2.2[a]	6.2
Quality			
Population covered by a mobile-cellular network (%)	20	..	..
Fixed (wired)-broadband subscriptions (% of total Internet)	45.7	11.3	30.9
International Internet bandwidth (bit/s per Internet user)	429	5,292	9,141
Affordability			
Fixed-telephone sub-basket ($ a month)	..	8.3	8.9
Mobile-cellular sub-basket ($ a month)	..	15.5	11.9
Fixed-broadband sub-basket ($ a month)	..	50.0	46.9
Trade			
ICT goods exports (% of total goods exports)	0.2	0.0	..
ICT goods imports (% of total goods imports)	2.2	3.6	..
ICT service exports (% of total service exports)	21.9	33.9	..
Applications			
Online service index (0–1, 1=highest presence)	0.16	0.32	0.20
Secure Internet servers (per million people)	0.1	1.0	1.1

Malta

	Country data		High-income group
	2005	2012	2012
Economic and social context			
Population (millions)	0.40	0.42	1,300
Urban population (% of total)	94	95	80
GNI per capita, World Bank Atlas method ($)	14,380	19,710	38,412
GDP growth, 2000–05 and 2005–12 (avg. annual %)	0.8	1.9	1.0
Adult literacy rate (% ages 15 and older)	92	..	..
Gross primary, secondary, tertiary school enrollment (%)	77	81	93
Sector structure			
Separate telecommunications/ICT regulator	Yes	Yes	
Status of main fixed-line telephone operator	Mixed	Private	
Level of competition (competition, partial comp., monopoly)			
International gateway(s)	C	C	
Mobile telephone service	C	C	
Internet service	C	C	
Foreign ownership (not allowed, restricted, allowed)	A	A	
Reg. treatment of VoIP (banned, closed, no framework, allowed)	A	A	
Sector efficiency and capacity			
Telecommunications revenue (% of GDP)	5.4	3.0	2.7
Telecommunications investment (% of revenue)	15.1	22.3	17.6
Sector performance			
Access			
Fixed-telephone subscriptions (per 100 people)	48.7	53.7	43.6
Mobile-cellular telephone subscriptions (per 100 people)	78.1	127.0	122.9
Fixed (wired)-broadband subscriptions (per 100 people)	12.4	32.0	26.2
Households with a computer (%)	46.0	78.0	77.7
Households with Internet access at home (%)	40.6	77.0	75.5
Usage			
Int'l. voice traffic, total (minutes/subscription/month)	..	10.3	..
Domestic mobile traffic (minutes/subscription/month)	40.3	86.3	113.6
Individuals using the Internet (%)	41.2	70.0	75.4
Quality			
Population covered by a mobile-cellular network (%)	99	100	100
Fixed (wired)-broadband subscriptions (% of total Internet)	57.9	100.0	95.9
International Internet bandwidth (bit/s per Internet user)	4,531	625,752	85,990
Affordability			
Fixed-telephone sub-basket ($ a month)	..	13.6	25.2
Mobile-cellular sub-basket ($ a month)	..	28.2	20.6
Fixed-broadband sub-basket ($ a month)	..	19.3	29.2
Trade			
ICT goods exports (% of total goods exports)	45.2	20.2	8.9
ICT goods imports (% of total goods imports)	25.5	10.9	10.8
ICT service exports (% of total service exports)	15.3	12.3	30.8
Applications			
Online service index (0–1, 1=highest presence)	0.66	0.61	0.67
Secure Internet servers (per million people)	331.8	1,488.0	827.6

Marshall Islands

East Asia & Pacific   **Upper middle income**

	Country data		Upper middle-income group
	2005	2012	2012
Economic and social context			
Population (millions)	0.05	0.05	2,391
Urban population (% of total)	70	72	61
GNI per capita, *World Bank Atlas* method ($)	3,560	4,040	6,969
GDP growth, 2000–05 and 2005–12 (avg. annual %)	1.8	1.2	6.2
Adult literacy rate (% ages 15 and older)	..	..	94
Gross primary, secondary, tertiary school enrollment (%)	69	..	76
Sector structure			
Separate telecommunications/ICT regulator	No	No	
Status of main fixed-line telephone operator	Mixed	Mixed	
Level of competition (competition, partial comp., monopoly)			
International gateway(s)	..	M	
Mobile telephone service	..	M	
Internet service	..	M	
Foreign ownership (not allowed, restricted, allowed)	..	A	
Reg. treatment of VoIP (banned, closed, no framework, allowed)	B	B	
Sector efficiency and capacity			
Telecommunications revenue (% of GDP)	5.0	..	2.5
Telecommunications investment (% of revenue)	..	..	18.2
Sector performance			
Access			
Fixed-telephone subscriptions (per 100 people)	10.6	..	19.4
Mobile-cellular telephone subscriptions (per 100 people)	1.3	..	92.4
Fixed (wired)-broadband subscriptions (per 100 people)	0.0	0.0	10.8
Households with a computer (%)	..	..	40.6
Households with Internet access at home (%)	..	..	36.3
Usage			
Int'l. voice traffic, total (minutes/subscription/month)	..	..	1.3
Domestic mobile traffic (minutes/subscription/month)	..	..	284.4
Individuals using the Internet (%)	3.9	10.0[a]	41.6
Quality			
Population covered by a mobile-cellular network (%)	..	..	99
Fixed (wired)-broadband subscriptions (% of total Internet)	0.0	..	95.5
International Internet bandwidth (bit/s per Internet user)	1,153	8,562	14,580
Affordability			
Fixed-telephone sub-basket ($ a month)	..	45.8	9.4
Mobile-cellular sub-basket ($ a month)	..	22.2	14.9
Fixed-broadband sub-basket ($ a month)	..	50.0	17.8
Trade			
ICT goods exports (% of total goods exports)	..	..	17.6
ICT goods imports (% of total goods imports)	..	..	14.7
ICT service exports (% of total service exports)	..	..	29.1
Applications			
Online service index (0–1, 1=highest presence)	0.00	0.14	0.42
Secure Internet servers (per million people)	19.2	113.2	18.5

Mauritania

Lower middle income

	Country data		Lower middle-income group
	2005	2012	2012
Economic and social context			
Population (millions)	3	4	2,507
Urban population (% of total)	40	42	39
GNI per capita, *World Bank Atlas* method ($)	690	1,110	1,893
GDP growth, 2000–05 and 2005–12 (avg. annual %)	4.5	4.2	6.0
Adult literacy rate (% ages 15 and older)	51	59	71
Gross primary, secondary, tertiary school enrollment (%)	45	49	64
Sector structure			
Separate telecommunications/ICT regulator	Yes	Yes	
Status of main fixed-line telephone operator	Mixed	Mixed	
Level of competition (competition, partial comp., monopoly)			
International gateway(s)	C	C	
Mobile telephone service	C	C	
Internet service	C	C	
Foreign ownership (not allowed, restricted, allowed)	A	A	
Reg. treatment of VoIP (banned, closed, no framework, allowed)	B	C	
Sector efficiency and capacity			
Telecommunications revenue (% of GDP)	5.8	5.7	2.5
Telecommunications investment (% of revenue)	19.2	20.0	20.5
Sector performance			
Access			
Fixed-telephone subscriptions (per 100 people)	1.3	1.7	5.4
Mobile-cellular telephone subscriptions (per 100 people)	23.7	106.0	83.1
Fixed (wired)-broadband subscriptions (per 100 people)	0.0	0.2	1.4
Households with a computer (%)	1.6[a]	3.7[a]	15.0
Households with Internet access at home (%)	0.6[a]	3.4[a]	12.4
Usage			
Int'l. voice traffic, total (minutes/subscription/month)	8.7	5.3	6.5
Domestic mobile traffic (minutes/subscription/month)	47.1	68.0	..
Individuals using the Internet (%)	0.7	5.4[a]	18.7
Quality			
Population covered by a mobile-cellular network (%)	26	62	86
Fixed (wired)-broadband subscriptions (% of total Internet)	7.2	95.5	58.2
International Internet bandwidth (bit/s per Internet user)	2,135	3,042	8,076
Affordability			
Fixed-telephone sub-basket ($ a month)	..	17.6	4.9
Mobile-cellular sub-basket ($ a month)	..	14.6	10.5
Fixed-broadband sub-basket ($ a month)	..	22.3	20.6
Trade			
ICT goods exports (% of total goods exports)	..	..	4.6
ICT goods imports (% of total goods imports)	1.4	1.2	7.2
ICT service exports (% of total service exports)	..	..	47.1
Applications			
Online service index (0–1, 1=highest presence)	0.20	0.08	0.32
Secure Internet servers (per million people)	0.3	2.1	4.4

Mauritius

	Country data		Upper middle-income group
	2005	2012	2012
Sub-Saharan Africa			**Upper middle income**

	Country data		Upper middle-income group
	2005	**2012**	**2012**
Economic and social context			
Population (millions)	1	1	2,391
Urban population (% of total)	42	42	61
GNI per capita, *World Bank Atlas* method ($)	5,360	8,570	6,969
GDP growth, 2000–05 and 2005–12 (avg. annual %)	3.3	4.3	6.2
Adult literacy rate (% ages 15 and older)	84	89	94
Gross primary, secondary, tertiary school enrollment (%)	77	86	76
Sector structure			
Separate telecommunications/ICT regulator	Yes	Yes	
Status of main fixed-line telephone operator	Mixed	Mixed	
Level of competition (competition, partial comp., monopoly)			
International gateway(s)	C	C	
Mobile telephone service	C	C	
Internet service	C	C	
Foreign ownership (not allowed, restricted, allowed)	A	A	
Reg. treatment of VoIP (banned, closed, no framework, allowed)	A	A	
Sector efficiency and capacity			
Telecommunications revenue (% of GDP)	4.4	3.1	2.5
Telecommunications investment (% of revenue)	12.9	55.5	18.2
Sector performance			
Access			
Fixed-telephone subscriptions (per 100 people)	29.5	28.2	19.4
Mobile-cellular telephone subscriptions (per 100 people)	54.2	119.9	92.4
Fixed (wired)-broadband subscriptions (per 100 people)	0.4	11.2	10.8
Households with a computer (%)	22.5[a]	40.6[a]	40.6
Households with Internet access at home (%)	15.0[a]	42.0[a]	36.3
Usage			
Int'l. voice traffic, total (minutes/subscription/month)	14.5	11.6	1.3
Domestic mobile traffic (minutes/subscription/month)	80.8	125.1	284.4
Individuals using the Internet (%)	15.2[a]	41.4[a]	41.6
Quality			
Population covered by a mobile-cellular network (%)	100	99	99
Fixed (wired)-broadband subscriptions (% of total Internet)	6.3	96.2	95.5
International Internet bandwidth (bit/s per Internet user)	832	16,125	14,580
Affordability			
Fixed-telephone sub-basket ($ a month)	..	5.4	9.4
Mobile-cellular sub-basket ($ a month)	..	6.5	14.9
Fixed-broadband sub-basket ($ a month)	..	12.2	17.8
Trade			
ICT goods exports (% of total goods exports)	13.3	0.8	17.6
ICT goods imports (% of total goods imports)	12.8	5.1	14.7
ICT service exports (% of total service exports)	18.5	35.4	29.1
Applications			
Online service index (0–1, 1=highest presence)	0.51	0.43	0.42
Secure Internet servers (per million people)	18.5	127.3	18.5

Mexico

Latin America & Caribbean			Upper middle income

	Country data		Upper middle-income group
	2005	2012	2012
Economic and social context			
Population (millions)	111	121	2,391
Urban population (% of total)	76	78	61
GNI per capita, *World Bank Atlas* method ($)	7,710	9,640	6,969
GDP growth, 2000–05 and 2005–12 (avg. annual %)	1.7	1.9	6.2
Adult literacy rate (% ages 15 and older)	92	94	94
Gross primary, secondary, tertiary school enrollment (%)	73	76	76
Sector structure			
Separate telecommunications/ICT regulator	Yes	Yes	
Status of main fixed-line telephone operator	Private	Private	
Level of competition (competition, partial comp., monopoly)			
International gateway(s)	..	..	
Mobile telephone service	C	C	
Internet service	C	C	
Foreign ownership (not allowed, restricted, allowed)	R	R	
Reg. treatment of VoIP (banned, closed, no framework, allowed)	No	No	
Sector efficiency and capacity			
Telecommunications revenue (% of GDP)	2.5	2.6	2.5
Telecommunications investment (% of revenue)	15.9	22.2	18.2
Sector performance			
Access			
Fixed-telephone subscriptions (per 100 people)	17.6	16.7	19.4
Mobile-cellular telephone subscriptions (per 100 people)	42.6	83.4	92.4
Fixed (wired)-broadband subscriptions (per 100 people)	1.7	10.5	10.8
Households with a computer (%)	18.6	32.2	40.6
Households with Internet access at home (%)	8.9	26.0	36.3
Usage			
Int'l. voice traffic, total (minutes/subscription/month)	..	..	1.3
Domestic mobile traffic (minutes/subscription/month)	45.8	111.8	284.4
Individuals using the Internet (%)	17.2[a]	38.4	41.6
Quality			
Population covered by a mobile-cellular network (%)	100	100	99
Fixed (wired)-broadband subscriptions (% of total Internet)	49.5	98.3	95.5
International Internet bandwidth (bit/s per Internet user)	708	15,670	14,580
Affordability			
Fixed-telephone sub-basket ($ a month)	..	19.2	9.4
Mobile-cellular sub-basket ($ a month)	..	23.4	14.9
Fixed-broadband sub-basket ($ a month)	..	17.6	17.8
Trade			
ICT goods exports (% of total goods exports)	18.0	16.9	17.6
ICT goods imports (% of total goods imports)	17.1	16.5	14.7
ICT service exports (% of total service exports)	..	..	29.1
Applications			
Online service index (0–1, 1=highest presence)	0.59	0.73	0.42
Secure Internet servers (per million people)	7.8	26.5	18.5

Micronesia, Fed. Sts.

East Asia & Pacific			Lower middle income

	Country data		Lower middle-income group
	2005	2012	2012
Economic and social context			
Population (millions)	0.11	0.10	2,507
Urban population (% of total)	22	23	39
GNI per capita, *World Bank Atlas* method ($)	2,550	3,230	1,893
GDP growth, 2000–05 and 2005–12 (avg. annual %)	0.4	0.2	6.0
Adult literacy rate (% ages 15 and older)	..	..	71
Gross primary, secondary, tertiary school enrollment (%)	75	..	64
Sector structure			
Separate telecommunications/ICT regulator	No	No	
Status of main fixed-line telephone operator	Public	Public	
Level of competition (competition, partial comp., monopoly)			
International gateway(s)	..	*M*	
Mobile telephone service	C	*M*	
Internet service	..	*M*	
Foreign ownership (not allowed, restricted, allowed)	..	R	
Reg. treatment of VoIP (banned, closed, no framework, allowed)	No	A	
Sector efficiency and capacity			
Telecommunications revenue (% of GDP)	4.8	..	2.5
Telecommunications investment (% of revenue)	13.2	..	20.5
Sector performance			
Access			
Fixed-telephone subscriptions (per 100 people)	11.7	8.1	5.4
Mobile-cellular telephone subscriptions (per 100 people)	13.3	30.2	83.1
Fixed (wired)-broadband subscriptions (per 100 people)	0.0	1.0	1.4
Households with a computer (%)	..	..	15.0
Households with Internet access at home (%)	..	..	12.4
Usage			
Int'l. voice traffic, total (minutes/subscription/month)	..	..	6.5
Domestic mobile traffic (minutes/subscription/month)	44.2	..	..
Individuals using the Internet (%)	11.9	26.0[a]	18.7
Quality			
Population covered by a mobile-cellular network (%)	..	..	86
Fixed (wired)-broadband subscriptions (% of total Internet)	2.0	46.9	58.2
International Internet bandwidth (bit/s per Internet user)	476	1,930	8,076
Affordability			
Fixed-telephone sub-basket ($ a month)	..	147.0	4.9
Mobile-cellular sub-basket ($ a month)	..	13.6	10.5
Fixed-broadband sub-basket ($ a month)	..	33.0	20.6
Trade			
ICT goods exports (% of total goods exports)	..	..	4.6
ICT goods imports (% of total goods imports)	..	..	7.2
ICT service exports (% of total service exports)	..	..	47.1
Applications			
Online service index (0–1, 1=highest presence)	0.00	0.21	0.32
Secure Internet servers (per million people)	18.8	19.2	4.4

Moldova

Lower middle income

	Country data		Lower middle-income group
	2005	2012	2012
Economic and social context			
Population (millions)	4	4	2,507
Urban population (% of total)	43	48	39
GNI per capita, *World Bank Atlas* method ($)	890	2,070	1,893
GDP growth, 2000–05 and 2005–12 (avg. annual %)	7.1	3.1	6.0
Adult literacy rate (% ages 15 and older)	97	99	71
Gross primary, secondary, tertiary school enrollment (%)	71	64	64
Sector structure			
Separate telecommunications/ICT regulator	Yes	Yes	
Status of main fixed-line telephone operator	Public	Public	
Level of competition (competition, partial comp., monopoly)			
International gateway(s)	C	C	
Mobile telephone service	C	C	
Internet service	C	C	
Foreign ownership (not allowed, restricted, allowed)	A	A	
Reg. treatment of VoIP (banned, closed, no framework, allowed)	No	A	
Sector efficiency and capacity			
Telecommunications revenue (% of GDP)	9.7	4.7	2.5
Telecommunications investment (% of revenue)	31.4	42.0	20.5
Sector performance			
Access			
Fixed-telephone subscriptions (per 100 people)	24.7	34.3	5.4
Mobile-cellular telephone subscriptions (per 100 people)	28.9	102.0	83.1
Fixed (wired)-broadband subscriptions (per 100 people)	0.3	11.9	1.4
Households with a computer (%)	7.0	44.5[a]	15.0
Households with Internet access at home (%)	2.3[a]	42.0[a]	12.4
Usage			
Int'l. voice traffic, total (minutes/subscription/month)	22.2	17.2	6.5
Domestic mobile traffic (minutes/subscription/month)	36.4	103.1	..
Individuals using the Internet (%)	14.6	43.4[a]	18.7
Quality			
Population covered by a mobile-cellular network (%)	97	..	86
Fixed (wired)-broadband subscriptions (% of total Internet)	17.0	100.0	58.2
International Internet bandwidth (bit/s per Internet user)	744	94,175	8,076
Affordability			
Fixed-telephone sub-basket ($ a month)	..	0.5	4.9
Mobile-cellular sub-basket ($ a month)	..	13.2	10.5
Fixed-broadband sub-basket ($ a month)	..	12.8	20.6
Trade			
ICT goods exports (% of total goods exports)	0.3	0.3	4.6
ICT goods imports (% of total goods imports)	3.6	3.3	7.2
ICT service exports (% of total service exports)	21.2	25.3	47.1
Applications			
Online service index (0–1, 1=highest presence)	0.45	0.52	0.32
Secure Internet servers (per million people)	4.2	25.3	4.4

Monaco

	Country data		High-income group
	2005	2012	2012
Economic and social context			
Population (millions)	0.03	0.04	1,300
Urban population (% of total)	100	100	80
GNI per capita, World Bank Atlas method ($)	128,380	186,950	38,412
GDP growth, 2000–05 and 2005–12 (avg. annual %)	1.7	..	1.0
Adult literacy rate (% ages 15 and older)	..	..	..
Gross primary, secondary, tertiary school enrollment (%)	..	..	93
Sector structure			
Separate telecommunications/ICT regulator	No	No	
Status of main fixed-line telephone operator	Private	Private	
Level of competition (competition, partial comp., monopoly)			
International gateway(s)	..	P	
Mobile telephone service	M	M	
Internet service	C	M	
Foreign ownership (not allowed, restricted, allowed)	A	A	
Reg. treatment of VoIP (banned, closed, no framework, allowed)	..	..	
Sector efficiency and capacity			
Telecommunications revenue (% of GDP)	5.4	..	2.7
Telecommunications investment (% of revenue)	7.6	..	17.6
Sector performance			
Access			
Fixed-telephone subscriptions (per 100 people)	100.5	121.7	43.6
Mobile-cellular telephone subscriptions (per 100 people)	50.8	88.3	122.9
Fixed (wired)-broadband subscriptions (per 100 people)	28.1	43.3	26.2
Households with a computer (%)	63.5[a]	73.5[a]	77.7
Households with Internet access at home (%)	40.1[a]	70.9[a]	75.5
Usage			
Int'l. voice traffic, total (minutes/subscription/month)	241.5	114.6	..
Domestic mobile traffic (minutes/subscription/month)	49.0	125.4	113.6
Individuals using the Internet (%)	55.5	87.0[a]	75.4
Quality			
Population covered by a mobile-cellular network (%)	100	100	100
Fixed (wired)-broadband subscriptions (% of total Internet)	96.9	100.0	95.9
International Internet bandwidth (bit/s per Internet user)	6,129	244,695	85,990
Affordability			
Fixed-telephone sub-basket ($ a month)	..	21.2	25.2
Mobile-cellular sub-basket ($ a month)	..	52.6	20.6
Fixed-broadband sub-basket ($ a month)	..	45.9	29.2
Trade			
ICT goods exports (% of total goods exports)	..	..	8.9
ICT goods imports (% of total goods imports)	..	..	10.8
ICT service exports (% of total service exports)	..	..	30.8
Applications			
Online service index (0–1, 1=highest presence)	0.00	0.36	0.67
Secure Internet servers (per million people)	709.9	2,736.8	827.6

Mongolia

Lower middle income

	Country data		Lower middle-income group
	2005	2012	2012
Economic and social context			
Population (millions)	3	3	2,507
Urban population (% of total)	62	69	39
GNI per capita, *World Bank Atlas* method ($)	900	3,160	1,893
GDP growth, 2000–05 and 2005–12 (avg. annual %)	6.7	8.0	6.0
Adult literacy rate (% ages 15 and older)	*98*	*97*	*71*
Gross primary, secondary, tertiary school enrollment (%)	79	93	64
Sector structure			
Separate telecommunications/ICT regulator	Yes	Yes	
Status of main fixed-line telephone operator	Mixed	Mixed	
Level of competition (competition, partial comp., monopoly)			
International gateway(s)	C	*P*	
Mobile telephone service	P	*P*	
Internet service	C	*C*	
Foreign ownership (not allowed, restricted, allowed)	R	R	
Reg. treatment of VoIP (banned, closed, no framework, allowed)	A	A	
Sector efficiency and capacity			
Telecommunications revenue (% of GDP)	3.3	4.2	*2.5*
Telecommunications investment (% of revenue)	15.1	19.1	*20.5*
Sector performance			
Access			
Fixed-telephone subscriptions (per 100 people)	6.2	6.3	5.4
Mobile-cellular telephone subscriptions (per 100 people)	22.1	120.7	83.1
Fixed (wired)-broadband subscriptions (per 100 people)	0.1	3.7	1.4
Households with a computer (%)	6.3[a]	30.3	15.0
Households with Internet access at home (%)	2.3[a]	14.0	12.4
Usage			
Int'l. voice traffic, total (minutes/subscription/month)	..	4.2	6.5
Domestic mobile traffic (minutes/subscription/month)	0.3	99.4	..
Individuals using the Internet (%)	9.0[a]	16.4	18.7
Quality			
Population covered by a mobile-cellular network (%)	29	91	*86*
Fixed (wired)-broadband subscriptions (% of total Internet)	20.0	98.8	*58.2*
International Internet bandwidth (bit/s per Internet user)	5,138	94,295	8,076
Affordability			
Fixed-telephone sub-basket ($ a month)	..	1.1	4.9
Mobile-cellular sub-basket ($ a month)	..	5.7	10.5
Fixed-broadband sub-basket ($ a month)	..	10.3	20.6
Trade			
ICT goods exports (% of total goods exports)	0.0	..	4.6
ICT goods imports (% of total goods imports)	5.0	..	7.2
ICT service exports (% of total service exports)	6.0	20.7	47.1
Applications			
Online service index (0–1, 1=highest presence)	0.47	0.59	0.32
Secure Internet servers (per million people)	3.2	22.2	4.4

Montenegro

	Country data		Upper middle-income group
	2005	2012	2012
Economic and social context			
Population (millions)	0.62	0.62	2,391
Urban population (% of total)	62	63	61
GNI per capita, *World Bank Atlas* method ($)	3,650	7,220	6,969
GDP growth, 2000–05 and 2005–12 (avg. annual %)	2.8	3.1	6.2
Adult literacy rate (% ages 15 and older)	..	98	94
Gross primary, secondary, tertiary school enrollment (%)	75	89	76
Sector structure			
Separate telecommunications/ICT regulator	Yes	Yes	
Status of main fixed-line telephone operator	Mixed	Mixed	
Level of competition (competition, partial comp., monopoly)			
International gateway(s)	C	C	
Mobile telephone service	C	C	
Internet service	C	C	
Foreign ownership (not allowed, restricted, allowed)	..	A	
Reg. treatment of VoIP (banned, closed, no framework, allowed)	No	A	
Sector efficiency and capacity			
Telecommunications revenue (% of GDP)	..	..	2.5
Telecommunications investment (% of revenue)	..	..	18.2
Sector performance			
Access			
Fixed-telephone subscriptions (per 100 people)	27.8	26.2[a]	19.4
Mobile-cellular telephone subscriptions (per 100 people)	88.2	181.3	92.4
Fixed (wired)-broadband subscriptions (per 100 people)	1.2	8.4	10.8
Households with a computer (%)	18.6	51.3	40.6
Households with Internet access at home (%)	13.0[a]	55.0	36.3
Usage			
Int'l. voice traffic, total (minutes/subscription/month)	..	..	1.3
Domestic mobile traffic (minutes/subscription/month)	110.7	..	284.4
Individuals using the Internet (%)	27.1[a]	56.8	41.6
Quality			
Population covered by a mobile-cellular network (%)	99	100	99
Fixed (wired)-broadband subscriptions (% of total Internet)	9.5	..	95.5
International Internet bandwidth (bit/s per Internet user)	1,438	60,621	14,580
Affordability			
Fixed-telephone sub-basket ($ a month)	..	8.3	9.4
Mobile-cellular sub-basket ($ a month)	..	17.5	14.9
Fixed-broadband sub-basket ($ a month)	..	19.5	17.8
Trade			
ICT goods exports (% of total goods exports)	..	0.4	17.6
ICT goods imports (% of total goods imports)	..	3.0	14.7
ICT service exports (% of total service exports)	9.5	7.9	29.1
Applications			
Online service index (0–1, 1=highest presence)	0.43	0.51	0.42
Secure Internet servers (per million people)	..	37.0	18.5

Morocco

	Country data		Lower middle-income group
	2005	2012	2012
Economic and social context			
Population (millions)	30	33	2,507
Urban population (% of total)	55	57	39
GNI per capita, World Bank Atlas method ($)	1,980	2,960	1,893
GDP growth, 2000–05 and 2005–12 (avg. annual %)	5.0	4.7	6.0
Adult literacy rate (% ages 15 and older)	52	67	71
Gross primary, secondary, tertiary school enrollment (%)	59	67	64
Sector structure			
Separate telecommunications/ICT regulator	Yes	Yes	
Status of main fixed-line telephone operator	Mixed	Mixed	
Level of competition (competition, partial comp., monopoly)			
International gateway(s)	C	C	
Mobile telephone service	C	C	
Internet service	C	C	
Foreign ownership (not allowed, restricted, allowed)	A	A	
Reg. treatment of VoIP (banned, closed, no framework, allowed)	C	A	
Sector efficiency and capacity			
Telecommunications revenue (% of GDP)	4.6	4.3	2.5
Telecommunications investment (% of revenue)	17.0	16.7	20.5
Sector performance			
Access			
Fixed-telephone subscriptions (per 100 people)	4.5	10.1	5.4
Mobile-cellular telephone subscriptions (per 100 people)	41.1	120.0	83.1
Fixed (wired)-broadband subscriptions (per 100 people)	0.8	2.1	1.4
Households with a computer (%)	13.2	43.1	15.0
Households with Internet access at home (%)	4.3	38.9	12.4
Usage			
Int'l. voice traffic, total (minutes/subscription/month)	12.7	9.9	6.5
Domestic mobile traffic (minutes/subscription/month)	7.8	68.2	..
Individuals using the Internet (%)	15.1	55.0	18.7
Quality			
Population covered by a mobile-cellular network (%)	98	99	86
Fixed (wired)-broadband subscriptions (% of total Internet)	95.0	99.7	58.2
International Internet bandwidth (bit/s per Internet user)	1,562	14,871	8,076
Affordability			
Fixed-telephone sub-basket ($ a month)	..	2.3	4.9
Mobile-cellular sub-basket ($ a month)	..	23.2	10.5
Fixed-broadband sub-basket ($ a month)	..	12.2	20.6
Trade			
ICT goods exports (% of total goods exports)	6.0	3.1	4.6
ICT goods imports (% of total goods imports)	7.0	3.5	7.2
ICT service exports (% of total service exports)	17.0	21.8	47.1
Applications			
Online service index (0–1, 1=highest presence)	0.29	0.54	0.32
Secure Internet servers (per million people)	0.7	3.6	4.4

Mozambique

	Country data		Low-income group
	2005	2012	2012
Economic and social context			
Population (millions)	21	25	846
Urban population (% of total)	30	31	28
GNI per capita, *World Bank Atlas* method ($)	290	510	590
GDP growth, 2000–05 and 2005–12 (avg. annual %)	8.5	6.9	5.9
Adult literacy rate (% ages 15 and older)	48	51	61
Gross primary, secondary, tertiary school enrollment (%)	52	61	60
Sector structure			
Separate telecommunications/ICT regulator	Yes	Yes	
Status of main fixed-line telephone operator	Mixed	Mixed	
Level of competition (competition, partial comp., monopoly)			
International gateway(s)	C	C	
Mobile telephone service	C	C	
Internet service	C	C	
Foreign ownership (not allowed, restricted, allowed)	R	R	
Reg. treatment of VoIP (banned, closed, no framework, allowed)	B	B	
Sector efficiency and capacity			
Telecommunications revenue (% of GDP)	1.5	6.2	5.0
Telecommunications investment (% of revenue)	24.6	21.7	..
Sector performance			
Access			
Fixed-telephone subscriptions (per 100 people)	0.3	0.3	1.0
Mobile-cellular telephone subscriptions (per 100 people)	7.2	36.2	47.2
Fixed (wired)-broadband subscriptions (per 100 people)	0.0	0.1	0.2
Households with a computer (%)	0.6[a]	5.9[a]	4.2
Households with Internet access at home (%)	0.8[a]	4.7[a]	3.4
Usage			
Int'l. voice traffic, total (minutes/subscription/month)	..	0.8	..
Domestic mobile traffic (minutes/subscription/month)	25.6	26.4	70.1
Individuals using the Internet (%)	0.9[a]	4.8[a]	6.2
Quality			
Population covered by a mobile-cellular network (%)	..	..	
Fixed (wired)-broadband subscriptions (% of total Internet)	..	132.8	30.9
International Internet bandwidth (bit/s per Internet user)	106	1,636	9,141
Affordability			
Fixed-telephone sub-basket ($ a month)	..	12.9	8.9
Mobile-cellular sub-basket ($ a month)	..	13.0	11.9
Fixed-broadband sub-basket ($ a month)	..	58.5	46.9
Trade			
ICT goods exports (% of total goods exports)	0.1	0.0	..
ICT goods imports (% of total goods imports)	4.5	2.3	..
ICT service exports (% of total service exports)	20.6	31.1	..
Applications			
Online service index (0–1, 1=highest presence)	0.26	0.37	0.20
Secure Internet servers (per million people)	0.1	1.6	1.1

Myanmar

Low income

	Country data		Low-income group
	2005	2012	2012
Economic and social context			
Population (millions)	50	53	846
Urban population (% of total)	29	33	28
GNI per capita, *World Bank Atlas* method ($)	..	..	590
GDP growth, 2000–05 and 2005–12 (avg. annual %)	12.8	..	5.9
Adult literacy rate (% ages 15 and older)	90	93	61
Gross primary, secondary, tertiary school enrollment (%)	53	..	60
Sector structure			
Separate telecommunications/ICT regulator	No	No	
Status of main fixed-line telephone operator	Public	Public	
Level of competition (competition, partial comp., monopoly)			
International gateway(s)	M	M	
Mobile telephone service	M	M	
Internet service	P	M	
Foreign ownership (not allowed, restricted, allowed)	..	A	
Reg. treatment of VoIP (banned, closed, no framework, allowed)	C	B	
Sector efficiency and capacity			
Telecommunications revenue (% of GDP)	..	..	5.0
Telecommunications investment (% of revenue)	8.6	..	..
Sector performance			
Access			
Fixed-telephone subscriptions (per 100 people)	1.0	1.1	1.0
Mobile-cellular telephone subscriptions (per 100 people)	0.3	10.3	47.2
Fixed (wired)-broadband subscriptions (per 100 people)	0.0	0.0	0.2
Households with a computer (%)	0.3[a]	2.3[a]	4.2
Households with Internet access at home (%)	0.2[a]	1.8[a]	3.4
Usage			
Int'l. voice traffic, total (minutes/subscription/month)	15.2	..	..
Domestic mobile traffic (minutes/subscription/month)	..	..	70.1
Individuals using the Internet (%)	0.1	1.1[a]	6.2
Quality			
Population covered by a mobile-cellular network (%)	10	2	..
Fixed (wired)-broadband subscriptions (% of total Internet)	3.8	72.8	30.9
International Internet bandwidth (bit/s per Internet user)	2,871	9,425	9,141
Affordability			
Fixed-telephone sub-basket ($ a month)	..	0.9	8.9
Mobile-cellular sub-basket ($ a month)	..	12.8	11.9
Fixed-broadband sub-basket ($ a month)	..	28.5	46.9
Trade			
ICT goods exports (% of total goods exports)	..	0.0	..
ICT goods imports (% of total goods imports)	..	1.7	..
ICT service exports (% of total service exports)	..	..	..
Applications			
Online service index (0–1, 1=highest presence)	0.29	0.10	0.20
Secure Internet servers (per million people)	0.0	0.1	1.1

Namibia

	Country data		Upper middle-income group
	2005	2012	2012
Economic and social context			
Population (millions)	2	2	2,391
Urban population (% of total)	35	39	61
GNI per capita, *World Bank Atlas* method ($)	3,390	5,610	6,969
GDP growth, 2000–05 and 2005–12 (avg. annual %)	5.4	4.1	6.2
Adult literacy rate (% ages 15 and older)	76	..	94
Gross primary, secondary, tertiary school enrollment (%)	71	..	76
Sector structure			
Separate telecommunications/ICT regulator	Yes	Yes	
Status of main fixed-line telephone operator	Public	Public	
Level of competition (competition, partial comp., monopoly)			
International gateway(s)	M	C	
Mobile telephone service	M	C	
Internet service	C	C	
Foreign ownership (not allowed, restricted, allowed)	R	R	
Reg. treatment of VoIP (banned, closed, no framework, allowed)	B	A	
Sector efficiency and capacity			
Telecommunications revenue (% of GDP)	*4.1*	3.2	2.5
Telecommunications investment (% of revenue)	*7.5*	12.3	18.2
Sector performance			
Access			
Fixed-telephone subscriptions (per 100 people)	6.9	7.6	19.4
Mobile-cellular telephone subscriptions (per 100 people)	22.1	95.0	92.4
Fixed (wired)-broadband subscriptions (per 100 people)	0.0	1.2	10.8
Households with a computer (%)	6.9[a]	14.3[a]	40.6
Households with Internet access at home (%)	3.0[a]	13.0[a]	36.3
Usage			
Int'l. voice traffic, total (minutes/subscription/month)	..	6.0	1.3
Domestic mobile traffic (minutes/subscription/month)	..	92.6	284.4
Individuals using the Internet (%)	4.0[a]	12.9[a]	41.6
Quality			
Population covered by a mobile-cellular network (%)	88	100	99
Fixed (wired)-broadband subscriptions (% of total Internet)	0.2	..	95.5
International Internet bandwidth (bit/s per Internet user)	443	3,564	14,580
Affordability			
Fixed-telephone sub-basket ($ a month)	..	12.8	9.4
Mobile-cellular sub-basket ($ a month)	..	16.0	14.9
Fixed-broadband sub-basket ($ a month)	..	68.7	17.8
Trade			
ICT goods exports (% of total goods exports)	0.5	0.6	17.6
ICT goods imports (% of total goods imports)	4.8	3.1	14.7
ICT service exports (% of total service exports)	4.7	27.0	29.1
Applications			
Online service index (0–1, 1=highest presence)	0.34	0.30	0.42
Secure Internet servers (per million people)	6.9	18.2	18.5

Nepal

	Country data		Low-income group
	2005	2012	2012
Economic and social context			
Population (millions)	25	27	846
Urban population (% of total)	15	17	28
GNI per capita, *World Bank Atlas* method ($)	320	700	590
GDP growth, 2000–05 and 2005–12 (avg. annual %)	3.3	4.5	5.9
Adult literacy rate (% ages 15 and older)	*49*	*57*	*61*
Gross primary, secondary, tertiary school enrollment (%)	64	77	60
Sector structure			
Separate telecommunications/ICT regulator	Yes	Yes	
Status of main fixed-line telephone operator	Public	Mixed	
Level of competition (competition, partial comp., monopoly)			
International gateway(s)	P	C	
Mobile telephone service	P	P	
Internet service	C	C	
Foreign ownership (not allowed, restricted, allowed)	R	R	
Reg. treatment of VoIP (banned, closed, no framework, allowed)	B	A	
Sector efficiency and capacity			
Telecommunications revenue (% of GDP)	0.9	..	*5.0*
Telecommunications investment (% of revenue)	*26.7*	..	..
Sector performance			
Access			
Fixed-telephone subscriptions (per 100 people)	1.9	3.0	1.0
Mobile-cellular telephone subscriptions (per 100 people)	0.9	59.6	47.2
Fixed (wired)-broadband subscriptions (per 100 people)	0.0	0.5	0.2
Households with a computer (%)	*1.9*	7.8[a]	4.2
Households with Internet access at home (%)	0.7[a]	4.1[a]	3.4
Usage			
Int'l. voice traffic, total (minutes/subscription/month)	..	..	..
Domestic mobile traffic (minutes/subscription/month)	..	..	70.1
Individuals using the Internet (%)	0.8	11.1[a]	6.2
Quality			
Population covered by a mobile-cellular network (%)	*10*	*35*	..
Fixed (wired)-broadband subscriptions (% of total Internet)	0.0	64.8	*30.9*
International Internet bandwidth (bit/s per Internet user)	226	1,632	9,141
Affordability			
Fixed-telephone sub-basket ($ a month)	..	2.7	8.9
Mobile-cellular sub-basket ($ a month)	..	3.5	11.9
Fixed-broadband sub-basket ($ a month)	..	8.0	46.9
Trade			
ICT goods exports (% of total goods exports)	..	*0.2*	..
ICT goods imports (% of total goods imports)	4.5	5.3	..
ICT service exports (% of total service exports)	27.2	41.5	..
Applications			
Online service index (0–1, 1=highest presence)	0.27	0.29	0.20
Secure Internet servers (per million people)	0.5	2.4	1.1

Netherlands

	Country data		High-income group
	2005	2012	2012
Economic and social context			
Population (millions)	16	17	1,300
Urban population (% of total)	80	84	80
GNI per capita, *World Bank Atlas* method ($)	39,880	48,000	38,412
GDP growth, 2000–05 and 2005–12 (avg. annual %)	1.2	0.7	1.0
Adult literacy rate (% ages 15 and older)	..	..	..
Gross primary, secondary, tertiary school enrollment (%)	97	106	93
Sector structure			
Separate telecommunications/ICT regulator	Yes	Yes	
Status of main fixed-line telephone operator	Mixed	Mixed	
Level of competition (competition, partial comp., monopoly)			
International gateway(s)	..	C	
Mobile telephone service	P	C	
Internet service	P	C	
Foreign ownership (not allowed, restricted, allowed)	A	A	
Reg. treatment of VoIP (banned, closed, no framework, allowed)	A	A	
Sector efficiency and capacity			
Telecommunications revenue (% of GDP)	2.2	1.7	2.7
Telecommunications investment (% of revenue)	13.2	26.3	17.6
Sector performance			
Access			
Fixed-telephone subscriptions (per 100 people)	46.6	43.0	43.6
Mobile-cellular telephone subscriptions (per 100 people)	97.1	118.0	122.9
Fixed (wired)-broadband subscriptions (per 100 people)	25.1	39.8	26.2
Households with a computer (%)	78.0	97.2[a]	77.7
Households with Internet access at home (%)	78.3	94.0	75.5
Usage			
Int'l. voice traffic, total (minutes/subscription/month)	..	..	..
Domestic mobile traffic (minutes/subscription/month)	38.8	95.0	113.6
Individuals using the Internet (%)	81.0	93.0	75.4
Quality			
Population covered by a mobile-cellular network (%)	100	100	100
Fixed (wired)-broadband subscriptions (% of total Internet)	73.2	100.0	95.9
International Internet bandwidth (bit/s per Internet user)	25,338	172,864	85,990
Affordability			
Fixed-telephone sub-basket ($ a month)	..	35.1	25.2
Mobile-cellular sub-basket ($ a month)	..	43.5	20.6
Fixed-broadband sub-basket ($ a month)	..	35.4	29.2
Trade			
ICT goods exports (% of total goods exports)	16.8	10.2	8.9
ICT goods imports (% of total goods imports)	18.7	12.1	10.8
ICT service exports (% of total service exports)	45.5	45.2	30.8
Applications			
Online service index (0–1, 1=highest presence)	0.86	0.96	0.67
Secure Internet servers (per million people)	327.1	2,391.3	827.6

New Caledonia

High income

	Country data		High-income group
	2005	2012	2012
Economic and social context			
Population (millions)	0.23	0.26	1,300
Urban population (% of total)	63	62	80
GNI per capita, *World Bank Atlas* method ($)	..	..	38,412
GDP growth, 2000–05 and 2005–12 (avg. annual %)	..	..	1.0
Adult literacy rate (% ages 15 and older)	..	97	..
Gross primary, secondary, tertiary school enrollment (%)	..	..	93
Sector structure			
Separate telecommunications/ICT regulator	..	..	
Status of main fixed-line telephone operator	..	..	
Level of competition (competition, partial comp., monopoly)			
International gateway(s)	..	..	
Mobile telephone service	..	..	
Internet service	..	..	
Foreign ownership (not allowed, restricted, allowed)	..	..	
Reg. treatment of VoIP (banned, closed, no framework, allowed)	B	A	
Sector efficiency and capacity			
Telecommunications revenue (% of GDP)	..	..	2.7
Telecommunications investment (% of revenue)	..	..	17.6
Sector performance			
Access			
Fixed-telephone subscriptions (per 100 people)	24.2	31.6	43.6
Mobile-cellular telephone subscriptions (per 100 people)	58.7	91.2	122.9
Fixed (wired)-broadband subscriptions (per 100 people)	4.2	18.9	26.2
Households with a computer (%)	18.2	28.2[a]	77.7
Households with Internet access at home (%)	8.0[a]	20.3[a]	75.5
Usage			
Int'l. voice traffic, total (minutes/subscription/month)	..	..	..
Domestic mobile traffic (minutes/subscription/month)	60.1	..	113.6
Individuals using the Internet (%)	32.4	58.0[a]	75.4
Quality			
Population covered by a mobile-cellular network (%)	75[a]	89	100
Fixed (wired)-broadband subscriptions (% of total Internet)	51.2	100.0	95.9
International Internet bandwidth (bit/s per Internet user)	1,784	20,432	85,990
Affordability			
Fixed-telephone sub-basket ($ a month)	..	..	25.2
Mobile-cellular sub-basket ($ a month)	..	..	20.6
Fixed-broadband sub-basket ($ a month)	..	..	29.2
Trade			
ICT goods exports (% of total goods exports)	0.2	0.2	8.9
ICT goods imports (% of total goods imports)	4.6	3.3	10.8
ICT service exports (% of total service exports)	8.6	12.7	30.8
Applications			
Online service index (0–1, 1=highest presence)	..	..	0.67
Secure Internet servers (per million people)	68.3	242.3	827.6

New Zealand

	Country data		High-income group
	2005	2012	2012
Economic and social context			
Population (millions)	4	4	1,300
Urban population (% of total)	86	86	80
GNI per capita, *World Bank Atlas* method ($)	25,150	36,900	38,412
GDP growth, 2000–05 and 2005–12 (avg. annual %)	4.0	1.2	1.0
Adult literacy rate (% ages 15 and older)	..	..	..
Gross primary, secondary, tertiary school enrollment (%)	106	107	93
Sector structure			
Separate telecommunications/ICT regulator	Yes	Yes	
Status of main fixed-line telephone operator	Private	Private	
Level of competition (competition, partial comp., monopoly)			
International gateway(s)	C	C	
Mobile telephone service	C	C	
Internet service	C	C	
Foreign ownership (not allowed, restricted, allowed)	A	A	
Reg. treatment of VoIP (banned, closed, no framework, allowed)	A	A	
Sector efficiency and capacity			
Telecommunications revenue (% of GDP)	4.3	2.5	2.7
Telecommunications investment (% of revenue)	6.1	24.1	17.6
Sector performance			
Access			
Fixed-telephone subscriptions (per 100 people)	41.8	42.2	43.6
Mobile-cellular telephone subscriptions (per 100 people)	85.4	110.4	122.9
Fixed (wired)-broadband subscriptions (per 100 people)	7.8	27.8	26.2
Households with a computer (%)	67.8a	91.2a	77.7
Households with Internet access at home (%)	62.1a	87.4a	75.5
Usage			
Int'l. voice traffic, total (minutes/subscription/month)	..	..	..
Domestic mobile traffic (minutes/subscription/month)	29.5	73.6	113.6
Individuals using the Internet (%)	62.7a	89.5a	75.4
Quality			
Population covered by a mobile-cellular network (%)	98	97	100
Fixed (wired)-broadband subscriptions (% of total Internet)	27.8	90.5	95.9
International Internet bandwidth (bit/s per Internet user)	1,764	31,062	85,990
Affordability			
Fixed-telephone sub-basket ($ a month)	..	53.4	25.2
Mobile-cellular sub-basket ($ a month)	..	51.6	20.6
Fixed-broadband sub-basket ($ a month)	..	59.2	29.2
Trade			
ICT goods exports (% of total goods exports)	1.7	1.1	8.9
ICT goods imports (% of total goods imports)	9.6	7.7	10.8
ICT service exports (% of total service exports)	12.5	18.6	30.8
Applications			
Online service index (0–1, 1=highest presence)	0.74	0.78	0.67
Secure Internet servers (per million people)	489.9	1,093.8	827.6

Nicaragua

	Country data		Lower middle-income group
	2005	2012	2012
Economic and social context			
Population (millions)	5	6	2,507
Urban population (% of total)	56	58	39
GNI per capita, World Bank Atlas method ($)	1,160	1,650	1,893
GDP growth, 2000–05 and 2005–12 (avg. annual %)	3.1	3.2	6.0
Adult literacy rate (% ages 15 and older)	78	..	71
Gross primary, secondary, tertiary school enrollment (%)	..	..	64
Sector structure			
Separate telecommunications/ICT regulator	Yes	Yes	
Status of main fixed-line telephone operator	Private	Private	
Level of competition (competition, partial comp., monopoly)			
International gateway(s)	..	M	
Mobile telephone service	C	C	
Internet service	C	C	
Foreign ownership (not allowed, restricted, allowed)	A	A	
Reg. treatment of VoIP (banned, closed, no framework, allowed)	B	A	
Sector efficiency and capacity			
Telecommunications revenue (% of GDP)	2.9	..	2.5
Telecommunications investment (% of revenue)	24.0	..	20.5
Sector performance			
Access			
Fixed-telephone subscriptions (per 100 people)	4.0	5.0	5.4
Mobile-cellular telephone subscriptions (per 100 people)	20.5	86.1	83.1
Fixed (wired)-broadband subscriptions (per 100 people)	0.2	1.6	1.4
Households with a computer (%)	3.8	9.9[a]	15.0
Households with Internet access at home (%)	0.1	7.4[a]	12.4
Usage			
Int'l. voice traffic, total (minutes/subscription/month)	..	..	6.5
Domestic mobile traffic (minutes/subscription/month)	..	..	..
Individuals using the Internet (%)	2.6	13.5[a]	18.7
Quality			
Population covered by a mobile-cellular network (%)	70	100	86
Fixed (wired)-broadband subscriptions (% of total Internet)	45.0	100.0	58.2
International Internet bandwidth (bit/s per Internet user)	43	24,725	8,076
Affordability			
Fixed-telephone sub-basket ($ a month)	..	3.8	4.9
Mobile-cellular sub-basket ($ a month)	..	27.8	10.5
Fixed-broadband sub-basket ($ a month)	..	22.2	20.6
Trade			
ICT goods exports (% of total goods exports)	0.1	0.2	4.6
ICT goods imports (% of total goods imports)	6.1	4.1	7.2
ICT service exports (% of total service exports)	..	18.7	47.1
Applications			
Online service index (0–1, 1=highest presence)	0.37	0.31	0.32
Secure Internet servers (per million people)	2.0	8.4	4.4

Niger

Sub-Saharan Africa   **Low income**

	Country data		Low-income group
	2005	2012	2012
Economic and social context			
Population (millions)	13	17	846
Urban population (% of total)	17	18	28
GNI per capita, *World Bank Atlas* method ($)	250	390	590
GDP growth, 2000–05 and 2005–12 (avg. annual %)	3.7	5.2	5.9
Adult literacy rate (% ages 15 and older)	29	..	61
Gross primary, secondary, tertiary school enrollment (%)	26	38	60
Sector structure			
Separate telecommunications/ICT regulator	Yes	Yes	
Status of main fixed-line telephone operator	Mixed	Mixed	
Level of competition (competition, partial comp., monopoly)			
International gateway(s)	..	..	
Mobile telephone service	C	C	
Internet service	M	M	
Foreign ownership (not allowed, restricted, allowed)	R	R	
Reg. treatment of VoIP (banned, closed, no framework, allowed)	B	B	
Sector efficiency and capacity			
Telecommunications revenue (% of GDP)	2.2	4.6	5.0
Telecommunications investment (% of revenue)	56.5	..	..
Sector performance			
Access			
Fixed-telephone subscriptions (per 100 people)	0.2	0.6	1.0
Mobile-cellular telephone subscriptions (per 100 people)	2.5	31.4	47.2
Fixed (wired)-broadband subscriptions (per 100 people)	0.0	0.0	0.2
Households with a computer (%)	0.1[a]	1.8[a]	4.2
Households with Internet access at home (%)	0.0[a]	1.4[a]	3.4
Usage			
Int'l. voice traffic, total (minutes/subscription/month)	..	..	..
Domestic mobile traffic (minutes/subscription/month)	..	18,471.9	70.1
Individuals using the Internet (%)	0.2[a]	1.4[a]	6.2
Quality			
Population covered by a mobile-cellular network (%)	15	75	
Fixed (wired)-broadband subscriptions (% of total Internet)	5.9	13.4	30.9
International Internet bandwidth (bit/s per Internet user)	1,028	3,499	9,141
Affordability			
Fixed-telephone sub-basket ($ a month)	..	11.7	8.9
Mobile-cellular sub-basket ($ a month)	..	16.6	11.9
Fixed-broadband sub-basket ($ a month)	..	59.6	46.9
Trade			
ICT goods exports (% of total goods exports)	0.2	0.2	..
ICT goods imports (% of total goods imports)	3.2	1.9	..
ICT service exports (% of total service exports)	34.3	5.4	..
Applications			
Online service index (0–1, 1=highest presence)	0.11	0.20	0.20
Secure Internet servers (per million people)	0.1	0.2	1.1

Nigeria

Sub-Saharan Africa **Lower middle income**

	Country data		Lower middle-income group
	2005	2012	2012
Economic and social context			
Population (millions)	140	169	2,507
Urban population (% of total)	46	50	39
GNI per capita, World Bank Atlas method ($)	630	1,440	1,893
GDP growth, 2000–05 and 2005–12 (avg. annual %)	6.6	6.9	6.0
Adult literacy rate (% ages 15 and older)	55	51	71
Gross primary, secondary, tertiary school enrollment (%)	56	..	64
Sector structure			
Separate telecommunications/ICT regulator	Yes	Yes	
Status of main fixed-line telephone operator	Public	Mixed	
Level of competition (competition, partial comp., monopoly)			
International gateway(s)	..	C	
Mobile telephone service	P	C	
Internet service	C	C	
Foreign ownership (not allowed, restricted, allowed)	A	A	
Reg. treatment of VoIP (banned, closed, no framework, allowed)	A	A	
Sector efficiency and capacity			
Telecommunications revenue (% of GDP)	3.1	2.6	2.5
Telecommunications investment (% of revenue)	0.4	75.5	20.5
Sector performance			
Access			
Fixed-telephone subscriptions (per 100 people)	0.9	0.2	5.4
Mobile-cellular telephone subscriptions (per 100 people)	13.3	66.8	83.1
Fixed (wired)-broadband subscriptions (per 100 people)	0.0	0.0	1.4
Households with a computer (%)	4.0	11.4[a]	15.0
Households with Internet access at home (%)	2.0[a]	9.1[a]	12.4
Usage			
Int'l. voice traffic, total (minutes/subscription/month)	6.2	4.6	6.5
Domestic mobile traffic (minutes/subscription/month)	27.4	37.6	..
Individuals using the Internet (%)	3.5	32.9[a]	18.7
Quality			
Population covered by a mobile-cellular network (%)	58	96	86
Fixed (wired)-broadband subscriptions (% of total Internet)	..	44.6	58.2
International Internet bandwidth (bit/s per Internet user)	30	306	8,076
Affordability			
Fixed-telephone sub-basket ($ a month)	..	9.5	4.9
Mobile-cellular sub-basket ($ a month)	..	9.8	10.5
Fixed-broadband sub-basket ($ a month)	..	39.0	20.6
Trade			
ICT goods exports (% of total goods exports)	0.0	0.0	4.6
ICT goods imports (% of total goods imports)	3.9	5.5	7.2
ICT service exports (% of total service exports)	1.6	4.4	47.1
Applications			
Online service index (0–1, 1=highest presence)	0.31	0.22	0.32
Secure Internet servers (per million people)	0.2	1.7	4.4

Northern Mariana Islands

High income

	Country data		High-income group
	2005	2012	2012
Economic and social context			
Population (millions)	0.06	0.05	1,300
Urban population (% of total)	91	92	80
GNI per capita, *World Bank Atlas* method ($)	..	..	38,412
GDP growth, 2000–05 and 2005–12 (avg. annual %)	..	..	1.0
Adult literacy rate (% ages 15 and older)	..	..	..
Gross primary, secondary, tertiary school enrollment (%)	..	..	93
Sector structure			
Separate telecommunications/ICT regulator	..	..	
Status of main fixed-line telephone operator	..	..	
Level of competition (competition, partial comp., monopoly)			
International gateway(s)	..	..	
Mobile telephone service	..	..	
Internet service	..	..	
Foreign ownership (not allowed, restricted, allowed)	..	..	
Reg. treatment of VoIP (banned, closed, no framework, allowed)	..	..	
Sector efficiency and capacity			
Telecommunications revenue (% of GDP)	..	..	2.7
Telecommunications investment (% of revenue)	..	..	17.6
Sector performance			
Access			
Fixed-telephone subscriptions (per 100 people)	36.2	43.1	43.6
Mobile-cellular telephone subscriptions (per 100 people)	*31.0*	..	122.9
Fixed (wired)-broadband subscriptions (per 100 people)	0.0	*0.0*	26.2
Households with a computer (%)	..	..	77.7
Households with Internet access at home (%)	30.9	..	75.5
Usage			
Int'l. voice traffic, total (minutes/subscription/month)	..	..	..
Domestic mobile traffic (minutes/subscription/month)	..	..	*113.6*
Individuals using the Internet (%)	..	..	75.4
Quality			
Population covered by a mobile-cellular network (%)	..	..	100
Fixed (wired)-broadband subscriptions (% of total Internet)	..	..	95.9
International Internet bandwidth (bit/s per Internet user)	..	..	85,990
Affordability			
Fixed-telephone sub-basket ($ a month)	..	..	25.2
Mobile-cellular sub-basket ($ a month)	..	..	20.6
Fixed-broadband sub-basket ($ a month)	..	..	29.2
Trade			
ICT goods exports (% of total goods exports)	..	..	8.9
ICT goods imports (% of total goods imports)	..	..	10.8
ICT service exports (% of total service exports)	..	..	30.8
Applications			
Online service index (0–1, 1=highest presence)	..	..	0.67
Secure Internet servers (per million people)	83.6	37.0	827.6

Norway

High income

	Country data		High-income group
	2005	2012	2012
Economic and social context			
Population (millions)	5	5	1,300
Urban population (% of total)	77	80	80
GNI per capita, World Bank Atlas method ($)	62,760	98,780	38,412
GDP growth, 2000–05 and 2005–12 (avg. annual %)	2.1	0.8	1.0
Adult literacy rate (% ages 15 and older)	..	..	..
Gross primary, secondary, tertiary school enrollment (%)	99	98	93
Sector structure			
Separate telecommunications/ICT regulator	Yes	Yes	
Status of main fixed-line telephone operator	Mixed	Mixed	
Level of competition (competition, partial comp., monopoly)			
International gateway(s)	..	C	
Mobile telephone service	P	C	
Internet service	C	C	
Foreign ownership (not allowed, restricted, allowed)	A	A	
Reg. treatment of VoIP (banned, closed, no framework, allowed)	A	A	
Sector efficiency and capacity			
Telecommunications revenue (% of GDP)	1.6	1.1	2.7
Telecommunications investment (% of revenue)	..	..	17.6
Sector performance			
Access			
Fixed-telephone subscriptions (per 100 people)	45.6	28.0	43.6
Mobile-cellular telephone subscriptions (per 100 people)	102.8	116.7	122.9
Fixed (wired)-broadband subscriptions (per 100 people)	21.4	36.3	26.2
Households with a computer (%)	74.0	92.0	77.7
Households with Internet access at home (%)	64.0	93.0	75.5
Usage			
Int'l. voice traffic, total (minutes/subscription/month)	..	..	..
Domestic mobile traffic (minutes/subscription/month)	119.3	174.7	113.6
Individuals using the Internet (%)	82.0	95.0	75.4
Quality			
Population covered by a mobile-cellular network (%)	..	..	100
Fixed (wired)-broadband subscriptions (% of total Internet)	69.8	100.0	95.9
International Internet bandwidth (bit/s per Internet user)	11,346	187,809	85,990
Affordability			
Fixed-telephone sub-basket ($ a month)	..	38.0	25.2
Mobile-cellular sub-basket ($ a month)	..	25.2	20.6
Fixed-broadband sub-basket ($ a month)	..	53.3	29.2
Trade			
ICT goods exports (% of total goods exports)	1.2	0.8	8.9
ICT goods imports (% of total goods imports)	8.8	7.1	10.8
ICT service exports (% of total service exports)	24.4	29.1	30.8
Applications			
Online service index (0–1, 1=highest presence)	0.89	0.86	0.67
Secure Internet servers (per million people)	308.9	1,741.9	827.6

Oman

	Country data		High-income group
	2005	2012	2012
Economic and social context			
Population (millions)	3	3	1,300
Urban population (% of total)	72	74	80
GNI per capita, World Bank Atlas method ($)	10,780	19,450	38,412
GDP growth, 2000–05 and 2005–12 (avg. annual %)	3.1	5.7	1.0
Adult literacy rate (% ages 15 and older)	81	87	..
Gross primary, secondary, tertiary school enrollment (%)	68	77	93
Sector structure			
Separate telecommunications/ICT regulator	Yes	Yes	
Status of main fixed-line telephone operator	Mixed	Mixed	
Level of competition (competition, partial comp., monopoly)			
International gateway(s)	M	C	
Mobile telephone service	P	P	
Internet service	M	C	
Foreign ownership (not allowed, restricted, allowed)	R	A	
Reg. treatment of VoIP (banned, closed, no framework, allowed)	B	A	
Sector efficiency and capacity			
Telecommunications revenue (% of GDP)	3.0	2.4	2.7
Telecommunications investment (% of revenue)	102.5	10.8	17.6
Sector performance			
Access			
Fixed-telephone subscriptions (per 100 people)	10.5	9.2	43.6
Mobile-cellular telephone subscriptions (per 100 people)	52.9	159.3	122.9
Fixed (wired)-broadband subscriptions (per 100 people)	0.5	2.1	26.2
Households with a computer (%)	37.2	62.7a	77.7
Households with Internet access at home (%)	15.5a	41.9a	75.5
Usage			
Int'l. voice traffic, total (minutes/subscription/month)	18.1	17.0	..
Domestic mobile traffic (minutes/subscription/month)	99.9	108.9	113.6
Individuals using the Internet (%)	6.7	60.0a	75.4
Quality			
Population covered by a mobile-cellular network (%)	92	98	100
Fixed (wired)-broadband subscriptions (% of total Internet)	24.4	92.1	95.9
International Internet bandwidth (bit/s per Internet user)	2,960	8,948	85,990
Affordability			
Fixed-telephone sub-basket ($ a month)	..	13.2	25.2
Mobile-cellular sub-basket ($ a month)	..	8.7	20.6
Fixed-broadband sub-basket ($ a month)	..	26.0	29.2
Trade			
ICT goods exports (% of total goods exports)	0.2	0.1	8.9
ICT goods imports (% of total goods imports)	4.4	3.0	10.8
ICT service exports (% of total service exports)	21.9	24.1	30.8
Applications			
Online service index (0–1, 1=highest presence)	0.47	0.67	0.67
Secure Internet servers (per million people)	4.0	62.8	827.6

Pakistan

	Country data 2005	2012	Lower middle-income group 2012
Economic and social context			
Population (millions)	158	179	2,507
Urban population (% of total)	34	37	39
GNI per capita, *World Bank Atlas* method ($)	710	1,260	1,893
GDP growth, 2000–05 and 2005–12 (avg. annual %)	5.0	3.1	6.0
Adult literacy rate (% ages 15 and older)	50	55	71
Gross primary, secondary, tertiary school enrollment (%)	41	45	64
Sector structure			
Separate telecommunications/ICT regulator	Yes	Yes	
Status of main fixed-line telephone operator	Public	Mixed	
Level of competition (competition, partial comp., monopoly)			
International gateway(s)	C	C	
Mobile telephone service	P	C	
Internet service	C	C	
Foreign ownership (not allowed, restricted, allowed)	A	A	
Reg. treatment of VoIP (banned, closed, no framework, allowed)	No	A	
Sector efficiency and capacity			
Telecommunications revenue (% of GDP)	2.2	2.0	2.5
Telecommunications investment (% of revenue)	61.0	39.7	20.5
Sector performance			
Access			
Fixed-telephone subscriptions (per 100 people)	3.3	3.2	5.4
Mobile-cellular telephone subscriptions (per 100 people)	8.1	67.1	83.1
Fixed (wired)-broadband subscriptions (per 100 people)	0.0	0.5	1.4
Households with a computer (%)	8.1	12.5[a]	15.0
Households with Internet access at home (%)	..	8.3[a]	12.4
Usage			
Int'l. voice traffic, total (minutes/subscription/month)	4.0	8.3	6.5
Domestic mobile traffic (minutes/subscription/month)	40.9	135.6	..
Individuals using the Internet (%)	6.3	10.0[a]	18.7
Quality			
Population covered by a mobile-cellular network (%)	36	92	86
Fixed (wired)-broadband subscriptions (% of total Internet)	0.7	25.6	58.2
International Internet bandwidth (bit/s per Internet user)	72	7,283	8,076
Affordability			
Fixed-telephone sub-basket ($ a month)	..	3.5	4.9
Mobile-cellular sub-basket ($ a month)	..	3.5	10.5
Fixed-broadband sub-basket ($ a month)	..	14.5	20.6
Trade			
ICT goods exports (% of total goods exports)	0.5	0.2	4.6
ICT goods imports (% of total goods imports)	8.7	4.4	7.2
ICT service exports (% of total service exports)	17.9	20.1	47.1
Applications			
Online service index (0–1, 1=highest presence)	0.32	0.37	0.32
Secure Internet servers (per million people)	0.3	1.3	4.4

Palau

			Upper middle-income group
East Asia & Pacific			**Upper middle income**
	Country data		
	2005	2012	2012
Economic and social context			
Population (millions)	0.02	0.02	2,391
Urban population (% of total)	78	85	61
GNI per capita, *World Bank Atlas* method ($)	8,910	9,860	6,969
GDP growth, 2000–05 and 2005–12 (avg. annual %)	3.2	-1.9	6.2
Adult literacy rate (% ages 15 and older)	..	..	94
Gross primary, secondary, tertiary school enrollment (%)	..	..	76
Sector structure			
Separate telecommunications/ICT regulator	..	..	
Status of main fixed-line telephone operator	Public	Public	
Level of competition (competition, partial comp., monopoly)			
International gateway(s)	..	..	
Mobile telephone service	..	..	
Internet service	..	..	
Foreign ownership (not allowed, restricted, allowed)	..	..	
Reg. treatment of VoIP (banned, closed, no framework, allowed)	..	..	
Sector efficiency and capacity			
Telecommunications revenue (% of GDP)	..	..	2.5
Telecommunications investment (% of revenue)	..	..	18.2
Sector performance			
Access			
Fixed-telephone subscriptions (per 100 people)	40.1	35.3	19.4
Mobile-cellular telephone subscriptions (per 100 people)	30.4	82.6	92.4
Fixed (wired)-broadband subscriptions (per 100 people)	0.5	4.4	10.8
Households with a computer (%)	18.5	..	40.6
Households with Internet access at home (%)	..	19.0	36.3
Usage			
Int'l. voice traffic, total (minutes/subscription/month)	50.7	23.8	1.3
Domestic mobile traffic (minutes/subscription/month)	..	..	284.4
Individuals using the Internet (%)	27.0	..	41.6
Quality			
Population covered by a mobile-cellular network (%)	30	98	99
Fixed (wired)-broadband subscriptions (% of total Internet)	7.6	79.2	95.5
International Internet bandwidth (bit/s per Internet user)	1,123	..	14,580
Affordability			
Fixed-telephone sub-basket ($ a month)	..	..	9.4
Mobile-cellular sub-basket ($ a month)	..	..	14.9
Fixed-broadband sub-basket ($ a month)	..	..	17.8
Trade			
ICT goods exports (% of total goods exports)	..	1.0	17.6
ICT goods imports (% of total goods imports)	..	2.5	14.7
ICT service exports (% of total service exports)	..	..	29.1
Applications			
Online service index (0–1, 1=highest presence)	0.00	0.18	0.42
Secure Internet servers (per million people)	50.5	95.2	18.5

Panama

Latin America & Caribbean			Upper middle income

	Country data		Upper middle-income group
	2005	2012	2012
Economic and social context			
Population (millions)	3	4	2,391
Urban population (% of total)	71	76	61
GNI per capita, *World Bank Atlas* method ($)	4,460	8,510	6,969
GDP growth, 2000–05 and 2005–12 (avg. annual %)	4.4	8.7	6.2
Adult literacy rate (% ages 15 and older)	92	94	94
Gross primary, secondary, tertiary school enrollment (%)	76	74	76
Sector structure			
Separate telecommunications/ICT regulator	Yes	Yes	
Status of main fixed-line telephone operator	Mixed	Mixed	
Level of competition (competition, partial comp., monopoly)			
International gateway(s)	..	C	
Mobile telephone service	P	C	
Internet service	C	C	
Foreign ownership (not allowed, restricted, allowed)	A	A	
Reg. treatment of VoIP (banned, closed, no framework, allowed)	No	A	
Sector efficiency and capacity			
Telecommunications revenue (% of GDP)	3.7	2.5	2.5
Telecommunications investment (% of revenue)	..	..	18.2
Sector performance			
Access			
Fixed-telephone subscriptions (per 100 people)	14.0	16.8	19.4
Mobile-cellular telephone subscriptions (per 100 people)	52.0	178.0	92.4
Fixed (wired)-broadband subscriptions (per 100 people)	0.5	7.8	10.8
Households with a computer (%)	14.6[a]	38.3	40.6
Households with Internet access at home (%)	8.1	31.6	36.3
Usage			
Int'l. voice traffic, total (minutes/subscription/month)	..	6.7	1.3
Domestic mobile traffic (minutes/subscription/month)	61.3	79.2	284.4
Individuals using the Internet (%)	11.5	45.2[a]	41.6
Quality			
Population covered by a mobile-cellular network (%)	75	96	99
Fixed (wired)-broadband subscriptions (% of total Internet)	21.3	98.4	95.5
International Internet bandwidth (bit/s per Internet user)	2,396	30,838	14,580
Affordability			
Fixed-telephone sub-basket ($ a month)	..	9.5	9.4
Mobile-cellular sub-basket ($ a month)	..	12.6	14.9
Fixed-broadband sub-basket ($ a month)	..	14.0	17.8
Trade			
ICT goods exports (% of total goods exports)	0.1	7.9	17.6
ICT goods imports (% of total goods imports)	9.1	8.1	14.7
ICT service exports (% of total service exports)	10.6	8.1	29.1
Applications			
Online service index (0–1, 1=highest presence)	0.47	0.46	0.42
Secure Internet servers (per million people)	54.1	89.8	18.5

Papua New Guinea

East Asia & Pacific			Lower middle income

	Country data		Lower middle-income group
	2005	2012	2012
Economic and social context			
Population (millions)	6	7	2,507
Urban population (% of total)	13	13	39
GNI per capita, World Bank Atlas method ($)	680	1,790	1,893
GDP growth, 2000–05 and 2005–12 (avg. annual %)	1.6	6.9	6.0
Adult literacy rate (% ages 15 and older)	57	62	71
Gross primary, secondary, tertiary school enrollment (%)	..	..	64
Sector structure			
Separate telecommunications/ICT regulator	Yes	Yes	
Status of main fixed-line telephone operator	Public	Public	
Level of competition (competition, partial comp., monopoly)			
International gateway(s)	..	..	
Mobile telephone service	M	M	
Internet service	P	P	
Foreign ownership (not allowed, restricted, allowed)	..	..	
Reg. treatment of VoIP (banned, closed, no framework, allowed)	A	A	
Sector efficiency and capacity			
Telecommunications revenue (% of GDP)	..	..	2.5
Telecommunications investment (% of revenue)	..	..	20.5
Sector performance			
Access			
Fixed-telephone subscriptions (per 100 people)	1.0	1.9	5.4
Mobile-cellular telephone subscriptions (per 100 people)	1.2	37.8	83.1
Fixed (wired)-broadband subscriptions (per 100 people)	0.0	0.1	1.4
Households with a computer (%)	2.0[a]	3.2[a]	15.0
Households with Internet access at home (%)	1.1[a]	2.7[a]	12.4
Usage			
Int'l. voice traffic, total (minutes/subscription/month)	..	..	6.5
Domestic mobile traffic (minutes/subscription/month)	..	..	..
Individuals using the Internet (%)	1.7	2.3[a]	18.7
Quality			
Population covered by a mobile-cellular network (%)	..	..	86
Fixed (wired)-broadband subscriptions (% of total Internet)	..	..	58.2
International Internet bandwidth (bit/s per Internet user)	57	4,849	8,076
Affordability			
Fixed-telephone sub-basket ($ a month)	..	11.5	4.9
Mobile-cellular sub-basket ($ a month)	..	30.4	10.5
Fixed-broadband sub-basket ($ a month)	..	185.6	20.6
Trade			
ICT goods exports (% of total goods exports)	0.0	0.0	4.6
ICT goods imports (% of total goods imports)	3.2	2.2	7.2
ICT service exports (% of total service exports)	72.8	49.3	47.1
Applications			
Online service index (0–1, 1=highest presence)	0.21	0.23	0.32
Secure Internet servers (per million people)	0.5	7.8	4.4

Paraguay

	Country data		Lower middle-income group
	2005	2012	2012
Economic and social context			
Population (millions)	6	7	2,507
Urban population (% of total)	58	62	39
GNI per capita, *World Bank Atlas* method ($)	1,210	3,400	1,893
GDP growth, 2000–05 and 2005–12 (avg. annual %)	2.2	4.3	6.0
Adult literacy rate (% ages 15 and older)	95	94	71
Gross primary, secondary, tertiary school enrollment (%)	72	74	64
Sector structure			
Separate telecommunications/ICT regulator	Yes	Yes	
Status of main fixed-line telephone operator	Public	Public	
Level of competition (competition, partial comp., monopoly)			
International gateway(s)	..	C	
Mobile telephone service	C	C	
Internet service	C	C	
Foreign ownership (not allowed, restricted, allowed)	R	A	
Reg. treatment of VoIP (banned, closed, no framework, allowed)	B	A	
Sector efficiency and capacity			
Telecommunications revenue (% of GDP)	3.5	3.7	2.5
Telecommunications investment (% of revenue)	..	..	20.5
Sector performance			
Access			
Fixed-telephone subscriptions (per 100 people)	5.4	6.1	5.4
Mobile-cellular telephone subscriptions (per 100 people)	32.0	101.6	83.1
Fixed (wired)-broadband subscriptions (per 100 people)	0.1	1.2	1.4
Households with a computer (%)	8.7	24.3[a]	15.0
Households with Internet access at home (%)	1.7	22.8[a]	12.4
Usage			
Int'l. voice traffic, total (minutes/subscription/month)	..	7.2	6.5
Domestic mobile traffic (minutes/subscription/month)	..	81.6	..
Individuals using the Internet (%)	7.9	27.1[a]	18.7
Quality			
Population covered by a mobile-cellular network (%)	..	94	86
Fixed (wired)-broadband subscriptions (% of total Internet)	9.3	98.3	58.2
International Internet bandwidth (bit/s per Internet user)	737	11,585	8,076
Affordability			
Fixed-telephone sub-basket ($ a month)	..	8.8	4.9
Mobile-cellular sub-basket ($ a month)	..	8.8	10.5
Fixed-broadband sub-basket ($ a month)	..	21.8	20.6
Trade			
ICT goods exports (% of total goods exports)	0.2	0.1	4.6
ICT goods imports (% of total goods imports)	17.4	19.1	7.2
ICT service exports (% of total service exports)	8.7	1.9	47.1
Applications			
Online service index (0–1, 1=highest presence)	0.47	0.46	0.32
Secure Internet servers (per million people)	1.4	15.4	4.4

Peru

		Country data	Upper middle-income group
Latin America & Caribbean			**Upper middle income**
	2005	2012	2012
Economic and social context			
Population (millions)	28	30	2,391
Urban population (% of total)	75	78	61
GNI per capita, *World Bank Atlas* method ($)	2,700	6,060	6,969
GDP growth, 2000–05 and 2005–12 (avg. annual %)	4.3	6.9	6.2
Adult literacy rate (% ages 15 and older)	88	..	94
Gross primary, secondary, tertiary school enrollment (%)	81	82	76
Sector structure			
Separate telecommunications/ICT regulator	Yes	Yes	
Status of main fixed-line telephone operator	Private	Private	
Level of competition (competition, partial comp., monopoly)			
International gateway(s)	..	..	
Mobile telephone service	C	C	
Internet service	C	C	
Foreign ownership (not allowed, restricted, allowed)	A	A	
Reg. treatment of VoIP (banned, closed, no framework, allowed)	A	A	
Sector efficiency and capacity			
Telecommunications revenue (% of GDP)	2.7	2.7	2.5
Telecommunications investment (% of revenue)	17.9	16.7	18.2
Sector performance			
Access			
Fixed-telephone subscriptions (per 100 people)	8.7	11.4	19.4
Mobile-cellular telephone subscriptions (per 100 people)	20.1	98.0	92.4
Fixed (wired)-broadband subscriptions (per 100 people)	1.3	4.7	10.8
Households with a computer (%)	8.2	29.9	40.6
Households with Internet access at home (%)	3.5	20.2	36.3
Usage			
Int'l. voice traffic, total (minutes/subscription/month)	13.7	9.5	1.3
Domestic mobile traffic (minutes/subscription/month)	40.5	58.6	284.4
Individuals using the Internet (%)	17.1[a]	38.2	41.6
Quality			
Population covered by a mobile-cellular network (%)	92	97	99
Fixed (wired)-broadband subscriptions (% of total Internet)	42.3	98.2	95.5
International Internet bandwidth (bit/s per Internet user)	2,109	13,094	14,580
Affordability			
Fixed-telephone sub-basket ($ a month)	..	12.3	9.4
Mobile-cellular sub-basket ($ a month)	..	12.8	14.9
Fixed-broadband sub-basket ($ a month)	..	18.0	17.8
Trade			
ICT goods exports (% of total goods exports)	0.2	0.1	17.6
ICT goods imports (% of total goods imports)	8.4	7.8	14.7
ICT service exports (% of total service exports)	13.9	15.1	29.1
Applications			
Online service index (0–1, 1=highest presence)	0.53	0.52	0.42
Secure Internet servers (per million people)	5.2	21.4	18.5

Philippines

East Asia & Pacific   **Lower middle income**

	Country data		Lower middle-income group
	2005	2012	2012
Economic and social context			
Population (millions)	86	97	2,507
Urban population (% of total)	48	49	39
GNI per capita, *World Bank Atlas* method ($)	1,210	2,500	1,893
GDP growth, 2000–05 and 2005–12 (avg. annual %)	4.7	4.8	6.0
Adult literacy rate (% ages 15 and older)	93	95	71
Gross primary, secondary, tertiary school enrollment (%)	78	76	64
Sector structure			
Separate telecommunications/ICT regulator	Yes	Yes	
Status of main fixed-line telephone operator	Private	Private	
Level of competition (competition, partial comp., monopoly)			
International gateway(s)	..	..	
Mobile telephone service	C	C	
Internet service	C	C	
Foreign ownership (not allowed, restricted, allowed)	R	R	
Reg. treatment of VoIP (banned, closed, no framework, allowed)	A	A	
Sector efficiency and capacity			
Telecommunications revenue (% of GDP)	4.2	2.4	2.5
Telecommunications investment (% of revenue)	24.4	24.0	20.5
Sector performance			
Access			
Fixed-telephone subscriptions (per 100 people)	3.9	4.1	5.4
Mobile-cellular telephone subscriptions (per 100 people)	40.5	106.5	83.1
Fixed (wired)-broadband subscriptions (per 100 people)	0.1	2.2	1.4
Households with a computer (%)	6.6[a]	16.9[a]	15.0
Households with Internet access at home (%)	4.3[a]	18.9[a]	12.4
Usage			
Int'l. voice traffic, total (minutes/subscription/month)	..	..	6.5
Domestic mobile traffic (minutes/subscription/month)	..	..	..
Individuals using the Internet (%)	5.4[a]	36.2[a]	18.7
Quality			
Population covered by a mobile-cellular network (%)	99	99[a]	86
Fixed (wired)-broadband subscriptions (% of total Internet)	8.5	34.5	58.2
International Internet bandwidth (bit/s per Internet user)	694	14,269	8,076
Affordability			
Fixed-telephone sub-basket ($ a month)	..	15.0	4.9
Mobile-cellular sub-basket ($ a month)	..	10.5	10.5
Fixed-broadband sub-basket ($ a month)	..	22.9	20.6
Trade			
ICT goods exports (% of total goods exports)	47.7	29.5	4.6
ICT goods imports (% of total goods imports)	45.8	24.8	7.2
ICT service exports (% of total service exports)	15.9	67.3	47.1
Applications			
Online service index (0–1, 1=highest presence)	0.50	0.50	0.32
Secure Internet servers (per million people)	2.4	8.1	4.4

Poland

High income

	Country data		High-income group
	2005	2012	2012
Economic and social context			
Population (millions)	38	39	1,300
Urban population (% of total)	61	61	80
GNI per capita, *World Bank Atlas* method ($)	7,270	12,660	38,412
GDP growth, 2000–05 and 2005–12 (avg. annual %)	3.2	4.2	1.0
Adult literacy rate (% ages 15 and older)	100	100	..
Gross primary, secondary, tertiary school enrollment (%)	87	90	93
Sector structure			
Separate telecommunications/ICT regulator	Yes	Yes	
Status of main fixed-line telephone operator	Mixed	Mixed	
Level of competition (competition, partial comp., monopoly)			
International gateway(s)	C	C	
Mobile telephone service	C	P	
Internet service	C	C	
Foreign ownership (not allowed, restricted, allowed)	A	A	
Reg. treatment of VoIP (banned, closed, no framework, allowed)	A	A	
Sector efficiency and capacity			
Telecommunications revenue (% of GDP)	3.8	2.7	2.7
Telecommunications investment (% of revenue)	16.1	14.9	17.6
Sector performance			
Access			
Fixed-telephone subscriptions (per 100 people)	31.0	15.6	43.6
Mobile-cellular telephone subscriptions (per 100 people)	76.3	140.3	122.9
Fixed (wired)-broadband subscriptions (per 100 people)	2.5	15.5	26.2
Households with a computer (%)	40.0	73.0	77.7
Households with Internet access at home (%)	30.4	70.0	75.5
Usage			
Int'l. voice traffic, total (minutes/subscription/month)	..	..	..
Domestic mobile traffic (minutes/subscription/month)	46.7	105.9	113.6
Individuals using the Internet (%)	38.8	65.0	75.4
Quality			
Population covered by a mobile-cellular network (%)	99	100	100
Fixed (wired)-broadband subscriptions (% of total Internet)	35.2	99.1	95.9
International Internet bandwidth (bit/s per Internet user)	1,442	70,620	85,990
Affordability			
Fixed-telephone sub-basket ($ a month)	..	21.6	25.2
Mobile-cellular sub-basket ($ a month)	..	11.3	20.6
Fixed-broadband sub-basket ($ a month)	..	19.9	29.2
Trade			
ICT goods exports (% of total goods exports)	4.0	7.0	8.9
ICT goods imports (% of total goods imports)	7.9	8.2	10.8
ICT service exports (% of total service exports)	19.6	33.7	30.8
Applications			
Online service index (0–1, 1=highest presence)	0.61	0.54	0.67
Secure Internet servers (per million people)	22.0	312.2	827.6

Portugal

	Country data		High-income group
	2005	2012	2012
Economic and social context			
Population (millions)	11	11	1,300
Urban population (% of total)	58	62	80
GNI per capita, *World Bank Atlas* method ($)	18,140	20,640	38,412
GDP growth, 2000–05 and 2005–12 (avg. annual %)	0.7	-0.2	1.0
Adult literacy rate (% ages 15 and older)	..	95	..
Gross primary, secondary, tertiary school enrollment (%)	89	97	93
Sector structure			
Separate telecommunications/ICT regulator	Yes	Yes	
Status of main fixed-line telephone operator	Mixed	Mixed	
Level of competition (competition, partial comp., monopoly)			
International gateway(s)	C	C	
Mobile telephone service	P	C	
Internet service	C	C	
Foreign ownership (not allowed, restricted, allowed)	A	A	
Reg. treatment of VoIP (banned, closed, no framework, allowed)	No	A	
Sector efficiency and capacity			
Telecommunications revenue (% of GDP)	4.8	4.0	2.7
Telecommunications investment (% of revenue)	9.9	11.6	17.6
Sector performance			
Access			
Fixed-telephone subscriptions (per 100 people)	40.3	43.0	43.6
Mobile-cellular telephone subscriptions (per 100 people)	108.9	116.1	122.9
Fixed (wired)-broadband subscriptions (per 100 people)	11.1	22.5	26.2
Households with a computer (%)	42.5	66.0	77.7
Households with Internet access at home (%)	31.5	61.0	75.5
Usage			
Int'l. voice traffic, total (minutes/subscription/month)	15.7	..	..
Domestic mobile traffic (minutes/subscription/month)	80.6	135.8	*113.6*
Individuals using the Internet (%)	35.0	64.0	75.4
Quality			
Population covered by a mobile-cellular network (%)	99	99	100
Fixed (wired)-broadband subscriptions (% of total Internet)	81.1	99.0	*95.9*
International Internet bandwidth (bit/s per Internet user)	2,378	195,537	85,990
Affordability			
Fixed-telephone sub-basket ($ a month)	..	25.0	25.2
Mobile-cellular sub-basket ($ a month)	..	25.3	20.6
Fixed-broadband sub-basket ($ a month)	..	29.2	29.2
Trade			
ICT goods exports (% of total goods exports)	7.8	3.4	8.9
ICT goods imports (% of total goods imports)	8.4	5.1	10.8
ICT service exports (% of total service exports)	16.1	17.8	30.8
Applications			
Online service index (0–1, 1=highest presence)	0.65	0.65	0.67
Secure Internet servers (per million people)	57.7	216.0	827.6

Puerto Rico

	Country data		High-income group
	2005	2012	2012
Economic and social context			
Population (millions)	4	4	1,300
Urban population (% of total)	98	99	80
GNI per capita, *World Bank Atlas* method ($)	14,120	18,000	38,412
GDP growth, 2000–05 and 2005–12 (avg. annual %)	1.5	-1.1	1.0
Adult literacy rate (% ages 15 and older)	91	90	..
Gross primary, secondary, tertiary school enrollment (%)	..	92	93
Sector structure			
Separate telecommunications/ICT regulator	..	..	
Status of main fixed-line telephone operator	..	..	
Level of competition (competition, partial comp., monopoly)			
International gateway(s)	..	..	
Mobile telephone service	..	..	
Internet service	..	..	
Foreign ownership (not allowed, restricted, allowed)	..	..	
Reg. treatment of VoIP (banned, closed, no framework, allowed)	..	..	
Sector efficiency and capacity			
Telecommunications revenue (% of GDP)	..	..	2.7
Telecommunications investment (% of revenue)	..	..	17.6
Sector performance			
Access			
Fixed-telephone subscriptions (per 100 people)	27.6[a]	19.1	43.6
Mobile-cellular telephone subscriptions (per 100 people)	53.0	82.6	122.9
Fixed (wired)-broadband subscriptions (per 100 people)	3.1	15.5	26.2
Households with a computer (%)	..	60.0[a]	77.7
Households with Internet access at home (%)	..	60.7[a]	75.5
Usage			
Int'l. voice traffic, total (minutes/subscription/month)	..	..	..
Domestic mobile traffic (minutes/subscription/month)	..	..	113.6
Individuals using the Internet (%)	23.4[a]	51.4[a]	75.4
Quality			
Population covered by a mobile-cellular network (%)	62	68	100
Fixed (wired)-broadband subscriptions (% of total Internet)	..	99.9	95.9
International Internet bandwidth (bit/s per Internet user)	2,272	136,866	85,990
Affordability			
Fixed-telephone sub-basket ($ a month)	..	..	25.2
Mobile-cellular sub-basket ($ a month)	..	..	20.6
Fixed-broadband sub-basket ($ a month)	..	..	29.2
Trade			
ICT goods exports (% of total goods exports)	..	..	8.9
ICT goods imports (% of total goods imports)	..	..	10.8
ICT service exports (% of total service exports)	..	..	30.8
Applications			
Online service index (0–1, 1=highest presence)	..	..	0.67
Secure Internet servers (per million people)	31.9	106.5	827.6

Qatar

High income

	Country data		High-income group
	2005	2012	2012
Economic and social context			
Population (millions)	0.82	2	1,300
Urban population (% of total)	97	99	80
GNI per capita, *World Bank Atlas* method ($)	40,320	74,600	38,412
GDP growth, 2000–05 and 2005–12 (avg. annual %)	8.7	14.9	1.0
Adult literacy rate (% ages 15 and older)	89	96	..
Gross primary, secondary, tertiary school enrollment (%)	79	..	93
Sector structure			
Separate telecommunications/ICT regulator	Yes	Yes	
Status of main fixed-line telephone operator	Mixed	Mixed	
Level of competition (competition, partial comp., monopoly)			
International gateway(s)	M	P	
Mobile telephone service	M	P	
Internet service	M	P	
Foreign ownership (not allowed, restricted, allowed)	A	R	
Reg. treatment of VoIP (banned, closed, no framework, allowed)	B	A	
Sector efficiency and capacity			
Telecommunications revenue (% of GDP)	1.8	1.1	2.7
Telecommunications investment (% of revenue)	26.3	14.2	17.6
Sector performance			
Access			
Fixed-telephone subscriptions (per 100 people)	25.0	19.2	43.6
Mobile-cellular telephone subscriptions (per 100 people)	87.3	126.9	122.9
Fixed (wired)-broadband subscriptions (per 100 people)	3.1	10.5	26.2
Households with a computer (%)	65.7[a]	91.5	77.7
Households with Internet access at home (%)	31.5[a]	88.1	75.5
Usage			
Int'l. voice traffic, total (minutes/subscription/month)	79.1	..	..
Domestic mobile traffic (minutes/subscription/month)	..	..	113.6
Individuals using the Internet (%)	24.7	88.1	75.4
Quality			
Population covered by a mobile-cellular network (%)	99	100	100
Fixed (wired)-broadband subscriptions (% of total Internet)	48.2	97.8	95.9
International Internet bandwidth (bit/s per Internet user)	3,816	33,212	85,990
Affordability			
Fixed-telephone sub-basket ($ a month)	..	9.1	25.2
Mobile-cellular sub-basket ($ a month)	..	18.7	20.6
Fixed-broadband sub-basket ($ a month)	..	54.9	29.2
Trade			
ICT goods exports (% of total goods exports)	0.0	0.0	8.9
ICT goods imports (% of total goods imports)	4.8	4.3	10.8
ICT service exports (% of total service exports)	..	..	30.8
Applications			
Online service index (0–1, 1=highest presence)	0.53	0.74	0.67
Secure Internet servers (per million people)	20.7	161.8	827.6

Romania

Europe & Central Asia		**Upper middle income**	

	Country data		Upper middle-income group
	2005	**2012**	**2012**
Economic and social context			
Population (millions)	21	20	2,391
Urban population (% of total)	53	53	61
GNI per capita, *World Bank Atlas* method ($)	3,920	8,560	6,969
GDP growth, 2000–05 and 2005–12 (avg. annual %)	6.0	1.8	6.2
Adult literacy rate (% ages 15 and older)	97	98	94
Gross primary, secondary, tertiary school enrollment (%)	75	81	76
Sector structure			
Separate telecommunications/ICT regulator	Yes	Yes	
Status of main fixed-line telephone operator	Mixed	Mixed	
Level of competition (competition, partial comp., monopoly)			
International gateway(s)	C	C	
Mobile telephone service	C	C	
Internet service	C	C	
Foreign ownership (not allowed, restricted, allowed)	A	A	
Reg. treatment of VoIP (banned, closed, no framework, allowed)	A	A	
Sector efficiency and capacity			
Telecommunications revenue (% of GDP)	3.8	1.8	2.5
Telecommunications investment (% of revenue)	23.0	19.0	18.2
Sector performance			
Access			
Fixed-telephone subscriptions (per 100 people)	19.8	21.4	19.4
Mobile-cellular telephone subscriptions (per 100 people)	60.4	105.0	92.4
Fixed (wired)-broadband subscriptions (per 100 people)	1.7	16.2	10.8
Households with a computer (%)	24.7	57.0	40.6
Households with Internet access at home (%)	9.8a	54.0	36.3
Usage			
Int'l. voice traffic, total (minutes/subscription/month)	10.2	11.6	1.3
Domestic mobile traffic (minutes/subscription/month)	57.2	224.7	284.4
Individuals using the Internet (%)	21.5a	50.0	41.6
Quality			
Population covered by a mobile-cellular network (%)	99	100	99
Fixed (wired)-broadband subscriptions (% of total Internet)	47.7	100.0	95.5
International Internet bandwidth (bit/s per Internet user)	2,835	114,917	14,580
Affordability			
Fixed-telephone sub-basket ($ a month)	..	13.0	9.4
Mobile-cellular sub-basket ($ a month)	..	25.7	14.9
Fixed-broadband sub-basket ($ a month)	..	9.5	17.8
Trade			
ICT goods exports (% of total goods exports)	2.2	5.0	17.6
ICT goods imports (% of total goods imports)	6.7	6.8	14.7
ICT service exports (% of total service exports)	19.2	37.3	29.1
Applications			
Online service index (0–1, 1=highest presence)	0.54	0.52	0.42
Secure Internet servers (per million people)	5.4	68.7	18.5

Russian Federation

	Country data		High-income group
	2005	2012	2012
Economic and social context			
Population (millions)	143	144	1,300
Urban population (% of total)	73	74	80
GNI per capita, *World Bank Atlas* method ($)	4,460	12,700	38,412
GDP growth, 2000–05 and 2005–12 (avg. annual %)	6.2	2.9	1.0
Adult literacy rate (% ages 15 and older)	99	100	..
Gross primary, secondary, tertiary school enrollment (%)	82	84	93
Sector structure			
Separate telecommunications/ICT regulator	No	No	
Status of main fixed-line telephone operator	Mixed	Mixed	
Level of competition (competition, partial comp., monopoly)			
International gateway(s)	..	..	
Mobile telephone service	C	C	
Internet service	..	..	
Foreign ownership (not allowed, restricted, allowed)	..	..	
Reg. treatment of VoIP (banned, closed, no framework, allowed)	No	No	
Sector efficiency and capacity			
Telecommunications revenue (% of GDP)	2.9	2.3	2.7
Telecommunications investment (% of revenue)	32.1	21.3	17.6
Sector performance			
Access			
Fixed-telephone subscriptions (per 100 people)	27.9	30.1	43.6
Mobile-cellular telephone subscriptions (per 100 people)	83.4	182.9	122.9
Fixed (wired)-broadband subscriptions (per 100 people)	1.1	14.5	26.2
Households with a computer (%)	25.0[a]	60.6[a]	77.7
Households with Internet access at home (%)	17.0[a]	51.2[a]	75.5
Usage			
Int'l. voice traffic, total (minutes/subscription/month)	..	..	..
Domestic mobile traffic (minutes/subscription/month)	..	115.2	113.6
Individuals using the Internet (%)	15.2	53.3[a]	75.4
Quality			
Population covered by a mobile-cellular network (%)	95	..	100
Fixed (wired)-broadband subscriptions (% of total Internet)	8.3	98.1	95.9
International Internet bandwidth (bit/s per Internet user)	655	32,838	85,990
Affordability			
Fixed-telephone sub-basket ($ a month)	..	4.1	25.2
Mobile-cellular sub-basket ($ a month)	..	11.1	20.6
Fixed-broadband sub-basket ($ a month)	..	10.2	29.2
Trade			
ICT goods exports (% of total goods exports)	0.2	0.3	8.9
ICT goods imports (% of total goods imports)	7.8	7.5	10.8
ICT service exports (% of total service exports)	23.7	31.9	30.8
Applications			
Online service index (0–1, 1=highest presence)	0.51	0.66	0.67
Secure Internet servers (per million people)	2.4	51.9	827.6

Rwanda

	Country data		Low-income group
	2005	2012	2012
Economic and social context			
Population (millions)	9	11	846
Urban population (% of total)	18	19	28
GNI per capita, *World Bank Atlas* method ($)	260	600	590
GDP growth, 2000–05 and 2005–12 (avg. annual %)	7.5	8.1	5.9
Adult literacy rate (% ages 15 and older)	65	66	61
Gross primary, secondary, tertiary school enrollment (%)	55	67	60
Sector structure			
Separate telecommunications/ICT regulator	Yes	Yes	
Status of main fixed-line telephone operator	Mixed	Mixed	
Level of competition (competition, partial comp., monopoly)			
International gateway(s)	..	P	
Mobile telephone service	C	C	
Internet service	C	C	
Foreign ownership (not allowed, restricted, allowed)	..	A	
Reg. treatment of VoIP (banned, closed, no framework, allowed)	B	A	
Sector efficiency and capacity			
Telecommunications revenue (% of GDP)	2.7	2.8	5.0
Telecommunications investment (% of revenue)	22.7	40.1	..
Sector performance			
Access			
Fixed-telephone subscriptions (per 100 people)	0.3	0.4	1.0
Mobile-cellular telephone subscriptions (per 100 people)	2.4	49.7	47.2
Fixed (wired)-broadband subscriptions (per 100 people)	0.0	0.0	0.2
Households with a computer (%)	0.2	2.4a	4.2
Households with Internet access at home (%)	0.1	2.4a	3.4
Usage			
Int'l. voice traffic, total (minutes/subscription/month)	12.8	3.3	..
Domestic mobile traffic (minutes/subscription/month)	11.8	48.9	70.1
Individuals using the Internet (%)	0.6a	8.0a	6.2
Quality			
Population covered by a mobile-cellular network (%)	75	98	..
Fixed (wired)-broadband subscriptions (% of total Internet)	40.0	69.6	30.9
International Internet bandwidth (bit/s per Internet user)	1,030	6,585	9,141
Affordability			
Fixed-telephone sub-basket ($ a month)	..	9.0	8.9
Mobile-cellular sub-basket ($ a month)	..	14.7	11.9
Fixed-broadband sub-basket ($ a month)	..	111.7	46.9
Trade			
ICT goods exports (% of total goods exports)	1.2	0.2	..
ICT goods imports (% of total goods imports)	8.4	7.8	..
ICT service exports (% of total service exports)	8.4	3.8	..
Applications			
Online service index (0–1, 1=highest presence)	0.29	0.34	0.20
Secure Internet servers (per million people)	..	2.5	1.1

Samoa

	Country data		Lower middle-income group
	2005	2012	2012
Economic and social context			
Population (millions)	0.18	0.19	2,507
Urban population (% of total)	21	20	39
GNI per capita, *World Bank Atlas* method ($)	2,100	3,260	1,893
GDP growth, 2000–05 and 2005–12 (avg. annual %)	4.9	0.7	6.0
Adult literacy rate (% ages 15 and older)	99	99	71
Gross primary, secondary, tertiary school enrollment (%)	..	..	64
Sector structure			
Separate telecommunications/ICT regulator	No	Yes	
Status of main fixed-line telephone operator	Public	Public	
Level of competition (competition, partial comp., monopoly)			
International gateway(s)	M	C	
Mobile telephone service	M	C	
Internet service	C	C	
Foreign ownership (not allowed, restricted, allowed)	R	R	
Reg. treatment of VoIP (banned, closed, no framework, allowed)	B	A	
Sector efficiency and capacity			
Telecommunications revenue (% of GDP)	5.0	..	2.5
Telecommunications investment (% of revenue)	..	..	20.5
Sector performance			
Access			
Fixed-telephone subscriptions (per 100 people)	10.8	..	5.4
Mobile-cellular telephone subscriptions (per 100 people)	13.3	..	83.1
Fixed (wired)-broadband subscriptions (per 100 people)	0.0	0.1	1.4
Households with a computer (%)	..	..	15.0
Households with Internet access at home (%)	..	..	12.4
Usage			
Int'l. voice traffic, total (minutes/subscription/month)	..	..	6.5
Domestic mobile traffic (minutes/subscription/month)	..	..	..
Individuals using the Internet (%)	3.4	12.9[a]	18.7
Quality			
Population covered by a mobile-cellular network (%)	..	..	86
Fixed (wired)-broadband subscriptions (% of total Internet)	..	..	58.2
International Internet bandwidth (bit/s per Internet user)	1,492	5,531	8,076
Affordability			
Fixed-telephone sub-basket ($ a month)	..	12.7	4.9
Mobile-cellular sub-basket ($ a month)	..	18.1	10.5
Fixed-broadband sub-basket ($ a month)	..	42.7	20.6
Trade			
ICT goods exports (% of total goods exports)	0.1	0.1	4.6
ICT goods imports (% of total goods imports)	2.0	2.7	7.2
ICT service exports (% of total service exports)	10.1	7.8	47.1
Applications			
Online service index (0–1, 1=highest presence)	0.38	0.28	0.32
Secure Internet servers (per million people)	5.6	26.3	4.4

San Marino

	Country data		High-income group
	2005	2012	2012
Economic and social context			
Population (millions)	0.03	0.03	1,300
Urban population (% of total)	94	94	80
GNI per capita, World Bank Atlas method ($)	41,080	51,470	38,412
GDP growth, 2000–05 and 2005–12 (avg. annual %)	3.2	..	1.0
Adult literacy rate (% ages 15 and older)	..	..	..
Gross primary, secondary, tertiary school enrollment (%)	..	86	93
Sector structure			
Separate telecommunications/ICT regulator	No	No	
Status of main fixed-line telephone operator	Mixed	Mixed	
Level of competition (competition, partial comp., monopoly)			
International gateway(s)	..	..	
Mobile telephone service	C	C	
Internet service	..	..	
Foreign ownership (not allowed, restricted, allowed)	..	..	
Reg. treatment of VoIP (banned, closed, no framework, allowed)	..	..	
Sector efficiency and capacity			
Telecommunications revenue (% of GDP)	0.4	..	2.7
Telecommunications investment (% of revenue)	50.0	..	17.6
Sector performance			
Access			
Fixed-telephone subscriptions (per 100 people)	70.0	59.8	43.6
Mobile-cellular telephone subscriptions (per 100 people)	57.6	115.2	122.9
Fixed (wired)-broadband subscriptions (per 100 people)	4.1	31.7	26.2
Households with a computer (%)	..	..	77.7
Households with Internet access at home (%)	..	..	75.5
Usage			
Int'l. voice traffic, total (minutes/subscription/month)	..	..	..
Domestic mobile traffic (minutes/subscription/month)	..	..	113.6
Individuals using the Internet (%)	50.3	50.9a	75.4
Quality			
Population covered by a mobile-cellular network (%)	..	98	100
Fixed (wired)-broadband subscriptions (% of total Internet)	22.2	75.4	95.9
International Internet bandwidth (bit/s per Internet user)	10,358	628,959	85,990
Affordability			
Fixed-telephone sub-basket ($ a month)	..	25.6	25.2
Mobile-cellular sub-basket ($ a month)	..	23.8	20.6
Fixed-broadband sub-basket ($ a month)	..	22.2	29.2
Trade			
ICT goods exports (% of total goods exports)	..	..	8.9
ICT goods imports (% of total goods imports)	..	..	10.8
ICT service exports (% of total service exports)	..	..	30.8
Applications			
Online service index (0–1, 1=highest presence)	0.00	0.29	0.67
Secure Internet servers (per million people)	369.4	1,451.6	827.6

São Tomé and Príncipe

Sub-Saharan Africa			Lower middle income

	Country data		Lower middle-income group
	2005	2012	2012
Economic and social context			
Population (millions)	0.15	0.19	2,507
Urban population (% of total)	58	63	39
GNI per capita, World Bank Atlas method ($)	740	1,310	1,893
GDP growth, 2000–05 and 2005–12 (avg. annual %)	4.1	4.9	6.0
Adult literacy rate (% ages 15 and older)	85	70	71
Gross primary, secondary, tertiary school enrollment (%)	65	74	64
Sector structure			
Separate telecommunications/ICT regulator	No	Yes	
Status of main fixed-line telephone operator	Mixed	Mixed	
Level of competition (competition, partial comp., monopoly)			
International gateway(s)	..	..	
Mobile telephone service	..	M	
Internet service	..	M	
Foreign ownership (not allowed, restricted, allowed)	..	..	
Reg. treatment of VoIP (banned, closed, no framework, allowed)	No	No	
Sector efficiency and capacity			
Telecommunications revenue (% of GDP)	9.1	5.8	2.5
Telecommunications investment (% of revenue)	14.9	51.2	20.5
Sector performance			
Access			
Fixed-telephone subscriptions (per 100 people)	4.6	4.3	5.4
Mobile-cellular telephone subscriptions (per 100 people)	7.7	65.0	83.1
Fixed (wired)-broadband subscriptions (per 100 people)	0.0	0.4	1.4
Households with a computer (%)	..	..	15.0
Households with Internet access at home (%)	..	..	12.4
Usage			
Int'l. voice traffic, total (minutes/subscription/month)	33.2	7.4	6.5
Domestic mobile traffic (minutes/subscription/month)	4.6	25.5	..
Individuals using the Internet (%)	13.8[a]	21.6[a]	18.7
Quality			
Population covered by a mobile-cellular network (%)	8	70	86
Fixed (wired)-broadband subscriptions (% of total Internet)	0.0	88.7	58.2
International Internet bandwidth (bit/s per Internet user)	94	7,689	8,076
Affordability			
Fixed-telephone sub-basket ($ a month)	..	8.6	4.9
Mobile-cellular sub-basket ($ a month)	..	13.2	10.5
Fixed-broadband sub-basket ($ a month)	..	116.8	20.6
Trade			
ICT goods exports (% of total goods exports)	0.0	0.2	4.6
ICT goods imports (% of total goods imports)	3.4	3.2	7.2
ICT service exports (% of total service exports)	13.2	8.3	47.1
Applications			
Online service index (0–1, 1=highest presence)	0.32	0.12	0.32
Secure Internet servers (per million people)	12.2	46.6	4.4

Saudi Arabia

High income

	Country data		High-income group
	2005	**2012**	**2012**
Economic and social context			
Population (millions)	25	28	1,300
Urban population (% of total)	81	82	80
GNI per capita, *World Bank Atlas* method ($)	12,460	24,310	38,412
GDP growth, 2000–05 and 2005–12 (avg. annual %)	5.2	6.1	1.0
Adult literacy rate (% ages 15 and older)	83	87	..
Gross primary, secondary, tertiary school enrollment (%)	75	92	93
Sector structure			
Separate telecommunications/ICT regulator	Yes	Yes	
Status of main fixed-line telephone operator	Mixed	Mixed	
Level of competition (competition, partial comp., monopoly)			
International gateway(s)	P	..	
Mobile telephone service	P	P	
Internet service	C	C	
Foreign ownership (not allowed, restricted, allowed)	No	R	
Reg. treatment of VoIP (banned, closed, no framework, allowed)	B	B	
Sector efficiency and capacity			
Telecommunications revenue (% of GDP)	2.8	2.7	2.7
Telecommunications investment (% of revenue)	0.0	0.0	17.6
Sector performance			
Access			
Fixed-telephone subscriptions (per 100 people)	15.6	17.0	43.6
Mobile-cellular telephone subscriptions (per 100 people)	57.4	187.4	122.9
Fixed (wired)-broadband subscriptions (per 100 people)	0.3	6.9	26.2
Households with a computer (%)	30.0	67.7a	77.7
Households with Internet access at home (%)	20.0	66.6a	75.5
Usage			
Int'l. voice traffic, total (minutes/subscription/month)	..	29.3	..
Domestic mobile traffic (minutes/subscription/month)	15.6	102.0	113.6
Individuals using the Internet (%)	12.7	54.0a	75.4
Quality			
Population covered by a mobile-cellular network (%)	96	99	100
Fixed (wired)-broadband subscriptions (% of total Internet)	5.4	100.0	95.9
International Internet bandwidth (bit/s per Internet user)	383	36,396	85,990
Affordability			
Fixed-telephone sub-basket ($ a month)	..	13.2	25.2
Mobile-cellular sub-basket ($ a month)	..	14.1	20.6
Fixed-broadband sub-basket ($ a month)	..	39.7	29.2
Trade			
ICT goods exports (% of total goods exports)	0.1	0.1	8.9
ICT goods imports (% of total goods imports)	6.5	8.0	10.8
ICT service exports (% of total service exports)	41.5	3.6	30.8
Applications			
Online service index (0–1, 1=highest presence)	0.49	0.80	0.67
Secure Internet servers (per million people)	3.1	34.2	827.6

Senegal

Lower middle income

	Country data		Lower middle-income group
	2005	2012	2012
Economic and social context			
Population (millions)	11	14	2,507
Urban population (% of total)	41	43	39
GNI per capita, *World Bank Atlas* method ($)	770	1,030	1,893
GDP growth, 2000–05 and 2005–12 (avg. annual %)	4.6	3.4	6.0
Adult literacy rate (% ages 15 and older)	42	50	71
Gross primary, secondary, tertiary school enrollment (%)	41	48	64
Sector structure			
Separate telecommunications/ICT regulator	Yes	Yes	
Status of main fixed-line telephone operator	Mixed	Mixed	
Level of competition (competition, partial comp., monopoly)			
International gateway(s)	C	C	
Mobile telephone service	C	P	
Internet service	C	C	
Foreign ownership (not allowed, restricted, allowed)	A	A	
Reg. treatment of VoIP (banned, closed, no framework, allowed)	B	A	
Sector efficiency and capacity			
Telecommunications revenue (% of GDP)	7.8	9.8	2.5
Telecommunications investment (% of revenue)	22.1	10.0	20.5
Sector performance			
Access			
Fixed-telephone subscriptions (per 100 people)	2.4	2.5	5.4
Mobile-cellular telephone subscriptions (per 100 people)	15.4	83.6	83.1
Fixed (wired)-broadband subscriptions (per 100 people)	0.2	0.7	1.4
Households with a computer (%)	2.9[a]	9.0[a]	15.0
Households with Internet access at home (%)	0.7[a]	5.8[a]	12.4
Usage			
Int'l. voice traffic, total (minutes/subscription/month)	36.4	9.3	6.5
Domestic mobile traffic (minutes/subscription/month)	42.6	68.1	..
Individuals using the Internet (%)	4.8	19.2[a]	18.7
Quality			
Population covered by a mobile-cellular network (%)	85	91	86
Fixed (wired)-broadband subscriptions (% of total Internet)	86.8	100.0	58.2
International Internet bandwidth (bit/s per Internet user)	1,437	5,122	8,076
Affordability			
Fixed-telephone sub-basket ($ a month)	..	12.5	4.9
Mobile-cellular sub-basket ($ a month)	..	19.5	10.5
Fixed-broadband sub-basket ($ a month)	..	38.1	20.6
Trade			
ICT goods exports (% of total goods exports)	0.4	0.3	4.6
ICT goods imports (% of total goods imports)	3.9	2.2	7.2
ICT service exports (% of total service exports)	28.0	32.3	47.1
Applications			
Online service index (0–1, 1=highest presence)	0.25	0.35	0.32
Secure Internet servers (per million people)	0.3	2.2	4.4

Serbia

Europe & Central Asia			Upper middle income

	Country data		Upper middle-income group
	2005	2012	2012
Economic and social context			
Population (millions)	7	7	2,391
Urban population (% of total)	54	57	61
GNI per capita, *World Bank Atlas* method ($)	3,430	5,280	6,969
GDP growth, 2000–05 and 2005–12 (avg. annual %)	5.3	1.3	6.2
Adult literacy rate (% ages 15 and older)	..	98	94
Gross primary, secondary, tertiary school enrollment (%)	78	79	76
Sector structure			
Separate telecommunications/ICT regulator	No	Yes	
Status of main fixed-line telephone operator	Mixed	Mixed	
Level of competition (competition, partial comp., monopoly)			
International gateway(s)	..	..	
Mobile telephone service	C	C	
Internet service	..	C	
Foreign ownership (not allowed, restricted, allowed)	..	A	
Reg. treatment of VoIP (banned, closed, no framework, allowed)	B	A	
Sector efficiency and capacity			
Telecommunications revenue (% of GDP)	4.7	5.3	2.5
Telecommunications investment (% of revenue)	22.9	15.0	18.2
Sector performance			
Access			
Fixed-telephone subscriptions (per 100 people)	30.9	38.4	19.4
Mobile-cellular telephone subscriptions (per 100 people)	67.4	117.8	92.4
Fixed (wired)-broadband subscriptions (per 100 people)	0.4	12.9	10.8
Households with a computer (%)	25.0	60.3[a]	40.6
Households with Internet access at home (%)	18.0	48.0[a]	36.3
Usage			
Int'l. voice traffic, total (minutes/subscription/month)	13.5	8.2	1.3
Domestic mobile traffic (minutes/subscription/month)	27.6	97.4	284.4
Individuals using the Internet (%)	26.3[a]	48.1[a]	41.6
Quality			
Population covered by a mobile-cellular network (%)	96	100	99
Fixed (wired)-broadband subscriptions (% of total Internet)	4.4	99.0	95.5
International Internet bandwidth (bit/s per Internet user)	799	89,563	14,580
Affordability			
Fixed-telephone sub-basket ($ a month)	..	7.0	9.4
Mobile-cellular sub-basket ($ a month)	..	12.5	14.9
Fixed-broadband sub-basket ($ a month)	..	21.2	17.8
Trade			
ICT goods exports (% of total goods exports)	..	2.1	17.6
ICT goods imports (% of total goods imports)	..	3.8	14.7
ICT service exports (% of total service exports)	36.5	42.0	29.1
Applications			
Online service index (0–1, 1=highest presence)	0.48	0.58	0.42
Secure Internet servers (per million people)	5.1	34.7	18.5

Seychelles

Sub-Saharan Africa   **Upper middle income**

	Country data		Upper middle-income group
	2005	2012	2012
Economic and social context			
Population (millions)	0.08	0.09	2,391
Urban population (% of total)	52	54	61
GNI per capita, *World Bank Atlas* method ($)	10,540	12,180	6,969
GDP growth, 2000–05 and 2005–12 (avg. annual %)	-1.0	4.0	6.2
Adult literacy rate (% ages 15 and older)	92	92	94
Gross primary, secondary, tertiary school enrollment (%)	82	71	76
Sector structure			
Separate telecommunications/ICT regulator	No	No	
Status of main fixed-line telephone operator	Private	Private	
Level of competition (competition, partial comp., monopoly)			
International gateway(s)	..	C	
Mobile telephone service	P	P	
Internet service	P	C	
Foreign ownership (not allowed, restricted, allowed)	A	A	
Reg. treatment of VoIP (banned, closed, no framework, allowed)	A	A	
Sector efficiency and capacity			
Telecommunications revenue (% of GDP)	6.4	3.8	2.5
Telecommunications investment (% of revenue)	24.9	..	18.2
Sector performance			
Access			
Fixed-telephone subscriptions (per 100 people)	24.6	22.7	19.4
Mobile-cellular telephone subscriptions (per 100 people)	67.5	147.8	92.4
Fixed (wired)-broadband subscriptions (per 100 people)	1.1	11.0	10.8
Households with a computer (%)	12.0[a]	51.9[a]	40.6
Households with Internet access at home (%)	6.0[a]	41.9[a]	36.3
Usage			
Int'l. voice traffic, total (minutes/subscription/month)	9.3	5.2	1.3
Domestic mobile traffic (minutes/subscription/month)	..	42.3	284.4
Individuals using the Internet (%)	25.4	47.1[a]	41.6
Quality			
Population covered by a mobile-cellular network (%)	98	98	99
Fixed (wired)-broadband subscriptions (% of total Internet)	24.5	94.2	95.5
International Internet bandwidth (bit/s per Internet user)	1,062	15,606	14,580
Affordability			
Fixed-telephone sub-basket ($ a month)	..	9.0	9.4
Mobile-cellular sub-basket ($ a month)	..	15.3	14.9
Fixed-broadband sub-basket ($ a month)	..	16.3	17.8
Trade			
ICT goods exports (% of total goods exports)	0.0	0.0	17.6
ICT goods imports (% of total goods imports)	1.5	2.1	14.7
ICT service exports (% of total service exports)	4.9	6.4	29.1
Applications			
Online service index (0–1, 1=highest presence)	0.49	0.33	0.42
Secure Internet servers (per million people)	482.5	604.4	18.5

Sierra Leone

	Country data		Low-income group
	2005	2012	2012
Economic and social context			
Population (millions)	5	6	846
Urban population (% of total)	37	40	28
GNI per capita, *World Bank Atlas* method ($)	310	580	590
GDP growth, 2000–05 and 2005–12 (avg. annual %)	9.0	6.3	5.9
Adult literacy rate (% ages 15 and older)	35	43	61
Gross primary, secondary, tertiary school enrollment (%)	..	..	60
Sector structure			
Separate telecommunications/ICT regulator	No	Yes	
Status of main fixed-line telephone operator	Public	Public	
Level of competition (competition, partial comp., monopoly)			
International gateway(s)	..	P	
Mobile telephone service	C	P	
Internet service	P	P	
Foreign ownership (not allowed, restricted, allowed)	..	..	
Reg. treatment of VoIP (banned, closed, no framework, allowed)	B	B	
Sector efficiency and capacity			
Telecommunications revenue (% of GDP)	..	..	5.0
Telecommunications investment (% of revenue)	..	..	..
Sector performance			
Access			
Fixed-telephone subscriptions (per 100 people)	0.5	0.3	1.0
Mobile-cellular telephone subscriptions (per 100 people)	14.3	37.0	47.2
Fixed (wired)-broadband subscriptions (per 100 people)	0.0	..	0.2
Households with a computer (%)	0.8	..	4.2
Households with Internet access at home (%)	..	..	3.4
Usage			
Int'l. voice traffic, total (minutes/subscription/month)	..	..	..
Domestic mobile traffic (minutes/subscription/month)	..	..	70.1
Individuals using the Internet (%)	0.2	1.3[a]	6.2
Quality			
Population covered by a mobile-cellular network (%)	70	..	..
Fixed (wired)-broadband subscriptions (% of total Internet)	..	..	30.9
International Internet bandwidth (bit/s per Internet user)	..	1,994	9,141
Affordability			
Fixed-telephone sub-basket ($ a month)	..	..	8.9
Mobile-cellular sub-basket ($ a month)	..	..	11.9
Fixed-broadband sub-basket ($ a month)	..	..	46.9
Trade			
ICT goods exports (% of total goods exports)	..	..	..
ICT goods imports (% of total goods imports)	..	..	..
ICT service exports (% of total service exports)	0.2	57.2	..
Applications			
Online service index (0–1, 1=highest presence)	0.15	0.17	0.20
Secure Internet servers (per million people)	0.7	0.8	1.1

Singapore

	Country data		High-income group
	2005	2012	2012
Economic and social context			
Population (millions)	4	5	1,300
Urban population (% of total)	100	100	80
GNI per capita, *World Bank Atlas* method ($)	27,240	47,210	38,412
GDP growth, 2000–05 and 2005–12 (avg. annual %)	5.1	5.5	1.0
Adult literacy rate (% ages 15 and older)	93	96	..
Gross primary, secondary, tertiary school enrollment (%)	..	..	93
Sector structure			
Separate telecommunications/ICT regulator	Yes	Yes	
Status of main fixed-line telephone operator	Mixed	Mixed	
Level of competition (competition, partial comp., monopoly)			
International gateway(s)	C	C	
Mobile telephone service	C	C	
Internet service	C	C	
Foreign ownership (not allowed, restricted, allowed)	A	A	
Reg. treatment of VoIP (banned, closed, no framework, allowed)	A	No	
Sector efficiency and capacity			
Telecommunications revenue (% of GDP)	3.5	2.6	2.7
Telecommunications investment (% of revenue)	12.6	..	17.6
Sector performance			
Access			
Fixed-telephone subscriptions (per 100 people)	41.0	37.5	43.6
Mobile-cellular telephone subscriptions (per 100 people)	97.5	152.1	122.9
Fixed (wired)-broadband subscriptions (per 100 people)	14.6	25.4	26.2
Households with a computer (%)	74.0	87.7[a]	77.7
Households with Internet access at home (%)	66.0	87.7[a]	75.5
Usage			
Int'l. voice traffic, total (minutes/subscription/month)	75.2	88.3	..
Domestic mobile traffic (minutes/subscription/month)	..	..	113.6
Individuals using the Internet (%)	61.0	74.2[a]	75.4
Quality			
Population covered by a mobile-cellular network (%)	100	100	100
Fixed (wired)-broadband subscriptions (% of total Internet)	29.1	98.3	95.9
International Internet bandwidth (bit/s per Internet user)	31,606	387,641	85,990
Affordability			
Fixed-telephone sub-basket ($ a month)	..	8.8	25.2
Mobile-cellular sub-basket ($ a month)	..	9.3	20.6
Fixed-broadband sub-basket ($ a month)	..	30.0	29.2
Trade			
ICT goods exports (% of total goods exports)	45.5	28.4	8.9
ICT goods imports (% of total goods imports)	37.9	23.4	10.8
ICT service exports (% of total service exports)	22.3	24.0	30.8
Applications			
Online service index (0–1, 1=highest presence)	0.70	1.00	0.67
Secure Internet servers (per million people)	275.4	610.1	827.6

Sint Maarten (Dutch part)

High income

	Country data		High-income group
	2005	**2012**	**2012**
Economic and social context			
Population (millions)	0.04	0.04	1,300
Urban population (% of total)	..	..	80
GNI per capita, *World Bank Atlas* method ($)	..	..	38,412
GDP growth, 2000–05 and 2005–12 (avg. annual %)	..	..	1.0
Adult literacy rate (% ages 15 and older)	..	..	..
Gross primary, secondary, tertiary school enrollment (%)	..	..	93
Sector structure			
Separate telecommunications/ICT regulator	..	..	
Status of main fixed-line telephone operator	..	..	
Level of competition (competition, partial comp., monopoly)			
International gateway(s)	..	..	
Mobile telephone service	..	..	
Internet service	..	..	
Foreign ownership (not allowed, restricted, allowed)	..	..	
Reg. treatment of VoIP (banned, closed, no framework, allowed)	..	..	
Sector efficiency and capacity			
Telecommunications revenue (% of GDP)	..	..	2.7
Telecommunications investment (% of revenue)	..	..	17.6
Sector performance			
Access			
Fixed-telephone subscriptions (per 100 people)	..	..	43.6
Mobile-cellular telephone subscriptions (per 100 people)	..	..	122.9
Fixed (wired)-broadband subscriptions (per 100 people)	..	..	26.2
Households with a computer (%)	..	..	77.7
Households with Internet access at home (%)	..	..	75.5
Usage			
Int'l. voice traffic, total (minutes/subscription/month)	..	..	..
Domestic mobile traffic (minutes/subscription/month)	..	..	113.6
Individuals using the Internet (%)	..	..	75.4
Quality			
Population covered by a mobile-cellular network (%)	..	..	100
Fixed (wired)-broadband subscriptions (% of total Internet)	..	..	95.9
International Internet bandwidth (bit/s per Internet user)	..	..	85,990
Affordability			
Fixed-telephone sub-basket ($ a month)	..	..	25.2
Mobile-cellular sub-basket ($ a month)	..	..	20.6
Fixed-broadband sub-basket ($ a month)	..	..	29.2
Trade			
ICT goods exports (% of total goods exports)	..	..	8.9
ICT goods imports (% of total goods imports)	..	..	10.8
ICT service exports (% of total service exports)	..	..	30.8
Applications			
Online service index (0–1, 1=highest presence)	..	..	0.67
Secure Internet servers (per million people)	..	..	827.6

Slovak Republic

High income

	Country data		High-income group
	2005	2012	2012
Economic and social context			
Population (millions)	5	5	1,300
Urban population (% of total)	56	55	80
GNI per capita, *World Bank Atlas* method ($)	11,070	17,190	38,412
GDP growth, 2000–05 and 2005–12 (avg. annual %)	4.9	3.5	1.0
Adult literacy rate (% ages 15 and older)	..	..	..
Gross primary, secondary, tertiary school enrollment (%)	78	82	93
Sector structure			
Separate telecommunications/ICT regulator	Yes	Yes	
Status of main fixed-line telephone operator	Mixed	Mixed	
Level of competition (competition, partial comp., monopoly)			
International gateway(s)	C	P	
Mobile telephone service	C	P	
Internet service	C	C	
Foreign ownership (not allowed, restricted, allowed)	A	A	
Reg. treatment of VoIP (banned, closed, no framework, allowed)	A	A	
Sector efficiency and capacity			
Telecommunications revenue (% of GDP)	3.0	2.6	2.7
Telecommunications investment (% of revenue)	22.6	11.0	17.6
Sector performance			
Access			
Fixed-telephone subscriptions (per 100 people)	22.2	17.9	43.6
Mobile-cellular telephone subscriptions (per 100 people)	84.2	111.9	122.9
Fixed (wired)-broadband subscriptions (per 100 people)	3.4	14.7	26.2
Households with a computer (%)	47.0	79.0	77.7
Households with Internet access at home (%)	23.0	76.6	75.5
Usage			
Int'l. voice traffic, total (minutes/subscription/month)	12.4	11.4	..
Domestic mobile traffic (minutes/subscription/month)	86.4	120.0	*113.6*
Individuals using the Internet (%)	55.2	80.0	75.4
Quality			
Population covered by a mobile-cellular network (%)	100	100	100
Fixed (wired)-broadband subscriptions (% of total Internet)	61.7	96.4	*95.9*
International Internet bandwidth (bit/s per Internet user)	4,772	11,477	85,990
Affordability			
Fixed-telephone sub-basket ($ a month)	..	18.9	25.2
Mobile-cellular sub-basket ($ a month)	..	17.5	20.6
Fixed-broadband sub-basket ($ a month)	..	27.6	29.2
Trade			
ICT goods exports (% of total goods exports)	9.4	16.6	8.9
ICT goods imports (% of total goods imports)	8.3	12.8	10.8
ICT service exports (% of total service exports)	24.2	31.7	30.8
Applications			
Online service index (0–1, 1=highest presence)	0.59	0.50	0.67
Secure Internet servers (per million people)	18.4	263.3	827.6

Slovenia

	Country data		High-income group
	2005	2012	2012
Economic and social context			
Population (millions)	2	2	1,300
Urban population (% of total)	50	50	80
GNI per capita, *World Bank Atlas* method ($)	18,070	22,810	38,412
GDP growth, 2000–05 and 2005–12 (avg. annual %)	3.6	0.6	1.0
Adult literacy rate (% ages 15 and older)	*100*	*100*	..
Gross primary, secondary, tertiary school enrollment (%)	92	94	93
Sector structure			
Separate telecommunications/ICT regulator	Yes	Yes	
Status of main fixed-line telephone operator	Mixed	Mixed	
Level of competition (competition, partial comp., monopoly)			
International gateway(s)	C	C	
Mobile telephone service	C	C	
Internet service	C	C	
Foreign ownership (not allowed, restricted, allowed)	A	A	
Reg. treatment of VoIP (banned, closed, no framework, allowed)	A	A	
Sector efficiency and capacity			
Telecommunications revenue (% of GDP)	3.3	2.5	2.7
Telecommunications investment (% of revenue)	23.8	20.0	17.6
Sector performance			
Access			
Fixed-telephone subscriptions (per 100 people)	51.0	39.9	43.6
Mobile-cellular telephone subscriptions (per 100 people)	87.9	108.6	122.9
Fixed (wired)-broadband subscriptions (per 100 people)	9.8	24.3	26.2
Households with a computer (%)	61.0	76.0	77.7
Households with Internet access at home (%)	48.2	74.0	75.5
Usage			
Int'l. voice traffic, total (minutes/subscription/month)	11.6	9.9	..
Domestic mobile traffic (minutes/subscription/month)	109.4	137.3	*113.6*
Individuals using the Internet (%)	46.8	70.0	75.4
Quality			
Population covered by a mobile-cellular network (%)	99	100	100
Fixed (wired)-broadband subscriptions (% of total Internet)	49.4	99.6	*95.9*
International Internet bandwidth (bit/s per Internet user)	2,681	94,652	85,990
Affordability			
Fixed-telephone sub-basket ($ a month)	..	18.7	25.2
Mobile-cellular sub-basket ($ a month)	..	25.1	20.6
Fixed-broadband sub-basket ($ a month)	..	36.2	29.2
Trade			
ICT goods exports (% of total goods exports)	1.3	1.8	8.9
ICT goods imports (% of total goods imports)	4.3	3.6	10.8
ICT service exports (% of total service exports)	20.4	22.2	30.8
Applications			
Online service index (0–1, 1=highest presence)	0.67	0.67	0.67
Secure Internet servers (per million people)	79.0	547.8	827.6

Solomon Islands

Lower middle income

	Country data		Lower middle-income group
	2005	2012	2012
Economic and social context			
Population (millions)	0.47	0.55	2,507
Urban population (% of total)	18	21	39
GNI per capita, *World Bank Atlas* method ($)	900	1,130	1,893
GDP growth, 2000–05 and 2005–12 (avg. annual %)	1.6	6.0	6.0
Adult literacy rate (% ages 15 and older)	..	..	71
Gross primary, secondary, tertiary school enrollment (%)	51	..	64
Sector structure			
Separate telecommunications/ICT regulator	No	Yes	
Status of main fixed-line telephone operator	Mixed	Mixed	
Level of competition (competition, partial comp., monopoly)			
International gateway(s)	..	..	
Mobile telephone service	..	..	
Internet service	..	..	
Foreign ownership (not allowed, restricted, allowed)	..	..	
Reg. treatment of VoIP (banned, closed, no framework, allowed)	B	B	
Sector efficiency and capacity			
Telecommunications revenue (% of GDP)	2.7	..	2.5
Telecommunications investment (% of revenue)	..	..	20.5
Sector performance			
Access			
Fixed-telephone subscriptions (per 100 people)	1.6	1.5	5.4
Mobile-cellular telephone subscriptions (per 100 people)	1.3	55.0	83.1
Fixed (wired)-broadband subscriptions (per 100 people)	0.1	0.4	1.4
Households with a computer (%)	..	5.1[a]	15.0
Households with Internet access at home (%)	..	4.2[a]	12.4
Usage			
Int'l. voice traffic, total (minutes/subscription/month)	..	..	6.5
Domestic mobile traffic (minutes/subscription/month)	..	..	..
Individuals using the Internet (%)	0.8	7.0[a]	18.7
Quality			
Population covered by a mobile-cellular network (%)	..	..	86
Fixed (wired)-broadband subscriptions (% of total Internet)	23.7	..	58.2
International Internet bandwidth (bit/s per Internet user)	2,044	3,614	8,076
Affordability			
Fixed-telephone sub-basket ($ a month)	..	10.3	4.9
Mobile-cellular sub-basket ($ a month)	..	14.5	10.5
Fixed-broadband sub-basket ($ a month)	..	259.2	20.6
Trade			
ICT goods exports (% of total goods exports)	..	0.0	4.6
ICT goods imports (% of total goods imports)	..	2.7	7.2
ICT service exports (% of total service exports)	57.5	2.4	47.1
Applications			
Online service index (0–1, 1=highest presence)	0.27	0.13	0.32
Secure Internet servers (per million people)	4.3	5.3	4.4

Somalia

Sub-Saharan Africa			Low income

	Country data		Low-income group
	2005	2012	2012
Economic and social context			
Population (millions)	8	10	846
Urban population (% of total)	35	38	28
GNI per capita, *World Bank Atlas* method ($)	..	..	590
GDP growth, 2000–05 and 2005–12 (avg. annual %)	..	..	5.9
Adult literacy rate (% ages 15 and older)	..	..	61
Gross primary, secondary, tertiary school enrollment (%)	..	..	60
Sector structure			
Separate telecommunications/ICT regulator	No	No	
Status of main fixed-line telephone operator	Private	Private	
Level of competition (competition, partial comp., monopoly)			
International gateway(s)	..	..	
Mobile telephone service	..	..	
Internet service	..	..	
Foreign ownership (not allowed, restricted, allowed)	..	..	
Reg. treatment of VoIP (banned, closed, no framework, allowed)	A	A	
Sector efficiency and capacity			
Telecommunications revenue (% of GDP)	..	..	5.0
Telecommunications investment (% of revenue)	..	..	..
Sector performance			
Access			
Fixed-telephone subscriptions (per 100 people)	1.2	0.7	1.0
Mobile-cellular telephone subscriptions (per 100 people)	5.9	22.6	47.2
Fixed (wired)-broadband subscriptions (per 100 people)	0.0	0.0	0.2
Households with a computer (%)	..	..	4.2
Households with Internet access at home (%)	..	..	3.4
Usage			
Int'l. voice traffic, total (minutes/subscription/month)	..	..	..
Domestic mobile traffic (minutes/subscription/month)	..	..	70.1
Individuals using the Internet (%)	1.1[a]	1.4[a]	6.2
Quality			
Population covered by a mobile-cellular network (%)	..	80	..
Fixed (wired)-broadband subscriptions (% of total Internet)	0.0	..	30.9
International Internet bandwidth (bit/s per Internet user)	33	..	9,141
Affordability			
Fixed-telephone sub-basket ($ a month)	..	..	8.9
Mobile-cellular sub-basket ($ a month)	..	..	11.9
Fixed-broadband sub-basket ($ a month)	..	..	46.9
Trade			
ICT goods exports (% of total goods exports)	..	..	..
ICT goods imports (% of total goods imports)	..	..	..
ICT service exports (% of total service exports)	..	..	..
Applications			
Online service index (0–1, 1=highest presence)	0.00	0.18	0.20
Secure Internet servers (per million people)	0.1	0.1	1.1

South Africa

Sub-Saharan Africa			Upper middle income

	Country data		Upper middle-income group
	2005	2012	2012

Economic and social context
Population (millions)	48	52	2,391
Urban population (% of total)	59	62	61
GNI per capita, *World Bank Atlas* method ($)	4,810	7,460	6,969
GDP growth, 2000–05 and 2005–12 (avg. annual %)	3.8	2.8	6.2
Adult literacy rate (% ages 15 and older)	89	93	94
Gross primary, secondary, tertiary school enrollment (%)	..	..	76

Sector structure
Separate telecommunications/ICT regulator	Yes	Yes	
Status of main fixed-line telephone operator	Mixed	Mixed	
Level of competition (competition, partial comp., monopoly)			
International gateway(s)	P	P	
Mobile telephone service	P	P	
Internet service	C	C	
Foreign ownership (not allowed, restricted, allowed)	R	R	
Reg. treatment of VoIP (banned, closed, no framework, allowed)	A	A	

Sector efficiency and capacity
Telecommunications revenue (% of GDP)	6.3	4.5	2.5
Telecommunications investment (% of revenue)	13.1	12.1	18.2

Sector performance
Access
Fixed-telephone subscriptions (per 100 people)	9.8	7.7	19.4
Mobile-cellular telephone subscriptions (per 100 people)	70.4	130.6	92.4
Fixed (wired)-broadband subscriptions (per 100 people)	0.3	2.1	10.8
Households with a computer (%)	13.0[a]	23.6[a]	40.6
Households with Internet access at home (%)	3.0[a]	25.5[a]	36.3

Usage
Int'l. voice traffic, total (minutes/subscription/month)	..	..	1.3
Domestic mobile traffic (minutes/subscription/month)	..	..	284.4
Individuals using the Internet (%)	7.5	41.0[a]	41.6

Quality
Population covered by a mobile-cellular network (%)	96	..	99
Fixed (wired)-broadband subscriptions (% of total Internet)	1.7	..	95.5
International Internet bandwidth (bit/s per Internet user)	244	18,111	14,580

Affordability
Fixed-telephone sub-basket ($ a month)	..	28.3	9.4
Mobile-cellular sub-basket ($ a month)	..	32.6	14.9
Fixed-broadband sub-basket ($ a month)	..	28.1	17.8

Trade
ICT goods exports (% of total goods exports)	1.2	1.0	17.6
ICT goods imports (% of total goods imports)	11.1	7.6	14.7
ICT service exports (% of total service exports)	9.9	10.6	29.1

Applications
Online service index (0–1, 1=highest presence)	0.51	0.46	0.42
Secure Internet servers (per million people)	20.2	87.7	18.5

South Sudan

	Country data		Low-income group
	2005	2012	2012
Economic and social context			
Population (millions)	8	11	846
Urban population (% of total)	17	18	28
GNI per capita, *World Bank Atlas* method ($)	..	790	590
GDP growth, 2000–05 and 2005–12 (avg. annual %)	..	-9.8	5.9
Adult literacy rate (% ages 15 and older)	..	..	61
Gross primary, secondary, tertiary school enrollment (%)	..	..	60
Sector structure			
Separate telecommunications/ICT regulator	No	No	
Status of main fixed-line telephone operator	Mixed	Mixed	
Level of competition (competition, partial comp., monopoly)			
International gateway(s)	..	..	
Mobile telephone service	..	..	
Internet service	..	..	
Foreign ownership (not allowed, restricted, allowed)	..	..	
Reg. treatment of VoIP (banned, closed, no framework, allowed)	..	C	
Sector efficiency and capacity			
Telecommunications revenue (% of GDP)	..	..	5.0
Telecommunications investment (% of revenue)	..	..	..
Sector performance			
Access			
Fixed-telephone subscriptions (per 100 people)	..	0.0	1.0
Mobile-cellular telephone subscriptions (per 100 people)	..	21.2	47.2
Fixed (wired)-broadband subscriptions (per 100 people)	..	0.0	0.2
Households with a computer (%)	..	..	4.2
Households with Internet access at home (%)	..	..	3.4
Usage			
Int'l. voice traffic, total (minutes/subscription/month)	..	10.2	..
Domestic mobile traffic (minutes/subscription/month)	..	63.0	70.1
Individuals using the Internet (%)	..	..	6.2
Quality			
Population covered by a mobile-cellular network (%)	..	..	..
Fixed (wired)-broadband subscriptions (% of total Internet)	..	..	30.9
International Internet bandwidth (bit/s per Internet user)	..	..	9,141
Affordability			
Fixed-telephone sub-basket ($ a month)	..	..	8.9
Mobile-cellular sub-basket ($ a month)	..	..	11.9
Fixed-broadband sub-basket ($ a month)	..	..	46.9
Trade			
ICT goods exports (% of total goods exports)	..	..	..
ICT goods imports (% of total goods imports)	..	..	..
ICT service exports (% of total service exports)	..	..	..
Applications			
Online service index (0–1, 1=highest presence)	..	0.14	0.20
Secure Internet servers (per million people)	..	..	1.1

Spain

High income

	Country data		High-income group
	2005	2012	2012
Economic and social context			
Population (millions)	44	47	1,300
Urban population (% of total)	77	78	80
GNI per capita, World Bank Atlas method ($)	25,310	29,270	38,412
GDP growth, 2000–05 and 2005–12 (avg. annual %)	3.2	0.1	1.0
Adult literacy rate (% ages 15 and older)	98	98	..
Gross primary, secondary, tertiary school enrollment (%)	96	106	93
Sector structure			
Separate telecommunications/ICT regulator	Yes	Yes	
Status of main fixed-line telephone operator	Private	Private	
Level of competition (competition, partial comp., monopoly)			
International gateway(s)	C	C	
Mobile telephone service	C	C	
Internet service	C	C	
Foreign ownership (not allowed, restricted, allowed)	A	A	
Reg. treatment of VoIP (banned, closed, no framework, allowed)	A	A	
Sector efficiency and capacity			
Telecommunications revenue (% of GDP)	3.1	2.3	2.7
Telecommunications investment (% of revenue)	19.6	15.4	17.6
Sector performance			
Access			
Fixed-telephone subscriptions (per 100 people)	44.9	41.9	43.6
Mobile-cellular telephone subscriptions (per 100 people)	98.4	108.4	122.9
Fixed (wired)-broadband subscriptions (per 100 people)	11.6	24.4	26.2
Households with a computer (%)	55.0	74.0	77.7
Households with Internet access at home (%)	35.5	68.0	75.5
Usage			
Int'l. voice traffic, total (minutes/subscription/month)	..	..	..
Domestic mobile traffic (minutes/subscription/month)	93.1	115.7	113.6
Individuals using the Internet (%)	47.9	72.0	75.4
Quality			
Population covered by a mobile-cellular network (%)	99	100	100
Fixed (wired)-broadband subscriptions (% of total Internet)	80.8	99.6	95.9
International Internet bandwidth (bit/s per Internet user)	5,799	81,365	85,990
Affordability			
Fixed-telephone sub-basket ($ a month)	..	33.5	25.2
Mobile-cellular sub-basket ($ a month)	..	39.9	20.6
Fixed-broadband sub-basket ($ a month)	..	33.5	29.2
Trade			
ICT goods exports (% of total goods exports)	3.7	1.3	8.9
ICT goods imports (% of total goods imports)	7.2	4.6	10.8
ICT service exports (% of total service exports)	23.3	30.0	30.8
Applications			
Online service index (0–1, 1=highest presence)	0.72	0.76	0.67
Secure Internet servers (per million people)	81.2	266.7	827.6

Sri Lanka

<table>
<tr><td>**South Asia**</td><td colspan="2"></td><td>**Lower middle income**</td></tr>
<tr><td></td><td colspan="2">Country data</td><td>Lower middle-income group</td></tr>
<tr><td></td><td>2005</td><td>2012</td><td>2012</td></tr>
</table>

	2005	2012	2012
Economic and social context			
Population (millions)	20	20	2,507
Urban population (% of total)	15	15	39
GNI per capita, *World Bank Atlas* method ($)	1,210	2,920	1,893
GDP growth, 2000–05 and 2005–12 (avg. annual %)	4.3	6.5	6.0
Adult literacy rate (% ages 15 and older)	91	91	71
Gross primary, secondary, tertiary school enrollment (%)	..	77	64
Sector structure			
Separate telecommunications/ICT regulator	Yes	Yes	
Status of main fixed-line telephone operator	Mixed	Mixed	
Level of competition (competition, partial comp., monopoly)			
International gateway(s)	..	P	
Mobile telephone service	C	P	
Internet service	C	P	
Foreign ownership (not allowed, restricted, allowed)	A	A	
Reg. treatment of VoIP (banned, closed, no framework, allowed)	No	C	
Sector efficiency and capacity			
Telecommunications revenue (% of GDP)	2.5	1.9	2.5
Telecommunications investment (% of revenue)	12.2	33.4	20.5
Sector performance			
Access			
Fixed-telephone subscriptions (per 100 people)	6.2	16.3	5.4
Mobile-cellular telephone subscriptions (per 100 people)	16.8	91.6	83.1
Fixed (wired)-broadband subscriptions (per 100 people)	0.1	1.7	1.4
Households with a computer (%)	5.0	15.0[a]	15.0
Households with Internet access at home (%)	1.1[a]	10.3[a]	12.4
Usage			
Int'l. voice traffic, total (minutes/subscription/month)	..	10.0	6.5
Domestic mobile traffic (minutes/subscription/month)	74.7	160.5	..
Individuals using the Internet (%)	1.8[a]	18.3[a]	18.7
Quality			
Population covered by a mobile-cellular network (%)	85	98	86
Fixed (wired)-broadband subscriptions (% of total Internet)	18.3	83.6	58.2
International Internet bandwidth (bit/s per Internet user)	1,396	5,995	8,076
Affordability			
Fixed-telephone sub-basket ($ a month)	..	3.4	4.9
Mobile-cellular sub-basket ($ a month)	..	1.1	10.5
Fixed-broadband sub-basket ($ a month)	..	4.5	20.6
Trade			
ICT goods exports (% of total goods exports)	1.1	0.5	4.6
ICT goods imports (% of total goods imports)	4.9	3.7	7.2
ICT service exports (% of total service exports)	20.4	24.6	47.1
Applications			
Online service index (0–1, 1=highest presence)	0.42	0.38	0.32
Secure Internet servers (per million people)	1.8	8.7	4.4

St. Kitts and Nevis

High income

	Country data		High-income group
	2005	2012	2012
Economic and social context			
Population (millions)	0.05	0.05	1,300
Urban population (% of total)	32	32	80
GNI per capita, World Bank Atlas method ($)	10,900	13,610	38,412
GDP growth, 2000–05 and 2005–12 (avg. annual %)	3.2	0.7	1.0
Adult literacy rate (% ages 15 and older)	..	..	..
Gross primary, secondary, tertiary school enrollment (%)	..	75	93
Sector structure			
Separate telecommunications/ICT regulator	No	No	
Status of main fixed-line telephone operator	Private	Private	
Level of competition (competition, partial comp., monopoly)			
International gateway(s)	..	..	
Mobile telephone service	..	..	
Internet service	..	..	
Foreign ownership (not allowed, restricted, allowed)	..	..	
Reg. treatment of VoIP (banned, closed, no framework, allowed)	No	No	
Sector efficiency and capacity			
Telecommunications revenue (% of GDP)	5.4	6.9	2.7
Telecommunications investment (% of revenue)	25.3	7.9	17.6
Sector performance			
Access			
Fixed-telephone subscriptions (per 100 people)	41.3	37.3[a]	43.6
Mobile-cellular telephone subscriptions (per 100 people)	103.8	156.8[a]	122.9
Fixed (wired)-broadband subscriptions (per 100 people)	13.2	27.2[a]	26.2
Households with a computer (%)	17.3[a]	54.7[a]	77.7
Households with Internet access at home (%)	..	..	75.5
Usage			
Int'l. voice traffic, total (minutes/subscription/month)	58.2	63.5	..
Domestic mobile traffic (minutes/subscription/month)	102.1	32.3	113.6
Individuals using the Internet (%)	34.0[a]	79.3[a]	75.4
Quality			
Population covered by a mobile-cellular network (%)	..	..	100
Fixed (wired)-broadband subscriptions (% of total Internet)	..	..	95.9
International Internet bandwidth (bit/s per Internet user)	..	67,860	85,990
Affordability			
Fixed-telephone sub-basket ($ a month)	..	12.6	25.2
Mobile-cellular sub-basket ($ a month)	..	22.1	20.6
Fixed-broadband sub-basket ($ a month)	..	36.7	29.2
Trade			
ICT goods exports (% of total goods exports)	2.4	22.5	8.9
ICT goods imports (% of total goods imports)	8.3	5.9	10.8
ICT service exports (% of total service exports)	14.0	16.7	30.8
Applications			
Online service index (0–1, 1=highest presence)	0.48	0.18	0.67
Secure Internet servers (per million people)	1,017.5	1,388.9	827.6

St. Lucia

Latin America & Caribbean		**Upper middle income**	

	Country data		Upper middle-income group
	2005	**2012**	**2012**
Economic and social context			
Population (millions)	0.17	0.18	2,391
Urban population (% of total)	23	17	61
GNI per capita, *World Bank Atlas* method ($)	5,110	6,890	6,969
GDP growth, 2000–05 and 2005–12 (avg. annual %)	2.0	2.2	6.2
Adult literacy rate (% ages 15 and older)	..	..	94
Gross primary, secondary, tertiary school enrollment (%)	73	71	76
Sector structure			
Separate telecommunications/ICT regulator	Yes	Yes.	
Status of main fixed-line telephone operator	Private	Private	
Level of competition (competition, partial comp., monopoly)			
International gateway(s)	C	C	
Mobile telephone service	C	C	
Internet service	M	C	
Foreign ownership (not allowed, restricted, allowed)	A	A	
Reg. treatment of VoIP (banned, closed, no framework, allowed)	No	A	
Sector efficiency and capacity			
Telecommunications revenue (% of GDP)	*8.5*	*6.7*	*2.5*
Telecommunications investment (% of revenue)	*9.4*	*8.4*	*18.2*
Sector performance			
Access			
Fixed-telephone subscriptions (per 100 people)	23.6	20.4	19.4
Mobile-cellular telephone subscriptions (per 100 people)	63.9	125.5	92.4
Fixed (wired)-broadband subscriptions (per 100 people)	4.2[a]	13.6	10.8
Households with a computer (%)	..	42.5[a]	40.6
Households with Internet access at home (%)	..	32.2[a]	36.3
Usage			
Int'l. voice traffic, total (minutes/subscription/month)	53.5	28.7	1.3
Domestic mobile traffic (minutes/subscription/month)	64.7	80.4	284.4
Individuals using the Internet (%)	21.6	48.6[a]	41.6
Quality			
Population covered by a mobile-cellular network (%)	80	*100*	99
Fixed (wired)-broadband subscriptions (% of total Internet)	91.2	98.5	95.5
International Internet bandwidth (bit/s per Internet user)	..	68,218	14,580
Affordability			
Fixed-telephone sub-basket ($ a month)	..	13.4	9.4
Mobile-cellular sub-basket ($ a month)	..	21.6	14.9
Fixed-broadband sub-basket ($ a month)	..	36.2	17.8
Trade			
ICT goods exports (% of total goods exports)	4.8	4.2	17.6
ICT goods imports (% of total goods imports)	5.5	3.9	14.7
ICT service exports (% of total service exports)	5.9	9.1	29.1
Applications			
Online service index (0–1, 1=highest presence)	0.47	0.35	0.42
Secure Internet servers (per million people)	36.3	71.4	18.5

St. Martin (French part)

	Country data		High-income group
	2005	2012	2012
Economic and social context			
Population (millions)	0.03	0.03	1,300
Urban population (% of total)	..	..	80
GNI per capita, *World Bank Atlas* method ($)	..	..	38,412
GDP growth, 2000–05 and 2005–12 (avg. annual %)	..	..	1.0
Adult literacy rate (% ages 15 and older)	..	..	..
Gross primary, secondary, tertiary school enrollment (%)	..	..	93
Sector structure			
Separate telecommunications/ICT regulator	..	..	
Status of main fixed-line telephone operator	..	..	
Level of competition (competition, partial comp., monopoly)			
International gateway(s)	..	..	
Mobile telephone service	..	..	
Internet service	..	..	
Foreign ownership (not allowed, restricted, allowed)	..	..	
Reg. treatment of VoIP (banned, closed, no framework, allowed)	..	..	
Sector efficiency and capacity			
Telecommunications revenue (% of GDP)	..	..	2.7
Telecommunications investment (% of revenue)	..	..	17.6
Sector performance			
Access			
Fixed-telephone subscriptions (per 100 people)	..	..	43.6
Mobile-cellular telephone subscriptions (per 100 people)	..	..	122.9
Fixed (wired)-broadband subscriptions (per 100 people)	..	..	26.2
Households with a computer (%)	..	..	77.7
Households with Internet access at home (%)	..	..	75.5
Usage			
Int'l. voice traffic, total (minutes/subscription/month)	..	..	..
Domestic mobile traffic (minutes/subscription/month)	..	..	113.6
Individuals using the Internet (%)	..	..	75.4
Quality			
Population covered by a mobile-cellular network (%)	..	..	100
Fixed (wired)-broadband subscriptions (% of total Internet)	..	..	95.9
International Internet bandwidth (bit/s per Internet user)	..	..	85,990
Affordability			
Fixed-telephone sub-basket ($ a month)	..	..	25.2
Mobile-cellular sub-basket ($ a month)	..	..	20.6
Fixed-broadband sub-basket ($ a month)	..	..	29.2
Trade			
ICT goods exports (% of total goods exports)	..	..	8.9
ICT goods imports (% of total goods imports)	..	..	10.8
ICT service exports (% of total service exports)	..	..	30.8
Applications			
Online service index (0–1, 1=highest presence)	..	..	0.67
Secure Internet servers (per million people)	..	32.3	827.6

St. Vincent and the Grenadines

Latin America & Caribbean			Upper middle income

	Country data		Upper middle-income group
	2005	2012	2012
Economic and social context			
Population (millions)	0.11	0.11	2,391
Urban population (% of total)	47	50	61
GNI per capita, *World Bank Atlas* method ($)	4,960	6,400	6,969
GDP growth, 2000–05 and 2005–12 (avg. annual %)	4.9	0.6	6.2
Adult literacy rate (% ages 15 and older)	..	..	94
Gross primary, secondary, tertiary school enrollment (%)	78	..	76
Sector structure			
Separate telecommunications/ICT regulator	Yes	Yes	
Status of main fixed-line telephone operator	Private	Private	
Level of competition (competition, partial comp., monopoly)			
International gateway(s)	C	C	
Mobile telephone service	C	C	
Internet service	C	C	
Foreign ownership (not allowed, restricted, allowed)	A	A	
Reg. treatment of VoIP (banned, closed, no framework, allowed)	No	A	
Sector efficiency and capacity			
Telecommunications revenue (% of GDP)	9.3	7.4	2.5
Telecommunications investment (% of revenue)	..	..	18.2
Sector performance			
Access			
Fixed-telephone subscriptions (per 100 people)	20.7	17.7	19.4
Mobile-cellular telephone subscriptions (per 100 people)	64.9	123.9	92.4
Fixed (wired)-broadband subscriptions (per 100 people)	3.4	12.4	10.8
Households with a computer (%)	16.8[a]	62.3[a]	40.6
Households with Internet access at home (%)	14.1[a]	49.7[a]	36.3
Usage			
Int'l. voice traffic, total (minutes/subscription/month)	58.9	34.7	1.3
Domestic mobile traffic (minutes/subscription/month)	49.4	82.2	284.4
Individuals using the Internet (%)	9.2	47.5[a]	41.6
Quality			
Population covered by a mobile-cellular network (%)	100	100	99
Fixed (wired)-broadband subscriptions (% of total Internet)	71.7	98.4	95.5
International Internet bandwidth (bit/s per Internet user)	1,719,474	577,211	14,580
Affordability			
Fixed-telephone sub-basket ($ a month)	..	10.9	9.4
Mobile-cellular sub-basket ($ a month)	..	24.6	14.9
Fixed-broadband sub-basket ($ a month)	..	33.6	17.8
Trade			
ICT goods exports (% of total goods exports)	1.4	2.5	17.6
ICT goods imports (% of total goods imports)	6.4	3.3	14.7
ICT service exports (% of total service exports)	24.8	23.8	29.1
Applications			
Online service index (0–1, 1=highest presence)	0.43	0.31	0.42
Secure Internet servers (per million people)	101.2	238.5	18.5

Sudan

Sub-Saharan Africa			Lower middle income

	Country data		Lower middle-income group
	2005	2012	2012
Economic and social context			
Population (millions)[b]	32	37	2,507
Urban population (% of total)[b]	33	33	39
GNI per capita, *World Bank Atlas* method ($)[c]	570	1,500	1,893
GDP growth, 2000–05 and 2005–12 (avg. annual %)[c]	6.3	2.8	6.0
Adult literacy rate (% ages 15 and older)	61	72	71
Gross primary, secondary, tertiary school enrollment (%)	..	..	64
Sector structure			
Separate telecommunications/ICT regulator	Yes	Yes	
Status of main fixed-line telephone operator	Mixed	Mixed	
Level of competition (competition, partial comp., monopoly)			
International gateway(s)	M	P	
Mobile telephone service	P	P	
Internet service	P	C	
Foreign ownership (not allowed, restricted, allowed)	R	R	
Reg. treatment of VoIP (banned, closed, no framework, allowed)	B	C	
Sector efficiency and capacity			
Telecommunications revenue (% of GDP)	3.9	2.1	2.5
Telecommunications investment (% of revenue)	384.0	332.4	20.5
Sector performance			
Access			
Fixed-telephone subscriptions (per 100 people)	1.5	1.1	5.4
Mobile-cellular telephone subscriptions (per 100 people)	4.8[a]	74.4	83.1
Fixed (wired)-broadband subscriptions (per 100 people)	0.0	0.1	1.4
Households with a computer (%)	3.0	14.0	15.0
Households with Internet access at home (%)	0.6	29.3	12.4
Usage			
Int'l. voice traffic, total (minutes/subscription/month)	5.6	5.6	6.5
Domestic mobile traffic (minutes/subscription/month)	81.1	80.2	..
Individuals using the Internet (%)	1.3	21.0	18.7
Quality			
Population covered by a mobile-cellular network (%)	34	88	86
Fixed (wired)-broadband subscriptions (% of total Internet)	4.7	72.4	58.2
International Internet bandwidth (bit/s per Internet user)	407	1,703	8,076
Affordability			
Fixed-telephone sub-basket ($ a month)	..	4.9	4.9
Mobile-cellular sub-basket ($ a month)	..	5.6	10.5
Fixed-broadband sub-basket ($ a month)	..	9.7	20.6
Trade			
ICT goods exports (% of total goods exports)	0.0	0.0	4.6
ICT goods imports (% of total goods imports)	4.2	3.8	7.2
ICT service exports (% of total service exports)	2.1	3.8	47.1
Applications			
Online service index (0–1, 1=highest presence)	0.22	0.25	0.32
Secure Internet servers (per million people)	0.0	0.0	4.4

Suriname

Latin America & Caribbean   **Upper middle income**

	Country data		Upper middle-income group
	2005	2012	2012
Economic and social context			
Population (millions)	0.50	0.53	2,391
Urban population (% of total)	67	70	61
GNI per capita, *World Bank Atlas* method ($)	3,330	8,680	6,969
GDP growth, 2000–05 and 2005–12 (avg. annual %)	5.9	4.2	6.2
Adult literacy rate (% ages 15 and older)	90	95	94
Gross primary, secondary, tertiary school enrollment (%)	..	..	76
Sector structure			
Separate telecommunications/ICT regulator	Yes	Yes	
Status of main fixed-line telephone operator	Public	Public	
Level of competition (competition, partial comp., monopoly)			
International gateway(s)	M	C	
Mobile telephone service	M	C	
Internet service	P	C	
Foreign ownership (not allowed, restricted, allowed)	R	R	
Reg. treatment of VoIP (banned, closed, no framework, allowed)	No	A	
Sector efficiency and capacity			
Telecommunications revenue (% of GDP)	5.7	1.0	2.5
Telecommunications investment (% of revenue)	32.4	15.9	18.2
Sector performance			
Access			
Fixed-telephone subscriptions (per 100 people)	16.2	16.2	19.4
Mobile-cellular telephone subscriptions (per 100 people)	46.6	106.5	92.4
Fixed (wired)-broadband subscriptions (per 100 people)	0.2	5.5	10.8
Households with a computer (%)	17.3[a]	34.3[a]	40.6
Households with Internet access at home (%)	5.2[a]	20.2[a]	36.3
Usage			
Int'l. voice traffic, total (minutes/subscription/month)	..	28.9	1.3
Domestic mobile traffic (minutes/subscription/month)	43.0	70.6	284.4
Individuals using the Internet (%)	6.4	34.7[a]	41.6
Quality			
Population covered by a mobile-cellular network (%)	..	100	99
Fixed (wired)-broadband subscriptions (% of total Internet)	15.9	67.9	95.5
International Internet bandwidth (bit/s per Internet user)	1,407	2,002	14,580
Affordability			
Fixed-telephone sub-basket ($ a month)	..	2.9	9.4
Mobile-cellular sub-basket ($ a month)	..	14.2	14.9
Fixed-broadband sub-basket ($ a month)	..	41.9	17.8
Trade			
ICT goods exports (% of total goods exports)	0.2	0.1	17.6
ICT goods imports (% of total goods imports)	3.3	2.8	14.7
ICT service exports (% of total service exports)	..	26.7	29.1
Applications			
Online service index (0–1, 1=highest presence)	0.35	0.16	0.42
Secure Internet servers (per million people)	10.0	33.4	18.5

Swaziland

        Lower middle income

	Country data		Lower middle-income group
	2005	2012	2012
Economic and social context			
Population (millions)	1	1	2,507
Urban population (% of total)	22	21	39
GNI per capita, *World Bank Atlas* method ($)	2,390	2,860	1,893
GDP growth, 2000–05 and 2005–12 (avg. annual %)	2.2	1.7	6.0
Adult literacy rate (% ages 15 and older)	*82*	*88*	*71*
Gross primary, secondary, tertiary school enrollment (%)	61	67	64
Sector structure			
Separate telecommunications/ICT regulator	No	No	
Status of main fixed-line telephone operator	Public	Public	
Level of competition (competition, partial comp., monopoly)			
International gateway(s)	..	M	
Mobile telephone service	*M*	M	
Internet service	C	P	
Foreign ownership (not allowed, restricted, allowed)	No	R	
Reg. treatment of VoIP (banned, closed, no framework, allowed)	B	B	
Sector efficiency and capacity			
Telecommunications revenue (% of GDP)	12.4	4.5	2.5
Telecommunications investment (% of revenue)	*13.2*	*6.8*	*20.5*
Sector performance			
Access			
Fixed-telephone subscriptions (per 100 people)	4.0	3.7	5.4
Mobile-cellular telephone subscriptions (per 100 people)	18.1	65.4	83.1
Fixed (wired)-broadband subscriptions (per 100 people)	0.0	0.3	1.4
Households with a computer (%)	8.6[a]	11.9[a]	15.0
Households with Internet access at home (%)	3.0[a]	11.4[a]	12.4
Usage			
Int'l. voice traffic, total (minutes/subscription/month)	..	8.3	6.5
Domestic mobile traffic (minutes/subscription/month)	..	45.2	..
Individuals using the Internet (%)	3.7[a]	20.8[a]	18.7
Quality			
Population covered by a mobile-cellular network (%)	*90*	*97*	*86*
Fixed (wired)-broadband subscriptions (% of total Internet)	0.0	90.0	58.2
International Internet bandwidth (bit/s per Internet user)	24	1,818	8,076
Affordability			
Fixed-telephone sub-basket ($ a month)	..	6.8	4.9
Mobile-cellular sub-basket ($ a month)	..	22.5	10.5
Fixed-broadband sub-basket ($ a month)	..	75.7	20.6
Trade			
ICT goods exports (% of total goods exports)	0.2	..	4.6
ICT goods imports (% of total goods imports)	2.2	..	7.2
ICT service exports (% of total service exports)	15.6	42.7	47.1
Applications			
Online service index (0–1, 1=highest presence)	0.35	0.14	0.32
Secure Internet servers (per million people)	1.8	8.8	4.4

Sweden

	Country data		High-income group
	2005	2012	2012
Economic and social context			
Population (millions)	9	10	1,300
Urban population (% of total)	84	85	80
GNI per capita, *World Bank Atlas* method ($)	42,920	56,120	38,412
GDP growth, 2000–05 and 2005–12 (avg. annual %)	2.8	1.4	1.0
Adult literacy rate (% ages 15 and older)	..	..	..
Gross primary, secondary, tertiary school enrollment (%)	95	92	93
Sector structure			
Separate telecommunications/ICT regulator	Yes	Yes	
Status of main fixed-line telephone operator	Mixed	Mixed	
Level of competition (competition, partial comp., monopoly)			
International gateway(s)	C	C	
Mobile telephone service	C	C	
Internet service	C	C	
Foreign ownership (not allowed, restricted, allowed)	A	A	
Reg. treatment of VoIP (banned, closed, no framework, allowed)	A	A	
Sector efficiency and capacity			
Telecommunications revenue (% of GDP)	1.8	1.5	2.7
Telecommunications investment (% of revenue)	17.8	13.5	17.6
Sector performance			
Access			
Fixed-telephone subscriptions (per 100 people)	62.4	43.8	43.6
Mobile-cellular telephone subscriptions (per 100 people)	100.8	124.6	122.9
Fixed (wired)-broadband subscriptions (per 100 people)	27.9	32.3	26.2
Households with a computer (%)	80.0	92.0	77.7
Households with Internet access at home (%)	72.5	92.0	75.5
Usage			
Int'l. voice traffic, total (minutes/subscription/month)	..	..	..
Domestic mobile traffic (minutes/subscription/month)	90.8	164.9	113.6
Individuals using the Internet (%)	84.8	94.0	75.4
Quality			
Population covered by a mobile-cellular network (%)	99	100	100
Fixed (wired)-broadband subscriptions (% of total Internet)	76.7	96.6	95.9
International Internet bandwidth (bit/s per Internet user)	20,578	279,287	85,990
Affordability			
Fixed-telephone sub-basket ($ a month)	..	28.3	25.2
Mobile-cellular sub-basket ($ a month)	..	20.6	20.6
Fixed-broadband sub-basket ($ a month)	..	36.8	29.2
Trade			
ICT goods exports (% of total goods exports)	11.2	7.2	8.9
ICT goods imports (% of total goods imports)	11.1	10.1	10.8
ICT service exports (% of total service exports)	46.2	46.6	30.8
Applications			
Online service index (0–1, 1=highest presence)	0.92	0.84	0.67
Secure Internet servers (per million people)	331.2	1,444.0	827.6

Switzerland

High income

	Country data		High-income group
	2005	**2012**	**2012**
Economic and social context			
Population (millions)	7	8	1,300
Urban population (% of total)	73	74	80
GNI per capita, *World Bank Atlas* method ($)	58,530	80,970	38,412
GDP growth, 2000–05 and 2005–12 (avg. annual %)	1.2	1.7	1.0
Adult literacy rate (% ages 15 and older)	..	..	..
Gross primary, secondary, tertiary school enrollment (%)	85	87	93
Sector structure			
Separate telecommunications/ICT regulator	Yes	Yes	
Status of main fixed-line telephone operator	Mixed	Mixed	
Level of competition (competition, partial comp., monopoly)			
International gateway(s)	C	C	
Mobile telephone service	P	C	
Internet service	C	C	
Foreign ownership (not allowed, restricted, allowed)	A	A	
Reg. treatment of VoIP (banned, closed, no framework, allowed)	A	A	
Sector efficiency and capacity			
Telecommunications revenue (% of GDP)	3.4	2.4	2.7
Telecommunications investment (% of revenue)	12.6	21.1	17.6
Sector performance			
Access			
Fixed-telephone subscriptions (per 100 people)	69.5	56.5	43.6
Mobile-cellular telephone subscriptions (per 100 people)	92.2	130.2	122.9
Fixed (wired)-broadband subscriptions (per 100 people)	22.5	39.9	26.2
Households with a computer (%)	76.5	85.8[a]	77.7
Households with Internet access at home (%)	67.0[a]	90.0[a]	75.5
Usage			
Int'l. voice traffic, total (minutes/subscription/month)	..	..	..
Domestic mobile traffic (minutes/subscription/month)	57.6	84.5	*113.6*
Individuals using the Internet (%)	70.1	85.2	75.4
Quality			
Population covered by a mobile-cellular network (%)	100	100	100
Fixed (wired)-broadband subscriptions (% of total Internet)	64.6	99.0	*95.9*
International Internet bandwidth (bit/s per Internet user)	13,760	312,015	85,990
Affordability			
Fixed-telephone sub-basket ($ a month)	..	34.6	25.2
Mobile-cellular sub-basket ($ a month)	..	51.3	20.6
Fixed-broadband sub-basket ($ a month)	..	38.3	29.2
Trade			
ICT goods exports (% of total goods exports)	2.6	1.4	8.9
ICT goods imports (% of total goods imports)	7.4	5.5	10.8
ICT service exports (% of total service exports)	-26.9	34.6	30.8
Applications			
Online service index (0–1, 1=highest presence)	0.76	0.67	0.67
Secure Internet servers (per million people)	472.8	2,222.0	827.6

Syrian Arab Republic

Middle East & North Africa			Lower middle income

	Country data		Lower middle-income group 2012
	2005	2012	2012
Economic and social context			
Population (millions)	18	22	2,507
Urban population (% of total)	54	56	39
GNI per capita, *World Bank Atlas* method ($)	1,520	..	1,893
GDP growth, 2000–05 and 2005–12 (avg. annual %)	4.7	5.0	6.0
Adult literacy rate (% ages 15 and older)	81	84	71
Gross primary, secondary, tertiary school enrollment (%)	70	73	64
Sector structure			
Separate telecommunications/ICT regulator	No	No	
Status of main fixed-line telephone operator	Public	Public	
Level of competition (competition, partial comp., monopoly)			
International gateway(s)	..	..	
Mobile telephone service	P	*P*	
Internet service	P	*P*	
Foreign ownership (not allowed, restricted, allowed)	A	R	
Reg. treatment of VoIP (banned, closed, no framework, allowed)	B	B	
Sector efficiency and capacity			
Telecommunications revenue (% of GDP)	2.6	..	2.5
Telecommunications investment (% of revenue)	7.5	15.1	20.5
Sector performance			
Access			
Fixed-telephone subscriptions (per 100 people)	16.0	20.2	5.4
Mobile-cellular telephone subscriptions (per 100 people)	16.2	59.3	83.1
Fixed (wired)-broadband subscriptions (per 100 people)	0.0a	1.1	1.4
Households with a computer (%)	28.0	43.0a	15.0
Households with Internet access at home (%)	26.0	38.0a	12.4
Usage			
Int'l. voice traffic, total (minutes/subscription/month)	13.6	11.6	6.5
Domestic mobile traffic (minutes/subscription/month)	130.2	72.2	..
Individuals using the Internet (%)	5.6a	24.3a	18.7
Quality			
Population covered by a mobile-cellular network (%)	92	90	86
Fixed (wired)-broadband subscriptions (% of total Internet)	1.3	60.5	58.2
International Internet bandwidth (bit/s per Internet user)	333	3,760	8,076
Affordability			
Fixed-telephone sub-basket ($ a month)	..	1.3	4.9
Mobile-cellular sub-basket ($ a month)	..	21.3	10.5
Fixed-broadband sub-basket ($ a month)	..	21.6	20.6
Trade			
ICT goods exports (% of total goods exports)	0.0	0.0	4.6
ICT goods imports (% of total goods imports)	3.3	2.2	7.2
ICT service exports (% of total service exports)	9.3	2.5	47.1
Applications			
Online service index (0–1, 1=highest presence)	0.36	0.23	0.32
Secure Internet servers (per million people)	0.1	0.5	4.4

Tajikistan

	Country data		Low-income group
	2005	2012	2012
Economic and social context			
Population (millions)	7	8	846
Urban population (% of total)	26	27	28
GNI per capita, *World Bank Atlas* method ($)	320	880	590
GDP growth, 2000–05 and 2005–12 (avg. annual %)	10.1	6.7	5.9
Adult literacy rate (% ages 15 and older)	99	100	61
Gross primary, secondary, tertiary school enrollment (%)	69	69	60
Sector structure			
Separate telecommunications/ICT regulator	No	No	
Status of main fixed-line telephone operator	Mixed	Mixed	
Level of competition (competition, partial comp., monopoly)			
International gateway(s)	..	..	
Mobile telephone service	..	..	
Internet service	..	..	
Foreign ownership (not allowed, restricted, allowed)	..	..	
Reg. treatment of VoIP (banned, closed, no framework, allowed)	No	A	
Sector efficiency and capacity			
Telecommunications revenue (% of GDP)	2.9	..	5.0
Telecommunications investment (% of revenue)	71.4	..	..
Sector performance			
Access			
Fixed-telephone subscriptions (per 100 people)	4.1	4.9	1.0
Mobile-cellular telephone subscriptions (per 100 people)	3.9	81.5	47.2
Fixed (wired)-broadband subscriptions (per 100 people)	0.1	0.1	0.2
Households with a computer (%)	1.0[a]	4.1[a]	4.2
Households with Internet access at home (%)	0.3	3.6[a]	3.4
Usage			
Int'l. voice traffic, total (minutes/subscription/month)	..	..	..
Domestic mobile traffic (minutes/subscription/month)	7.3	..	70.1
Individuals using the Internet (%)	0.3	14.5[a]	6.2
Quality			
Population covered by a mobile-cellular network (%)	..	..	..
Fixed (wired)-broadband subscriptions (% of total Internet)	2.2	..	30.9
International Internet bandwidth (bit/s per Internet user)	98	..	9,141
Affordability			
Fixed-telephone sub-basket ($ a month)	..	0.9	8.9
Mobile-cellular sub-basket ($ a month)	..	8.5	11.9
Fixed-broadband sub-basket ($ a month)	..	362.5	46.9
Trade			
ICT goods exports (% of total goods exports)	..	..	..
ICT goods imports (% of total goods imports)	..	..	..
ICT service exports (% of total service exports)	19.2	40.7	..
Applications			
Online service index (0–1, 1=highest presence)	0.32	0.24	0.20
Secure Internet servers (per million people)	..	1.2	1.1

Tanzania

Low income

	Country data		Low-income group
	2005	2012	2012
Economic and social context			
Population (millions)	39	48	846
Urban population (% of total)	24	27	28
GNI per capita, *World Bank Atlas* method ($)	380	570	590
GDP growth, 2000–05 and 2005–12 (avg. annual %)	7.1	6.8	5.9
Adult literacy rate (% ages 15 and older)	69	68	61
Gross primary, secondary, tertiary school enrollment (%)	..	56	60
Sector structure			
Separate telecommunications/ICT regulator	Yes	Yes	
Status of main fixed-line telephone operator	Mixed	Mixed	
Level of competition (competition, partial comp., monopoly)			
International gateway(s)	M	M	
Mobile telephone service	C	C	
Internet service	C	C	
Foreign ownership (not allowed, restricted, allowed)	R	R	
Reg. treatment of VoIP (banned, closed, no framework, allowed)	A	A	
Sector efficiency and capacity			
Telecommunications revenue (% of GDP)	..	..	5.0
Telecommunications investment (% of revenue)	..	..	..
Sector performance			
Access			
Fixed-telephone subscriptions (per 100 people)	0.4	0.4	1.0
Mobile-cellular telephone subscriptions (per 100 people)	7.6	57.0	47.2
Fixed (wired)-broadband subscriptions (per 100 people)	0.0	0.0	0.2
Households with a computer (%)	2.1[a]	3.2[a]	4.2
Households with Internet access at home (%)	0.5[a]	3.3[a]	3.4
Usage			
Int'l. voice traffic, total (minutes/subscription/month)	3.2	0.5	..
Domestic mobile traffic (minutes/subscription/month)	7.1	51.5	70.1
Individuals using the Internet (%)	1.1[a]	4.0[a]	6.2
Quality			
Population covered by a mobile-cellular network (%)	45	95	..
Fixed (wired)-broadband subscriptions (% of total Internet)	1.6	..	30.9
International Internet bandwidth (bit/s per Internet user)	234	3,974	9,141
Affordability			
Fixed-telephone sub-basket ($ a month)	..	8.9	8.9
Mobile-cellular sub-basket ($ a month)	..	7.7	11.9
Fixed-broadband sub-basket ($ a month)	..	19.1	46.9
Trade			
ICT goods exports (% of total goods exports)	0.3	0.1	..
ICT goods imports (% of total goods imports)	5.8	3.6	..
ICT service exports (% of total service exports)	10.1	13.3	..
Applications			
Online service index (0–1, 1=highest presence)	0.29	0.35	0.20
Secure Internet servers (per million people)	0.1	1.1	1.1

Thailand

East Asia & Pacific		**Upper middle income**	

	Country data		Upper middle-income group
	2005	2012	2012
Economic and social context			
Population (millions)	66	67	2,391
Urban population (% of total)	32	34	61
GNI per capita, *World Bank Atlas* method ($)	2,600	5,210	6,969
GDP growth, 2000–05 and 2005–12 (avg. annual %)	5.5	3.0	6.2
Adult literacy rate (% ages 15 and older)	94	..	94
Gross primary, secondary, tertiary school enrollment (%)	72	76	76
Sector structure			
Separate telecommunications/ICT regulator	Yes	Yes	
Status of main fixed-line telephone operator	Public	Public	
Level of competition (competition, partial comp., monopoly)			
International gateway(s)	M	C	
Mobile telephone service	P	C	
Internet service	C	C	
Foreign ownership (not allowed, restricted, allowed)	R	R	
Reg. treatment of VoIP (banned, closed, no framework, allowed)	B	A	
Sector efficiency and capacity			
Telecommunications revenue (% of GDP)	3.2	2.3	2.5
Telecommunications investment (% of revenue)	10.0	23.5	18.2
Sector performance			
Access			
Fixed-telephone subscriptions (per 100 people)	10.7	9.5	19.4
Mobile-cellular telephone subscriptions (per 100 people)	46.5	127.3	92.4
Fixed (wired)-broadband subscriptions (per 100 people)	0.8	8.2	10.8
Households with a computer (%)	15.5	26.9	40.6
Households with Internet access at home (%)	7.2[a]	18.4	36.3
Usage			
Int'l. voice traffic, total (minutes/subscription/month)	..	1.8	1.3
Domestic mobile traffic (minutes/subscription/month)	..	38.0	284.4
Individuals using the Internet (%)	15.0	26.5	41.6
Quality			
Population covered by a mobile-cellular network (%)	26	100	99
Fixed (wired)-broadband subscriptions (% of total Internet)	99.6	94.4	95.5
International Internet bandwidth (bit/s per Internet user)	691	26,649	14,580
Affordability			
Fixed-telephone sub-basket ($ a month)	..	6.2	9.4
Mobile-cellular sub-basket ($ a month)	..	10.6	14.9
Fixed-broadband sub-basket ($ a month)	..	20.7	17.8
Trade			
ICT goods exports (% of total goods exports)	23.4	16.0	17.6
ICT goods imports (% of total goods imports)	17.4	11.8	14.7
ICT service exports (% of total service exports)	25.7	16.2	29.1
Applications			
Online service index (0–1, 1=highest presence)	0.50	0.51	0.42
Secure Internet servers (per million people)	4.8	18.1	18.5

Timor-Leste

Lower middle income

	Country data		Lower middle-income group
	2005	2012	2012
Economic and social context			
Population (millions)	1	1	2,507
Urban population (% of total)	26	29	39
GNI per capita, *World Bank Atlas* method ($)	890	3,620	1,893
GDP growth, 2000–05 and 2005–12 (avg. annual %)	1.0	9.8	6.0
Adult literacy rate (% ages 15 and older)	51	58	71
Gross primary, secondary, tertiary school enrollment (%)	66	72	64
Sector structure			
Separate telecommunications/ICT regulator	No	No	
Status of main fixed-line telephone operator	..	..	
Level of competition (competition, partial comp., monopoly)			
International gateway(s)	..	..	
Mobile telephone service	..	..	
Internet service	..	..	
Foreign ownership (not allowed, restricted, allowed)	..	..	
Reg. treatment of VoIP (banned, closed, no framework, allowed)	B	B	
Sector efficiency and capacity			
Telecommunications revenue (% of GDP)	3.6	6.0	2.5
Telecommunications investment (% of revenue)	16.9	28.6	20.5
Sector performance			
Access			
Fixed-telephone subscriptions (per 100 people)	0.2	0.3	5.4
Mobile-cellular telephone subscriptions (per 100 people)	3.3	55.7	83.1
Fixed (wired)-broadband subscriptions (per 100 people)	0.0	0.1	1.4
Households with a computer (%)	..	..	15.0
Households with Internet access at home (%)	..	..	12.4
Usage			
Int'l. voice traffic, total (minutes/subscription/month)	20.0	..	6.5
Domestic mobile traffic (minutes/subscription/month)	70.6	36.8	..
Individuals using the Internet (%)	0.1	0.9[a]	18.7
Quality			
Population covered by a mobile-cellular network (%)	50	92	86
Fixed (wired)-broadband subscriptions (% of total Internet)	3.4	51.5	58.2
International Internet bandwidth (bit/s per Internet user)	5,071	17,467	8,076
Affordability			
Fixed-telephone sub-basket ($ a month)	..	20.8	4.9
Mobile-cellular sub-basket ($ a month)	..	16.3	10.5
Fixed-broadband sub-basket ($ a month)	..	99.0	20.6
Trade			
ICT goods exports (% of total goods exports)	5.2	..	4.6
ICT goods imports (% of total goods imports)	3.4	..	7.2
ICT service exports (% of total service exports)	..	..	47.1
Applications			
Online service index (0–1, 1=highest presence)	0.25	0.22	0.32
Secure Internet servers (per million people)	1.0	0.8	4.4

Togo

	Country data		Low-income group
	2005	2012	2012
Economic and social context			
Population (millions)	6	7	846
Urban population (% of total)	35	39	28
GNI per capita, *World Bank Atlas* method ($)	370	500	590
GDP growth, 2000–05 and 2005–12 (avg. annual %)	1.5	3.6	5.9
Adult literacy rate (% ages 15 and older)	57	60	61
Gross primary, secondary, tertiary school enrollment (%)	61	73	60
Sector structure			
Separate telecommunications/ICT regulator	Yes	Yes	
Status of main fixed-line telephone operator	Public	Public	
Level of competition (competition, partial comp., monopoly)			
International gateway(s)	P	P	
Mobile telephone service	P	C	
Internet service	C	C	
Foreign ownership (not allowed, restricted, allowed)	R	R	
Reg. treatment of VoIP (banned, closed, no framework, allowed)	A	A	
Sector efficiency and capacity			
Telecommunications revenue (% of GDP)	6.3	9.2	5.0
Telecommunications investment (% of revenue)	34.7	23.6	..
Sector performance			
Access			
Fixed-telephone subscriptions (per 100 people)	1.1	0.9	1.0
Mobile-cellular telephone subscriptions (per 100 people)	7.8	49.9	47.2
Fixed (wired)-broadband subscriptions (per 100 people)	0.0	0.1	0.2
Households with a computer (%)	1.0	2.3	4.2
Households with Internet access at home (%)	..	1.4	3.4
Usage			
Int'l. voice traffic, total (minutes/subscription/month)	22.5	7.6	..
Domestic mobile traffic (minutes/subscription/month)	22.0	29.4	70.1
Individuals using the Internet (%)	1.8[a]	4.0[a]	6.2
Quality			
Population covered by a mobile-cellular network (%)	85	91	..
Fixed (wired)-broadband subscriptions (% of total Internet)	1.9	16.9	30.9
International Internet bandwidth (bit/s per Internet user)	143	5,224	9,141
Affordability			
Fixed-telephone sub-basket ($ a month)	..	10.5	8.9
Mobile-cellular sub-basket ($ a month)	..	17.8	11.9
Fixed-broadband sub-basket ($ a month)	..	47.2	46.9
Trade			
ICT goods exports (% of total goods exports)	0.1	0.0	..
ICT goods imports (% of total goods imports)	3.9	1.9	..
ICT service exports (% of total service exports)	23.8	23.2	..
Applications			
Online service index (0–1, 1=highest presence)	0.22	0.14	0.20
Secure Internet servers (per million people)	0.4	3.1	1.1

Tonga

	Country data		Upper middle-income group
	2005	2012	2012
Economic and social context			
Population (millions)	0.10	0.10	2,391
Urban population (% of total)	23	24	61
GNI per capita, *World Bank Atlas* method ($)	2,550	4,220	6,969
GDP growth, 2000–05 and 2005–12 (avg. annual %)	2.4	1.1	6.2
Adult literacy rate (% ages 15 and older)	99	..	94
Gross primary, secondary, tertiary school enrollment (%)	88	..	76
Sector structure			
Separate telecommunications/ICT regulator	No	No	
Status of main fixed-line telephone operator	Public	Public	
Level of competition (competition, partial comp., monopoly)			
International gateway(s)	..	C	
Mobile telephone service	..	C	
Internet service	P	C	
Foreign ownership (not allowed, restricted, allowed)	..	A	
Reg. treatment of VoIP (banned, closed, no framework, allowed)	C	C	
Sector efficiency and capacity			
Telecommunications revenue (% of GDP)	..	..	2.5
Telecommunications investment (% of revenue)	..	..	18.2
Sector performance			
Access			
Fixed-telephone subscriptions (per 100 people)	13.6	28.6	19.4
Mobile-cellular telephone subscriptions (per 100 people)	29.6	53.4	92.4
Fixed (wired)-broadband subscriptions (per 100 people)	0.6	1.4	10.8
Households with a computer (%)	..	15.5[a]	40.6
Households with Internet access at home (%)	..	12.0[a]	36.3
Usage			
Int'l. voice traffic, total (minutes/subscription/month)	..	..	1.3
Domestic mobile traffic (minutes/subscription/month)	..	..	284.4
Individuals using the Internet (%)	4.9[a]	34.9[a]	41.6
Quality			
Population covered by a mobile-cellular network (%)	70	..	99
Fixed (wired)-broadband subscriptions (% of total Internet)	37.0	16.2	95.5
International Internet bandwidth (bit/s per Internet user)	404	2,733	14,580
Affordability			
Fixed-telephone sub-basket ($ a month)	..	6.4	9.4
Mobile-cellular sub-basket ($ a month)	..	11.0	14.9
Fixed-broadband sub-basket ($ a month)	..	62.3	17.8
Trade			
ICT goods exports (% of total goods exports)	..	1.1	17.6
ICT goods imports (% of total goods imports)	2.8	3.8	14.7
ICT service exports (% of total service exports)	16.3	12.2	29.1
Applications			
Online service index (0–1, 1=highest presence)	0.40	0.24	0.42
Secure Internet servers (per million people)	9.8	19.0	18.5

Trinidad and Tobago

High income

	Country data		High-income group
	2005	**2012**	**2012**
Economic and social context			
Population (millions)	1	1	1,300
Urban population (% of total)	12	14	80
GNI per capita, *World Bank Atlas* method ($)	11,060	14,710	38,412
GDP growth, 2000–05 and 2005–12 (avg. annual %)	8.7	1.4	1.0
Adult literacy rate (% ages 15 and older)	98	99	..
Gross primary, secondary, tertiary school enrollment (%)	67	..	93
Sector structure			
Separate telecommunications/ICT regulator	Yes	Yes	
Status of main fixed-line telephone operator	Mixed	Mixed	
Level of competition (competition, partial comp., monopoly)			
International gateway(s)	M	..	
Mobile telephone service	M	P	
Internet service	C	P	
Foreign ownership (not allowed, restricted, allowed)	A	A	
Reg. treatment of VoIP (banned, closed, no framework, allowed)	No	A	
Sector efficiency and capacity			
Telecommunications revenue (% of GDP)	2.4	2.9	2.7
Telecommunications investment (% of revenue)	..	8.7	17.6
Sector performance			
Access			
Fixed-telephone subscriptions (per 100 people)	24.9	21.4	43.6
Mobile-cellular telephone subscriptions (per 100 people)	71.3	140.8	122.9
Fixed (wired)-broadband subscriptions (per 100 people)	0.8	13.8	26.2
Households with a computer (%)	31.0	61.0[a]	77.7
Households with Internet access at home (%)	17.0	40.0[a]	75.5
Usage			
Int'l. voice traffic, total (minutes/subscription/month)	27.0	19.6	..
Domestic mobile traffic (minutes/subscription/month)	272.8	205.7	113.6
Individuals using the Internet (%)	29.0[a]	59.5[a]	75.4
Quality			
Population covered by a mobile-cellular network (%)	100	100	100
Fixed (wired)-broadband subscriptions (% of total Internet)	16.6	99.1	95.9
International Internet bandwidth (bit/s per Internet user)	1,304	18,442	85,990
Affordability			
Fixed-telephone sub-basket ($ a month)	..	15.6	25.2
Mobile-cellular sub-basket ($ a month)	..	15.1	20.6
Fixed-broadband sub-basket ($ a month)	..	12.3	29.2
Trade			
ICT goods exports (% of total goods exports)	0.2	0.1	8.9
ICT goods imports (% of total goods imports)	4.0	3.1	10.8
ICT service exports (% of total service exports)	8.9	85.3	30.8
Applications			
Online service index (0–1, 1=highest presence)	0.53	0.48	0.67
Secure Internet servers (per million people)	21.6	93.2	827.6

Tunisia

Middle East & North Africa			Upper middle income

	Country data		Upper middle-income group
	2005	2012	2012
Economic and social context			
Population (millions)	10	11	2,391
Urban population (% of total)	65	67	61
GNI per capita, *World Bank Atlas* method ($)	3,200	4,150	6,969
GDP growth, 2000–05 and 2005–12 (avg. annual %)	4.5	3.3	6.2
Adult literacy rate (% ages 15 and older)	74	79	94
Gross primary, secondary, tertiary school enrollment (%)	77	78	76
Sector structure			
Separate telecommunications/ICT regulator	Yes	Yes	
Status of main fixed-line telephone operator	Public	Mixed	
Level of competition (competition, partial comp., monopoly)			
International gateway(s)	..	P	
Mobile telephone service	C	C	
Internet service	C	C	
Foreign ownership (not allowed, restricted, allowed)	..	R	
Reg. treatment of VoIP (banned, closed, no framework, allowed)	C	A	
Sector efficiency and capacity			
Telecommunications revenue (% of GDP)	3.8	3.9	2.5
Telecommunications investment (% of revenue)	21.7	18.2	18.2
Sector performance			
Access			
Fixed-telephone subscriptions (per 100 people)	12.5	10.2	19.4
Mobile-cellular telephone subscriptions (per 100 people)	56.5	118.1	92.4
Fixed (wired)-broadband subscriptions (per 100 people)	0.2	4.9	10.8
Households with a computer (%)	7.2	22.8[a]	40.6
Households with Internet access at home (%)	2.1	20.6[a]	36.3
Usage			
Int'l. voice traffic, total (minutes/subscription/month)	7.1	9.3	1.3
Domestic mobile traffic (minutes/subscription/month)	35.5	136.7	284.4
Individuals using the Internet (%)	9.7	41.4[a]	41.6
Quality			
Population covered by a mobile-cellular network (%)	98	99	99
Fixed (wired)-broadband subscriptions (% of total Internet)	11.7	96.3	95.5
International Internet bandwidth (bit/s per Internet user)	773	18,745	14,580
Affordability			
Fixed-telephone sub-basket ($ a month)	..	6.0	9.4
Mobile-cellular sub-basket ($ a month)	..	10.6	14.9
Fixed-broadband sub-basket ($ a month)	..	7.0	17.8
Trade			
ICT goods exports (% of total goods exports)	2.0	7.4	17.6
ICT goods imports (% of total goods imports)	4.6	6.6	14.7
ICT service exports (% of total service exports)	5.1	9.6	29.1
Applications			
Online service index (0–1, 1=highest presence)	0.35	0.48	0.42
Secure Internet servers (per million people)	1.4	17.0	18.5

Turkey

	Country data		Upper middle-income group
	2005	2012	2012
Economic and social context			
Population (millions)	68	74	2,391
Urban population (% of total)	67	72	61
GNI per capita, *World Bank Atlas* method ($)	6,520	10,830	6,969
GDP growth, 2000–05 and 2005–12 (avg. annual %)	5.2	3.4	6.2
Adult literacy rate (% ages 15 and older)	88	94	94
Gross primary, secondary, tertiary school enrollment (%)	74	85	76
Sector structure			
Separate telecommunications/ICT regulator	Yes	Yes	
Status of main fixed-line telephone operator	Mixed	Mixed	
Level of competition (competition, partial comp., monopoly)			
International gateway(s)	C	..	
Mobile telephone service	P	..	
Internet service	C	C	
Foreign ownership (not allowed, restricted, allowed)	A	A	
Reg. treatment of VoIP (banned, closed, no framework, allowed)	No	A	
Sector efficiency and capacity			
Telecommunications revenue (% of GDP)	2.6	2.1	2.5
Telecommunications investment (% of revenue)	11.0	19.0	18.2
Sector performance			
Access			
Fixed-telephone subscriptions (per 100 people)	28.0	18.7	19.4
Mobile-cellular telephone subscriptions (per 100 people)	64.4	91.5	92.4
Fixed (wired)-broadband subscriptions (per 100 people)	2.3	10.6	10.8
Households with a computer (%)	12.0	50.2	40.6
Households with Internet access at home (%)	7.7	47.2	36.3
Usage			
Int'l. voice traffic, total (minutes/subscription/month)	3.9	5.6	1.3
Domestic mobile traffic (minutes/subscription/month)	68.3	209.0	284.4
Individuals using the Internet (%)	15.5	45.1	41.6
Quality			
Population covered by a mobile-cellular network (%)	96	100	99
Fixed (wired)-broadband subscriptions (% of total Internet)	70.6	99.2	95.5
International Internet bandwidth (bit/s per Internet user)	2,788	40,629	14,580
Affordability			
Fixed-telephone sub-basket ($ a month)	..	13.7	9.4
Mobile-cellular sub-basket ($ a month)	..	31.4	14.9
Fixed-broadband sub-basket ($ a month)	..	12.5	17.8
Trade			
ICT goods exports (% of total goods exports)	4.4	1.7	17.6
ICT goods imports (% of total goods imports)	6.1	4.2	14.7
ICT service exports (% of total service exports)	2.2	1.6	29.1
Applications			
Online service index (0–1, 1=highest presence)	0.48	0.46	0.42
Secure Internet servers (per million people)	18.1	50.4	18.5

Turkmenistan

Europe & Central Asia   **Upper middle income**

	Country data		Upper middle-income group
	2005	2012	2012
Economic and social context			
Population (millions)	5	5	2,391
Urban population (% of total)	47	49	61
GNI per capita, *World Bank Atlas* method ($)	1,600	5,410	6,969
GDP growth, 2000–05 and 2005–12 (avg. annual %)	4.5	10.9	6.2
Adult literacy rate (% ages 15 and older)	..	100	94
Gross primary, secondary, tertiary school enrollment (%)	..	..	76
Sector structure			
Separate telecommunications/ICT regulator	No	No	
Status of main fixed-line telephone operator	Public	Public	
Level of competition (competition, partial comp., monopoly)			
International gateway(s)	..	..	
Mobile telephone service	C	C	
Internet service	..	..	
Foreign ownership (not allowed, restricted, allowed)	..	..	
Reg. treatment of VoIP (banned, closed, no framework, allowed)	B	B	
Sector efficiency and capacity			
Telecommunications revenue (% of GDP)	1.5	..	2.5
Telecommunications investment (% of revenue)	..	..	18.2
Sector performance			
Access			
Fixed-telephone subscriptions (per 100 people)	8.4	11.1	19.4
Mobile-cellular telephone subscriptions (per 100 people)	2.2	76.4	92.4
Fixed (wired)-broadband subscriptions (per 100 people)	..	0.0	10.8
Households with a computer (%)	1.9[a]	13.7[a]	40.6
Households with Internet access at home (%)	0.9[a]	6.7[a]	36.3
Usage			
Int'l. voice traffic, total (minutes/subscription/month)	..	..	1.3
Domestic mobile traffic (minutes/subscription/month)	..	..	284.4
Individuals using the Internet (%)	1.0[a]	7.2[a]	41.6
Quality			
Population covered by a mobile-cellular network (%)	14	..	99
Fixed (wired)-broadband subscriptions (% of total Internet)	..	..	95.5
International Internet bandwidth (bit/s per Internet user)	1,605	1,075	14,580
Affordability			
Fixed-telephone sub-basket ($ a month)	..	..	9.4
Mobile-cellular sub-basket ($ a month)	..	..	14.9
Fixed-broadband sub-basket ($ a month)	..	..	17.8
Trade			
ICT goods exports (% of total goods exports)	..	..	17.6
ICT goods imports (% of total goods imports)	..	..	14.7
ICT service exports (% of total service exports)	..	..	29.1
Applications			
Online service index (0–1, 1=highest presence)	0.33	0.19	0.42
Secure Internet servers (per million people)	..	0.2	18.5

Turks and Caicos Islands

High income

	Country data		High-income group
	2005	2012	2012
Economic and social context			
Population (millions)	0.03	0.03	1,300
Urban population (% of total)	90	94	80
GNI per capita, *World Bank Atlas* method ($)	..	..	38,412
GDP growth, 2000–05 and 2005–12 (avg. annual %)	..	..	1.0
Adult literacy rate (% ages 15 and older)	..	..	..
Gross primary, secondary, tertiary school enrollment (%)	..	..	93
Sector structure			
Separate telecommunications/ICT regulator	..	..	
Status of main fixed-line telephone operator	..	..	
Level of competition (competition, partial comp., monopoly)			
International gateway(s)	..	..	
Mobile telephone service	..	..	
Internet service	..	..	
Foreign ownership (not allowed, restricted, allowed)	..	..	
Reg. treatment of VoIP (banned, closed, no framework, allowed)	..	..	
Sector efficiency and capacity			
Telecommunications revenue (% of GDP)	..	..	2.7
Telecommunications investment (% of revenue)	..	..	17.6
Sector performance			
Access			
Fixed-telephone subscriptions (per 100 people)	..	..	43.6
Mobile-cellular telephone subscriptions (per 100 people)	..	..	122.9
Fixed (wired)-broadband subscriptions (per 100 people)	..	..	26.2
Households with a computer (%)	..	..	77.7
Households with Internet access at home (%)	..	..	75.5
Usage			
Int'l. voice traffic, total (minutes/subscription/month)	..	..	..
Domestic mobile traffic (minutes/subscription/month)	..	..	*113.6*
Individuals using the Internet (%)	..	..	75.4
Quality			
Population covered by a mobile-cellular network (%)	..	..	100
Fixed (wired)-broadband subscriptions (% of total Internet)	..	..	95.9
International Internet bandwidth (bit/s per Internet user)	..	..	85,990
Affordability			
Fixed-telephone sub-basket ($ a month)	..	..	25.2
Mobile-cellular sub-basket ($ a month)	..	..	20.6
Fixed-broadband sub-basket ($ a month)	..	..	29.2
Trade			
ICT goods exports (% of total goods exports)	4.0	1.9	8.9
ICT goods imports (% of total goods imports)	4.6	3.0	10.8
ICT service exports (% of total service exports)	..	..	30.8
Applications			
Online service index (0–1, 1=highest presence)	..	..	0.67
Secure Internet servers (per million people)	..	333.3	827.6

Tuvalu

Upper middle income

	Country data		Upper middle-income group
	2005	2012	2012
Economic and social context			
Population (millions)	0.01	0.01	2,391
Urban population (% of total)	48	51	61
GNI per capita, *World Bank Atlas* method ($)	3,740	5,650	6,969
GDP growth, 2000–05 and 2005–12 (avg. annual %)	0.2	2.3	6.2
Adult literacy rate (% ages 15 and older)	..	..	94
Gross primary, secondary, tertiary school enrollment (%)	..	..	76
Sector structure			
Separate telecommunications/ICT regulator	No	No	
Status of main fixed-line telephone operator	Public	Public	
Level of competition (competition, partial comp., monopoly)			
International gateway(s)	..	..	
Mobile telephone service	M	..	
Internet service	M	M	
Foreign ownership (not allowed, restricted, allowed)	R	R	
Reg. treatment of VoIP (banned, closed, no framework, allowed)	..	..	
Sector efficiency and capacity			
Telecommunications revenue (% of GDP)	..	..	2.5
Telecommunications investment (% of revenue)	..	..	18.2
Sector performance			
Access			
Fixed-telephone subscriptions (per 100 people)	9.2	14.7	19.4
Mobile-cellular telephone subscriptions (per 100 people)	13.4	28.4	92.4
Fixed (wired)-broadband subscriptions (per 100 people)	1.5	5.6	10.8
Households with a computer (%)	..	23.4[a]	40.6
Households with Internet access at home (%)	..	19.7[a]	36.3
Usage			
Int'l. voice traffic, total (minutes/subscription/month)	..	..	1.3
Domestic mobile traffic (minutes/subscription/month)	2.9	..	284.4
Individuals using the Internet (%)	10.0[a]	35.0[a]	41.6
Quality			
Population covered by a mobile-cellular network (%)	13	..	99
Fixed (wired)-broadband subscriptions (% of total Internet)	28.8	..	95.5
International Internet bandwidth (bit/s per Internet user)	3,073	1,159	14,580
Affordability			
Fixed-telephone sub-basket ($ a month)	..	..	9.4
Mobile-cellular sub-basket ($ a month)	..	..	14.9
Fixed-broadband sub-basket ($ a month)	..	..	17.8
Trade			
ICT goods exports (% of total goods exports)	7.3	..	17.6
ICT goods imports (% of total goods imports)	6.1	2.1	14.7
ICT service exports (% of total service exports)	..	..	29.1
Applications			
Online service index (0–1, 1=highest presence)	0.00	0.05	0.42
Secure Internet servers (per million people)	..	102.2	18.5

Uganda

	Country data		Low-income group
	2005	2012	2012
Economic and social context			
Population (millions)	29	36	846
Urban population (% of total)	13	16	28
GNI per capita, *World Bank Atlas* method ($)	290	480	590
GDP growth, 2000–05 and 2005–12 (avg. annual %)	6.9	7.3	5.9
Adult literacy rate (% ages 15 and older)	71	73	61
Gross primary, secondary, tertiary school enrollment (%)	64	67	60
Sector structure			
Separate telecommunications/ICT regulator	Yes	Yes	
Status of main fixed-line telephone operator	Mixed	Mixed	
Level of competition (competition, partial comp., monopoly)			
International gateway(s)	P	C	
Mobile telephone service	P	C	
Internet service	C	C	
Foreign ownership (not allowed, restricted, allowed)	A	A	
Reg. treatment of VoIP (banned, closed, no framework, allowed)	No	A	
Sector efficiency and capacity			
Telecommunications revenue (% of GDP)	3.2	3.7	5.0
Telecommunications investment (% of revenue)	23.4	32.6	..
Sector performance			
Access			
Fixed-telephone subscriptions (per 100 people)	0.3	0.9	1.0
Mobile-cellular telephone subscriptions (per 100 people)	4.6	45.0	47.2
Fixed (wired)-broadband subscriptions (per 100 people)	0.0	0.1	0.2
Households with a computer (%)	0.8[a]	4.0[a]	4.2
Households with Internet access at home (%)	0.1[a]	4.2[a]	3.4
Usage			
Int'l. voice traffic, total (minutes/subscription/month)	..	..	..
Domestic mobile traffic (minutes/subscription/month)	119.4	61.3	70.1
Individuals using the Internet (%)	1.7	14.7[a]	6.2
Quality			
Population covered by a mobile-cellular network (%)	70	100	..
Fixed (wired)-broadband subscriptions (% of total Internet)	8.9	40.0	30.9
International Internet bandwidth (bit/s per Internet user)	121	4,670	9,141
Affordability			
Fixed-telephone sub-basket ($ a month)	..	9.2	8.9
Mobile-cellular sub-basket ($ a month)	..	9.0	11.9
Fixed-broadband sub-basket ($ a month)	..	14.0	46.9
Trade			
ICT goods exports (% of total goods exports)	2.0	6.5	..
ICT goods imports (% of total goods imports)	7.5	6.6	..
ICT service exports (% of total service exports)	13.4	14.1	..
Applications			
Online service index (0–1, 1=highest presence)	0.31	0.29	0.20
Secure Internet servers (per million people)	0.0	1.2	1.1

Ukraine

	Country data		Lower middle-income group
	2005	**2012**	**2012**
Economic and social context			
Population (millions)	47	46	2,507
Urban population (% of total)	68	69	39
GNI per capita, *World Bank Atlas* method ($)	1,540	3,500	1,893
GDP growth, 2000–05 and 2005–12 (avg. annual %)	8.0	0.5	6.0
Adult literacy rate (% ages 15 and older)	99	100	71
Gross primary, secondary, tertiary school enrollment (%)	88	94	64
Sector structure			
Separate telecommunications/ICT regulator	Yes	Yes	
Status of main fixed-line telephone operator	Public	Mixed	
Level of competition (competition, partial comp., monopoly)			
International gateway(s)	..	C	
Mobile telephone service	C	C	
Internet service	..	C	
Foreign ownership (not allowed, restricted, allowed)	..	A	
Reg. treatment of VoIP (banned, closed, no framework, allowed)	No	A	
Sector efficiency and capacity			
Telecommunications revenue (% of GDP)	5.9	3.4	2.5
Telecommunications investment (% of revenue)	32.8	13.6	20.5
Sector performance			
Access			
Fixed-telephone subscriptions (per 100 people)	24.8	26.8	5.4
Mobile-cellular telephone subscriptions (per 100 people)	63.7	130.3	83.1
Fixed (wired)-broadband subscriptions (per 100 people)	0.3	8.0	1.4
Households with a computer (%)	11.5	40.5	15.0
Households with Internet access at home (%)	3.0	36.5[a]	12.4
Usage			
Int'l. voice traffic, total (minutes/subscription/month)	..	..	6.5
Domestic mobile traffic (minutes/subscription/month)	..	..	..
Individuals using the Internet (%)	3.7	33.7[a]	18.7
Quality			
Population covered by a mobile-cellular network (%)	96	100	86
Fixed (wired)-broadband subscriptions (% of total Internet)	3.5	72.0	58.2
International Internet bandwidth (bit/s per Internet user)	461	14,143	8,076
Affordability			
Fixed-telephone sub-basket ($ a month)	..	3.7	4.9
Mobile-cellular sub-basket ($ a month)	..	7.8	10.5
Fixed-broadband sub-basket ($ a month)	..	7.5	20.6
Trade			
ICT goods exports (% of total goods exports)	0.5	1.1	4.6
ICT goods imports (% of total goods imports)	4.0	3.8	7.2
ICT service exports (% of total service exports)	7.6	19.2	47.1
Applications			
Online service index (0–1, 1=highest presence)	0.57	0.42	0.32
Secure Internet servers (per million people)	1.3	26.8	4.4

United Arab Emirates

High income

	Country data		High-income group
	2005	**2012**	**2012**
Economic and social context			
Population (millions)	4	9	1,300
Urban population (% of total)	82	85	80
GNI per capita, *World Bank Atlas* method ($)	41,470	38,620	38,412
GDP growth, 2000–05 and 2005–12 (avg. annual %)	5.8	2.1	1.0
Adult literacy rate (% ages 15 and older)	90	..	..
Gross primary, secondary, tertiary school enrollment (%)	..	..	93
Sector structure			
Separate telecommunications/ICT regulator	Yes	Yes	
Status of main fixed-line telephone operator	Mixed	Mixed	
Level of competition (competition, partial comp., monopoly)			
International gateway(s)	P	*P*	
Mobile telephone service	P	*P*	
Internet service	P	*P*	
Foreign ownership (not allowed, restricted, allowed)	..	R	
Reg. treatment of VoIP (banned, closed, no framework, allowed)	B	A	
Sector efficiency and capacity			
Telecommunications revenue (% of GDP)	1.9	2.0	2.7
Telecommunications investment (% of revenue)	9.8	22.6	17.6
Sector performance			
Access			
Fixed-telephone subscriptions (per 100 people)	29.8	21.4	43.6
Mobile-cellular telephone subscriptions (per 100 people)	109.3	149.6	122.9
Fixed (wired)-broadband subscriptions (per 100 people)	3.1	10.3	26.2
Households with a computer (%)	36.5[a]	85.0	77.7
Households with Internet access at home (%)	30.4[a]	72.0	75.5
Usage			
Int'l. voice traffic, total (minutes/subscription/month)	..	41.8	..
Domestic mobile traffic (minutes/subscription/month)	..	110.4	*113.6*
Individuals using the Internet (%)	40.0[a]	85.0	75.4
Quality			
Population covered by a mobile-cellular network (%)	100	100	100
Fixed (wired)-broadband subscriptions (% of total Internet)	24.5	99.4	*95.9*
International Internet bandwidth (bit/s per Internet user)	3,082	32,445	85,990
Affordability			
Fixed-telephone sub-basket ($ a month)	..	4.1	25.2
Mobile-cellular sub-basket ($ a month)	..	9.1	20.6
Fixed-broadband sub-basket ($ a month)	..	40.6	29.2
Trade			
ICT goods exports (% of total goods exports)	4.3	*2.0*	8.9
ICT goods imports (% of total goods imports)	8.1	*4.5*	10.8
ICT service exports (% of total service exports)	..	..	30.8
Applications			
Online service index (0–1, 1=highest presence)	0.63	0.86	0.67
Secure Internet servers (per million people)	53.7	194.2	827.6

United Kingdom

	Country data		High-income group
	2005	2012	2012
Economic and social context			
Population (millions)	60	64	1,300
Urban population (% of total)	79	80	80
GNI per capita, *World Bank Atlas* method ($)	39,560	38,500	38,412
GDP growth, 2000–05 and 2005–12 (avg. annual %)	3.0	0.0	1.0
Adult literacy rate (% ages 15 and older)	..	..	..
Gross primary, secondary, tertiary school enrollment (%)	92	89	93
Sector structure			
Separate telecommunications/ICT regulator	Yes	Yes	
Status of main fixed-line telephone operator	Private	Private	
Level of competition (competition, partial comp., monopoly)			
International gateway(s)	..	..	
Mobile telephone service	C	C	
Internet service	C	..	
Foreign ownership (not allowed, restricted, allowed)	A	A	
Reg. treatment of VoIP (banned, closed, no framework, allowed)	A	A	
Sector efficiency and capacity			
Telecommunications revenue (% of GDP)	3.7	1.8	2.7
Telecommunications investment (% of revenue)	..	15.2	17.6
Sector performance			
Access			
Fixed-telephone subscriptions (per 100 people)	56.5	52.9	43.6
Mobile-cellular telephone subscriptions (per 100 people)	108.6	135.3	122.9
Fixed (wired)-broadband subscriptions (per 100 people)	16.4	34.0	26.2
Households with a computer (%)	70.0	87.0	77.7
Households with Internet access at home (%)	60.2	88.6[a]	75.5
Usage			
Int'l. voice traffic, total (minutes/subscription/month)	..	..	..
Domestic mobile traffic (minutes/subscription/month)	87.6	123.0	113.6
Individuals using the Internet (%)	70.0	87.0[a]	75.4
Quality			
Population covered by a mobile-cellular network (%)	99	100	100
Fixed (wired)-broadband subscriptions (% of total Internet)	60.7	98.6	95.9
International Internet bandwidth (bit/s per Internet user)	52,831	188,920	85,990
Affordability			
Fixed-telephone sub-basket ($ a month)	..	36.2	25.2
Mobile-cellular sub-basket ($ a month)	..	47.8	20.6
Fixed-broadband sub-basket ($ a month)	..	20.8	29.2
Trade			
ICT goods exports (% of total goods exports)	14.0	4.2	8.9
ICT goods imports (% of total goods imports)	12.3	7.3	10.8
ICT service exports (% of total service exports)	37.6	39.0	30.8
Applications			
Online service index (0–1, 1=highest presence)	0.79	0.97	0.67
Secure Internet servers (per million people)	464.8	1,200.3	827.6

United States

	Country data		High-income group
	2005	2012	2012
Economic and social context			
Population (millions)	296	314	1,300
Urban population (% of total)	81	83	80
GNI per capita, World Bank Atlas method ($)	46,350	52,340	38,412
GDP growth, 2000–05 and 2005–12 (avg. annual %)	2.6	0.8	1.0
Adult literacy rate (% ages 15 and older)	..	..	..
Gross primary, secondary, tertiary school enrollment (%)	93	97	93
Sector structure			
Separate telecommunications/ICT regulator	Yes	Yes	
Status of main fixed-line telephone operator	Private	Private	
Level of competition (competition, partial comp., monopoly)			
International gateway(s)	..	C	
Mobile telephone service	C	C	
Internet service	C	C	
Foreign ownership (not allowed, restricted, allowed)	A	A	
Reg. treatment of VoIP (banned, closed, no framework, allowed)	A	A	
Sector efficiency and capacity			
Telecommunications revenue (% of GDP)	2.9	3.4	2.7
Telecommunications investment (% of revenue)	18.7	14.0	17.6
Sector performance			
Access			
Fixed-telephone subscriptions (per 100 people)	58.7	44.4	43.6
Mobile-cellular telephone subscriptions (per 100 people)	68.3	95.4	122.9
Fixed (wired)-broadband subscriptions (per 100 people)	17.2	28.3	26.2
Households with a computer (%)	67.1	79.3[a]	77.7
Households with Internet access at home (%)	58.1[a]	75.0[a]	75.5
Usage			
Int'l. voice traffic, total (minutes/subscription/month)	20.1	18.5	..
Domestic mobile traffic (minutes/subscription/month)	..	383.7	113.6
Individuals using the Internet (%)	68.0[a]	81.0[a]	75.4
Quality			
Population covered by a mobile-cellular network (%)	99	100	100
Fixed (wired)-broadband subscriptions (% of total Internet)	90.0	97.0	95.9
International Internet bandwidth (bit/s per Internet user)	7,185	61,938	85,990
Affordability			
Fixed-telephone sub-basket ($ a month)	..	15.0	25.2
Mobile-cellular sub-basket ($ a month)	..	35.6	20.6
Fixed-broadband sub-basket ($ a month)	..	15.0	29.2
Trade			
ICT goods exports (% of total goods exports)	14.3	9.0	8.9
ICT goods imports (% of total goods imports)	13.7	12.8	10.8
ICT service exports (% of total service exports)	19.3	22.1	30.8
Applications			
Online service index (0–1, 1=highest presence)	0.86	1.00	0.67
Secure Internet servers (per million people)	785.2	1,304.0	827.6

Uruguay

High income

	Country data		High-income group
	2005	2012	2012
Economic and social context			
Population (millions)	3	3	1,300
Urban population (% of total)	92	93	80
GNI per capita, *World Bank Atlas* method ($)	4,720	13,580	38,412
GDP growth, 2000–05 and 2005–12 (avg. annual %)	0.0	5.8	1.0
Adult literacy rate (% ages 15 and older)	98	98	..
Gross primary, secondary, tertiary school enrollment (%)	90	90	93
Sector structure			
Separate telecommunications/ICT regulator	Yes	Yes	
Status of main fixed-line telephone operator	Public	Public	
Level of competition (competition, partial comp., monopoly)			
International gateway(s)	..	..	
Mobile telephone service	C	C	
Internet service	C	P	
Foreign ownership (not allowed, restricted, allowed)	A	..	
Reg. treatment of VoIP (banned, closed, no framework, allowed)	No	A	
Sector efficiency and capacity			
Telecommunications revenue (% of GDP)	*3.8*	2.5	2.7
Telecommunications investment (% of revenue)	*8.0*	49.7	17.6
Sector performance			
Access			
Fixed-telephone subscriptions (per 100 people)	30.3	29.8	43.6
Mobile-cellular telephone subscriptions (per 100 people)	34.7	147.1	122.9
Fixed (wired)-broadband subscriptions (per 100 people)	1.5	16.6	26.2
Households with a computer (%)	22.1	63.7	77.7
Households with Internet access at home (%)	13.5	48.4	75.5
Usage			
Int'l. voice traffic, total (minutes/subscription/month)	*8.9*	5.9	..
Domestic mobile traffic (minutes/subscription/month)	28.1	97.0	*113.6*
Individuals using the Internet (%)	20.1	55.1[a]	75.4
Quality			
Population covered by a mobile-cellular network (%)	100	100	100
Fixed (wired)-broadband subscriptions (% of total Internet)	27.8	100.0	95.9
International Internet bandwidth (bit/s per Internet user)	2,395	40,635	85,990
Affordability			
Fixed-telephone sub-basket ($ a month)	..	12.0	25.2
Mobile-cellular sub-basket ($ a month)	..	22.4	20.6
Fixed-broadband sub-basket ($ a month)	..	14.9	29.2
Trade			
ICT goods exports (% of total goods exports)	0.1	0.1	8.9
ICT goods imports (% of total goods imports)	6.3	5.6	10.8
ICT service exports (% of total service exports)	11.6	15.9	30.8
Applications			
Online service index (0–1, 1=highest presence)	0.56	0.55	0.67
Secure Internet servers (per million people)	27.1	75.1	827.6

Uzbekistan

		Europe & Central Asia	**Lower middle income**

	Country data		Lower middle-income group
	2005	2012	2012
Economic and social context			
Population (millions)	26	30	2,507
Urban population (% of total)	37	36	39
GNI per capita, World Bank Atlas method ($)	530	1,720	1,893
GDP growth, 2000–05 and 2005–12 (avg. annual %)	5.3	8.5	6.0
Adult literacy rate (% ages 15 and older)	99	99	71
Gross primary, secondary, tertiary school enrollment (%)	75	70	64
Sector structure			
Separate telecommunications/ICT regulator	No	No	
Status of main fixed-line telephone operator	Public	Public	
Level of competition (competition, partial comp., monopoly)			
International gateway(s)	..	..	
Mobile telephone service	C	C	
Internet service	..	..	
Foreign ownership (not allowed, restricted, allowed)	..	..	
Reg. treatment of VoIP (banned, closed, no framework, allowed)	No	No	
Sector efficiency and capacity			
Telecommunications revenue (% of GDP)	2.2	..	2.5
Telecommunications investment (% of revenue)	31.7	..	20.5
Sector performance			
Access			
Fixed-telephone subscriptions (per 100 people)	6.9	6.9	5.4
Mobile-cellular telephone subscriptions (per 100 people)	2.8	71.0	83.1
Fixed (wired)-broadband subscriptions (per 100 people)	0.0	0.7	1.4
Households with a computer (%)	1.0	8.0a	15.0
Households with Internet access at home (%)	0.9a	9.6a	12.4
Usage			
Int'l. voice traffic, total (minutes/subscription/month)	..	22.1	6.5
Domestic mobile traffic (minutes/subscription/month)	..	154.3	..
Individuals using the Internet (%)	3.3	36.5a	18.7
Quality			
Population covered by a mobile-cellular network (%)	75	92	86
Fixed (wired)-broadband subscriptions (% of total Internet)	7.4	85.0	58.2
International Internet bandwidth (bit/s per Internet user)	164	959	8,076
Affordability			
Fixed-telephone sub-basket ($ a month)	..	1.4	4.9
Mobile-cellular sub-basket ($ a month)	..	2.4	10.5
Fixed-broadband sub-basket ($ a month)	..	11.5	20.6
Trade			
ICT goods exports (% of total goods exports)	..	..	4.6
ICT goods imports (% of total goods imports)	..	..	7.2
ICT service exports (% of total service exports)	..	..	47.1
Applications			
Online service index (0–1, 1=highest presence)	0.41	0.50	0.32
Secure Internet servers (per million people)	0.0	0.8	4.4

Vanuatu

Lower middle income

	Country data		Lower middle-income group
	2005	2012	2012
Economic and social context			
Population (millions)	0.21	0.25	2,507
Urban population (% of total)	23	25	39
GNI per capita, *World Bank Atlas* method ($)	1,780	3,000	1,893
GDP growth, 2000–05 and 2005–12 (avg. annual %)	1.0	3.9	6.0
Adult literacy rate (% ages 15 and older)	78	83	71
Gross primary, secondary, tertiary school enrollment (%)	64	..	64
Sector structure			
Separate telecommunications/ICT regulator	No	Yes	
Status of main fixed-line telephone operator	Mixed	Mixed	
Level of competition (competition, partial comp., monopoly)			
International gateway(s)	..	C	
Mobile telephone service	..	C	
Internet service	..	C	
Foreign ownership (not allowed, restricted, allowed)	..	R	
Reg. treatment of VoIP (banned, closed, no framework, allowed)	No	A	
Sector efficiency and capacity			
Telecommunications revenue (% of GDP)	3.5	4.8	2.5
Telecommunications investment (% of revenue)	20.0	24.6	20.5
Sector performance			
Access			
Fixed-telephone subscriptions (per 100 people)	3.3	2.2	5.4
Mobile-cellular telephone subscriptions (per 100 people)	6.1	59.1	83.1
Fixed (wired)-broadband subscriptions (per 100 people)	0.0	0.1	1.4
Households with a computer (%)	4.0	10.7[a]	15.0
Households with Internet access at home (%)	..	3.5	12.4
Usage			
Int'l. voice traffic, total (minutes/subscription/month)	..	..	6.5
Domestic mobile traffic (minutes/subscription/month)	..	99.1	..
Individuals using the Internet (%)	5.1	10.6[a]	18.7
Quality			
Population covered by a mobile-cellular network (%)	20	92	86
Fixed (wired)-broadband subscriptions (% of total Internet)	3.7	11.9	58.2
International Internet bandwidth (bit/s per Internet user)	376	2,290	8,076
Affordability			
Fixed-telephone sub-basket ($ a month)	..	40.4	4.9
Mobile-cellular sub-basket ($ a month)	..	25.1	10.5
Fixed-broadband sub-basket ($ a month)	..	105.2	20.6
Trade			
ICT goods exports (% of total goods exports)	0.2	0.0	4.6
ICT goods imports (% of total goods imports)	2.8	3.1	7.2
ICT service exports (% of total service exports)	6.5	2.0	47.1
Applications			
Online service index (0–1, 1=highest presence)	0.25	0.22	0.32
Secure Internet servers (per million people)	133.7	43.5	4.4

Venezuela, RB

Latin America & Caribbean			Upper middle income

	Country data		Upper middle-income group
	2005	2012	2012
Economic and social context			
Population (millions)	27	30	2,391
Urban population (% of total)	92	94	61
GNI per capita, *World Bank Atlas* method ($)	4,920	12,460	6,969
GDP growth, 2000–05 and 2005–12 (avg. annual %)	1.5	3.1	6.2
Adult literacy rate (% ages 15 and older)	95	96	94
Gross primary, secondary, tertiary school enrollment (%)	76	89	76
Sector structure			
Separate telecommunications/ICT regulator	Yes	Yes	
Status of main fixed-line telephone operator	Mixed	Public	
Level of competition (competition, partial comp., monopoly)			
International gateway(s)	C	..	
Mobile telephone service	C	C	
Internet service	C	C	
Foreign ownership (not allowed, restricted, allowed)	A	R	
Reg. treatment of VoIP (banned, closed, no framework, allowed)	No	C	
Sector efficiency and capacity			
Telecommunications revenue (% of GDP)	3.5	2.9	2.5
Telecommunications investment (% of revenue)	27.5	14.7	18.2
Sector performance			
Access			
Fixed-telephone subscriptions (per 100 people)	13.7	25.5	19.4
Mobile-cellular telephone subscriptions (per 100 people)	46.8	101.9	92.4
Fixed (wired)-broadband subscriptions (per 100 people)	1.3	6.7	10.8
Households with a computer (%)	10.3	20.2[a]	40.6
Households with Internet access at home (%)	2.5	20.2[a]	36.3
Usage			
Int'l. voice traffic, total (minutes/subscription/month)	6.3	3.8	1.3
Domestic mobile traffic (minutes/subscription/month)	91.6	99.3	284.4
Individuals using the Internet (%)	12.6	44.0[a]	41.6
Quality			
Population covered by a mobile-cellular network (%)	90	..	99
Fixed (wired)-broadband subscriptions (% of total Internet)	55.2	89.1	95.5
International Internet bandwidth (bit/s per Internet user)	399	10,914	14,580
Affordability			
Fixed-telephone sub-basket ($ a month)	..	1.7	9.4
Mobile-cellular sub-basket ($ a month)	..	14.9	14.9
Fixed-broadband sub-basket ($ a month)	..	15.4	17.8
Trade			
ICT goods exports (% of total goods exports)	0.0	0.0	17.6
ICT goods imports (% of total goods imports)	11.9	6.4	14.7
ICT service exports (% of total service exports)	13.8	11.9	29.1
Applications			
Online service index (0–1, 1=highest presence)	0.51	0.48	0.42
Secure Internet servers (per million people)	4.6	11.1	18.5

Vietnam

East Asia & Pacific   **Lower middle income**

	Country data		Lower middle-income group
	2005	2012	2012
Economic and social context			
Population (millions)	82	89	2,507
Urban population (% of total)	27	32	39
GNI per capita, *World Bank Atlas* method ($)	680	1,550	1,893
GDP growth, 2000–05 and 2005–12 (avg. annual %)	6.9	6.1	6.0
Adult literacy rate (% ages 15 and older)	90	93	71
Gross primary, secondary, tertiary school enrollment (%)	..	..	64
Sector structure			
Separate telecommunications/ICT regulator	No	Yes	
Status of main fixed-line telephone operator	Public	Public	
Level of competition (competition, partial comp., monopoly)			
International gateway(s)	C	C	
Mobile telephone service	C	C	
Internet service	C	C	
Foreign ownership (not allowed, restricted, allowed)	..	R	
Reg. treatment of VoIP (banned, closed, no framework, allowed)	C	A	
Sector efficiency and capacity			
Telecommunications revenue (% of GDP)	4.3	6.5	2.5
Telecommunications investment (% of revenue)	..	..	20.5
Sector performance			
Access			
Fixed-telephone subscriptions (per 100 people)	10.0	11.2	5.4
Mobile-cellular telephone subscriptions (per 100 people)	11.3	147.7	83.1
Fixed (wired)-broadband subscriptions (per 100 people)	0.2	4.9	1.4
Households with a computer (%)	6.3[a]	17.5[a]	15.0
Households with Internet access at home (%)	1.5[a]	15.6[a]	12.4
Usage			
Int'l. voice traffic, total (minutes/subscription/month)	..	..	6.5
Domestic mobile traffic (minutes/subscription/month)	..	..	..
Individuals using the Internet (%)	12.7	39.5[a]	18.7
Quality			
Population covered by a mobile-cellular network (%)	70	..	86
Fixed (wired)-broadband subscriptions (% of total Internet)	7.2	30.6	58.2
International Internet bandwidth (bit/s per Internet user)	334	13,359	8,076
Affordability			
Fixed-telephone sub-basket ($ a month)	..	2.0	4.9
Mobile-cellular sub-basket ($ a month)	..	4.1	10.5
Fixed-broadband sub-basket ($ a month)	..	11.8	20.6
Trade			
ICT goods exports (% of total goods exports)	2.8	11.6	4.6
ICT goods imports (% of total goods imports)	6.1	10.2	7.2
ICT service exports (% of total service exports)	..	..	47.1
Applications			
Online service index (0–1, 1=highest presence)	0.46	0.42	0.32
Secure Internet servers (per million people)	0.1	8.2	4.4

Virgin Islands (U.S.)

High income

	Country data		High-income group
	2005	2012	2012
Economic and social context			
Population (millions)	0.11	0.11	1,300
Urban population (% of total)	94	96	80
GNI per capita, *World Bank Atlas* method ($)	..	..	38,412
GDP growth, 2000–05 and 2005–12 (avg. annual %)	..	..	1.0
Adult literacy rate (% ages 15 and older)	..	..	..
Gross primary, secondary, tertiary school enrollment (%)	..	..	93
Sector structure			
Separate telecommunications/ICT regulator	..	..	
Status of main fixed-line telephone operator	..	..	
Level of competition (competition, partial comp., monopoly)			
International gateway(s)	..	..	
Mobile telephone service	..	..	
Internet service	..	..	
Foreign ownership (not allowed, restricted, allowed)	..	..	
Reg. treatment of VoIP (banned, closed, no framework, allowed)	..	..	
Sector efficiency and capacity			
Telecommunications revenue (% of GDP)	..	..	2.7
Telecommunications investment (% of revenue)	:.	..	17.6
Sector performance			
Access			
Fixed-telephone subscriptions (per 100 people)	66.5	71.3	43.6
Mobile-cellular telephone subscriptions (per 100 people)	74.5[a]	..	122.9
Fixed (wired)-broadband subscriptions (per 100 people)	2.8[a]	8.6[a]	26.2
Households with a computer (%)	..	..	77.7
Households with Internet access at home (%)	..	..	75.5
Usage			
Int'l. voice traffic, total (minutes/subscription/month)	..	..	..
Domestic mobile traffic (minutes/subscription/month)	..	..	113.6
Individuals using the Internet (%)	27.3[a]	40.5[a]	75.4
Quality			
Population covered by a mobile-cellular network (%)	..	..	100
Fixed (wired)-broadband subscriptions (% of total Internet)	..	..	95.9
International Internet bandwidth (bit/s per Internet user)	1,527	..	85,990
Affordability			
Fixed-telephone sub-basket ($ a month)	..	..	25.2
Mobile-cellular sub-basket ($ a month)	..	..	20.6
Fixed-broadband sub-basket ($ a month)	..	..	29.2
Trade			
ICT goods exports (% of total goods exports)	..	..	8.9
ICT goods imports (% of total goods imports)	..	..	10.8
ICT service exports (% of total service exports)	..	..	30.8
Applications			
Online service index (0–1, 1=highest presence)	..	..	0.67
Secure Internet servers (per million people)	213.2	396.2	827.6

West Bank and Gaza

Middle East & North Africa			Lower middle income

	Country data		Lower middle-income group
	2005	2012	2012
Economic and social context			
Population (millions)	3	4	2,507
Urban population (% of total)	73	75	39
GNI per capita, World Bank Atlas method ($)	1,340	..	1,893
GDP growth, 2000–05 and 2005–12 (avg. annual %)	-0.9	..	6.0
Adult literacy rate (% ages 15 and older)	93	95	71
Gross primary, secondary, tertiary school enrollment (%)	79	77	64
Sector structure			
Separate telecommunications/ICT regulator	..	..	
Status of main fixed-line telephone operator	..	..	
Level of competition (competition, partial comp., monopoly)			
International gateway(s)	..	..	
Mobile telephone service	..	..	
Internet service	..	..	
Foreign ownership (not allowed, restricted, allowed)	..	..	
Reg. treatment of VoIP (banned, closed, no framework, allowed)	No	A	
Sector efficiency and capacity			
Telecommunications revenue (% of GDP)	0.8	..	2.5
Telecommunications investment (% of revenue)	5.1	..	20.5
Sector performance			
Access			
Fixed-telephone subscriptions (per 100 people)	9.5	9.3	5.4
Mobile-cellular telephone subscriptions (per 100 people)	15.9	75.6	83.1
Fixed (wired)-broadband subscriptions (per 100 people)	0.2	..	1.4
Households with a computer (%)	29.5[a]	53.9[a]	15.0
Households with Internet access at home (%)	15.9	33.4[a]	12.4
Usage			
Int'l. voice traffic, total (minutes/subscription/month)	..	..	6.5
Domestic mobile traffic (minutes/subscription/month)	..	..	..
Individuals using the Internet (%)	16.0[a]	41.1[a]	18.7
Quality			
Population covered by a mobile-cellular network (%)	95	..	86
Fixed (wired)-broadband subscriptions (% of total Internet)	9.6	..	58.2
International Internet bandwidth (bit/s per Internet user)	421	10,906	8,076
Affordability			
Fixed-telephone sub-basket ($ a month)	..	..	4.9
Mobile-cellular sub-basket ($ a month)	..	..	10.5
Fixed-broadband sub-basket ($ a month)	..	..	20.6
Trade			
ICT goods exports (% of total goods exports)	0.5	1.0	4.6
ICT goods imports (% of total goods imports)	2.3	3.1	7.2
ICT service exports (% of total service exports)	27.7	4.4	47.1
Applications			
Online service index (0–1, 1=highest presence)	..	..	0.32
Secure Internet servers (per million people)	0.6	4.6	4.4

Yemen, Rep.

Lower middle income

	Country data		Lower middle-income group
	2005	**2012**	**2012**
Economic and social context			
Population (millions)	20	24	2,507
Urban population (% of total)	29	33	39
GNI per capita, *World Bank Atlas* method ($)	700	1,270	1,893
GDP growth, 2000–05 and 2005–12 (avg. annual %)	4.1	1.9	6.0
Adult literacy rate (% ages 15 and older)	55	65	71
Gross primary, secondary, tertiary school enrollment (%)	56	56	64
Sector structure			
Separate telecommunications/ICT regulator	No	No	
Status of main fixed-line telephone operator	Public	Public	
Level of competition (competition, partial comp., monopoly)			
International gateway(s)	M	M	
Mobile telephone service	C	C	
Internet service	C	C	
Foreign ownership (not allowed, restricted, allowed)	..	No	
Reg. treatment of VoIP (banned, closed, no framework, allowed)	B	B	
Sector efficiency and capacity			
Telecommunications revenue (% of GDP)	1.2	3.4	2.5
Telecommunications investment (% of revenue)	25.2	29.4	20.5
Sector performance			
Access			
Fixed-telephone subscriptions (per 100 people)	4.5ª	4.6	5.4
Mobile-cellular telephone subscriptions (per 100 people)	11.3	58.3	83.1
Fixed (wired)-broadband subscriptions (per 100 people)	0.0	0.7	1.4
Households with a computer (%)	1.9ª	5.1ª	15.0
Households with Internet access at home (%)	1.4ª	4.7ª	12.4
Usage			
Int'l. voice traffic, total (minutes/subscription/month)	14.7	13.4	6.5
Domestic mobile traffic (minutes/subscription/month)	..	..	..
Individuals using the Internet (%)	1.0ª	17.4ª	18.7
Quality			
Population covered by a mobile-cellular network (%)	68	84	86
Fixed (wired)-broadband subscriptions (% of total Internet)	1.4	14.4	58.2
International Internet bandwidth (bit/s per Internet user)	28	2,788	8,076
Affordability			
Fixed-telephone sub-basket ($ a month)	..	0.9	4.9
Mobile-cellular sub-basket ($ a month)	..	11.1	10.5
Fixed-broadband sub-basket ($ a month)	..	14.7	20.6
Trade			
ICT goods exports (% of total goods exports)	0.0	0.0	4.6
ICT goods imports (% of total goods imports)	2.1	1.0	7.2
ICT service exports (% of total service exports)	15.8	8.7	47.1
Applications			
Online service index (0–1, 1=highest presence)	0.21	0.18	0.32
Secure Internet servers (per million people)	0.1	0.7	4.4

Zambia

Sub-Saharan Africa			Lower middle income

	Country data		Lower middle-income group
	2005	2012	2012
Economic and social context			
Population (millions)	11	14	2,507
Urban population (% of total)	37	40	39
GNI per capita, *World Bank Atlas* method ($)	490	1,350	1,893
GDP growth, 2000–05 and 2005–12 (avg. annual %)	4.8	6.6	6.0
Adult literacy rate (% ages 15 and older)	61	..	71
Gross primary, secondary, tertiary school enrollment (%)	..	85	64
Sector structure			
Separate telecommunications/ICT regulator	Yes	Yes	
Status of main fixed-line telephone operator	Public	Mixed	
Level of competition (competition, partial comp., monopoly)			
International gateway(s)	C	C	
Mobile telephone service	P	C	
Internet service	P	C	
Foreign ownership (not allowed, restricted, allowed)	R	R	
Reg. treatment of VoIP (banned, closed, no framework, allowed)	B	B	
Sector efficiency and capacity			
Telecommunications revenue (% of GDP)	2.6	0.1	2.5
Telecommunications investment (% of revenue)	29.3	..	20.5
Sector performance			
Access			
Fixed-telephone subscriptions (per 100 people)	0.8	0.6	5.4
Mobile-cellular telephone subscriptions (per 100 people)	8.3	74.8	83.1
Fixed (wired)-broadband subscriptions (per 100 people)	0.0	0.1	1.4
Households with a computer (%)	1.4[a]	3.1[a]	15.0
Households with Internet access at home (%)	0.1[a]	2.8[a]	12.4
Usage			
Int'l. voice traffic, total (minutes/subscription/month)	..	1.8	6.5
Domestic mobile traffic (minutes/subscription/month)	28.2	57.8	..
Individuals using the Internet (%)	2.9[a]	13.5[a]	18.7
Quality			
Population covered by a mobile-cellular network (%)	65	78	86
Fixed (wired)-broadband subscriptions (% of total Internet)	31.8	93.9	58.2
International Internet bandwidth (bit/s per Internet user)	67	2,721	8,076
Affordability			
Fixed-telephone sub-basket ($ a month)	..	7.4	4.9
Mobile-cellular sub-basket ($ a month)	..	16.5	10.5
Fixed-broadband sub-basket ($ a month)	..	82.3	20.6
Trade			
ICT goods exports (% of total goods exports)	0.0	0.0	4.6
ICT goods imports (% of total goods imports)	4.6	3.0	7.2
ICT service exports (% of total service exports)	5.5	6.8	47.1
Applications			
Online service index (0–1, 1=highest presence)	0.23	0.31	0.32
Secure Internet servers (per million people)	0.2	2.8	4.4

Zimbabwe

	Country data		Low-income group
	2005	2012	2012
Economic and social context			
Population (millions)	13	14	846
Urban population (% of total)	36	39	28
GNI per capita, *World Bank Atlas* method ($)	430	650	590
GDP growth, 2000–05 and 2005–12 (avg. annual %)	-8.5	0.2	5.9
Adult literacy rate (% ages 15 and older)	..	84	61
Gross primary, secondary, tertiary school enrollment (%)	54	..	60
Sector structure			
Separate telecommunications/ICT regulator	Yes	Yes	
Status of main fixed-line telephone operator	Public	Public	
Level of competition (competition, partial comp., monopoly)			
International gateway(s)	M	P	
Mobile telephone service	C	P	
Internet service	C	C	
Foreign ownership (not allowed, restricted, allowed)	R	R	
Reg. treatment of VoIP (banned, closed, no framework, allowed)	B	A	
Sector efficiency and capacity			
Telecommunications revenue (% of GDP)	..	..	5.0
Telecommunications investment (% of revenue)	4.1	..	..
Sector performance			
Access			
Fixed-telephone subscriptions (per 100 people)	2.6	2.2	1.0
Mobile-cellular telephone subscriptions (per 100 people)	5.1	91.9	47.2
Fixed (wired)-broadband subscriptions (per 100 people)	0.1	0.5	0.2
Households with a computer (%)	2.0[a]	6.5[a]	4.2
Households with Internet access at home (%)	0.9[a]	4.9[a]	3.4
Usage			
Int'l. voice traffic, total (minutes/subscription/month)	..	4.0	..
Domestic mobile traffic (minutes/subscription/month)	51.7	30.3	70.1
Individuals using the Internet (%)	8.0[a]	17.1[a]	6.2
Quality			
Population covered by a mobile-cellular network (%)	70	81	..
Fixed (wired)-broadband subscriptions (% of total Internet)	10.6	99.3	30.9
International Internet bandwidth (bit/s per Internet user)	54	2,643	9,141
Affordability			
Fixed-telephone sub-basket ($ a month)	..	9.8	8.9
Mobile-cellular sub-basket ($ a month)	..	20.6	11.9
Fixed-broadband sub-basket ($ a month)	..	30.0	46.9
Trade			
ICT goods exports (% of total goods exports)	0.1	0.0	..
ICT goods imports (% of total goods imports)	2.5	3.4	..
ICT service exports (% of total service exports)	..	..	..
Applications			
Online service index (0–1, 1=highest presence)	0.30	0.30	0.20
Secure Internet servers (per million people)	0.2	3.2	1.1

Notes

a. ITU estimate.

b. Excludes South Sudan.

c. Excludes South Sudan after July 9, 2011.

Glossary

Adult literacy rate is the percentage of people ages 15 and older who can, with understanding, read and write a short, simple statement about their everyday life. (United Nations Educational, Scientific, and Cultural Organization Institute for Statistics) (w)

Domestic mobile-telephone traffic refers to the total number of minutes of calls made by mobile subscribers within a country (including minutes to fixed-telephone and minutes to mobile-phone subscribers). (International Telecommunication Union) (w)

Fixed-broadband sub-basket refers to the price of the monthly subscription to an entry-level fixed broadband plan. For comparability reasons, the fixed broadband sub-basket is based on a monthly usage of (a minimum of) 1 gigabyte (GB). For plans that limit the monthly amount of data transferred by including caps below 1 gigabyte, the cost for additional bytes is added to the sub-basket. The minimum speed of a broadband connection is 256 kbit/s. (International Telecommunication Union) (m)

Fixed (wired)-broadband subscriptions refers to subscriptions to high-speed access to the public Internet (a TCP/IP connection), at downstream speeds equal to, or greater than, 256 kbit/s. This includes cable modem, DSL, fiber-to-the-home/building, and other fixed (wired)-broadband subscriptions. This total is measured irrespective of the method of payment. It excludes subscriptions that have access to data communications (including the Internet) via mobile-cellular networks. It excludes technologies listed under the wireless-broadband category. (International Telecommunication Union) (w)

Fixed-telephone sub-basket refers to the monthly price charged for subscribing to the Public Switched Telephone Network (PSTN), plus the cost of 30 local calls to the same (fixed) network (15 peak and 15 off-peak calls) of three minutes each. The service refers to the traditional fixed telephone line and does not refer to, for example, prices for managed VoIP. (International Telecommunication Union) (m)

Fixed-telephone subscriptions refers to the sum of active number of analog fixed-telephone lines, Voice over Internet Protocol (VoIP) subscriptions, fixed wireless local loop (WLL) subscriptions, ISDN voice-channel equivalents, and fixed public payphones. (International Telecommunication Union) (w)

Foreign ownership refers to the allowance of foreign participation or owner-ship in facility-based and spectrum-based operators as well as in Internet Service Providers (ISPs). (No = not allowed, R = allowed with restrictions, A = allowed without restrictions) (International Telecommunication Union)

GDP growth is the annual percentage growth rate of gross domestic product (GDP) at market prices based on constant local currency. Aggregates are based on constant 2005 U.S. dollars. GDP is the sum of gross value added by all resident producers in the economy plus any product taxes and minus any subsidies not included in the value of the products. It is calculated without

Glossary

making deductions for depreciation of fabricated assets or for depletion and degradation of natural resources. (World Bank and Organisation for Economic Co-operation and Development) (w)

GNI per capita, *World Bank Atlas* method, is gross national income (GNI) converted to U.S. dollars using the *World Bank Atlas* method divided by the midyear population. GNI is the sum of value added by all resident producers plus any product taxes (less subsidies) not included in the valuation of output plus net receipts of primary income (compensation of employees and property income) from abroad. GNI, calculated in national currency, is usually converted to U.S. dollars at official exchange rates for comparisons across economies. The *World Bank Atlas* method is used to smooth fluctuations in prices and exchange rates. It averages the exchange rate for a given year and the two preceding years, adjusted for differences in rates of inflation between the country and the Euro area, Japan, the United Kingdom, and the United States. (World Bank) (w)

Gross primary, secondary, and tertiary enrollment is the combined number of students enrolled in primary, secondary, and tertiary levels of education, regardless of age, as a percentage of the population of official school age for the three levels. (United Nations Educational, Scientific and Cultural Organization Institute for Statistics) (w)

Households with a computer refers to the percentage of households with a computer at home. A computer includes a desktop computer, a laptop (portable) computer, or a tablet (or similar handheld computer). It does not include equipment with some embedded computing abilities such as smart TV sets, and devices with telephony as their primary function, such as smartphones. (International Telecommunication Union) (w)

Households with Internet access at home refers to the percentage of households with Internet access at home. Access is not assumed to be only via a computer—it may also be by mobile phone, tablet, PDA, games machine, digital TV, etc. (International Telecommunication Union) (w)

ICT goods exports and imports are goods that are intended to fulfill the function of information processing and communication by electronic means, including transmission and display, or that use electronic processing to detect, measure, or record physical phenomena or to control a physical process. They include telecommunications, audio and video, computer and related equipment; electronic components; and other information and communication technology goods. Software is excluded. Re-exports (exports of foreign goods in the same state as previously imported) are included. (United Nations Conference on Trade and Development) (w)

ICT service exports comprise communications services (telecommunications, business network services, teleconferencing, support services, and postal services) and computer and information services (database, data processing, software design and development, maintenance and repair, and news-related service transactions). (International Monetary Fund) (w)

Glossary

Individuals using the Internet refers to the percentage of individuals who have used the Internet (from any location) in the last 12 months. Internet can be used via a computer, mobile phone, personal digital assistant, games machine, digital TV, etc. (International Telecommunication Union) (w)

International Internet bandwidth refers to the total used capacity of international Internet bandwidth, in bits per second per Internet user. It is measured as the sum of used capacity of all Internet exchanges (locations where Internet traffic is exchanged) offering international bandwidth. If capacity is asymmetric (i.e., more incoming [downlink] than outgoing [uplink] capacity), then the incoming (downlink) capacity should be provided. (International Telecommunication Union) (w)

International voice traffic, total is the sum of international incoming and outgoing telephone fixed and mobile telephone traffic (in minutes). (International Telecommunication Union) (w)

Level of competition, international gateway, is the level of competition for international gateway(s). International gateway is any facility that provides an interface to send and receive electronic communications (i.e., voice, data and multimedia images/video) traffic between one country's domestic network facilities and those in another country. (M = monopoly, P = partial competition, C = full competition). (International Telecommunication Union)

Level of competition, Internet service, is the level of competition for retail Internet access service. (M = monopoly, P = partial competition, C = full competition). (International Telecommunication Union)

Level of competition, mobile telephone service, is the level of competition for digital cellular mobile services. (M = monopoly, P = partial competition, C = full competition). (International Telecommunication Union)

Mobile-cellular sub-basket refers to the price of a standard basket of mobile monthly usage for 30 outgoing calls per month (on-net, off-net, to a fixed line, and for peak and off-peak times) in predetermined ratios, plus 100 SMS messages. The mobile-cellular sub-basket is based on prepaid tariffs although postpaid tariffs may be used for countries where prepaid subscriptions make up less than three percent of all mobile-cellular subscriptions. The mobile-cellular prepaid sub-basket is largely based, but does not entirely follow, the 2009 methodology of the OECD low-user basket. (International Telecommunication Union) (m)

Mobile-cellular telephone subscriptions refers to the number of subscriptions to a public mobile-telephone service that provide access to the PSTN (public switched telephone network) using cellular technology. The indicator includes (and is split into) the number of postpaid subscriptions, and the number of active prepaid accounts (i.e., that have been used during the last three months). The indicator applies to all mobile-cellular subscriptions that offer voice communications. It excludes subscriptions via data cards or

Glossary

USB modems, subscriptions to public mobile data services, private trunked mobile radio, telepoint, radio paging, and telemetry services. (International Telecommunication Union) (w)

Online service index is one of the three component indicators for the United Nation's e-Government Development Index (EGDI). Online service index measures the level of sophistication of a government's online presence based on four stages of e-government evolution: emerging presence, enhanced presence, transactional presence, and connected presence. A value of 0 indicates the lowest presence, a value of 1 the highest. (United Nations Department of Economic and Social Affairs and United Nations Public Administration Network) (m)

Population is based on the de facto definition of population, which counts all residents regardless of legal status or citizenship, except for refugees not permanently settled in the country of asylum, who are generally considered part of the population of their country of origin. Data are midyear estimates. (World Bank) (s)

Population covered by a mobile-cellular network refers to the percentage of people within range of a mobile-cellular signal, irrespective of whether they are subscribers or users or not. This is calculated by dividing the number of people within range of a mobile-cellular signal by the total population and multiplying by 100. (International Telecommunication Union) (w)

Regulatory treatment of VoIP indicates whether the country has any regulatory treatment on Voice over Internet Protocol (VoIP), a generic term to describe the techniques used to carry voice traffic over IP. The status are categorized as banned, closed, no framework, or allowed. "Closed" means that wholesale VoIP is permitted, but retail VoIP is banned, as well as cases where only the incumbent is licensed to provide VoIP. (B = banned, C = closed, No = no framework, A = allowed) (International Telecommunication Union)

Secure Internet servers are the number of servers using encryption technology for Internet transactions. Data listed for 2012 are for December 2013. (Netcraft) (w)

Separate telecommunications/ICT regulator indicates whether the country has a separate telecommunications/ICT Regulatory Authority independent in terms of finance, structure, and decision making from the operators and the sector Ministry. (International Telecommunication Union)

Status of main fixed-line telephone operator indicates whether the incumbent fixed-line operator is a public or private entity. Public refers to a fully state-owned operator that has remained 100 percent government-owned since its creation or has been re/nationalized; private refers to a fully private operator that is 100 percent private, either as a result of a privatization or created as such; and mixed refers to a partially private operator that has a portion of its shares sold to either a private operator or to the public (e.g., through Initial

Glossary

Public Offerings or Employee Stock Ownership Plan), with the government remaining one of its shareholders. (International Telecommunication Union)

Telecommunications investment refers to the investment during the financial year in telecommunication services (including fixed, mobile, and Internet services) for acquiring or upgrading property and networks. Property includes tangible assets such as plant, intellectual and non-tangible assets such as computer software. The indicator is a measure of investment in tele-communication infrastructure in the country, and includes expenditure on initial installations and additions to existing installations where the usage is expected to be over an extended period of time. It excludes expenditure on research and development (R&D), annual fees for operating licenses and the use of radio spectrum. (International Telecommunication Union) (m)

Telecommunications revenue refers to revenue earned from retail fixed telephone, mobile-cellular, Internet, and data services offered by telecom-munication operators (both network and virtual) offering services within the country. Revenue (turnover) consists of retail telecommunication ser-vice earnings (therefore excluding revenue from wholesaling activities) dur-ing the financial year under review. It is calculated as percentage of GDP. (International Telecommunication Union) (w)

Urban population is the midyear population of areas defined as urban in each country and reported to the United Nations. (United Nations) (s)

VoIP is Voice over Internet Protocol, a generic term.